The
COMPLETE
BOOK
OF
BiRTHDAYS

THE COMPLETE BOOK OF BIRTHDAYS

PERSONALITY PREDICTIONS FOR EVERY DAY OF THE YEAR

CLARE GIBSON

wellfleet
press

This edition published in 2023 by Wellfleet Press,
an imprint of The Quarto Group,
142 West 36th Street, 4th Floor,
New York, NY 10018, USA
T (212) 779-4972 **F** (212) 779-6058
www.Quarto.com

First published in 2016 by Wellfleet Press, an imprint of The Quarto Group, 142 West 36th Street, 4th Floor, New York, NY 10018, USA.

Wellfleet Press titles are also available at discount for retail, wholesale, promotional, and bulk purchase. For details, contact the Special Sales Manager by email at specialsales@quarto.com or by mail at The Quarto Group, Attn: Special Sales Manager, 100 Cummings Center, Suite 265D Beverly, MA 01915, USA.

10 9 8 7 6 5 4 3 2

ISBN: 978-1-57715-401-3

Library of Congress Control Number: 2023938741

Created and produced by Saraband
Suite 202, 98 Woodlands Road, Glasgow, UK

Printed in China

AUTHOR'S NOTE

This book is based largely on the astrological principles and research compiled for *The Ultimate Birthday Book*, first published in 1998. This revised and updated volume includes some modifications and additional features. The more detailed compatibility predictions included for each date of birth have been contributed by a colleague whose specializes in this field. All predictions relating to careers, relationships and other characteristics will be more accurate if the year of birth is taken into account, and therefore it is recommended that a personal chart be commissioned if further details are sought.

CONTENTS

THE HISTORY AND PRINCIPLES
OF ASTROLOGY

It is the stars,
The stars above us, govern our conditions.

William Shakespeare, *King Lear* (1605–06), Act 4, Scene 3.1

Since time immemorial the heavenly bodies—luminaries, planets and stars—have exerted a mysterious fascination upon their Earth-bound observers. Even today, when the scientific precepts of astronomy have come to marginalize (some even say, discredit) the astrological beliefs that prevailed for millennia, we remain captivated by their ethereal beauty and elusive promise of worlds as yet undiscovered.

Ancient stargazers, who lacked instruments like the telescope with which to study the heavens in accurate detail, still discerned that certain astral bodies comprised fixed formations that moved in predictable fashion through the night sky, their appearance and disappearance heralding the changes of season. They believed that the universe was geocentric, and that the positions and majestic progressions of the Sun, Moon, planets and stars influenced the lives of human beings and all of the events that occurred on Earth. This concept is encapsulated in the word "astrology," a composite of the Greek words *astron* ("star") and *legetin* ("speak"). It was only through the groundbreaking work of such later astronomers as Nicolaus Copernicus (1473–1543), who first postulated that the Earth did not, in fact, occupy the center of the universe, but

rotated on its axis while revolving around the Sun; and Galileo Galilei (1564–1642), who described it as part of a solar system, that the geocentric view began to change, if slowly. (The Vatican, for example, did not formally accept Galileo's findings until 1979). Their successors built upon the work of these pioneering astronomers to provide us with knowledge undreamed of by the ancients. In learning more about our universe and the celestial bodies that it contains, we have learned that many aspects of the astrological beliefs professed by our ancestors were correct. We also know that numerous cosmic truths have yet to be discovered.

Today astronomy is regarded as a scientific discipline distinct from astrology, which most scientists dismiss as simply a naive divinatory system. Yet our affinity with astrology endures: Why is it that even astrological nonbelievers cannot resist sneaking a glance at their "stars" for the day? The human psyche, through the collective unconscious that we all share, clearly has a profound and complex connection to the stars. In order to understand the reasons underlying this attraction, we need to trace the history of astrology through time to its ancient origins.

The Origins of Western Astrology

Blessed as we are with our inherited legacy of millennia of human thought, experience and discovery, our current level of intellectual sophistication and knowledge—though still increasing—is unprecedented in human history. Scientific advances have enriched our lives and understanding immeasurably, but have also in some respects detracted from the awe with which our forebears regarded the natural world. Especially mysterious to them were the celestial bodies: the life-giving, yet also destructive, powers of the brightly burning Sun; the apparently magical ability of its nocturnal counterpart, the Moon, to regulate the ebb and flow of the oceanic tides; and the regular cycles of these two luminaries (as well as those of the constellations), which helped humans to determine the measurement of time—night and day, months and years. In fact, the regular movements of the heavenly bodies, and their corresponding influence over the passage of the seasons, have long been understood as related to one another.

In trying to comprehend the role of the luminaries in governing natural life on Earth, many ancient cultures ascribed supernatural properties to the Sun and Moon, and later also to the planets and stars: the subsequent personification of the solar, lunar, planetary and stellar bodies as deities was an entirely logical progression. Star-worship (also termed astrolatry or Sabaism) was practiced in differing degrees by most of the world's early civilizations, especially those that depended upon agriculture for subsistence. Thus, for example, the ancient Egyptians venerated their supreme deity, the Sun god Re, who was believed to traverse the sky in his solar boat. Such megalithic structures as the standing stones of northern Europe (many aligned with the position at which the Sun rises on the summer and winter solstices), the Native American medicine wheels of North America, the pyramids of ancient Egypt and the ziggurats of Mesoamerica and Mesopotamia also attest to a widespread veneration of the celestial bodies.

Historians believe that the roots of Western astrology are embedded in Mesopotamia—the Near Eastern region comprising the land between the rivers Tigris and Euphrates, which was ruled successively by the Sumerians, Babylonians and Assyrians. Elements of the preceding culture's beliefs were adopted by each subsequent civilization, and yet although the Babylonians absorbed many Sumerian sacred concepts, it is they who are generally believed to have formalized the first astrological precepts. (It should be noted that there is some confusion as to whether the credit for the evolution of this astrological expertise should be given to the Babylonians or the Chaldeans. Chaldea was a region of Babylonia, and the two terms have become interchangeable, although there is reason to believe that the Chaldean astrologers, as priests of Baal, were especially renowned astrologers. Even the Bible refers to the astrological prowess of the Chaldeans, and during the classical period all astrologers

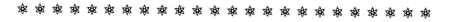

Ancient stone circles were constructed in alignment with the stars.

were generically known as Chaldeans.)

It is estimated that by 3000 BC the Babylonians believed that their Sun god, Shamash; their lunar deity, Sin; and the goddess of the Morning Star (Ishtar) had special power to regulate Earthly life. To keep track of their movements, the Babylonians built stepped pyramids, or ziggurats, which served as both observatories and temples (as they had in Sumeria). By about 500 BC, the Babylonians had extended their concept of stellar influence to the individual: they introduced the idea that the position of the luminaries, planets and stars at the time of a person's birth had a direct bearing on the course of his or her life. One of the world's oldest horoscopes was cast in Mesopotamia for a baby born on April 29, 410 BC. It would be some time, however, before astrology's primary purpose would shift from its role as a leading form of state divination—used to ascertain, for example, the most auspicious time to undertake military campaigns—to

that of predicting an individual's destiny.

Mesopotamia was the cradle that nurtured nascent astrology. From there it spread eastward, to India and beyond, evolving into different astrological traditions. In terms of Western astrology, it was the assimilation of the Babylonian tradition by the ancient Greeks that proved the most significant, both in clarifying astrological precepts and extending them to Greece's Mediterranean neighbors, and thence to other parts of the European continent. It is estimated that the ancient Greeks—enthusiastic diviners and readers of many different oracles—embraced Babylonian astrological beliefs between 600 and 500 BC. The first written Greek allusion to astrology was made during the following century by the philosopher Plato. Through Hellenistic influence, it reached into Macedonia and, after Alexander the Great's conquest, to Egypt and the Roman Empire, where it was probably introduced around 250 BC by Greek slaves.

The Greco-Roman formalization of astrological concepts shaped the system into one that is recognizable today. The Romans adopted the Greek pantheon of Olympic gods virtually wholesale, although they endowed them with Latin names. Thus the leading Greek deities who were associated with the planets were renamed as follows: Zeus became Jupiter; Ares, Mars; Aphrodite, Venus; Hermes, Mercury; and Kronos, Saturn. The luminaries did not enjoy such a simple translation, however. The Moon and its several phases was variously associated with Diana, Selen and Luna, among other goddesses, while the all-powerful Sun was the shared province of Apollo, Sol Invictus ("the unconquered Sun") and Mithras. The

Medieval astronomers.

cult of the latter deity was particularly associated with astrological tenets, for it had seven grades of initiation, each of which corresponded to a planet.

Just as astrology thrived in imperial Rome, so it spread to the outposts of its empire—a vast entity that dominated much of Europe, the Near East and northern Africa. It was the advent of Christianity that heralded astrology's decline, for the emphasis that the former placed on individual free will and potential redemption contradicted the principles inherent in the latter, especially the belief that an individual's destiny is preordained, or "written in the stars." The first Christian emperor, Constantine (AD 274–337), pronounced astrology "demonic" in 333: from then on, Christianity's ascent in Europe was inversely paralleled by astrology's decline. However, not all parts of Europe became Christianized. Some regions were subject to the influence of Islamic culture—specifically Spain, which was conquered by the Arab-Berber Moors in 711 and reconquered by Christian forces by 1250 (apart from Granada, which remained Islamic until 1492).

There are many reasons why, during Europe's astrological dark age, the tradition continued to be the subject of serious and concerted study in Islamic lands, initially according to the translation of the *Almagest* along Ptolemaic lines. Between the eighth and tenth centuries, astrological treatises from India, Persia and Syria, as well as Greece, were also transcribed into Arabic. For the ritual observance of the Islamic believer, it was important that both the correct times for prayer and the direction of Mecca be identified accurately, and they could be determined only by charting the movements of the various celestial bodies. Scientific knowledge was encouraged as a means of attaining *tawhid*, or "the oneness of Allah." The simultaneous flowering of such mathematical disciplines as trigonometry advanced the Arab astrologers' understanding of the "science of the decrees of the stars," and dedicated observatories were established at Maragha in Azerbaijan in 1259 and at Samarquand during the fifteenth century. There astronomers worked meticulously with such instruments as the astrolabe and quadrant.

Following the fall of Arab Granada to the Spanish monarchs Ferdinand and Isabella, Christians were reintroduced to astrology at the city's celebrated Moorish universities, partly as a result of the influence of Judeo-Spanish scholars, who reconciled many astrological principles with those governing their own mystical system of belief, the Kabbalah. From the fifteenth century, astrology enjoyed an unprecedented renaissance in Europe. Taught as a science at universities, it was regarded as a vital source of medical knowledge and treatment, for according to the macrocosmic-microcosmic principles of melothesia, the human body was a microcosm of the celestial macrocosm, or *imago mundi* ("image of the world [or universe]"). Hence each of its component parts was subject to the influence of the planet that rules it. It was also considered a prophetic system, and as a result, such astrological practitioners to royalty as

Medieval representation of a constellation.

John Dee (1527–1608) and Nostradamus— Michel de Nostredame—(1503–66) enjoyed the respective patronage of the English monarch Elizabeth I and the French queen Catherine de' Medici and her son Charles IX. Ordinary citizens, too, consulted popular astrologers like the Englishman William Lilly (who is said to have predicted London's plague year of 1665 and the city's great fire in 1666), and printers could barely satisfy the demand for astrological almanacs.

Even the previously hostile Roman Catholic Church now accepted the system that it had so vehemently condemned. The dates of papal coronations were set according to the auspices indicated by the stars, while zodiacal symbols decorated churches, their presence subtly justified by their reinterpretation as Christian symbols (Virgo, for example, representing the Virgin Mary, and Pisces referring to Christ's role as the fisher of men). Yet although Roman Catholic authorities now acknowledged the influence of the constellations as indicators

Physical correspondences of the constellations.

around 7 BC); or the "dog star." A related theory is that the three wise men were astrologers from Persia, who followed the star in the belief that it indicated the imminent fulfillment of a prophecy made by Zoroaster (c.628–551 BC).

Another school of astrological beliefs reconciles the characteristics of the zodiacal signs said to govern two-thousand-year eras with human, and specifically Judeo-Christian, behavior. Thus the astrological age of Taurus, the bull (from about 4000 to 2000 BC), was indicated by the idolatrous worship of the golden calf; that of Aries, the ram (lasting for 2000 years from c.2000 BC), by the near-sacrifice of Isaac by Abraham and the substitution of a ram in his place. These episodes occurred in the Old Testament, while the birth of Christ heralded the age of Pisces, the fish, predicted to end about AD 2000. Because the vernal equinox has slipped over the millennia, the age of Aquarius has been calculated as starting at any time between 1904 and 2160).

Inevitably, the cumulative result of the discoveries made by such notable astronomers as Copernicus, Tycho Brahe (1546–1601), Galileo, Johann Kepler (1571–1630) and Isaac Newton (1642–1727), was a diversion of the study of the celestial bodies into two discrete spheres. Astronomy was considered "scientific," while astrology was a dubious kind of divinatory art. The discovery of three planets unknown to the ancient stargazers—Uranus (in 1781), Neptune (1846) and Pluto (1930)—seemed to cast new doubt on astrological principles. However, modern astrologers have reconciled such

of fate, they never regarded them as agents of destiny. Furthermore, the roles of the planets, with their dangerously pagan names, were minimized in relation to those of the zodiacal signs.

It is interesting to note that some commentators have suggested fascinating parallels between many events described in the Bible and possible astrological occurrences. For example, the star that Matthew mentions hovering over Bethlehem, guiding the Magi from the east to the birthplace of Jesus Christ (2:1–12), has been variously interpreted as: a supernova; Halley's Comet (thought to have been visible in the skies around 11 BC); the conjunction of Jupiter and Saturn in the constellation of Pisces (believed to have occurred findings with traditional principles (which provide the answers to previously puzzling anomalies), and astrology remains as significant and enlightening a subject today as it was four thousand years ago.

ASTROLOGY RE-EVALUATED

During the last century or so, in conjunction with the emergence of the discipline of psychology, the role of astrology has undergone a change of emphasis. The work of American astrologer Marc Jones (1888–1980) popularized the Sabian symbols (channeled by a clairvoyant in 1925), which impart an evocative image to each degree of the zodiac to enable psychological inspiration and illumination through free association and meditation. In this respect, "the battles of life actually are fought, and won or lost, in the purely psychological and intangible areas of being.... Here, in the individual's ability to create at will, is the dynamic of his being and the essence of his functional or actual identity. It is with this that any effective astrology must have its primary concern," wrote Jones in his seminal work *The Sabian Symbols in Astrology* (1953).

The pioneering psychologist Carl Gustav Jung (1875–1961), who also made a serious study of alchemy and mythology, thought that astrology and its symbols were an integral part of humanity's collective unconscious—that part of the human psyche that contains the archetypes, the universal blueprints of human experience. Through studying the horoscopes of certain clients, he

A personification of Saturn.

also came to believe in synchronicity ("the 'acausal' correspondences between mutually independent psychic and physical events"). After evaluating a study of nearly five hundred married couples' horoscopes to ascertain whether mutual compatibility was determined by astrological influences, he stated: "The statistical material shows that a practical as well as a theoretically improbable chance combination star occurred which coincides in the most remarkable way with traditional astrological expectations."

Some scientists are still unwilling to deny the possible truth of astrological tenets. The noted German astrologer and psychologist Reinhold Ebertin (b. 1901) was responsible for initiating a new realm

Arab astronomers during the Islamic Golden Age.

of study: cosmobiology, "a scientific discipline concerned with the possible correlations between cosmos and organic life and the effect of cosmic rhythms and stellar motions on man...plant and animal life as a whole." Undeniably, the gravitational pull of the Moon affects the tides. The decreasing Apogean tide, for example, occurs when the Moon is farthest from the Earth, while the increasing Perigean tide flows when the Earth is nearest to the Moon. Since ancient times, it has been observed that the Moon (Latin, *luna*) directly affects some people's behavior—hence the words "lunacy" and "lunatic" (the latter derived from *lunaticus*, meaning "moonstruck"). Statistical evidence indicates that violent crime tends to increase when the Moon is full. Why, then, should the other "planets" be disbarred from exerting a similar influence?

Many scientific studies have, in fact, attested to the macrocosmic influence of other planets over the microcosmic Earth. Noted German seismologist Rudolf Tomascheck, for instance, discovered that when Uranus is positioned within 15° of the meridian, violent earthquakes sometimes occur, a phenomenon that could be explained by the gravitational influence exerted by Uranus over the Earth's molten core. And although the French psychologist and statistician Michel Gauquelin, in a series of tests begun in 1949, concluded that he had disproved many astrological precepts, he did identify a curiously frequent series of "coincidences" in examining the birthdates of selected physicians, athletes and high achievers in other professional spheres, which he termed the "Mars effect." In noting the common occurrence of a shared Sun, Moon or rising sign between parents and their off-spring, he also suggested that humans may somehow be biologically attuned to celestial forces, and that the fetus may unconsciously "choose" the moment of its birth.

The South African-born astronomer Dr. Percy Seymour, in his compelling study *Astrology: the Evidence of Science* (1988), concurs: "According to my theory, [in the womb] we are all genetically 'tuned' to receiving a different set of 'melodies' from the magnetic 'symphony' of the Solar System." He goes on to state that: "the cosmos cannot alter our inherited characteristics but, by causing the actual moment of birth,… [our connection with the cosmos] is determined by our genes." Many scientists are becoming increasingly willing to explore, rather than reject outright, the ancient theory that human characteristics and behavioral patterns, along with those of other Earthly components, may be conditioned by the planets.

THE PRINCIPLES OF WESTERN ASTROLOGY

There are four leading systems of Western astrology: horary astrology, which is used to answer questions; electional astrology, employed to determine the optimum time when an intended course of action should be undertaken in order to ensure its success; mundane (or judicial) astrology, which is concerned with the forecasting of global, national or communal events; and natal astrology, whereby a person's characteristics and prospects are interpreted through the birth chart, or horoscope (a word derived from the Greek for "I look the hour," or "hour-watch"). Another type, natural astrology, has since been eclipsed by astronomy. It was used for practical purposes, for example, to set calendrical dates (such as Easter). Astrology is still sometimes used for predictive purposes, by calculating the planets' progressions or transits, their future positions or aspects, and then relating them to a specific birth chart.

THE ZODIAC

The zodiac may be defined as a circular belt extending for 8° on each side of the ecliptic, the path followed each solar year by the Sun, through which the twelve constellations pass cyclically. It is represented symbolically as a circle with the Sun at its center, with the zodiacal constellation arranged in a band around the perimeter, each occupying 30° of the 360° circle.

In the interests of scientific precision, it should be noted that because of the precession (simply described as a sort of wobble caused by the Earth's revolution on its axis) of the equinoxes—the vernal, around March 21, and the fall, around September 23—when the Sun crosses the celestial equator, the zodiacal constellations no longer occupy the same areas and dates traditionally assigned to them. For example, the Sun now traverses Leo between August 16 and September 15, whereas Leo's traditional dates ranged from July 23 to August 22. Therefore, effectively there are two zodiacs: the astrological zodiac, which is discussed here, and the movable.

Ancient star-gazers from many cultures observed that the constellations and planets seemed to follow the same cycle every year, each constellation reappearing at the same point in the night sky annually. Thus it was that the zodiacal cycle came to be used as a method of measuring time. The concept of the zodiac—derived from the Greek words *zodiakos kuklos*, "circus/circle of animated creatures," or *zoe* ("life") and *diakos* ("wheel")—is now believed to have originated in Mesopotamia around 3000 BC. During the earliest periods of astronomical observation, the Moon was considered more significant than the Sun, for not only were the constellations visible at night, but many ancient cultures venerated a lunar (often feminine) over a solar (usually masculine) deity. In contrast to today's convention, it was the Moon's, rather than the Sun's, progress through the zodiac that was charted. It is

An early Jewish zodiac.

believed that the ancient Egyptians assimilated the Mesopotamian zodiac, incorporating a new refinement: the decans (the three periods of approximately ten days into which the zodiacal "month" is divided). Each of the thirty-six divisions that resulted was equated with an astral deity.

Many of these deities were allotted patronage of a specific constellation, according to the image that the starry pattern appeared to paint in the sky: Isis, for example, was associated with the creature whose shape was seen in Virgo. Indeed, it is probably this pairing of astral spirit and zodiacal constellation that resulted in some members of the original "circus" (comprised solely of animals) assuming human or demihuman form. By extension, the influence of the macrocosm (the zodiacal constellation) on the microcosm (a person born under that sign) was seen as imparting the characteristics inherent in, for instance, Aries, to the natal Arian: like the heavenly ram, people born under this sign were said to be headstrong and energetic. This astrological belief has endured over the millennia, although modern astrologers recognize that many other natal influences must also be taken into account.

The zodiacal signs were also thought to affect human health. In microcosmic-macrocosmic thought ("as above, so below"), the macrocosm comprised the celestial components of the universe, which were mirrored exactly in the microcosm (the human body), over which they exerted a corresponding influence. This belief is graphically demonstrated in the medieval melothesic figure of "zodiacal man," in which each sign of the zodiac is strategically placed over the part of the body that it is said to govern. The theory underlying such representations profoundly influenced both medical diagnosis and treatment.

The symbolism associated with the twelve zodiacal signs is reflected in both the Jewish as well as the Christian religions. Eusebius (c.260–c.340), bishop of Caesarea (the modern city of Qisarya in Israel), chronicled the Jewish belief that Abraham was the father of the zodiac, and that each of the twelve tribes of Israel (named for the twelve patriarchs, the sons of Jacob) was associated symbolically with a sign of the zodiac. Within Christianity, not only are there twelve apostles, but St. John's Book of Revelation in the New Testament describes the post-Apocalyptic holy city of Jerusalem as resting on twelve cornerstones inscribed with the apostles' names, and as having twelve pearly gates. Medieval Church authorities Christianized the name of the zodiac itself to the Latin *corona seu circulus sanctorium apostolorum,* "the crown of the circle of the Holy Apostles." They also tried to reinterpret the pagan signs into Christian symbols (Aries, for example, becoming the lamb of God), but this attempt never captured the popular imagination. The zodiac also assumed a symbolic role in Christian legends, as when King Arthur's knights took their places at the table equated with its circular form.

By astrological convention, the zodiacal signs have various groupings, all of which add symbolic meaning to their interpretations.

The medieval humors.

Aries, Taurus, Gemini, Cancer, Virgo and Leo—called the septentironal signs from the Latin *septem* ("seven") and *triones* ("oxen") for the seven stars in the constellation of the Great Bear or Plow—are found in the northern hemisphere; Libra, Scorpio, Sagittarius, Capricorn, Aquarius and Pisces are southern-hemisphere constellations. Each sign is also accorded either feminine or masculine characteristics, which Ptolemy mentioned: "as the day is followed by the night, and as the male is coupled with the female." Each may also be balanced against its opposite, or polar, counterpart in a conflicting-complementing relationship similar to that of yin and yang. Thus Aries is paired with Libra; Taurus with Scorpio; Gemini with Sagittarius; Cancer with Capricorn; Leo with Aquarius; and Virgo with Pisces.

Also important to defining the type of character imparted by each zodiacal sign is its mode (or "quadruplicity," denoting the four signs allocated to it, each of which represents a different element), which is said to reflect a quality of life. These can be one of three: cardinal (representing creativity and activity—Aries, Cancer, Libra and Capricorn); fixed (signifying preservation and passivity—Taurus, Leo, Scorpio and Aquarius); and mutable (denoting destruction and changeability—Gemini, Virgo, Sagittarius and Pisces).

THE PLANETS

"Observe how system into system runs/ What other planets circle other suns," wrote Alexander Pope in his work *An Essay on Man,* Epistle I, li.25 (1733). And, indeed, the extent to which the astrological, calendrical and esoteric systems of world cultures and beliefs interact is astonishing, even in the light of syncretization and cross-fertilization of ideas. Nowhere is this more evident than in the influences associated with the planets, elements and seasons.

Perhaps the most significant figure in the history of astrology is Ptolemy (AD c.100–c.170), the Greco-Egyptian astronomer who grouped more than a thousand stars into forty-eight constellations. His key astrological treatise *Tetrabiblios*, written around AD 140, and specifically his *Almagest*, postulated that the Earth stood at the center of the universe, while the celestial bodies revolved around it. The Ptolemaic system prevailed until Copernicus disproved it in his posthumous opus *De Revolutionibus*

Orbium Coelestium (1544), but by then the belief that the planets and constellations orbited the Earth, rather than the Sun, had become deeply entrenched in astrological theory and symbolism. In examining the role of the planets, it must also be remembered that early astrologers not only regarded the Sun and Moon—the luminaries—as planets, but that the existence of the three planets mentioned earlier was unknown. For millennia the "planets' were defined as seven bodies: the Sun, Moon, Mercury, Venus, Mars, Jupiter and Saturn.

Modern astrologers follow Copernican rather than Ptolemaic principles, but many of the concepts popularized by Ptolemy endure, especially in terms of symbolic associations. The original seven "planets," for instance, were equated with the seven heavens, directions, days of the week, metals, and also—with the ascendance of Christianity—the cardinal virtues and sins, and gifts of the Holy Spirit. Yet Ptolemy did not originate, but rather perpetuated, the symbolic significance of the seven planets. The seven stepped levels that make up the Mesopotamian ziggurat, for example, were believed to represent the hierarchy of the seven "wandering stars" within the structure (the word "planet" is derived from the Greek *planetes*, "wanderer," because they appeared to move erratically in comparison to the fixed stars). They also signified the ascending stages leading from Earth to the heavens (representing increasing spiritual enlightenment). Called *etemenanki*, the "temple of the seven spheres of the world," or "house of the seven directions of heaven and Earth," the ziggurat's seven levels were painted to accord with the colors associated with the deities (whose Romanized names are given here): black (Saturn), orange (Jupiter), red (Mars), gold (the Sun), yellow (Venus), blue (Mercury) and silver (the Moon). The Mesopotamians regarded the Moon, rather than the Sun, as being most important, both in astronomical and sacred belief, and placed it at the ziggurat's zenith.

In microcosmic-macrocosmic thought, astrologers credit the planets with a more important role than the zodiacal constellations, for it is their position in the sky that is said to exert the greatest influence over everything that occurs on Earth, as well as over personalities. While the sign of the zodiac under which a person is born may be said to impart potential, the planets are the energizing factors that activate and direct these innate possibilities. For example, while each zodiacal sign was believed to hold sway over a specific part of the human body—the Sun was said to be the spirit and the Moon, the soul— the remaining planets were assigned one of the five senses. According to a related theory from antiquity—that of the Greek philosopher Pythagoras (570–496 BC)—the seven planetary spheres were arranged hemispherically above the Earth: their independent turning created the "music of the spheres" (as our musical scale consists of seven principal notes). When a human soul descended to Earth from the eighth sphere (the Empyrean), traveling down through each level, it received the attributes of the individual ruling planet, so that when it was manifested on Earth as a new-born baby it possessed the corresponding virtues—and vices. Given the awesome power supposedly invested in them, it is hardly surprising that the planets were believed to be gods, and under Greco-Roman influence, the older Mesopotamian deities were transformed first into the Olympians and then into Roman gods.

The geocentric Ptolemaic system ordered the cosmos as follows: the Earth at the center, surrounded by the circular spheres of the Moon, Mercury, Venus, the Sun, Mars, Jupiter and Saturn. In a further refinement, Plato (427–347 BC) regarded the universe as a "cosmic soul" rotating on its own axis, while Tycho Brahe believed that while the Sun and Moon revolved around the Earth, the planets rotated round the Sun. Today the order of precedence used by astrologers accords with the updated heliocentric Copernican system, in which the Sun—the center of the solar system—is followed by the Moon (actually the Earth's satellite), then the nearest planet, Mercury, and subsequently by Venus, (Earth), Mars, Jupiter, Saturn, Uranus, Neptune and Pluto. In astrological interpretation the planets are categorized into three groups, indicating the level of influence that each exerts over people and the Earth: the fast-moving, "personal" planets, the Sun, Moon, Mercury, Venus, and Mars; the middle, or "transpersonal," planets, Jupiter and Saturn, which revolve at a more stately and sedate pace; and the "impersonal" planets: Uranus, Neptune and Pluto, which move so slowly that they are thus described as having a generational, rather than a personal, effect.

The Sun ☉

Sigil: a dot within a circle
Zodiacal rulership: Leo
Associated deity: Apollo, the Roman god of the Sun, music, poetry and prophecy
Day: Sunday
Zodiacal cycle: 1 year
Characteristics bestowed: vitality and individual consciousness

The Moon ☽

Sigil: a crescent
Zodiacal rulership: Cancer
Associated deity: Diana/Artemis, goddess of the Moon and of the hunt
Day: Monday
Zodiacal cycle: approximately 28 days
Characteristics bestowed: profound emotions and intuition

Mercury ☿

Sigil: the caduceus
Zodiacal rulership: Gemini and Virgo
Associated deity: Mercury/Hermes messenger of the gods
Color: dark blue
Metal: mercury/quicksilver
Day: Wednesday
Zodiacal cycle: 88 days
Characteristics bestowed: intellectual ability and communication skills

Venus ♀

Sigil: a mirror or necklace
Zodiacal rulership: Taurus and Libra
Associated deity: Venus/Aphrodite, goddess of love and beauty

Day: Friday
Zodiacal cycle: 225 days
Characteristics bestowed: the quest for beauty and harmony; benevolence

Mars ♂

Sigil: a shield and spear
Zodiacal rulership: Aries (traditionally, also Scorpio)
Associated deity: Mars/Ares, the god of warfare and bloodshed
Day: Tuesday
Zodiacal cycle: 687 days
Characteristics bestowed: energy, leadership and aggression

Jupiter ♃

Sigil: the Greek letter zeta (Z)
Zodiacal rulership: Sagittarius (traditionally, also Pisces)
Associated deity: Jupiter/Zeus, the chief Greco-Roman god and deity of the sky
Day: Thursday
Zodiacal cycle: 11 years, 315 days
Characteristics bestowed: expansive energy and optimism

Saturn ♄

Sigil: a sickle
Zodiacal rulership: Capricorn (traditionally, also Aquarius)
Associated deity: Saturn/Kronos god of agriculture and time
Day: Saturday
Zodiacal cycle: 29 years, 167 days
Characteristics bestowed: growing wisdom and maturity

Uranus ♅

Sigil: the letter "H" bisected by
  an orb
Zodiacal rulership:
  Aquarius
Associated deity:
  Uranus/Ouranos,
  the sky god
Zodiacal cycle:
  84 years
Characteristics bestowed:
  transcendental
  energy, unpredictabil-
  ity and inventiveness

Neptune ♆

Sigil: a trident
Zodiacal rulership: Pisces
Associated deity: Neptune/
  Poseidon, god of the sea
Zodiacal cycle: 168 years, 292
  days
Characteristics bestowed:
  psychic powers, idealism, escapism and
  confusion

Pluto ♇

Sigil: an orb enclosed by a crescent; the
  initials "P" and "L"
Zodiacal rulership: Scorpio
Associated deity: Hades, god of the
  underworld
Zodiacal cycle: 248 years, 183 days
Characteristics bestowed: the power to effect
  transformation

A representation of the constellations.

THE ELEMENTS

Just as the numbers twelve (the total zodiacal signs) and seven (the sum of the traditional planets) are symbolically important
within astrology, so the number four
assumes additional significance, for each of
the four elements (fire, air, water and earth)
is associated with three signs of the zodiac.

From classical through medieval times,
and even for some centuries later, it was
believed that everything in the universe
was made up of the four elements, differences in form and character arising from the
attractive and repulsive properties and relationships of elements, as well as the varying

proportions of the four vital ingredients. Solid matter (represented by the element of earth), liquid (water) and vapor (air) were each believed to be inherent in any object or living being, while fire provided animating energy. The basest or heaviest element was earth, followed by water, the lightest or most elevated elements being air and fire. (In esoteric thought, originated by the ancient Greeks, there is also a rarefied fifth element, ether, the perfect element which contains and generates the other four, from which the ethereal stellar and planetary bodies are made, and which exists only in the heavenly sphere.)

Although it was the ancient Greeks, and specifically Empedocles (c.490–30 BC), who formalized the elemental theory, they had inherited a concept so ancient that scholars believe it stretches back to Neolithic times, and perhaps even beyond. Some speculate that it was derived from the early human realization that corpses can only be disposed of satisfactorily by four means: burying them in the earth; throwing them into a body of water, there to sink to the bottom of a river, sea or lake bed; allowing carrion birds, such as vultures, to swoop from the air and feast on the remains; or cremating them on a pyre. Thus the human body was perceived to be reclaimed by the elements after death, to dissolve into its elemental component parts, and then to be ecologically reconstituted. And just as the planets were personified as gods, so most sacred beliefs elevated the elements to deified status, venerating an Earth Mother, such as the Greco-Roman Demeter (Ceres) or a

divine ruler of the Underworld like Hades (Pluto); a god of water, such as Poseidon (Neptune); a deity whose realm was the air, most notably Zeus (Jupiter); and a fire god like Hephaestos (Vulcan).

In medieval times, and also in alchemical thought, each element was associated with an appropriate spirit: gnomes represented the earth; undines, water; sylphs, air; and salamanders, fire. In this respect, too, astrological and Christian symbolism are linked, for the form of the "astrologer's cross" was traditionally used to represent the Evangelists: St. John's eagle (equated with Scorpio and the element of air) standing on the northerly point; St. Luke's ox (related to Taurus and the element of earth) in the south; St. Matthew's angel (Aquarius and water) in the west; and St. Mark's lion (Leo and fire) in the east.

In a further refinement of the macrocosmic-microcosmic elemental concept in relation to the human body, medieval physicians not only believed that each zodiacal sign governed a particular limb or organ, but also that four elemental "humors" flowed through the body, and that certain ailments were caused by an imbalance of these. The element of earth was equated with black bile, and the melancholic humor; water with phlegm, and thus the phlegmatic humor; air was associated with the blood, and hence with the sanguine humor; and fire with choler (yellow bile), and the choleric humor.

The twelve zodiacal signs are divided into four trigons, or triplicities, each of which corresponds to an element: the fiery (masculine) trigon, comprising Aries, Leo and Sagittarius; the airy (masculine) trigon, containing Gemini, Libra and Aquarius; the watery (feminine) trigon, consisting of Cancer, Scorpio and Pisces; and the earthy (feminine) trigon of Taurus, Virgo and Capricorn. Each element is believed to influence the personality: fire bestows vitality and aggression; air, intellectual aspiration and volatility; water, gentleness and changeability; and earth, patience and solidity. People born under the first zodiacal sign within each trigon (e.g., Aries within the fiery trigon) are said to manifest these characteristics in their purest form, while those whose natal signs are second and third in a trigon will possess these traits in gradually decreasing degrees.

ASTROLOGICAL GOVERNANCE OF TIME

Astrological precepts are inextricably linked with the measurement of time—cosmic and Earthly. Thus the symbolism of the number four is harnessed to the planets, which are associated with the idea of dividing time into "world periods," a concept that exists within most sacred traditions, from the Mesoamerican to the Zoroastrian, to the Hindu, Greco-Roman and Christian, among others. Ovid (43 BC–AD 18), in his work *Metamorphoses I*, specifies four such ages, of decreasing levels of perfection: the Golden Age, under the rulership of Saturn; the Silver Age, dominated by Jupiter; the Bronze/Brazen Age, and the Iron Age (the governing deities of the latter are not specified). St. Augustine of Hippo (354–430) specified seven ages in *De Civitate Dei* (The City of God), connected to the number

From Kepler's *The Rudolphine Tables* (1627).

of days listed in the Old Testament book of creation, Genesis (but also, in esoteric thought, with the planets).

The four elements are said to correspond to the cardinal directions and seasons: earth representing the south and fall; water, the west and winter; air, the north and spring; and fire, the east and summer (although these designations can vary). The Mesopotamian civilizations distinguished three seasons: spring, summer and winter; while the inhabitants of more northerly, harsher, climes recognized only two: summer and winter. As with so many conventions, it was the ancient Greeks who introduced the additional season of fall, thus harmonizing the seasons both numerically and symbolically with the elements and directions. In fact, the Greek word *horae* ("hours"), signifying the four goddesses who represented the seasons, was also used to describe the four quadrants of the cosmos.

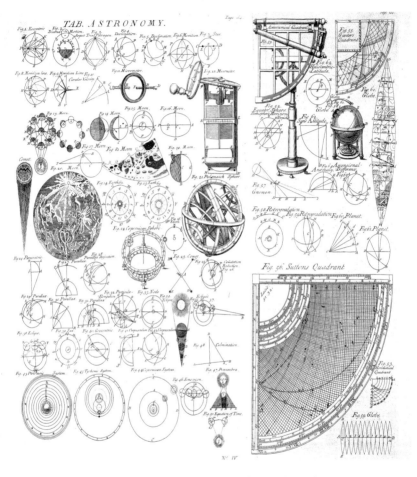

Astronomical diagrams in the 1728 publication *Cyclopedia*.

Spring denotes the time when nature awakens after its long sleep. The vernal equinox, which falls around March 21, was especially significant in sacred pagan rites: for example, it marked the beginning of the ancient Roman *hieros gamos* (held between March 22 and 24). By April 30, May Eve, the burgeoning of nature was evident, and the Romans dedicated their licentious festivities of May 1 to the fertility goddesses Floralia or Maia, while the Celts honored their Sun god Beli at the feast of Beltane. In the medieval Christian books of hours, the spring zodiacal constellations were equated with agricultural "labors of the months," Aries being associated with the pruning of vines, for instance; Taurus with the planting of flowers and training of vines; and Gemini with the scything of grass.

The arrival of summer is heralded by the summer solstice, which usually falls around June 21, a time when the prospect of the Sun's descent and the coming winter caused pagan peoples to burn fires to the Sun to encourage its eventual return. Important summer festivals included the Celtic Lughnasha on August 1—a sociable occasion when the grain god Lug was celebrated with games and feasting. Traditional summer activities include the reaping of harvests sown in spring, and the summer zodiacal signs reflected this emphasis— Cancer, haymaking; Leo, the scything and threshing of corn; and Virgo, the gathering of fruits.

Fall is a somewhat melancholy period, a transitional season when winter's chill begins to manifest itself even while the Sun still warm the Earth. The labors over which the zodiacal signs held sway reflect this duality, for Libra presided over the trading of grapes; Scorpio over the distillation of wine into casks; and Sagittarius over the harvesting of olives and the collection of kindling. Pagan tribes held ceremonial rites to mark the fall equinox around September 21, but perhaps the most important Celtic festival was that of Samhain, on November 1, when, according to the lunar calendar, it was believed that the old year ended and the new one began. The fact that it was regarded as a dangerous night, when a cosmic crack in time allowed the ghostly inhabitants of the "other world" to roam abroad, is still reflected in today's Hallowe'en celebrations.

Winter is a barren, cheerless season, but also promises the coming of spring, and at the winter solstice (around December 21), which ancient civilizations equated with the rebirth of the solar god, this promise of regeneration was celebrated in such festivities as the Roman Saturnalia, those in honor of Sol Invictus, and the Teutonic Yule. (Thus the Christian commemoration of the birth of Christ on December 25, and the riotous behavior associated with New Year's Eve in modern times, both recall ancient pagan festivals). Other fertility rites, including the Celtic Imbolc (February 1), also looked forward to the spring with activities traditionally associated with the zodiacal signs of winter: Capricorn governing the slaughter of pigs and baking; Aquarius, the felling of trees; and Pisces the grafting of fruit-bearing trees.

Lunar Calendars

Today the Western world measures time in accordance with the solar calendar, and dates its years from the birth of Christ. (Since 1582, when the Gregorian calendar of Pope Gregory XIII replaced the Julian calendar devised by Julius Caesar in 46 BC, inaccuracies have been prevented by restricting century leap years to those divisible by four hundred.) Yet many of the world's major religions order their sacred calendars by lunar months according to ancient custom. Archaeological and historical evidence indicates that the Mesopotamian astronomers disregarded the position of the Sun in their observations, concentrating on that of the Moon for the purposes of lunar worship. Indeed, most ancient religions venerated the Moon, both because of its constantly changing shape which associated it with the cycle of life: birth (the new Moon); growth (the waxing, crescent Moon); maturity (the full Moon); decline (the waning, crescent Moon); death (the "black" Moon, comprising the three or four days when the Moon appears to be invisible); and rebirth (the new Moon again.) Another factor in its worship was the mysterious lunar effect on the ebb and flow of tides and its apparent effect upon menstrual cycles. It is said that the Roman emperor Numa Pomphilius (8th century BC) increased the number of months comprising a year from ten to twelve in order to regulate the lunar and solar cycles, thus instigating a conscious shift in importance from the Moon to the Sun in Western thought.

The Jewish calendar (*huach ha-shanah*) is primarily lunar, although it includes adjustments (the addition of an extra month between February and March seven times within every nineteen years) related to the solar cycle. Thus ritual celebrations of agricultural origin, such as the *sukkoth* harvest festival, do not fall out of synchronicity with the seasons (the lunar year is some eleven days shorter than the solar). Such is the ancient importance of the Moon in Judaism that it is symbolically equated with the children of Israel, while the Sun represents Gentiles (all other peoples). At the start of each month, the birth of the new Moon (*molad*) may be greeted with ritual rejoicing called *rosh chodesh*. Since medieval times, years have been counted from the date when God is believed to have created the world, that is, 3760 BC.

Like the Jewish calendar, that of Hinduism is lunar-based, although it is modified by the addition of a month every two-and-a-half years to bring it into line with the solar cycle. Each lunar month is thought of as consisting of two light (*shukra*), positive weeks, indicated by the waxing of the Moon, and two dark (*krishna*), negative weeks, heralded by the Moon's waning. The Islamic religious calendar is also lunar-based, from the date of Mohammed's migration (*hejira*) from Mecca to Medina (September 622 ad). This is the starting point not only for the calculation of years, but also for the month (in this case *muharram*) that opens the new year. Even Christianity, most of whose feasts and saints' days are celebrated on fixed annual dates, retains the influence of the lunar calendar in the moveable date of Easter Sunday (commemorating Christ's resurrection), which may fall on any Sunday between March 21 and April 25, according to when the Moon first becomes full after the vernal equinox. (Christianity and Judaism's shared sacred history closely links this date with that of the Jewish Passover, when Christ suffered).

Although astrology is heliocentric rather than lunacentric today, the Moon remains an extremely significant force: as

it progresses through the zodiacal signs, it exerts a strong influence over the Earth and its inhabitants. During those periods when it is between the signs, it is said to be "void in course," its absence threatening dangerous instability.

Of further significance in astrological calculations are the Moon's two nodes, or "dragon points" (so called because a dragon was envisaged as swallowing and then regurgitating the celestial bodies). The Dragon's Head (*Caput Draconis)*, the ascending, northern node, denotes where the Moon's orbit crosses that of the Earth's ecliptic as the latter rotates around the Sun; and the Dragon's tail (*Carda Draconis)*, or southern node, which lies directly opposite. The Dragon's Head and Tail are respectively termed Lo-hou and Chi-tu by Chinese astrologers, and Ratu and Ketu by Indian astrological practitioners. In ancient times the lunar nodes were important to the calculation of solar and lunar eclipses, but today Chinese and Indian astrologers consider them especially important for the interpretation of horoscopes. They are believed to represent the subject's karma—the northern node showing areas in which improvements should be made in life; and the southern, the subject's genetic inheritance (or the characteristics that stem from a former existence).

CHINESE ASTROLOGY

The Chinese calendar is among the most ancient of the world's surviving cultures. Based primarily on the lunar cycle, along with numerical and other astronomical observations, it is not only extremely complex, but is inseparable from the indigenous system of astrology—one that now rivals that of the West in terms of popularity. In a modified form, Chinese astrology also forms the basis of the Japanese tradition, as well as that practiced by Lamaist priests in Tibet Region of China. Chinese astrology, *ming shu* ("the reckoning of fate"), is said to have been instituted by the "Yellow Emperor," Huang Ti, in 2637 BC. He and his successors were divinely generated—"sons of heaven," who were considered directly responsible for ensuring celestial harmony in the realm. Chinese astrologers regard their craft as more predictive than that of their Western counterparts (who prefer to regard their conclusions as indicative), and in order to ascertain a person's destiny, knowledge of the precise time and place of birth is crucial.

THE CHINESE ZODIAC

Although they are said to date back to 3000 BC, it is speculated that the creatures now associated with the zodiac entered Chinese astrology around the first century AD, and that they were derived from

a Western exemplar brought to China by Turkish traders. The more conventional view is that they were introduced during the T'ang dynasty, around AD 600, and indicated the animals that should be sacrificed on the opening of each month or year, for unlike the Western signs, these creatures do not represent the names of the zodiacal constellations. The identities of the twelve signs are explained by the Buddhist legend that before his death Buddha summoned all the animals on Earth to him: only twelve responded (the rat narrowly beating the ox to arrive first), and he rewarded them by naming a year after each. The twelve are neatly divided into two additional categories: wild creatures (the rat, tiger, rabbit, dragon, snake and monkey) and domesticated ones (the ox, horse, goat, cock, dog and pig); and those that are respectively yin and yang. Such signs alternate throughout the cycle of the zodiac, with each yang creature paired with a yin animal (the yang rat and yin ox, for example) in a conflicting-complementing partnership.

Although the animals are now said to govern each month, as well as two hours of every day, their real importance lies in each creature's rulership of a year, resulting in a zodiacal cycle of twelve lunar years. The zodiac itself is represented as a "year tree," consisting of twelve branches under which the creatures graze. People's personalities are said to be influenced by the nature of the creature in whose year they were born. Just as Western astrology acknowledges the importance of the ascendant sign at time of birth, so in the Chinese system the influence of the creature that prevailed at the hour of birth is said to affect the way in which people present themselves to others, according to the "personality" of the animal that governs the double-hour concerned.

The Rat *(da shu)*
Polarity: yang
Element: water
Direction: north
Western equivalent: Sagittarius
Hours of ascendance: 11 p.m. to 1 p.m.
Characteristics bestowed: positive action, fortune, wealth and expansion

The Ox (buffalo or cow, *nion*)
Polarity: yin
Element: water
Direction: north-northeast
Western equivalent: Capricorn
Hours of ascendance: 1 a.m. to 3 a.m.
Characteristics bestowed: patience, industriousness and responsibility

The Tiger *(po hon)*
Polarity: yang
Element: wood
Direction: east-northeast
Western equivalent: Aquarius
Hours of ascendance: 3 a.m. to 5 a.m.
Characteristics bestowed: power, aggression and impulsiveness

The Rabbit (or hare, *tu ze*)
Polarity: yin
Element: wood
Direction: east

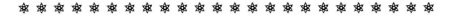

Western equivalent: Pisces
Hours of ascendance: 5 a.m. to 7 a.m.
Characteristics bestowed: good fortune, harmony and sensitivity

The **Dragon** *(long)*

Polarity: yang
Element: wood
Direction: east-southeast
Western equivalent: Aries
Hours of ascendance: 7 a.m. to 9 a.m.
Characteristics bestowed: energy, egotism and enthusiasm

The **Snake** (or serpent, *sue*)

Polarity: yin
Element: fire
Direction: south-southeast
Western equivalent: Taurus
Hours of ascendance: 9 a.m. to 11 a.m.
Characteristics bestowed: shrewdness, stealth and mystery

The **Horse** *(ma)*

Polarity: yang
Element: fire
Direction: south
Western equivalent: Gemini
Hours of ascendance: 11 a.m. to 1 p.m.
Characteristics bestowed: determination, optimism and fickleness

The **Goat** (ram or sheep, *yang*)

Polarity: yin
Element: fire
Direction: south-southwest
Western equivalent: Cancer
Hours of ascendance: 1 p.m. to 3 p.m.

Characteristics bestowed: sensitivity, compassion and gentleness

The **Monkey** *(hou)*

Polarity: yang
Element: metal
Direction: west-southwest
Western equivalent: Leo
Hours of ascendance: 3 p.m. to 5 p.m.
Characteristics bestowed: intelligence, versatility and humor

The **Rooster** *(cock, ji)*

Polarity: yin
Element: metal
Direction: west
Western equivalent: Virgo
Hours of ascendance: 5 p.m. to 7 p.m.
Characteristics bestowed: critical faculties, pride and independence

The **Dog** *(gou)*

Polarity: yang
Element: metal
Direction: west-northwest
Western equivalent: Libra
Hours of ascendance: 7 p.m. to 9 p.m.
Characteristics bestowed: loyalty, fairness and straightforwardness

The **Pig** (or boar, *zhu*)

Polarity: yin
Element: water
Direction: north-northwest
Western equivalent: Scorpio
Hours of ascendance: 9 p.m. to 11 p.m.
Characteristics bestowed: good humor, sensuality and honesty

THE LUNAR MANSIONS

Another significant convention to be considered is the Chinese custom of dividing the year into twenty-eight lunar *hsiu*, "mansions" (the palaces in which the Moon goddess resides every night in rotation during her passage across the sky). Each is equated with a ruling spirit and animal, as well as a Taoist disciple of the immortal T'ung-t'ien Chiao-chu (the first, for example, is the dragon's horn, whose animal is the scaly dragon; whose spirit is Teng Yo, and whose disciple is named as Po-lin Tao-jen), and whose name also corresponds to a day. In many respects, a greater parallel can be drawn between these lunar mansions and the Western zodiacal constellations than between the latter and the twelve Chinese beasts of the constellations, for the *hsiu* are said to exist within the constellations that lie along the celestial equator, through which the Moon passes.

THE CHINESE ELEMENTS

A vital component of Chinese astrology, as of Western astrology, is the modifying influence of the elements (*wu hsing*). However, in Chinese astrological thought—also said to have been originated by Huang Ti, but formalized by Tsou Yen (305–240 BC)—these number five, rather than four: water, fire, earth, metal and wood (the latter two replacing and supplementing the fourth Western element of air, which the Chinese regard as *ch'i*, the breath of life). The Chinese elemental theory is bound up with the Taoist belief in the cosmic polarities of yin and yang, which exist in opposition yet possess the potential to produce perfection when in harmony, each element possessing both yang (the masculine, solar, active principle), and yin (the female, lunar, passive force) aspects. The twelve zodiacal creatures and the years over which they preside are, however, one or the other—each positive year (perhaps that of the rat), being followed by a negative one (the year of the ox).

The theory underlying the five elements is similar to the Western view: all manifestations of cosmic energy (also called ch'i) are contained within them. The elements exist in a constant, cyclical state of engagement and battle for supremacy, explained by the fact that metal implements can be used to fell trees (wood); wood takes essential nourishment from the earth; earth hinders the flow of water; water extinguishes fire; and fire can melt metal. In the reverse aspect, metal can be used to contain water; water gives life to trees, and thus wood; wood gives energy to fire; the ashes produced by fire nurture the earth; and metal ore comes from the earth.

As in Western thought, the five Chinese elements are also associated with the seasons (the fifth season briefly separating summer and fall). The twenty-eight constellations are traditionally divided among the four quarters of the universe, each quadrant being allocated a season and guardian creature. East is the season of spring, protected by the green dragon; south, summer, and the scarlet phoenix (*feng huang*); west, fall and the white tiger or unicorn (*kylin*); and north, winter, with a black tortoise encircled by a snake. The center of this quadrant represents

China. Just as much Western symbolism is largely informed by the number four—the number of the Western elements—so the elemental number of five is used to represent such sacred concepts as the number of virtues, blessings and books of ritual, as well as the five emperors of heaven *(wu ti)*. The elements also play a vital part in the practice of feng shui, which seeks to identify and rectify any kind of elemental imbalance in the landscape.

In order to determine your own personal element, it is necessary to consult tables to discover, in order of their significance: the element of your year of birth (perhaps positive fire); the element associated with the animal sign that governs your natal year (perhaps the rooster, which is negative); the element that governs your hour of birth; the element that presides over the month of your birth; and the element that is linked with your country of birth. The element that occurs most frequently is regarded as your dominant sign, and thus the strongest personality indicator, although ideally each element should be represented within this grouping of five in order to produce a well-balanced personality.

Metal
Direction: west
Season: fall
Color: white
Characteristics bestowed: fairness, determination, inflexibility and melancholy

Water
Direction: north

Season: winter
Color: blue
Characteristics bestowed: compassion, flexibility, nervousness and hypersensitivity

Wood
Direction: east
Season: spring
Color: green
Characteristics bestowed: creativity, cooperation, impatience and lack of focus

Fire
Direction: south
Season: summer
Color: red
Characteristics bestowed: dynamism, passion, egotism, pride, frustration and recklessness

Earth
Direction: the center
Color: yellow
Characteristics bestowed: patience, practical skills, caution and stubbornness

OTHER TRADITIONS

It is generally (though not universally) accepted that the form of astrology practiced in India today originated in Mesopotamia, the "cradle of civilization." Indian astrology is closely interlinked with other forms of Hindu mystical tradition, such as *kundalini* yoga, and shares the microcosmic-macrocosmic theories that assumed such vital importance in traditional Western astrology. Thus, for example, it is said that while a fetus is growing in the womb two chakras ("wheels") are simultaneously being formed within the unborn child. One, the twelve-segmented *pingala*, corresponds to the signs of the solar zodiac, and the other, the *ina*, comprises twenty-eight components, each of which is equated with a house of the lunar zodiac. This theory implies that people harbor these dual forms of physical horoscope within their bodies.

Based primarily on the Chinese system of astrology, the Tibetan tradition tradition differs subtly from its parent. The Chinese rat, for instance, is replaced by a mouse, the rabbit by a hare, and the rooster by an unspecified bird. The influence of Indian astrological beliefs is also evident in those of its geographical neighbor, and the Lamaist astrologers *(tsi-pa)* practice any of three types of interpretation and prediction: the Chinese-influenced system of *jung-tsi*, in which yin and yang, the five elements, and twelve animals all play a crucial part; *kar-tsi*, whose origins are believed to lie in Hindu *kalachakra* tantric principles, and which employs nine planets, twelve houses (i.e., zodiacal signs), and twenty-seven constellations; and *wang-char*, a numerological and talismanic system that its adherents believe was taught to human beings by the Hindu god Shiva himself.

Indian astrology.

CONSTRUCTING A HOROSCOPE

Astrologers believe that by charting the positions of the luminaries, planets and zodiacal constellations at the exact time of a person's birth (or, indeed, a nation's inception), valuable conclusions as to that person's personality and potential, as well as possible future challenges, can be drawn by interpreting the influences that prevailed when they came into the world.

The charting of a horoscope is a highly skilled art, which requires a profound knowledge and understanding of the complex principles and interrelationships that govern astrology. Consulting an experienced astrologer, or perhaps taking advantage of the detailed, but now readily accessible, information stored in dedicated computer-software packages, is recommended. In order to compile as accurate a picture as possible, it is vital to know the subject's exact time of birth, and also his or her birthplace: any variation in these two crucial factors can lead to a distorted or false reading.

Once armed with the date and place of the subject's birth, the astrologer will consult a tabular daily listing (ephemeris) to ascertain the positions of the Sun, Moon and planets within the zodiac at that particular moment in "sidereal" time (astronomical, rather than artificially regulated time, such as Greenwich Mean Time). An atlas is also needed to calculate the latitude and longitude of the place of birth, which will then be added or subtracted from the sidereal time to calculate the astronomically correct time of birth. This information, in turn, will enable the astrologer to draw up a horoscope according to a prescribed circular format, in which the zodiacal signs occupy the outer band at 30° intervals, with the sigils of the luminaries and planets placed at the appropriate points. The tenth and twentieth degree of the circle are often differentiated by long lines, while the fifth, fifteenth and twenty-fifth are identified by dotted, or shorter, lines. Within the elliptic of each sign are further subdivisions: the thirty degrees themselves, and the three groups consisting of ten degrees (the decans).

THE HEMISPHERES

The circle is further divided into four quarters, or hemispheres, signifying the four cardinal points: the ascendant (ASC) in the east; the descendent (DSC) in the west; midheaven, or *mediumcoeli* (MC) in the north; and the *immum coeli* (IC) in the south. Thus the horoscope may be regarded as a sort of cosmic map of the heavens at the time of the subject's birth. The Sun sign, that is, the zodiacal constellation occupied by the Sun at the time of birth, is the most important component in the horoscope, for this indicates the subject's dominant personal characteristics. The second most significant

indicator is the ascendant, or rising sign (for which knowledge of the subject's time and date of birth is especially vital). Situated on the cusp of the first house, it reveals further information about the subject's personality, especially his or her means of expression. The planet that rules the zodiac sign situated on the ascendant is the subject's ruling planet. The descendant sign, on the cusp of the seventh house, imparts information about the subject's unconscious mind, while the midheaven sign, on the cusp of the fourth house, represents the zenith, or highest point in terms of potential success, and the *imum coeli*, on the cusp of the tenth house, indicates a person's lowest point, or nadir.

THE HOUSES

Next the astrologer will consider the implications of the planets' position within the twelve houses (represented as twelve segments) that hold sway over various aspects of daily life, and through which the zodiacal bodies pass every twenty-four hours. According to the mundane-house system, which equates the houses with the zodiacal signs, each house has a specific area of influence traditionally dictated by its zodiacal sign and its ruling planet:

I: personality, appearance and beginnings (Aries/Mars)
II: financial concerns, possessions and growth (Taurus/Venus)
III: communication skills, siblings and mundane matters (Gemini/Mercury)
IV: the childhood environment, parents and background (Cancer/The Moon)

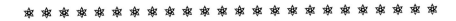

V: creativity and children (Leo/The Sun)
VI: health and work (Virgo/Mercury)
VII: relationships (Libra/Venus)
VIII: spirituality, inner motivations and change (Scorpio/Pluto)
IX: philosophical considerations and learning (Sagittarius/Jupiter)
X: professional concerns and ambition (Capricorn/Saturn)
XI: friendship and group activities (Aquarius/Uranus)
XII: uncertainty, privacy and karma (Pisces/Neptune)

If planets fall within their "own" houses, they are said to exert a harmonious influence. Yet just as the location of planets within zodiacal signs can cause subtle changes in personality, their placement within the houses also indicates a distinctive synergy between house and planet (the Moon in the first house, for example, indicates a self-absorbed character, while Jupiter suggests an expansive, optimistic personality). The houses are numbered counterclockwise from the eastern horizon, running full circle through the zenith. Those houses that fall within the eastern half of the circle are in the ascendant (as indicated by the first), and those on the western are descendant (marked by the seventh). The houses are further categorized as angular (comprising I, IV, VII, and X); succeedent (II, V, VIII, and XI); and cadent (III, VI, IX, and XII), in which the angularly placed planets initiate particular circumstances, to be modified by the succeedent and finally the cadent houses.

THE ASPECTS

Another consideration to be evaluated is the planetary aspects, or the angular relation of the planets to each other according to the number or degrees between them. Because each planet travels through the zodiac at a different speed, their position varies, and may be determined either by calculation or by a useful device termed an aspect finder. The aspects may exert either a positive or negative influence. The conjunction (and the self-explanatory parallel), in which planets occupy the same point, within 8° of each other, can be either beneficial or difficult, depending on the characteristics of the specific planets. The quincunx or inconjunct, in which planets are placed 150° apart, can indicate complications, while the quintile (72°) and biquintile (144°) exert a mildly positive influence.

The positive, or "benefic" aspects are: The semisextile, 30°=an easy relationship; the sextile, 60°=communication ability; the trine, 120°=great creativity. The negative, or "malefic" aspects are: the semisquare, 45°=difficulties; the square, 90°=a tense relationship; the sesquiquadrate, 135°=stressful interaction; and the opposition, 180°=conflict and frustration.

Note that conflicting aspects may cancel each other out. The aspects of the planets should be recorded in the following order: the Moon in relation to Mercury, Venus, the Sun, Mars, Jupiter, Saturn, Uranus, Neptune and Pluto; then Mercury in relation to the subsequent planets, followed by a similar process for Venus, the Sun, Mars, Jupiter, Saturn, Uranus, Neptune and Pluto.

THE CUSPS

Some individuals are born on the "cusp" of two zodiacal signs, that is, "on the line" between the ending of one zodiacal sign and the beginning of another, may be said to have a combination of the characteristics inherent in each. Because the exact date of the Sun's entry into each zodiacal sign varies from year to year, a natal chart specific to the individual is necessary, in order to determine exactly where the subject's birthday lies in relation to the two, and therefore whether the influence of the departing sign is greater, or (more usually), if it is that of the incoming sign. In determining potential compatibility with others born under different signs, those born on the cusp should be especially aware of their decanates, which must be determined accurately to serve as reliable clues to harmonious relationships.

WELL–STARRED?

"We must resemble each other a little in order to understand each other, but we must be a little different to love each other." So said Paul Géraldy in *L'Homme et L'Amour* (1951), and this appears to hold true in astrological compatibility patterns. Cancerians and Pisceans are perhaps the exceptions to this rule, since they are often most compatible with those of their own sign, whereas most people are more likely to be best suited to partners born under another sign. For water-ruled Pisces and Cancer, each partner can give the other the tenderness and supportive nurturing that both crave.

Compatibility is an inexact science...

The astrologer's ability to predict a successful love match is subject to many vagaries and qualifications, of course. Reading an astrological analysis of how you and your lover's signs or dates of birth relate to one another can give you valuable insight into your relationship, but don't be despondent if your planetary influences, elements or or polarities clash. In this book the most well-starred relationships are indicated for each day of the year, but there are so many other influences that can interact with the date of birth (such as your year of birth, for example) that you should try to regard all astrological advice as a potential source of empowerment for improving your relationship, where your characteristics clash.

ADVICE TO READERS

The personality profiles and listings of significant events for each day of the year that follow have been constructed broadly on the principles of the Western astrological tradition. In discussing the evolution and tenets of the various forms of astrology and calendrical traditions that were—and still are—practiced throughout the world, it is clear that no system stands alone: each is predicated upon similar, and sometimes identical, beliefs—especially with regard to macrocosmic-microcosmic theory—even if specific names and refinements of practice vary to some degree. Thus astrology is both global and holistic in its nature and resonance, and no variant should be regarded as separate from, or contradictory to, another. Indeed, each could be regarded as a vital strand in a richly variegated fabric.

There are a number of points that the reader should bear in mind when consulting this book. The day on which the Sun enters each sign of the zodiac is not a fixed date, but varies from year to year. Therefore, while the dates marking the beginning and end of each zodiacal period (sign and decan) as given here are traditional, they were originally instigated for reasons of convenience rather than accuracy. This means, for example, that a person born on July 21, 1929—on the cusp of Cancer and Leo—should be aware that the degree of the zodiacal sign—the correct indicator—may not accord with the day of the month on which he or she was born, and that the

Galileo consulting the constellations.

nearest personality profiles on either side of this birth date may be more pertinent to the individual than that given for July 21.

Each degree (or day) is part of a larger grouping of ten—a decan, or decanate—a system devised by the ancient Egyptians to help them locate fixed stars. Each sign is subdivided into three decans (the first decanate covering 0° to 10° of the segment of the zodiacal circle occupied by the sign; the second, 11° to 20°; and the third 21° to 30°). In this book, the decans have their traditional positions, but remember that just as the correspondence of degrees to dates varies by specific years, so do the starting and ending dates of each decan's period of influence (because there are 360 degrees in the zodiacal circle, but 365 days in the year—except for leap years).

To gain more than a general understanding of, and guide to, the astrological influences that govern an individual's personality, it is vital to consult a reputable astrologer, who will draw up a detailed horoscope showing the exact position of the planets and zodiacal constellations that prevailed at the time of birth, and will help interpret and draw lessons from the complex information revealed. Astrology does not promise concrete answers to specific questions: like life itself, it operates in subtle and infinitely variable ways. The information that it yields should be regarded as an enlightening guide to one's potential rather than as tablets set in stone.

The noted British astrologer Robert Currey urges his clients to remember while they are digesting the "cosmic inheritance" detailed in the horoscopes that he prepares for them: "Your genes and environmental conditions, such as your upbringing, are also key influences...astrology can reveal the impact of these conditions and your perception of them in surprising ways." Every person is an individual—no one else shares the genetic inheritance, the experiences that have shaped him or her since birth, his or her knowledge, perceptions and desires. So in reading the natal observations and advice contained here, the birthday person should remember that they represent a framework within which individual characteristics and predilections may vary greatly.

Remember, too that we are all constantly evolving, so that while one may not immediately recognize or concur with the personality summary presented, the passage of time and intervening events may make the words ring truer when consulted later. Do use the space provided on each page for notes of any observations that may be transient, or perhaps puzzle you at first reading. Alternatively, this space may be used to record relevant notes about friends or family members.

Finally, the question of free will must be taken into account. Throughout their lives people are presented with choices, faced with paths whose direction, if followed, may change them irrevocably. Astrology guides, but does not dictate, and while it offers sound advice, it is up to individuals to take responsibility for themselves and determine their own destiny—for better or for worse. For, as Paracelsus commented astutely in *Astronomia Magna* (1537): "The stars must obey man and be subject to him, and not he to the stars. Even if he is a child of Saturn and if Saturn has overshadowed his birth, he can master Saturn and become a child of the Sun."

The Days of the

YEAR

✳ ✳

✳ ✳

♈ ARIES

March 21 to April 20

RULING PLANET: *Mars* ELEMENT: *Cardinal fire*
SYMBOL: *Ram* POLARITY: *Positive (masculine)* COLORS: *White, red*
PHYSICAL CORRESPONDENCE: *Head, brain*
STONES: *Amethyst, ruby, diamond*
FLOWERS: *Hollyhock, carnation, poppy, thistle, geranium*

Aries is traditionally the first sign of the zodiac. Its ascendancy during the first month of the Northern Hemisphere's spring associates it with the burgeoning of life and the renewal of solar energy following winter, and thus with new beginnings. The ancient Egyptians identified the ram with their creator deity, the Sun-god Amon Ra, who was usually portrayed crowned with rams' horns. According to the Arab astronomer Abumsasr, the cosmos itself was created when the major planets were conjoined within the sign of Aries. While the Hindu zodiac equates Aries, as Mesha or Aja, with a ram or goat respectively, and the Persians termed it "the lamb," Varak, the Babylonian astronomers regarded the sign as either Zappu, "the hair," or Hungra, "the worker." The ancient Greeks called the ram of their zodiac Krios, and linked it with the golden-fleeced ram, which in turn was linked with Ares, the Greek god of war. The golden fleece subsequently adorned Ares's temple at Colchis, guarded by a fire-breathing serpent, until it was later claimed by Jason and his Argonauts. The association of this mythical ram with the zodiacal sign is confirmed by the shared Greek name for Mars, the ruling planet of this constellation.

It is Aries's association with the qualities traditionally attributed to the planet Mars—leadership, courage, aggression, and egotism—that in part defines the personal characteristics of those born under this sign, complemented by those that are suggested by the element of fire: heated emotions, vitality, and enthusiasm, but also the potential for impatience, impulsiveness, and destruction. And, of course, the headstrong and active nature of the ram itself further reinforces these dual associations.

MARCH 21

ZEALOUS LEADERS ♂ ♆

PLANETARY INFLUENCES
Ruling planets: Mars and Neptune
First decan: Personal planet is Mars
First cusp: Aries with Piscean
   qualities

VIRTUES
Ambitious, passionate, practical

VICES
Intimidating, temperamental,
impatient

CAREERS
Soldier, educator, CEO,
motivational speaker

SKILLS & APTITUDES
Organization, passion for progress,
leadership potential

FAMOUS BIRTHS
Johann Sebastian Bach (1685)
Gary Oldman (1958)
Rosie O'Donnell (1962)
Matthew Broderick (1962)

COMPATIBLE WITH
March 18–20, November 22–24

Others respect March 21 people for their forthright directness and the practical way in which they approach life. Although they are intuitive people, they prefer to express themselves through activity rather than remaining passive in the face of a stimulating challenge. This is not to say that those born on this day do not possess great powers of perception and reflection—on the contrary—just that they have a deep-rooted urge to act upon their convictions, and to see progress being made. These individuals are often attracted to extremes, espousing the highest ideals and the most radical solutions, and displaying a remarkable level of tenacity in promoting them.

As a result of their considerable energy and vision, combined with their practical gifts of logic and organization, little withstands March 21 people's drive and determination to succeed and to set an example for others. Furthermore, they have real leadership potential, which they will put to especially good use in business or military careers, or as educators, where they can blaze an inspirational trail.

These people have a tendency, however, to isolate themselves inadvertently from others, for not only can they intimidate weaker characters with the intensity and strength of their opinions, but they are also prone to spectacular bouts of temper when frustrated or opposed. Particularly in regard to their personal lives, it is vital that these people relax their standards and expectations and demonstrate the pragmatism of which they are unquestionably capable. By slowing down and opening themselves up to others, they will find that they will receive greater understanding and affection.

MARCH 22

✳ ✳ ✳ ✳ ✳ ✳ ✳ ✳ ✳ ✳ ✳ ✳ ✳ ✳

♂ ♆　　　OUTSPOKEN INDEPENDENTS

The sort of people who will bluntly speak their minds, sometimes oblivious to the offense they might cause, those individuals born on March 22 are uncompromisingly honest, valuing truth over anything else. Since they are brave and persistent types, they furthermore have no fear of the consequences of either discovering or expressing the actual facts of a situation.

It is just as well that these rabble-rousing independent agents are generally impervious to opposition, because few people relish hearing an unvarnished critique of their faults, while those who harbour ulterior agendas will resent having their real motives exposed to the world. It is not that these people are insensitive—on the contrary, they are extremely intuitive, and use this skill to bolster their position— it is merely that they are willing to jeopardize their popularity by refusing to pander to flattery or to submit to subterfuge.

Such uncompromising qualities suit them especially well to such technical areas as scientific or medical research, in which concepts can indeed be seen in black-and-white terms, but they will be less successful in those professions in which interpersonal and diplomatic skills are an important component. In their personal liaisons, the onus is on these people to temper their natural predilection for criticism—particularly if they were also born in the Chinese year of the dragon—and to realize that not only are they not always right, but that they will run the risk of driving away those who care for them.

PLANETARY INFLUENCES
Ruling planets: Mars and Neptune
First decan: Personal planet is Mars
First cusp: Aries with Piscean qualities

VIRTUES
Energetic, honorable, honest

VICES
Outspoken, stubborn, brash

CAREERS
Scientist, researcher, engineer, IT specialist

SKILLS & APTITUDES
Valuing truth, independence, intuition

FAMOUS BIRTHS
Louis L'Amour (1908)
William Shatner (1931)
Andrew Lloyd Webber (1948)
Reese Witherspoon (1976)

COMPATIBLE WITH
March 19–20, November 23–25

MARCH 23

EAGER OBSERVERS ♂ ♆

March 23 individuals are fascinated by the workings of the world—with what makes things tick—and this propensity is especially pronounced in their dealings with other people. Although they will use their intuition and keen powers of observation to gather information, these people are generally too objective and emotionally detached to be truly fired by compassionate sentiments and, if asked for advice, will give a detailed summary of the situation as they perceive it, unclouded by emotion.

Yet although they may be somewhat lacking in empathy, human behavior as a whole intrigues those born on this day, and they are therefore clearly well equipped for careers in teaching, psychotherapy or, indeed, for any type of medical specialty or academic research. They also have the potential to be gifted actors, for they possess the ability to model their fictitious characters on the traits of individuals whom they have closely observed in life.

Yet this highly developed capacity to keep their intellects and emotions separate does not mean that these people are cold fish—far from it. They enjoy the company of others, are blessed with an infectious sense of fun—particularly if they were also born in the Chinese year of the goat—and approach most ventures in an enthusiastic and positive manner. In their personal relationships they should, however, try to moderate their critical tendencies, and offer those closest to them a greater level of unquestioning support. They are rarely aware of the potential their stinging words may have for hurting those close to them, often unintentionally.

PLANETARY INFLUENCES
Ruling planets: Mars and Neptune
First decan: Personal planet is Mars
First cusp: Aries with Piscean qualities

VIRTUES
Observant, inquisitive, analytical

VICES
Critical, narcissistic, tactless

CAREERS
Teacher, therapist, actor

SKILLS & APTITUDES
Desire to understand human relationships, possession of clear viewpoint, intellectual sharpness

FAMOUS BIRTHS
Joan Crawford (1908)
Doc Watson (1923)
Chaka Khan (1953)
Perez Hilton (1978)

COMPATIBLE WITH
March 20, November 23–26

MARCH 24

♂ ♆   ALLURING INTELLECTUALS

These charismatic individuals prefer simple solutions and a direct approach in favour of more complicated and difficult alternatives, a result of their incisive intellectual powers and their predilection to take action rather than prevaricate. These are the sort of people who make snap decisions—often influenced by their intuitive perceptions—and then stick to their initial resolutions through thick and thin, regardless of any obstacles that may be put in their paths.

While the typically straightforward methods of March 24 people frequently results in success, it does, however, mean that these individuals may either blindly follow an unfortunate course, or that they may ignore small, but important, details. Since they are multitalented people, they will find fulfilment in any professional field in which they can act independently and imaginatively to achieve tangible results, but will be miserable if relegated to a passive role or required to deal with excessive bureaucracy.

Others are attracted to the optimistic, invigorating qualities that March 24 people radiate, and hence they may find themselves in popular demand, a position which they rather enjoy. Indeed, they are quick to reciprocate displays of affection and, as in all other things, are open and honest in their dealings with other people. Although they generally make excellent partners, parents and friends, they should ensure—especially if they are men—that they take care to moderate their natural propensity to speak their minds bluntly on all occasions, and that they do not ignore other people's emotional needs when fired by an all-consuming interest in a project.

PLANETARY INFLUENCES
Ruling planets: Mars and Neptune
First decan: Personal planet is Mars
First cusp: Aries with Piscean
qualities

VIRTUES
Vigorous, imaginative, confident

VICES
Impulsive, blunt, thoughtless

CAREERS
Writer, social-media manager, graphic designer

SKILLS & APTITUDES
Action-oriented, rising to challenges, ambition

FAMOUS BIRTHS
Harry Houdini (1874)
Steve McQueen (1930)
Jim Parsons (1973)
Alyson Hannigan (1974)

COMPATIBLE WITH
March 20, November 24–27

ARIES

MARCH 25

✳ ✳ ✳ ✳ ✳ ✳ ✳ ✳ ✳ ✳ ✳ ✳ ✳ ✳

LOYAL PROTECTORS   ♂

PLANETARY INFLUENCES
Ruling planet: Mars
First decan: Personal planet is Mars

VIRTUES
Self-reliant, generous,
compassionate

VICES
Sensitive, introspective, persistent

CAREERS
Police officer, social worker, lawyer,
nurse

SKILLS & APTITUDES
Generosity, empathy, compassion

FAMOUS BIRTHS
Gloria Steinem (1934)
Aretha Franklin (1942)
Elton John (1947)
Sarah Jessica Parker (1965)

COMPATIBLE WITH
November 25–27, December 1–3

March 25 people are regarded as rocks of support by those who depend on them for advice, practical help and empathetic commiseration. And indeed, these compassionate individuals have a highly developed sense of natural justice, while their strong protective instincts arouse in them a fierce desire to champion the underdog and reverse any perceived social abuses. It helps that they are also emotionally robust, self-confident and vigorous individuals, who, when certain of their motives and mission, will not allow their sense of purpose to be swayed by the censure of those who hold conflicting convictions. Neither are they afraid of taking an independent—even isolated—stance when convinced of the need to do so. All these qualities equip these people extremely well for such public-service-oriented careers as the military, medicine, law enforcement or social work, and this is especially true if they were also born in the Chinese year of the tiger.

Despite their externally directed energies, March 25 people also have a profound requirement for periods of solitude and reflection. It is essential that they make time in which to relax and be themselves, away from the demands of those who seek their assistance. Since they are loving and generous in their personal liaisons, they will find great comfort in the simple joys of friendship and domesticity, but will understandably be deeply wounded if the loyalty that they proffer to others is unreciprocated or—far worse—betrayed. Their nearest and dearest should therefore remember that, despite their apparent strength and invincibility, these people are also vulnerable.

MARCH 26

✳ ✳ ✳ ✳ ✳ ✳ ✳ ✳ ✳ ✳ ✳ ✳ ✳ ✳ ✳

♂ PERCEPTIVE VISIONARIES

To many who do not know them well, it appears that those born on March 26 are easy-going people who wish for nothing more than a simple life, and this is, to some extent, the case. This does not mean that they are intellectually or physically lazy—quite the reverse—just that they do not believe in making things unnecessarily difficult or complicated for themselves. Because they are inherently perceptive and quick-thinking people, they are blessed with the enviable gifts of clarity of vision and purpose, having the capacity both to cut straight to the heart of a problem and to fix their sights firmly on a long-term target. This mental directness is furthermore complemented by their vigor, tenacity and preference for taking positive action rather than endlessly prevaricating. Along with these personal qualities, those born on this day have an intuitive sense of right and wrong, and both their human empathy and high ethical standards suit them especially for public-service careers.

Hand in hand with their intellectual abilities also go marked qualities of sensuality and sensitivity, and hence these people often make talented artists, writers, musicians or actors. When "off duty," they will pursue their relationships, interests and hobbies with the energy and enthusiasm that characterizes their approach to their work, and thus they make popular friends and much-loved family members. These people will often find themselves in great demand, but it is vital for their emotional equilibrium that they periodically withdraw from the company of others and find time to be themselves.

PLANETARY INFLUENCES
Ruling planet: Mars
First decan: Personal planet is Mars

VIRTUES
Straightforward, clear-sighted, practical

VICES
Stubborn, narrow-minded, inflexible

CAREERS
Paramedic, firefighter, artist, musician

SKILLS & APTITUDES
Quick-witted mind, empathy, drive

FAMOUS BIRTHS
Robert Frost (1874)
Sandra Day O'Connor (1930)
Leonard Nimoy (1931)
Steven Tyler (1948)
Kiera Knightley (1985)

COMPATIBLE WITH
November 26–29, December 1–4

MARCH 27

✳ ✳ ✳ ✳ ✳ ✳ ✳ ✳ ✳ ✳ ✳ ✳ ✳

CHARMING INTELLECTUALS ♂

PLANETARY INFLUENCES
Ruling planet: Mars
First decan: Personal planet is Mars

VIRTUES
Sociable, determined, autonomous

VICES
Workaholic, zealous, introspective

CAREERS
Professor, lawyer, lecturer

SKILLS & APTITUDES
Empathy, work ethic, ambition

FAMOUS BIRTHS
Sarah Vaughan (1924)
Quentin Tarantino (1963)
Mariah Carey (1970)
Brenda Song (1988)

COMPATIBLE WITH
November 27–30, December 1–4

Appearances can be deceptive, and especially so in the case of March 27 people, who frequently hide their steely determination and capacity for incisive thought beneath a delightfully laid-back manner. Although they are blessed with considerable social skills—in part a result of their recognition that more can be achieved by charming rather than alienating people—they are generally concerned less with gaining the approval of others than with following their own original path through life. Indeed, those born on this day are independent thinkers who set themselves high targets and then work single-mindedly to achieve them.

While they may be fired by social ideals, those born on this day are usually far more interested in getting to the heart of a more abstract or technical issue and then reinterpreting it in their characteristically logical manner—but also with some flair. These people typically make gifted and dedicated academics, scientists or lawyers, particularly if they were also born in the Chinese year of the rooster.

Because March 27 people are intellectually curious, they are interested in soliciting other people's opinions, but sometimes more because they want to know what makes them tick than out of a sense of empathy or a need to be advised. As well as being sociable, they are extremely self-reliant people, and cope equally well alone or within group situations. Usually supportive and nonjudgemental with regard to their friends and family, they should try to ensure, however, that they do not ignore the basic emotional needs of those closest to them when carried along by a cause or an enthusiasm.

MARCH 28

✱ ✱ ✱ ✱ ✱ ✱ ✱ ✱ ✱ ✱ ✱ ✱ ✱ ✱

♂   REFLECTIVE RECLUSES

Paradoxically, although March 28 people are naturally somewhat solitary and reflective individuals, they frequently find themselves at the center of attention and beset with others' demands—requests either for the pleasure of their company or for their services. Other people admire them for their optimistic and practical approach to life, as well as for their personal charm and perceived empathy, and therefore turn to them for advice and support. And, indeed, these individuals respond magnificently to a crisis, mustering their great qualities of originality and steadfastness in the face of a challenge and thereby often achieving the desired outcome.

Rather than being motivated by feelings of profound compassion, however, it is the testing of their intellectual powers and stamina to which March 28 people respond. This quality of emotional detachment when occupied with the details of an issue will benefit them in such professions as the police or military, as well as in business and the building trades.

Although they are blessed with the ability to be objective and realistic in their dealings with the outside world, those born on this day need to feel cocooned by the loving devotion of those closest to them at home. It would surprise those who do not know them well to discover that these apparently confident and capable individuals are often subject to nagging feelings of self-doubt—which is perhaps the reason why they feel compelled to prove their worth. A stable domestic framework within which they can retreat from outer demands and be themselves is therefore crucial to these people's emotional well-being.

PLANETARY INFLUENCES
Ruling planet: Mars
First decan: Personal planet is Mars

VIRTUES
Clear-sighted, positive, determined

VICES
Insecure, overambitious, perfectionist

CAREERS
Police officer, soldier, architect

SKILLS & APTITUDES
Problem-solving, attention to detail, confidence

FAMOUS BIRTHS
Rudolf Serkin (1903)
Diane Wiest (1948)
Reba McEntire (1955)
Vince Vaughn (1970)
Lady Gaga (1986)

COMPATIBLE WITH
November 29–30, December 1–5

MARCH 29

✵ ✵ ✵ ✵ ✵ ✵ ✵ ✵ ✵ ✵ ✵ ✵ ✵

PERCEPTIVE LEADERS   ♂

PLANETARY INFLUENCES
Ruling planet: Mars
First decan: Personal planet is Mars

VIRTUES
Intelligent, perceptive, logical

VICES
Opinionated, stubborn, critical

CAREERS
Manager, administrator, politician, civil servant

SKILLS & APTITUDES
Observational skills, strategic thinking, reliability

FAMOUS BIRTHS
John Tyler (1790)
Sam Walton (1918)
Walt "Clyde" Frazier (1945)
Lucy Lawless (1968)

COMPATIBLE WITH
November 30, December 1–6

Although not driven by burning ambitions for personal success, those individuals born on this day may—somewhat to their surprise—find themselves in positions of authority, for while self-glorification is not one of their qualities, tenacity, perceptiveness and reliability are. March 29 people typically approach life in a calm and steady manner, their laid-back style and tendency toward self-effacement often masking the critical and astute way in which they observe everything that is going on around them. Undoubtedly sensitive, they will nevertheless use their intuitive powers like tools, considering every aspect of a situation, carefully working out their strategy, and then implementing it with unwavering determination—a method that will rarely prove unsuccessful. So positive and varied are their many talents, that they will thrive in almost any career, especially one in which their observational and organizational skills can be best employed.

These self-disciplined individuals generally keep their emotions to themselves in professional scenarios, but are, in fact, highly opinionated, having arrived at their ideological convictions by means of the same considered route that characterizes their response to any intellectual challenge. However, because they are extremely confident of their ground, they will stubbornly assert the validity of their convictions, even while remaining emotionally detached. March 29 individuals are deeply affectionate and supportive in their personal liaisons—perhaps instinctively recognizing that family ties and friendship offer a vital emotional release from work constraints—and are valued by their nearest and dearest for their loyal and steadfast qualities.

MARCH 30

♂ ☿   HEADSTRONG CREATIVES

March 30 people cannot help but arouse strong emotions in others—and not always positive ones—for not only are they larger-than-life characters who dominate their immediate surroundings but, like their Arian attribute, the ram, will typically put their heads down and charge at a challenge, regardless of the consequences. Inevitably, their stubbornness and drive will lead them to make mistakes, but these people have the intelligence to learn from past experiences.

Such is their relish for experiencing everything that the world has to offer, that March 30 individuals will discover far more from life than from books. They approach everything with passionate enthusiasm in their quest for stimulation, knowledge and success, and are the types to make things happen rather than standing passively on the sidelines. In doing so, they will either elicit feelings of intense admiration or, conversely, of profound irritation in others, but will never be ignored.

Because of their great sensuality and creative abilities, these people will often achieve outstanding success in the arts, although their talents will usually only be recognized later in life, when their youthful rebelliousness has been tempered by maturity. Because they react negatively to external constraints, they are unsuited to being small cogs in large organizations, and will only flourish when they can act independently. If their personal relationships are to succeed, their friends and partners will have to match their strength of character, but will also have to provide the emotional stability necessary to ground March 30 individuals.

PLANETARY INFLUENCES
Ruling planet: Mars
First decan: Personal planet is Mars

VIRTUES
Driven, imaginative, fearless

VICES
Compulsive, forceful, impulsive

CAREERS
Artist, sculptor, historian

SKILLS & APTITUDES
Working independently, creativity, thoroughness

FAMOUS BIRTHS
Vincent van Gogh (1853)
Warren Beatty (1937)
Eric Clapton (1945)
M.C. Hammer (1962)

COMPATIBLE WITH
November 30, December 1–7

ARIES

MARCH 31

✳ ✳ ✳ ✳ ✳ ✳ ✳ ✳ ✳ ✳ ✳ ✳ ✳ ✳

STEADFAST PROGRESSIVES ♂

Individuals born on this day are valued by their coworkers and family alike for their calm and steady qualities. They typically keep firm control, imposing their logical methods on everything and everyone that they encounter, thereby ensuring that their professional and personal environments remain organized to their liking.

Although they work determinedly toward their ideals and ambitions, these are never unrealistic or unachievable, and, indeed, the world view of March 31 people is conditioned by the pragmatism that allows them to readjust their approach—and compromise if necessary—if this will give them a better chance of success. Such willingness to be flexible if the circumstances require it is an undoubted asset in the business world, to which these people's qualities suit them extremely well, especially if they were also born in the Chinese year of the monkey.

Inherent in these individuals' desire to effect progress in an orderly and direct manner is their impatience with what they regard as unnecessary complications—be they impersonal obstacles impeding their path, or the objections of others. And while they will eventually accommodate most differences of opinion in the interests of pushing ahead, the sources of their irritation will first have been subject to their wrath. In their personal liaisons, March 31 people—particularly if they are men—display magnanimity, affection and loyalty, and expect those closest to them to reciprocate in kind. If, however, they perceive signs of insubordination, they have a tendency to lose their tempers spectacularly.

APRIL 1

♂ ☉   TRUSTWORTHY OPTIMISTS

Those born on April 1 exude an aura of quiet confidence that instantly inspires the trust of others. Nor is this faith in their abilities misplaced, for they are consistently competent and reliable in all their undertakings. Indeed, in many respects they represent the complete antithesis of the fool with which their birthday is popularly associated: dignified rather than madcap personalities; focused and tenacious instead of flighty; and prudently cautious rather than impulsively daring. Probably the only similarity that can be identified between the archetypal jester and those born on this day is the affection that they arouse in other people. They are admired for their typically perceptive, methodical and determined approach to life, an approach, moreover, that is always positive. And, although their main motivation is to achieve success in everything that they do, their ideals are usually realistic and rarely prompted by a desire for self-aggrandizement.

Because they are primarily task-oriented, they work equally well as independent agents or as team members, and in the latter situation will often find themselves elected to leadership positions—a tribute to their great professionalism, thoughtfulness and personal magnetism. So varied are their talents that they will usually excel in any career they choose, but they are probably best suited to those fields in which practical action is required. They generally make concerned and caring partners, parents and friends, whose loved ones rely on their unfailing support. An inherent disadvantage of being regarded as a pillar of strength, however, is that their own emotional needs may not be perceived or nurtured by others.

PLANETARY INFLUENCES
Ruling planet: Mars
Second decan: Personal planet is Sun

VIRTUES
Positive, organized, energetic

VICES
Self-sacrificing, emotional, nosy

CAREERS
Volunteer, principal, CEO

SKILLS & APTITUDES
Goal-orientation, orderly mindset, systematic approach

FAMOUS BIRTHS
Sergei Rachmaninov (1837)
Toshiro Mifune (1920)
Debbie Reynolds (1932)
Susan Boyle (1961)

COMPATIBLE WITH
November 3–4, December 3–9

APRIL 2

✻ ✻ ✻ ✻ ✻ ✻ ✻ ✻ ✻ ✻ ✻ ✻ ✻

FANCIFUL PHILANTHROPISTS   ♂ ☉

Inherent in the characters of those born on April 2 is a curious mixture of prodigious organizational skills and extreme idealism that almost tends toward the otherworldly. Hence although they exhibit a propensity for taking direct and practical action—a gift of their ruling planet, Mars—the causes that fire them may seem to others to be inadvisable at best, and ludicrously fanciful at worst. Because those born on this day possess an intuitive sense of social justice and therefore feel compelled to channel their energies toward protecting the vulnerable, weak or abused, their ambitions are typically of the humanitarian variety. The problem, however, is that while their motivations are eminently laudable, they have difficulty in inspiring others with a similar sense of zeal in the pursuit of their mission. It may be that they express their convictions too forcibly and hence frighten more cautious types, or when in the thrall of all-encompassing visions appear to lose their sense of realism and thus fail to convince others of the veracity of their beliefs.

Professionally, they find greatest satisfaction in those situations in which they can promote their progressive visions, but not necessarily within conventional structures—they are too libertarian to submit to someone else's party line or method. When they can express themselves independently—especially as writers or artists—however, they have the potential to achieve success and acclaim, although the recognition of others will probably not come immediately. During all of life's trials, they find enormous solace in the close emotional bonds that they typically form, and they are valued by their nearest and dearest for the loving concern that they display.

APRIL 3

♂ ☉   SOCIABLE LEADERS

Those born on April 3 are highly sociable individuals, who enjoy surrounding themselves with other people and directing their activities. They do not necessarily crave leadership positions out of a desire to dominate, merely that their energy, natural charisma and strong views tend to attract less vibrant people. It is, however, indubitably the case that these strong-minded people believe that their convictions and organizational methods are unquestionably correct and therefore seek to promote them by enlisting the support of those around them. Their considerable powers of persuasion are aided by intuitive gifts that also play a large part in informing their opinions: others' moods are assessed and then their own words and actions are adjusted appropriately to achieve optimum results. Such interpersonal skills equip them well for positions in which they can take charge of teams, and their capabilities are such that they may achieve success in any profession they choose, although they have the potential to star especially well as politicians, movie directors or actors.

There are dangers inherent in their self-certainty and predilection to guide others. Although they usually display a sunny, outgoing face to the world when things are going their way, in difficult situations their introverted, insecure side comes to the fore. When they are crossed or let down by others, they have a tendency to react badly, typically either exploding with anger, or retreating into their shell and brooding introspectively over the cause of their annoyance. It is therefore important that they become more realistic in their personal relationships, and do not punish others who fail to meet their own sometimes unreasonably high expectations.

PLANETARY INFLUENCES
Ruling planet: Mars
Second decan: Personal planet is Sun

VIRTUES
Perceptive, empathetic, inspiring

VICES
Oversensitive, headstrong, ornery

CAREERS
Senator, movie director, actor

SKILLS & APTITUDES
Team leader, persuasive skills, motivational ability

FAMOUS BIRTHS
Marlon Brando and
Doris Day (1924)
Jane Goodall (1934)
Alec Baldwin (1958)
Eddie Murphy (1961)

COMPATIBLE WITH
November 4–6, December 5–11

APRIL 4

✳ ✳ ✳ ✳ ✳ ✳ ✳ ✳ ✳ ✳ ✳ ✳ ✳

STRONG–WILLED PARADOXES   ♂ ☉

PLANETARY INFLUENCES
Ruling planet: Mars
Second decan: Personal planet is Sun

VIRTUES
Strategic, decisive, ambitious

VICES
Introspective, egocentric, inflexible

CAREERS
Accountant, literary professor,
cultural-events coordinator

SKILLS & APTITUDES
Coordination, strategy, ability to
produce successful outcomes

FAMOUS BIRTHS
Hans Richter (1843)
Muddy Waters (1915)
Maya Angelou (1928)
Robert Downey, Jr. (1965)

COMPATIBLE WITH
November 5–7, December 6–12

Underlying all of the actions of those born on April 4 is a compulsion to effect their visions, and to do so on their own terms. Their ambitions may well be humanitarian ones, for these protective people typically exhibit great compassion and kindness to the vulnerable as a collective entity, and may therefore become fired with enthusiasm to implement social progress. Surprisingly, however, they are less empathetic toward individuals. This apparent paradox may have various explanations: they may feel that the concerns of those closest to them are less urgent or serious than those of the world's downtrodden as a whole; they may have a misplaced suspicion of others' motives as a result of disappointments experienced in the past; or they may simply be uninterested in the problems of those for whom they do not feel personal sympathy. When they are inspired, however, they will typically throw their considerable energies, tenacity and organizational talents into a project, giving them immense potential for success, especially in the business and financial spheres, but also in the literary and performing arts.

Those born on this day possess a great sense of self-certainty; so convinced are they of the veracity of their convictions and approach to life that they expect others to conform to their views unquestioningly. Although they are typically affectionate and involved parents, partners and friends, they tend to demand that their personal liaisons operate on the terms that they have set. Just as they impatiently dismiss the validity of alternative opinions in the workplace, so do they regard any incidences of nonconformity by their nearest and dearest as tantamount to betrayal—an emotional reaction that they must strive to temper.

APRIL 5

✼ ✼ ✼ ✼ ✼ ✼ ✼ ✼ ✼ ✼ ✼ ✼ ✼ ✼

♂ ☉   EARNEST IDEALISTS

Those born on this day are admired for their strength of purpose and the forceful, determined way in which they work toward achieving their ambitions. Indeed, once enthralled by the light emanating from a star of inspiration, they will firmly set their eyes on their vision and refuse to allow themselves to be deflected from making steady progress toward its attainment. The motivations that inspire such tenacity may be varied: some April 5 people are fired by a social or humanitarian mission, others by their desire to achieve perfect artistry, while all yearn to be the best.

This determination to achieve their goals is even more pronounced in those also born in the Chinese year of the dragon. The urge to climb to the top of their professions is not fuelled by personal vanity or a craving to be showered with acclaim: rather it arises because they are perfectionists and feel compelled to conquer any challenge that presents itself. Their prodigious organizational powers, as well as their steadfast and logical approach, bestow on them enormous potential to realize their lofty aims.

Despite the seriousness that they accord to their intellectual pursuits, they are not wholly absorbed by their work and, when "off duty," play hard and enjoy themselves. They are caring friends and family members, who enjoy bringing pleasure to others and are typically extremely indulgent with their children. Particularly for the men, however, their attention may frequently be distracted by the irresistible lure of their impersonal ambitions, and insufficient attention may be paid to meeting the emotional needs of their intimate associates.

PLANETARY INFLUENCES
Ruling planet: Mars
Second decan: Personal planet is Sun

VIRTUES
Intellectual, visionary, methodical

VICES
Focused, imbalanced, self-absorbed

CAREERS
Social worker, sculptor, athletic coach

SKILLS & APTITUDES
Persistence, pursuit of aims, unshakable nature

FAMOUS BIRTHS
Booker T. Washington (1856)
Bette Davis (1908)
Colin Powell (1937)
Pharrell Williams (1973)

COMPATIBLE WITH
November 6–8, December 6–13

APRIL 6

✳ ✳ ✳ ✳ ✳ ✳ ✳ ✳ ✳ ✳ ✳ ✳ ✳

ENLIGHTENED INTELLECTUALS ♂ ☉

The driving force behind those born on April 6 is their restless quest for knowledge, their urge to uncover the true nature of a person or situation. And, because they learn from experience, the discoveries that they make upon their voyages of learning not only inform their future actions, but also bestow upon them the ability to be open-minded, and to accept the possibility of sometimes otherworldly concepts.

Yet despite their intellectual restlessness, these people are by no means deficient in staying power, and when they meet a subject that truly absorbs their interest, they will employ their considerable powers of logic, mental organization and tenacity in analyzing and subsequently building upon their findings.

Such talents give those individuals born on April 6 the potential to be real innovators, especially in the scientific field, although since they are typically all-rounders, they may also make gifted musicians, writers, researchers or even philosophers.

Indeed, such is the variety of talents and interests with which they are blessed that those born on April 6 may initially have difficulty in either settling on their life's vocation or committing to a life partner. Once they are finally established in a stable domestic situation they generally make loyal and supportive partners and family members, and are particularly cherished as generous and indulgent parents. The irresistible siren call of a fascinating idea, however, may cause them to drop everything in its hot pursuit, which can temporarily distract them from their parenting duties.

APRIL 7

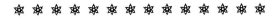

✻ ✻ ✻ ✻ ✻ ✻ ✻ ✻ ✻ ✻ ✻ ✻ ✻ ✻

♂ ☉   PASSIONATE VISIONARIES

There are two distinct sides to the characters of those born on April 7: a positive and idealistic side, which inspires them to work unstintingly toward progress; and a more negative, impatient side, which has a tendency to manifest itself when these individuals are frustrated. Although it may seem that these characteristics are in direct opposition to each other, they are, in fact, interlinked by cause and effect. When April 7 people are seized by the desire to bring about improvement—be it in the humanitarian sphere or, more specifically, with regard to a work-related task—they will enthusiastically and whole-heartedly invest their considerable gifts of imagination, logic and tenacity into the project. When, however, they encounter obstacles in their paths, they are prone to rush headlong at them, and then, like the Arian goat that is their astrological attribute, explode with anger when their repeated butts fail to clear the way. This temperamental reaction is even more pronounced if they were also born in the Chinese year of the dragon.

The talents of those born on April 7 are versatile: their idealism and sensitivity indicates potential success in literary, musical and dramatic pursuits, while their inquiring minds and methodical approach suits them for scientific research. In whatever field they make their profession, they need to be given as much autonomy as possible; they make good leaders, but usually only on their own terms. Similarly, although generally sunny and relaxed in their personal relationships, they will chafe if restricted by others' ground rules—especially in adolescence—and here again, if things are not going their way, they are prone to temperamental outbursts.

PLANETARY INFLUENCES
Ruling planet: Mars
Second decan: Personal planet is Sun

VIRTUES
Motivated, confident, progressive

VICES
Aggressive, combative, cantankerous

CAREERS
Medical-research analyst, band director, playwright

SKILLS & APTITUDES
Invest without equivocation, hardworking, progressive

FAMOUS BIRTHS
William Wordsworth (1770)
Wayne Rogers (1933)
Francis Ford Coppola (1939)
Jackie Chan (1954)

COMPATIBLE WITH
November 8–10, December 7–14

APRIL 8

✵ ✵ ✵ ✵ ✵ ✵ ✵ ✵ ✵ ✵ ✵ ✵ ✵ ✵

COMPASSIONATE MORALISTS ♂ ☉

PLANETARY INFLUENCES
Ruling planet: Mars
Second decan: Personal planet is Sun

VIRTUES
Benevolent, empathetic, protective

VICES
Sacrificing, distant, stubborn

CAREERS
Judge, military officer, police officer

SKILLS & APTITUDES
Vigilance, compassion, standing up for team members

FAMOUS BIRTHS
Betty Ford (1918)
John Gavin (1931)
Patricia Arquette (1968)
Chris Kyle (1974)

COMPATIBLE WITH
November 9–11, December 8–15

The ambitions that fuel the actions of those born on April 8 are rather noble ones, for they yearn to bring about global improvement, especially in social issues. Their humanitarian concerns and consequent ideals are motivated in part by feelings of compassion for unfortunate individuals suffering abuse, and in part by their inherent recognition of what is correct and morally just behavior. Such characteristics and ideals equip them especially well for careers in the judiciary, military or other law-enforcement agencies, but the attainment of sporting goals is also starred by this day and, whether or not they pursue athletics professionally, most will derive great enjoyment from energetic physical pursuits. In the great race of life, these strong-willed individuals typically map out well-considered and direct courses of action, which they then follow single-mindedly, a strategy that augurs well for success.

Despite their great empathy, the incisive and logical intellects of those born on April 8, as well as their desire to effect justice, give them a propensity to see the world in black-and-white terms, impatiently dismissing the myriad shades of gray opinion as being manifestations of mental and emotional confusion, or even unequivocally wrong. Since they furthermore keep their emotions on a tight leash, they may appear to others to be somewhat remote, lofty beings who find it hard to form truly intimate relationships. When among trusted friends and family members they are, however, generally deeply loyal and affectionate, and may develop a specially close rapport with their children.

APRIL 9

♂ ☉   PRACTICAL PROGRESSIVES

Those born on April 9 are resolutely practical, preferring action to reflection, and displaying great vigor and competence in the process. They are not given to abstract ideological visions, instead concentrating upon the immediate aims of their professional and domestic lives. In doing so, their drive, tenacity and strength of purpose come to the fore, and their capacity for organizing both their own ideas and other people's resources is put to good use. Such methodical and determined qualities, as well as a remarkable clarity of focus, augur well for their success.

However, their tendency to see things in black-and-white terms, and their impatience with those who do not concur with their approach may ultimately hinder their progress. Because they manifest both artistic and scientific talents, they are suited to careers in either field, but will probably find greatest satisfaction in those areas where tangible results can be achieved, such as in business, the military or as mechanics.

Many of those born on this day regard their home environment as being of greater importance than their careers, and they will typically run it—and their immediate family—with enormous efficiency. Indeed, such is their energy and compulsion to be active, that they frequently devote their leisure hours to home improvements and other domestic activities. While offering considerable practical support and stability to those nearest to them, they do have a propensity to dominate their loved ones, and should try to develop a more relaxed and accepting view of any differences of opinion.

PLANETARY INFLUENCES
Ruling planet: Mars
Second decan: Personal planet is Sun

VIRTUES
Energetic, focused, ambitious

VICES
Stubborn, opinionated, overbearing

CAREERS
Mechanic, pharmacist, business manager

SKILLS & APTITUDES
Efficiency, practical skills, organizational skills

FAMOUS BIRTHS
Tom Lehrer (1928)
Dennis Quaid (1954)
Paulina Porizkova (1957)
Marc Jacobs (1963)

COMPATIBLE WITH
November 10–11, December 8–15

ARIES

APRIL 10

✳ ✳ ✳ ✳ ✳ ✳ ✳ ✳ ✳ ✳ ✳ ✳ ✳

CAREFUL RISK-TAKERS ♂ ☉

PLANETARY INFLUENCES
Ruling planet: Mars
Second decan: Personal planet is Sun

VIRTUES
Observant, strategic, logical

VICES
Obsessive, dogmatic, zealous

CAREERS
Stockbroker, advertising director, copywriter

SKILLS & APTITUDES
Multiple talents, vision, analytical skills

FAMOUS BIRTHS
Joseph Pulitzer (1847)
Omar Sharif (1932)
Don Meredith (1938)
Steven Segal (1951)

COMPATIBLE WITH
November 11, December 9–15

Whatever it is that especially motivates those born on April 10—be it a humanitarian, spiritual, scientific or artistic vision—they will typically devote all of their single-minded attention and enormous energy to its exploration, shrewdly examining its inherent aspects in minute detail and then evolving a soundly considered plan of action with which to take it farther.

Although they are geared toward achieving results, these pragmatic people are rarely impulsive, and will first employ their incisive intellects and practical skills in researching and formulating the most feasible strategy with which to realize their ambitions. So while those who do not know them well are sometimes taken aback by what they perceive to be their radical approach, April 10 people are, in fact, confident of success, secure in the knowledge that they have carefully evaluated any potential risks. This conjunction of methodical and adventurous characteristics equips them for a variety of careers, but professions such as stockbroking, surveying, advertising or marketing are likely to be especially fertile fields.

Although those born on this day place great value on the bonds of family and friendship, and genuinely desire the happiness of those closest to them, their propensity to become overly involved in work-related projects may result in an unequal division of their interests. This tendency is particularly pronounced in men born on this day, as well as in those individuals who were also born in the Chinese year of the tiger, who are similarly often distracted by more pressing—but no less important—interests outside the home.

APRIL 11

♂ ♃   EMPHATIC IDEALISTS

Grand ideas fascinate those born on April 11, especially those that promise progress for humanity—either in terms of global social advancement or by means of scientific and technical advances. Blessed by an inherent sense of natural justice and a desire to champion the causes of those who are disadvantaged, they have both a strong sense of empathy with those who experience suffering and the determination to improve their lot. Eternally optimistic when it comes to the development of a strategy with which to realize their ambitions, these people will typically invest their prodigious energy, clarity of vision and considerable interpersonal skills in the formulation of a plan of action, and then promote it with single-minded tenacity. Not only are they intellectually incisive, but they are realistic and practical enough to know that they will need to enlist the support of others if they are to succeed. As a result, they will often consciously set out to charm potential opponents and convert them to their cause by means of skilled diplomacy.

Such skills and concerns suit them especially well for public-service careers, including the spheres of politics, the diplomatic service, social work or scientific research. They perform particularly well when given charge of a team, and have the capability to encourage and inspire their coworkers. For many of them, however, their personal environments may be less than harmonious, and within which their drive and tenacity may be struggling to find a satisfying outlet. They may, moreover, be bored by mundane domestic chores and may therefore gain a reputation for shirking their responsibilities in the home because of their preference for more stimulating pursuits.

PLANETARY INFLUENCES
Ruling planet: Mars
Third decan: Personal planet is Jupiter

VIRTUES
Persuasive, discerning, diplomatic

VICES
Impatient, prying, anxious

CAREERS
Public-relations executive, political analyst, counselor

SKILLS & APTITUDES
Credibility, strategy, strength as a team player

FAMOUS BIRTHS
James Parkinson (1775)
Nick La Rocca (1889)
Ethel Kennedy (1928)
Joss Stone (1987)

COMPATIBLE WITH
December 10–16

APRIL 12

✾ ✾ ✾ ✾ ✾ ✾ ✾ ✾ ✾ ✾ ✾ ✾ ✾

WITTY PHILANTHROPISTS   ♂ ♃

PLANETARY INFLUENCES
Ruling planet: Mars
Third decan: Personal planet is Jupiter

VIRTUES
Progressive, idealistic, driven

VICES
Tendency to alienate others, high standards, detached

CAREERS
Columnist, bureaucrat, military or police officer

SKILLS & APTITUDES
Articulacy, work ethic, energy

FAMOUS BIRTHS
Herbie Hancock (1940)
David Letterman (1947)
Shannen Doherty (1971)
Claire Danes (1979)

COMPATIBLE WITH
December 11–17

Those born on April 12 are externally oriented, typically projecting their ideals and humanitarian visions outward in their desire to create a more perfect, just and effective society. They are impatient with those who espouse personal interests, believing that achieving the greater good is of far more importance than, for example, making money or drifting idly through life. Indeed, although their commitment and strength of purpose may intimidate less driven people, they generally manage to mitigate their almost magisterial, aloof image by means of both their often self-deprecating wit and their concern not to alienate others. They are prone to employing their considerable verbally persuasive talents in enlisting and encouraging support for their mission, but are prepared to strike out courageously on a solitary—but morally justified—path if diplomatic methods fail. They have the potential to achieve success in whatever profession excites their interest, but are especially well equipped for military and political careers, as well as for those artistic styles—such as satire—in which they can make a moral statement.

It is ironic, given that these people are motivated by the desire to further human progress, that away from work they may be somewhat lonely individuals. Because they set others—as well as themselves—such high standards, they may not only find it difficult to find a partner who lives up to them, but also experience profound disappointment when the behavior of friends and family members incurs their disapproval. Yet once they moderate their propensity for criticism and become more indulgent of the failings of others, they can be extremely supportive of, and generous toward, their nearest and dearest.

APRIL 13

♂ ♃　　QUIET REVOLUTIONARIES

It may seem paradoxical, in the opinion of those who do not know April 13 people well, that these solitary, strong-willed and silent types are totally geared toward moving humankind forward. And, indeed, it is through their work that these essentially private and rather introverted individuals connect with the world, sometimes even making their indelible mark on history. Yet their external orientation is not as contradictory as it might appear at first sight, for when one considers their intellectual curiosity, their power of penetrating thought, their methodical approach, as well as their predilection toward progressive ideals, it is logical that they should employ their prodigious talents in projects for the benefit of humanity. Professionally, success beckons from a diversity of areas—politics, the judiciary and military, scientific research, and also such artistic spheres as music, literature and drama, in which they can translate their frequently radical visions into reality.

They are skeptical of conventional truths, and therefore feel compelled to seek out their own interpretations and solutions to social issues. Their quest may inevitably, however, either baffle or alienate less intellectually adventurous souls, who may respond to their ideas with incomprehension or derision. And, since they are deeply sensitive to the opinions of others, they will thus experience personal hurt, while nevertheless refusing to be deflected from the pursuance of their chosen course of action—particularly if they were also born in the Chinese year of the ox. Should they be fortunate enough to enjoy the understanding of friends and family, they will derive great comfort and encouragement from the support of those who know them best, and will reciprocate many times over.

PLANETARY INFLUENCES
Ruling planet: Mars
Third decan: Personal planet is Jupiter

VIRTUES
Intellectual, realistic, enlightened

VICES
Sensitive, timid, withdrawn

CAREERS
Novelist, clinical researcher, administrative assistant

SKILLS & APTITUDES
Empathy, foresight, curiosity

FAMOUS BIRTHS
Thomas Jefferson (1743)
Samuel Beckett (1906)
Lyle Waggoner (1935)
Al Green (1946)

COMPATIBLE WITH
December 11–17

APRIL 14

✳ ✳ ✳ ✳ ✳ ✳ ✳ ✳ ✳ ✳ ✳ ✳ ✳

CURIOUS SOCIAL BUTTERFLIES   ♂ ♃

PLANETARY INFLUENCES
Ruling planet: Mars
Third decan: Personal planet is
  Jupiter

VIRTUES
Optimistic, energetic, confident

VICES
Domineering, bossy, arrogant

CAREERS
Tour guide, director, bookseller

SKILLS & APTITUDES
Organizational skills, reliability,
leadership skills

FAMOUS BIRTHS
Loretta Lynn (1935)
Pete Rose (1941)
Julian Lloyd Webber (1951)
Sarah Michelle Geller (1977)

COMPATIBLE WITH
December 12–18

Their surroundings are of supreme importance to the well-being of those born on April 14, be it their professional or domestic environment or, indeed, the country in which they live. They possess a curious conjunction of apparently conflicting qualities: intellectual and physical restlessness and yet a strong emotional need to feel grounded within a societal group—usually the family. When each characteristic is taken to its extreme, they may be intrepid travelers, who delight in exploring foreign lands and cultures, or committed home-bodies, who direct their considerable energy and enthusiasm into beautifying their home and taking charge of the activities of their families and friends. And there is no doubt that they like to be in control, a predilection that may be manifested in their urge to act as independent agents, or in their tendency to impose their own regulations and methods on others.

Because they are capable organizers, with a practical turn of mind, they thrive in professions in which they can combine their love of creating order with their enjoyment of personal contact. Therefore tourism augurs well as a career choice, as does the retail trade, a variety of business pursuits and also the performing arts. Despite the autocratic conduct to which they are prone, they are extremely intuitive; since they are blessed with the ability to tune into others' moods, and because they wish to receive approval, they will generally quickly realize when their behavior is annoying others and adjust it accordingly. They should remember, however, to adopt a similarly flexible approach toward their nearest and dearest—who, moreover, provide them with the security that they crave—whom they would otherwise expect to conform unquestioningly to their views.

APRIL 15

♂ ♃   INDIVIDUALISTIC CREATIVES

Those born on April 15 possess a remarkable grasp of practicalities, and are methodical in the extreme. Their intellectual incisiveness enables them to formulate a well-structured strategy in response to a stimulating challenge, and they are extraordinarily tenacious when it comes to implementation, capably overseeing the contributions of others and refusing to be deflected from their objective. Although the methodology underlying their actions is sound, the visions that inspire them may be regarded by others as being uncharacteristically unrealistic and fanciful, if not downright bizarre. And, indeed, it may be that the world is not yet ready for such imaginative ideas: yet no matter how strange they may seem to others, their feasibility will generally have been researched in depth by their originators. Many areas may inspire them, including commerce and business issues, but they have a gift for working with their hands, especially when they can also be creative, as chefs, caterers, beauticians, interior designers or decorators, for example, where their talents can be accepted and admired by more conventional types.

Because these dynamic people are convinced of the validity of their ideals, they will not only be infuriated when others do not take them seriously, but will also suffer great personal hurt, so bound up are their identities with their idealistic ambitions. And this inherent inability to accept dissent also applies to their personal liaisons, within which (particularly if they are men) they typically expect the unwavering loyalty and support of their partners, friends and family members. Consequently, they may inadvertently suppress in others the individuality and freedom of thought which they themselves hold so dear.

PLANETARY INFLUENCES
Ruling planet: Mars
Third decan: Personal planet is Jupiter

VIRTUES
Innovative, inspirational, original

VICES
Eccentric, inflexible, stubborn

CAREERS
Hair stylist, interior designer, carpenter

SKILLS & APTITUDES
Creativity, vision, ambition

FAMOUS BIRTHS
Leonardo da Vinci (1452)
Henry James (1843)
Bessie Smith (1894)
Emma Watson (1990)

COMPATIBLE WITH
May 1–4, December 13–18

APRIL 16

✻ ✻ ✻ ✻ ✻ ✻ ✻ ✻ ✻ ✻ ✻ ✻ ✻ ✻

INTELLECTUAL CARETAKERS   ♂ ♃

PLANETARY INFLUENCES
Ruling planet: Mars
Third decan: Personal planet is
  Jupiter

VIRTUES
Caring, intellectual, dedicated

VICES
Easily overburdened, tendency to
overwork, self-sacrificing

CAREERS
Professor, lawyer, research scientist

SKILLS & APTITUDES
Introspection, wisdom, nurturing

FAMOUS BIRTHS
Wilbur Wright (1867)
Charlie Chaplin (1889)
Martin Lawrence (1965)
Selena Quintanilla (1971)

COMPATIBLE WITH
May 1–4, December 12–18

Those born on this day are very aware of their roots, of their place within their family and community, perhaps instinctively recognizing that they need to feel grounded within their home environment before taking flight from this solidly stable base. For while they cherish the familial bonds that surround them with the supportive and affectionate framework that is so important to their emotional well-being, April 16 individuals are adventurous thinkers, who feel compelled to seek out knowledge and truths and then, having assimilated as much information as they can, build upon their interests and move forward.

There are thus two sides to the natures of April 16 people: the side that desires a quietly happy domestic life, causing them generously to nurture the needs of their friends and family members, and the side that adopts a determinedly individualistic approach to the wider world and fiercely fights for those issues that motivate them. They are usually cheerful, balanced and popular.

Many subject matters interest those born on April 16, but underlying all is a concern with humanitarian issues and making progress. Because they are blessed with great powers of logic, organizational skills and unwavering steadfastness, whatever profession they choose to follow—be it within the scientific or technical fields, jurisprudence or academia, or the various pursuits that the artistic sphere encompasses—they will bring a solid backing to their imaginative visions. They also have great leadership potential, for not only do others admire them for their inspirational strength of purpose, but their fine sense of humor and gentle demeanor attract others to them.

APRIL 17

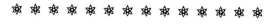

♂ ♀ ♃   PROTECTIVE INFLUENCERS

The impression that those born on this day make on others is a strong one, for they promote their lofty ambitions with unrelenting certainty and expect others to fall in line with their convictions. Because they have a highly developed sense of natural justice and possess a burning, protective desire to champion the cause of the downtrodden, April 17 people will often make their careers in such humanitarian-related fields as politics, jurisprudence or the military, although their predilection for paying attention to detail and their prodigious organizational skills will also equip them superbly as accountants or businessmen. And, because they typically translate their profound thoughts into energetic action, they may frequently find themselves leading the less imaginative or dynamic, or—especially if they are women—working as self-employed people on their own account.

Yet despite the laudable nature of their ideological concerns and their considerable practical talents, April 17 people may find enlisting the support of others an arduous task. One inherent problem with their direct, often forceful, approach—which is particularly pro-nounced if they were also born in the Chinese year of the dragon—is that they may appear somewhat unyielding individuals, who are furthermore not afraid to voice their criticism if they feel it is justified. Others may be intimidated by the austere, judgemental image that they project, and hasten to remove themselves from the line of fire. Those nearest to them may simi-larly believe themselves unable to live up to their high ideals and expectations, and thus these people may become emotionally isolated and prone to feelings of disillusionment and depression.

PLANETARY INFLUENCES
Ruling planets: Mars and Venus
Third decan: Personal planet is Jupiter
Second cusp: Aries with Taurean tendencies

VIRTUES
Methodical, ambitious, organized

VICES
Critical, judgmental, forceful

CAREERS
Lawyer, CEO, financial advisor

SKILLS & APTITUDES
Attention to detail, coordination, vigilance

FAMOUS BIRTHS
J.P. Morgan (1837)
William Holden (1918)
Jennifer Garner (1972)
Rooney Mara (1985)

COMPATIBLE WITH
May 1–4, July 27–28, December 12–18

APRIL 18

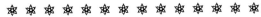

COMPASSIONATE HUMANITARIANS ♂ ♀ ♃

PLANETARY INFLUENCES
Ruling planets: Mars and Venus
Third decan: Personal planet is Jupiter
Second cusp: Aries with Taurean tendencies

VIRTUES
Idealistic, practical, warmhearted

VICES
Detached, emotional, obsessive

CAREERS
Judge, soldier, police officer

SKILLS & APTITUDES
Focus, enthusiasm, improvisation

FAMOUS BIRTHS
Eric Roberts (1956)
Conan O'Brien (1963)
David Tennant (1971)
Melissa Joan Hart (1976)

COMPATIBLE WITH
July 28–29, December 13–19

April 18 individuals may secretly regard themselves variously as the upholders of tradition, the torchbearers of justice or the champions of the vulnerable and abused. Possessed as they are of clear-cut views regarding the governance of human society and the importance of implementing justice, the driving forces behind their actions are often the maintenance of social order and the promotion of human equality. They will therefore often find a fulfilling outlet for their concerns and ambitions in those professions in which they can effect tangible improvements—national or civic politics, for example, the military, judiciary or other public-service bodies, as well as the caring professions. When engaged in their battles for the furtherance of human civilization, April 18 people will typical marshal their prodigious talents of energy, zeal and intellectual focus and employ them with determination and tenacity.

Despite their seriousness of intent, however, most people born on this day are redeemed from becoming overly obsessive in their single-mindedness by their intuitive recognition of the need to recharge their batteries by means of relaxation and fun. Indeed, some April 18 people have a markedly mischievous streak, and relish playing devil's advocate for the sheer enjoyment of provoking a stimulating argument. Concerned and magnanimous friends, partners and parents, they will stick loyally to those closest to them, but will inevitably suffer deep disappointment if they feel personally let down in any way, either through perceived abuses of their kindness, or by others failing to live up to their exceptionally high standards.

APRIL 19

✳ ✳ ✳ ✳ ✳ ✳ ✳ ✳ ✳ ✳ ✳ ✳ ✳ ✳

♂ ♀ ♃　　ORDERLY PERFECTIONISTS

Those born on this day cannot bear disorder, indecisiveness or stagnation, and therefore seek to introduce efficient, smoothly running and progressive systems into both their work and domestic environments. Nothing gives them more satisfaction than setting a drifting individual firmly upon a focused course of action, or turning an unprofitable operation into a success. Attaining tangible results is important to April 19 people, who regard the fruits of their labors as the validation of their efforts. Whatever career they choose to pursue, they will therefore experience the greatest fulfillment when their input is counterbalanced—if not outweighed—by the output, the physical proof of their success, that they generate. Such professions as teaching, manufacturing, project management, construction, design and the creative arts are especially well starred, as well as business pursuits, although it should be stressed that they rarely hunger for materialistic rewards.

Their highly achievement-driven determination can, however, lead them to become overly controlling. Because they possess great confidence in their intellectual capability, as well as in their practical and organizational talents, they are often reluctant to relinquish the reins of control to others that are, as yet, unproven. When they do delegate, they will sometimes succumb to the urge to point out how they think things could be better done, this tendency being particularly pronounced in women born on this day. Despite this regulatory predilection, they generally make generous and affectionate partners, parents and friends, who unselfishly wish for the greatest happiness and success of those closest to them.

PLANETARY INFLUENCES
Ruling planets: Mars and Venus
Third decan: Personal planet is Jupiter
Second cusp: Aries with Taurean tendencies

VIRTUES
Driven, persevering, goal-oriented

VICES
Controlling, demanding, fault-finding

CAREERS
Interior designer, teacher, project manager

SKILLS & APTITUDES
Attention to detail, self-motivation, focus

FAMOUS BIRTHS
Herbert Wilcox (1890)
Tim Curry (1946)
Paloma Picasso (1949)
Maria Sharapova (1987)

COMPATIBLE WITH
July 29–30, December 14–20

APRIL 20

✳ ✳ ✳ ✳ ✳ ✳ ✳ ✳ ✳ ✳ ✳ ✳ ✳

AMBITIOUS CRITICS   ♂ ♀ ♃

PLANETARY INFLUENCES
Ruling planets: Mars and Venus
Third decan: Personal planet is
   Jupiter
Second cusp: Aries with Taurean
   tendencies

VIRTUES
Incisive, energetic, driven

VICES
Domineering, intolerant,
unrealistic

CAREERS
Writer, college lecturer, laboratory
worker

SKILLS & APTITUDES
Determination, efficiency,
pragmatism

FAMOUS BIRTHS
Adolf Hitler (1889)
Joán Miró (1893)
Jessica Lange (1949)
Luther Vandross (1951)

COMPATIBLE WITH
July 30, December 15–21

Those born on April 20 hunger for success, partly because of their desire to realize their ambitions, and—since they may often be insecure—partly to feel validated by the approval of their peers. It is this quest for perfection that fuels their zeal, and these people typically observe their surroundings critically, noting shortcomings and then formulating complex strategies for bringing about improvement. When in the thrall of a vision, they will devote their energy, tenacity and organizational skills toward its achievement, allowing nothing to stand in their way. And although they are intuitive, this quality is not usually manifested in empathetic action, but rather in the manipulation of others in order to enlist support for the mission which they regard as being of paramount importance. Such focus, ambition and pragmatism augurs well for April 20 people, especially if they work as freelancers.

Their extreme clarity of vision and strength of purpose will inevitably incur extreme reactions, and these people will inspire either ardent support or strident opposition. Since they are convinced of the veracity of their ideas and methods and, moreover, crave the recognition of others, those born on this day will feel profoundly hurt when their opinions are subjected to criticism or derision, and have a tendency to close their ears to negative comments in order to protect their sensibilities. It is important that they recognize this propensity, as well as the inherent dangers of such an inflexible approach. By grounding themselves in the love and support of their families and diversifying their interests and priorities, they will gain a greater level of emotional equilibrium.

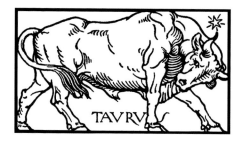

♉ TAURUS

April 21 to May 20

RULING PLANET: *Venus* ELEMENT: *Fixed earth* SYMBOL: *Bull*
POLARITY: *Negative (feminine)* COLORS: *Pale blue, lilac, pink*
PHYSICAL CORRESPONDENCE: *Neck, ears, throat*
STONES: *Alabaster, topaz, rose quartz, emerald*
FLOWERS: *Lily, lilac, daisy, mallow, poppy, violet*

Virtually every astrological tradition has equated the constellation of Taurus with a bull. A sign that is governed by the planet Venus, this astral grouping includes the seven stars known as the Pleiades, or the "Seven Sisters," who, in Greco-Roman mythology, guarded Aphrodite/Venus's "pearly gates." The bull's association with the goddess of sexual love is clear, for this creature not only embodies fecundity and procreative powers, but its horns may be said to represent the crescent Moon, and its head the full Moon, and the Moon is the preserve and symbol of the Goddess, as is the element of earth that governs this sign. Many ancient peoples sacrificed bulls at the time of the Taurean new Moon in the belief that the bull's body and blood gave birth to, and nurtured, all forms of vegetal and animal life. It is therefore appropriate that Taurus presides over the seasonal period in which spring life burgeons and thrives.

Those born under this sign are said to be influenced by the earthy element that rules their birth sign in that they are regarded as practical and materialistic types who have the capacity to initiate and steadily cultivate plans of actions, while Venus is said to bestow her sensuality, love of pleasure, and artistic affinity upon Taureans. Less positively, however, the Taurean personality may sometimes be obstinately resistant to change, fiercely possessive of loved ones, and roused to spectacular displays of anger when its plans are thwarted—all forms of behavior that may be said to be demonstrated by the bull.

APRIL 21

✤ ✤ ✤ ✤ ✤ ✤ ✤ ✤ ✤ ✤ ✤ ✤ ✤ ✤

PROUD PERFECTIONISTS   ♀ ♂

PLANETARY INFLUENCES
Ruling planets: Venus and Mars
First decan: Personal planet is Venus
First cusp: Taurus with Arian
  qualities

VIRTUES
Self-reliant, tenacious, sympathetic

VICES
Hedonistic, controlling, indulgent

CAREERS
Teacher, entrepreneur, art director,
producer, author

SKILLS & APTITUDES
Ability to balance professional and
personal life, objective intellectual
clarity, perfectionist tendencies

FAMOUS BIRTHS
Charlotte Brontë (1816)
Queen Elizabeth II (1926)
Andie MacDowell (1958)
James McAvoy (1979)

COMPATIBLE WITH
July 23–26, October 23–25

Those born on April 21 are proud individuals who set themselves high standards and are mortified if circumstances prevent their being achieved. Such is their capability, efficiency and self-discipline that when faced with a task, its completion will usually be hindered only by unforeseeable obstacles beyond their control. These are dignified and self-possessed people, who typically harness their prodigious powers of perspicacity and reflection (qualities born of their sensitivity), and their organizational skills and single-minded tenacity, in their drive to succeed. Because they are both reliable and unafraid of voicing their deeply held opinions, they will often find themselves assuming leadership roles, and will be accorded respect for both their ability and their talent for motivating others. These qualities bode well for success in such interpersonal careers as teaching, although their inherent distaste of being dictated to means that they will generally be unhappy in large, rigidly structured organizations.

April 21 people are bent on achieving perfection rather than receiving financial rewards, but they appreciate money for the good things that it can buy, for these are somewhat sybaritic types who relish sensual stimulation and therefore have a profound affinity with all things artistic. People are drawn to them for their infectious, pleasure-seeking propensity, as well as their endearing desire to bring happiness to others. They typically make indulgent, yet responsible, friends, parents and partners, but may occasionally annoy others by their tendency to control or impose their personal outlook on them.

APRIL 22

♀ ♂   TRUSTWORTHY CONSULTANTS

Others admire those born on April 22 for their instant grasp of potential problems inherent in a situation and their apparently effortless ability to counter and overcome them. The efficiency, energy and positive outlook manifested by these capable people means that not only are they often consulted for objective and realistic advice, but they are also frequently entrusted with projects. In such circumstances, they will accept total responsibility for the tasks and work tirelessly, with deceptive ease, to achieve beneficial outcomes, motivated by both their personal desire to test their abilities and their sneaking wish to elicit the approval and gratitude of others. There is a risk, however, that the cooperation and goodwill that they offer may be abused by others, and that they may end up overburdened and exhausted, while less scrupulous characters claim the glory for their achievements.

In their personal lives, they display a similar level of magnaminity and dependability, also bringing an element of fun to their interpersonal relationships since they are themselves deeply receptive to sensual stimuli. In their professional lives, they supplement their organizational talents with a combination of clear-sighted vision, a pragmatic outlook and a tendency to take risks, thus endowing them with great entrepreneurial potential. Such a conjunction of meticulous and far-sighted qualities augurs well for careers in business as well as in the realm of scientific research. They do, however, crave material rewards, both as recognition of their efforts and as a means of enabling them to indulge themselves when work is over.

PLANETARY INFLUENCES
Ruling planets: Venus and Mars
First decan: Personal planet is Venus
First cusp: Taurus with Arian qualities

VIRTUES
Steadfast, helpful, empathetic

VICES
Obsessive, overworked, stressed

CAREERS
Entrepreneur, business consultant, science researcher, corporate executive, project manager

SKILLS & APTITUDES
Organizational talents, strong work ethic, positive outlook

FAMOUS BIRTHS
Immanuael Kant (1724)
Glen Campbell (1936)
Jack Nicholson (1937)
Machine Gun Kelly (1990)

COMPATIBLE WITH
July 23–26, October 23–25

TAVRVS

APRIL 23

PLANETARY INFLUENCES
Ruling planets: Venus and Mars
First decan: Personal planet is Venus
First cusp: Taurus with Arian
  qualities

VIRTUES
Compassionate, inquisitive,
tenacious

VICES
Self-sacrificing, overburdened,
hedonistic

CAREERS
Philosopher, poet, counselor, actor

SKILLS & APTITUDES
Abstract thinking, sense of justice,
good people skills

FAMOUS BIRTHS
William Shakespeare (1564)
Shirley Temple (1928)
John Oliver (1977)
Taio Cruz (1985)
Gigi Hadid (1995)

COMPATIBLE WITH
July 23–26, October 23–25

....
....
....

Those born on April 23 possess a rare combination of introverted and extroverted qualities—namely, intellectual individuality and, conversely, a marked social orientation. These perceptive and curious individuals need to be able to explore the abstract concepts that hold their interest yet, at the same time, seek to ground themselves in a stable base from which to launch themselves on their quest for knowledge, perhaps intuitively recognizing that without such an anchor of security their darting imagination may lead them into fantasy worlds, causing them to lose touch with life's realities. Despite their independent leanings, however, they are gregarious types blessed with a sense of natural justice, born of their keen empathy with others. Such a well-balanced combination of characteristics enables them to find success in any professional situation in which they can exercise their talents for innovation and interpersonal contact; the various possibilities offered by artistic pursuits would therefore appear ideal career options for those born on April 23.

In their personal lives, April 23 people display a similar interest and concern for the well-being of those closest to them. They aim to create a happy and relaxed domestic environment, within which, while emotional bonds are paramount, the capacity for having fun is also encouraged. Others are drawn to them both for the steady aura of reliability that they exude and the infectious joie de vivre that they generate: the disadvantage of such popularity is that they may become overburdened with the expectations of less dynamic individuals.

APRIL 24

♀ ♂   COOPERATIVE COLLEAGUES

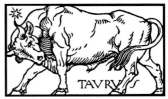

Those born on April 24 often feel torn between their careers and their families, for the urge to devote their whole-hearted attention to both is strong, and they do nothing by half measures. At work, they are driven by the desire to perform tasks as perfectly as humanly possible. Their searching intellects are supported by their methodical approach and organizational talents, as well as their sometimes obstinate refusal to quit until they have accomplished their aims.

A further facet of the natures of April 24 people is manifested by their great humanitarianism and concern with the feelings of others which, in professional scenarios, makes them cooperative and approachable colleagues. They have the potential to succeed in any field that they chose, provided that they have interpersonal contact, as well as the scope to act relatively independently. That they can be relied upon to deliver whatever is required of them is rarely in doubt, particularly if they were also born in the Chinese year of the ox.

Away from the workplace, April 24 people typically make loving and protective friends, partners and parents, whose somewhat controlling behavior is motivated by the desire to set their loved ones on stable and productive paths. Although undoubtedly sensible and steady types, they have a prodigious sense of fun, which bestows upon them an endearing ability to enjoy life and thereby also bring pleasure to others, qualities for which they are valued and which inspire genuine affection in others.

PLANETARY INFLUENCES
Ruling planets: Venus and Mars
First decan: Personal planet is Venus
First cusp: Taurus with Arian qualities

VIRTUES
Kind, devoted, approachable

VICES
Overburdened, unbalanced, obstinate

CAREERS
Team manager, charity organizer, project developer, counselor

SKILLS & APTITUDES
Single-minded focus, organizational skills, teamwork

FAMOUS BIRTHS
Shirley MacLaine (1934)
Barbra Streisand (1942)
Cedric the Entertainer (1964)
Kelly Clarkson (1982)

COMPATIBLE WITH
July 23–26

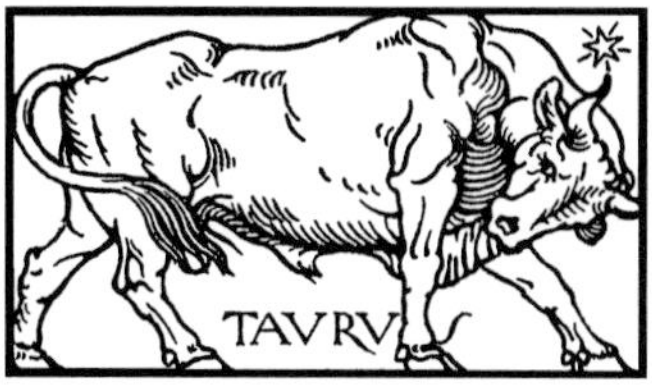

APRIL 25

Self-Assured Activists ♀

Planetary Influences
Ruling planet: Venus
First decan: Personal planet is Venus

Virtues
Energetic, dynamic, determined

Vices
Inflexible, blunt, impatient

Careers
Police officer, politician, project or team manager, artist, actor

Skills & Aptitudes
Leadership skills, desire to achieve active progress, single-minded focus

Famous Births
Oliver Cromwell (1559)
Al Pacino (1940)
Hank Azaria (1964)
Renée Zellweger (1969)

Compatible With
July 23–26

....

....

....

Those born on April 25 typically favor action over reflection, possessed as they are of a burning need to actually make progress rather than just musing on the possibility of achieving it. These are strong-minded types, whose enormous vigor and desire to effect tangible manifestations of their drive to succeed often inspires the somewhat intimidated awe of those who are less self-assured. Very little can resist the combined will and energy of April 25 people, despite their unwitting tendency to sabotage their own efforts by considering neither their personal motivations nor the implications of their actions sufficiently. Indeed, such is their aversion to both mental and physical inactivity that they are prone to make snap decisions and then tenaciously stick to them, steadfastly ignoring the objections of others. Such unwavering sense of purpose and single-minded commitment equips them for a variety of business, scientific or artistic careers, but the fields of law enforcement and politics are especially well starred.

Although they are natural leaders and seem to effortlessly command respect, April 25 people have a tendency to be overly blunt in their dealings with others, a propensity that applies equally to their colleagues and their family and friends, and one that can be deeply wounding. Although they play every bit as hard as they work, and moreover have a deep-rooted urge to protect and promote the well-being of their nearest and dearest, they tend to run their interpersonal relationships on their own terms and may thereby engender—and merit—resentment and rebellion.

APRIL 26

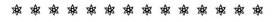

♀   METICULOUS PLANNERS

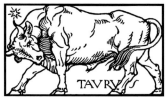

It may seem contradictory to those who do not know them well that although those born on April 26 are proponents of bold and visionary ideas, they also manifest a meticulous attention to detail. Yet these propensities are not so paradoxical when one understands that these realistic people recognize that a project's success cannot generally be achieved without careful forethought and planning involving the minute examination of all inherent issues and the subsequent setting in place of sound systems of organization, with contingency plans.

Having considered and catered for all eventualities, those born on this day will find themselves with the potential to preside over smooth-running and effective projects which they control with great capability while rarely relinquishing their focus on their ultimate objective. They are admired for their efficiency and reliability, and will therefore flourish in any profession they chose as long as they are able to retain their autonomy of thought and action.

It is perhaps inevitable, given their efficacy and practical talents, that April 26 people are extremely self-confident as regards to the veracity of their outlook and methods. There is a risk, however, that they will become too rigid in their beliefs, and will seek to mold others—or else dismiss them—into their preferred form. This controlling predilection will not generally result in harmonious personal relationships—particularly with their children—and it is therefore important that they should learn to relax their expectations of others, respect individuality and embrace diversity of conviction.

PLANETARY INFLUENCES
Ruling planet: Venus
First decan: Personal planet is Venus

VIRTUES
Reliable, independent, careful

VICES
Close-minded, controlling, rigid

CAREERS
Manager, project developer, consultant, military leader, teacher

SKILLS & APTITUDES
Strategic thinking, careful planning and forethought, clear-cut vision, single-minded focus

FAMOUS BIRTHS
Marcus Aurelius (AD 121)
Carol Burnett (1933)
Kevin James (1965)
Channing Tatum (1980)

COMPATIBLE WITH
July 27–31

TAVRV

APRIL 27

Thoughtful Independents ♀

PLANETARY INFLUENCES
Ruling planet: Venus
First decan: Personal planet is Venus

VIRTUES
Reflective, thoughtful, sensitive

VICES
Isolated, reserved, shy

CAREERS
Science researcher or theorist, humanitarian, painter, author

SKILLS & APTITUDES
Abstract thinking, self-reliance, intuition, refined taste

FAMOUS BIRTHS
Samuel Morse (1791)
Ulysses S. Grant (1822)
Coretta Scott King (1927)
Jenna Coleman (1986)
Lizzo (1988)

COMPATIBLE WITH
July 27–31

....
....
....

Those born on April 27 have a tendency to direct their attention and energies inward, preferring the exploration of their rich inner world of ideas and visions over the distraction of more trivial or unproductive pursuits. These are self-reliant and somewhat solitary types, who are rarely lonely in their own company and do not need to feel validated by the affirmation of others, especially if they are also women. More extroverted people may regard them as diffident or even antisocial, but this perception is far from the case; indeed, not only are these people comfortable with themselves, but they are furthermore blessed with qualities of profound intuition and compassion and will rarely withhold their help when it is truly required.

Those born on this day will typically be happiest when working on their own account, or within small organizations where their individuality and imagination can be given full rein, and will often find great fulfillment in the humanitarian, artistic or scientific realms. Alternatively, if their imagination and communication skills are also good, they might make excellent social-media marketers, being more sociable behind their computer screens than in person.

Despite their natural reserve and need for periods when they can be alone, April 27 individuals do not confine themselves exclusively to their self-imposed ivory towers and can often amaze those who do not know them well with their marked sensuality, appreciation of beauty and highly developed sense of humor. While rarely gregarious, they display great affection and loyalty to their friends, partners and family, who in turn cherish them for the emotional support and stability that they offer.

APRIL 28

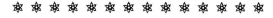

♀   SUCCESSFUL LEADERS

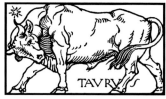
TAVRVS

Those born on April 28 are geared toward achievement, be it the attainment of personal goals or the realization of more abstract visions—either way, their drive for success compels them constantly to push forward until they finally reach their objectives. They are aided in their quest by their acute perspicacity, their great physical and mental vigor, their formidable organizational talents and their stubborn refusal to be deflected from their course. And because they are sensitive and intuitive individuals, they may not only direct their energies toward bringing about humanitarian progress, but also in so doing manifest a remarkable facility for tuning in to the emotions of others; they are not above using this ability to manipulate other people in order to enlist their support.

Their independence of thought and action, as well as their interpersonal skills, mark April 28 individuals out as potentially inspirational leaders in whatever field they choose to make their careers, especially if they nurture their creative potential and if they were also born in the Chinese year of the dragon.

April 28 people typically project a similar intensity of focus onto their private lives. Since they are averse to inactivity, they fill their private time with physical and sensual pursuits, a tendency which, when taken to its extreme, may result in uninhibited hedonism. Although they feel deep affection for those closest to them, they generally seek to direct the lives of their children in particular, without perceiving that they may be thereby suppressing the individual expression that they themselves hold so dear.

PLANETARY INFLUENCES
Ruling planet: Venus
First decan: Personal planet is Venus

VIRTUES
Resourceful, pragmatic, ambitious

VICES
Hedonistic, vain, dismissive

CAREERS
Team leader, counselor, international relations, politician

SKILLS & APTITUDES
Physical and mental vigor, desire for tangible results, resourcefulness, organizational talents

FAMOUS BIRTHS
Harper Lee (1926)
Terry Pratchett (1948)
Penelope Cruz (1974)
Jessica Alba (1981)

COMPATIBLE WITH
July 27–31

TAVRVS

APRIL 29

✿ ✿ ✿ ✿ ✿ ✿ ✿ ✿ ✿ ✿ ✿ ✿ ✿ ✿

ZESTFUL STRATEGISTS♀

PLANETARY INFLUENCES
Ruling planet: Venus
First decan: Personal planet is Venus

VIRTUES
Self-confident, optimistic, dependable

VICES
Obdurate, inconstant, liable to be overcommitted

CAREERS
Marketing consultant, advertiser, public-relations officer, project developer

SKILLS & APTITUDES
Attention to detail, strategic thinking, foresight, research skills, intellectual dynamism

FAMOUS BIRTHS
Willie Nelson (1933)
Jerry Seinfeld (1955)
Daniel Day-Lewis (1957)
Uma Thurman (1970)

COMPATIBLE WITH
July 27–31

The conjunction of their meticulous and determined approach to work with the often flamboyant personal image that April 29 people present to the world is a rare combination. These people are incisive and independent thinkers, who may be inspired by bold concepts but would rarely start to implement them without careful prior consideration. When planning a project they will typically examine every inherent aspect, anticipating potential pitfalls and then working out an appropriate course of action, with the result that although they may champion daring strategies, these will be soundly researched. And, because they understand the importance of image, they will "sell" their conceptual package to the skeptical with their enthusiasm and persuasive skills. Such talents are clearly suited to the world of business—and especially marketing, advertising and public relations—but they will also be effective in any professional area in which interpersonal relationships are important components.

Physically as well as intellectually dynamic, those born on this day are admired for their vigor, strength of will and infectious zest for life. In their personal lives, they are bent on having a good time, on enjoying to the full all that the world has to offer, and thereby they effortlessly attract friends and followers. Yet even when caught up in the excitement of a giddy social life, they never abandon their more sober and realistic characteristics, perhaps instinctively realizing the importance of grounding themselves in emotionally stable and supportive domestic relationships.

APRIL 30

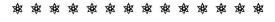

♀ MULTITALENTED CHILLAXERS

Those born on April 30 are deceptively calm individuals, their pronounced sense of humor, appreciation of the good things in life and relaxed and affectionate approach to other people often masking their highly perceptive and tenacious professionalism. Indeed, contrary to initial appearances, such is their intellectual drive that they will feel unfulfilled unless they can immerse themselves in their work, and this will often be directed toward achieving progress of a humanitarian nature—a result both of their empathy and of their ability incisively to identify faults in existing systems and then formulate strategies for improvement.

Because April 30 people wish to attain their aims as quickly and effectively as possible, and realistically recognize that they will be much more successful by winning others over to their cause rather than alienating them, they are very adept at using their considerable charm in the cultivation of open and friendly interpersonal relationships.

These multitalented individuals have the potential to make their mark on whichever area of professional expertise interests them. They are valued by their coworkers for their optimistic and encouraging outlook, as well as their great reliability. Within their personal liaisons, too, they are generally at the center of their social and domestic circles, for their ability to combine the provision of solid emotional support with a light-hearted, fun-loving approach is a rare and invigorating one and furthermore makes them especially gifted parents.

PLANETARY INFLUENCES
Ruling planet: Venus
First decan: Personal planet is Venus

VIRTUES
Calm, independent, practical

VICES
Overburdened, self-sacrificing, restless

CAREERS
Social worker, educational reformer, humanitarian, teacher, writer

SKILLS & APTITUDES
Relaxed approach, desire to be immersed in work, ability to formulate strategic improvements, skills in persuasion

FAMOUS BIRTHS
Cloris Leachman (1926)
Sam Heughan (1980)
Kirsten Dunst (1982)
Dianna Agron (1986)

COMPATIBLE WITH
July 27–31

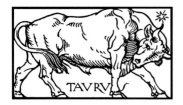

TAVRV

MAY 1

✳ ✳ ✳ ✳ ✳ ✳ ✳ ✳ ✳ ✳ ✳ ✳ ✳ ✳

BALANCED ALTRUISTS   ♀ ♀

PLANETARY INFLUENCES
Ruling planet: Venus
Second decan: Personal planet is
  Mercury

VIRTUES
Compassionate, tenacious,
nurturing

VICES
Biased, temperamental, distant

CAREERS
Salesperson, chef, charitable worker,
psychiatrist or counselor

SKILLS & APTITUDES
Empathetic disposition, intuitive
thinking, ability to balance the
professional with the personal

FAMOUS BIRTHS
Calamity Jane (1852)
Tim McGraw (1967)
Wes Anderson (1969)
Jamie Dornan (1982)

COMPATIBLE WITH
April 15–17, August 1–5

Perspicacity is the greatest strength of those born on May 1. There is very little that escapes these observant individuals—neither the occurrences of the physical world, nor actions reflecting the more nebulous range of human emotions. For, blessed as they are with acute powers of intellectual perception, these are also highly intuitive types, who often rely upon their instincts in forming their initial opinions of people, situations and predicaments. Then, once they have gleaned sufficient information, they will typically apply their talent for sound, logical and realistic thought to building an effective strategy for action. Their great sensitivity toward the feelings of others makes them kind and empathetic people, who will generally do their utmost to help when approached—as they frequently are—with a problem. This propensity, coupled with their other natural abilities, equips those born on this day especially well for the caring professions in general and for psychiatry or counseling in particular, although less altruistic types also have the potential to make gifted salespeople.

Within their personal relationships, also, May 1 individuals usually find themselves playing an actively supportive role, bolstering the confidence of those closest to them while at the same time encouraging them to enjoy life, for they love company, as well as such sensual domestic pleasures as cooking for others. But in assuming somewhat static positions as linchpins, around whom others revolve, they will need to guard against the risk of being taken for granted and, furthermore, of neglecting their own personal development.

MAY 2

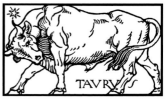

♀ ☿

CANDID ORATORS

As those who enjoy stable and harmonious interpersonal relationships, it might seem strange that those born on this day often upset others with their propensity to express themselves bluntly. Yet these honest individuals do not consciously set out to wound others, it is just that, as acutely perceptive people possessed of an almost clinical fascination with what makes others tick, they tend to reach logical conclusions unclouded by emotional complications and then to voice their findings with undiplomatic objectivity. Such people-oriented qualities of curiosity and interest, as well as their tenacious determination to effect improvement, bestow upon May 2 individuals a marked potential for success not only in the more technical of the caring professions, such as medicine and scientific research, but also in social campaigning.

In the domestic sphere, these people long to create steady and enduring ties of affection and greatly value the bonds that they form with their family and friends. They are often extremely gregarious types who are stimulated by social gatherings and relish seeing others enjoying themselves, yet they will also derive profound pleasure from being alone with nature—a predilection that often makes them inspired gardeners. They have a dangerous tendency, however, to apply their own standards to their nearest and dearest, expecting them to unquestioningly conform to their mores: thus they may themselves generate the sort of confrontational situations that they abhor by engendering a clash of wills. It is vital, therefore, that they should learn to relax their high, albeit well-meaning, expectations of others.

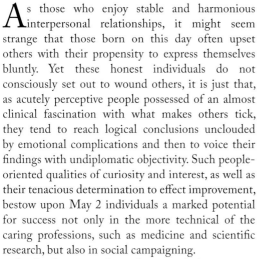

PLANETARY INFLUENCES
Ruling planet: Venus
Second decan: Personal planet is Mercury

VIRTUES
Curious, candid, driven

VICES
Impatient, tactless, inflexible

CAREERS
Landscape architect, environmentalist, doctor, researcher, event or wedding planner

SKILLS & APTITUDES
No-nonsense outlook, ability to think objectively, gregarious disposition, honesty

FAMOUS BIRTHS
Dwayne Johnson (1972)
David Beckham (1975)
Ellie Kemper (1980)
Princess Charlotte (2015)

COMPATIBLE WITH
April 15–17, August 1–5

TAVRV

MAY 3

✶ ✶ ✶ ✶ ✶ ✶ ✶ ✶ ✶ ✶ ✶ ✶ ✶

PERCEPTIVE EVALUATORS   ♀ ☿

T hose born on May 3 are astute judges of character, utilizing their highly developed skills of intuition, perception and intellectual objectivity to make often extremely realistic assessments of others. They can also apply these interpersonal talents to collective human situations, thus giving them a profound understanding of the reasons underlying both individual behavior and group dynamics. They are driven by an almost scientific curiosity, and the nature of this inquisitiveness, together with the information they glean in the process, endows them with genuine concern for their fellow beings. Linked with the necessary emotional detachment, this equips them admirably to become psychologists, psychiatrists or counselors: careers as market researchers or advertising executives are also favored. Combined with their human awareness, their ability to think pragmatically additionally promises success in the political sphere.

Although those born on this day manifest a healthy hedonistic streak, which enables them to discard their professional personae and enjoy life to the full when appropriate, they may have difficulty in committing themselves to a single partner, a problem that derives from their inherent propensity to judge people with their head rather than their heart. While others are attracted to May 3 people for the fun that they generate, as well as the sound advice that they proffer, those seeking more enduring relationships may be disappointed. Once strong emotional bonds are formed, however, these people remain steadfastly affectionate and caring toward those closest to them.

PLANETARY INFLUENCES
Ruling planet: Venus
Second decan: Personal planet is
   Mercury

VIRTUES
Insightful, optimistic, sociable

VICES
Judgmental, detached,
noncommittal

CAREERS
Market researcher, advertising
executive, psychologist, politician,
actor or singer

SKILLS & APTITUDES
Ability to judge character, objective
perception, inquisitive nature

FAMOUS BIRTHS
Niccolò Machiavelli (1469)
Bing Crosby (1903)
Frankie Valli (1934)
Cheryl Burke (1984)

COMPATIBLE WITH
April 15–17, August 1–5

MAY 4

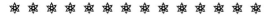

♀ ☿   HELPING HANDS

One of the strongest—and most endearing—qualities manifested by those born on May 4 is their concern with the well-being of others and their commensurate desire to place their considerable talents and energy at the disposal of those who require their help. Their enlightened powers of perspicacity and realism, in conjunction with their genuine empathy, steadiness and optimistic outlook, not only give them the potential to help solve others' problems effectively, but also win for them esteem and gratitude.

Their ability to combine their great intellectual and practical skills with their typically emotion-driven gifts of compassion and kindness is an unusually potent talent often seen in May 4 people, and whether they make a career of counseling or not, they will generally find that their sound advice is much sought after by others. Indeed, whatever profession they choose, they will generally flourish best in those work-based situations which offer a significant degree of personal interaction.

Within their personal relationships too, May 4 individuals make heartening friends, partners and parents, who typically tend to place the needs and desires of those closest to them above their own. Because they are so used to being consulted for their advice, there is a danger that, if their carefully considered words of wisdom are ignored, they will feel deeply disappointed and express their annoyance forcefully. They should guard against subsuming their own—equally important—ambitions to those of others.

PLANETARY INFLUENCES
Ruling planet: Venus
Second decan: Personal planet is Mercury

VIRTUES
Sensible, imaginative, generous

VICES
Resentful, self-sacrificing, frustrated

CAREERS
Social worker, counselor, doctor, firefighter, activist

SKILLS & APTITUDES
Problem-solving skills, propensity for teamwork, ability to listen and be open to new ideas

FAMOUS BIRTHS
Audrey Hepburn (1929)
Will Arnett (1970)
Kimora Lee Simmons (1975)
Lance Bass (1979)

COMPATIBLE WITH
April 15–17, August 1–5

TAVRVS

MAY 5

✳ ✳ ✳ ✳ ✳ ✳ ✳ ✳ ✳ ✳ ✳ ✳ ✳

INSPIRING PRAGMATISTS   ♀ ☿

PLANETARY INFLUENCES
Ruling planet: Venus
Second decan: Personal planet is
 Mercury

VIRTUES
Inspirational, helpful, self-assured

VICES
Controlling, dominant, prescriptive

CAREERS
Salesperson, policymaker, business
manager, philosopher, museum
director

SKILLS & APTITUDES
Progressive thinking, approachable
persona, attention to detail, ability
to inspire and motivate

FAMOUS BIRTHS
Karl Marx (1818)
Michael Palin (1943)
Henry Cavill (1983)
Adele (1988)

COMPATIBLE WITH
August 1–5

....
....
....

Those born on May 5 are convinced of the veracity of their remarkably strong opinions, which they feel compelled to transmit to others in order to convert them to their viewpoints. Since they are extremely concerned with the welfare of people as a collective entity, and furthermore blessed with a highly developed sense of fairness and justice, their convictions are more than likely to be inspired by a radical humanitarian vision—a desire to bring the greatest happiness to the greatest number of people.

When working toward the implementation of their aims, they typically manifest great pragmatism, using every weapon in their armory of skills to affect their ambitions: talents that include objective perspicacity, meticulous attention to detail, profoundly methodical organizational abilities, and enormous energy and tenacity. It is also pertinent that those born on this day are natural salespeople, who instinctively understand how to motivate and inspire others—and thereby, sometimes, to manipulate them toward their own ends, too.

Careers in the retail trade, as well as in politics, therefore augur especially well for May 5 individuals, but they also have the potential to find fulfillment in such academic areas as philosophy or medical studies, as well as in the arts, with which they have a remarkable affinity. For, however serious the purpose that drives their intellects, these are sensual people who relish such pleasurable experiences as fine food, haunting music and aesthetic beauty, this being especially true if they were also born in the Chinese year of the goat.

MAY 6

♀ ☿   FIERCE PROTECTORS

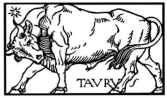

In common with many of their Taurean fellows, those intuitive people born on May 6 are acutely attuned to the emotions of others, and moreover often feel profound empathy with less fortunate individuals, who arouse a fiercely protective instinct in them. Whether or not their interest in humanity takes an active compassionate form, these people cannot help but be fascinated by the mechanics of the human psyche, seeking to understand what exactly it is that motivates others. And, because these are perceptive, articulate and logically thinking individuals, who feel compelled to pass on their wisdom to others, they typically make gifted and insightful problem-solvers, whose advice is frequently sought.

Given such inherently people-oriented talents and inclinations, they will usually find career fulfillment in the medical, psychiatric or caring professions, but they are also suited to politics and the arts, both areas in which they can utilize their sensitivity and urge to help humanity progress.

Despite the seriousness with which they apply themselves to their work, however, May 6 individuals retain the capacity to enjoy the simpler things in life, perhaps instinctively appreciating that relaxation is a vital release from intellectual pressure. They typically make deeply supportive and affectionate friends, partners and parents, whose marked sense of humor, infectious optimism and generosity draw others to them, particularly if they were also born in the Chinese year of the horse.

PLANETARY INFLUENCES
Ruling planet: Venus
Second decan: Personal planet is Mercury

VIRTUES
Sensitive, supportive, strong-minded

VICES
Indulgent, easily led, gullible

CAREERS
Doctor, nurse, psychologist, scientific researcher, actor

SKILLS & APTITUDES
Empathetic disposition, logical thinking, problem-solving skills, interest in the human psyche

FAMOUS BIRTHS
Sigmund Freud (1856)
Orson Welles (1915)
George Clooney (1961)
Gabourey Sidibe (1983)

COMPATIBLE WITH
August 6–10

MAY 7

✵ ✵ ✵ ✵ ✵ ✵ ✵ ✵ ✵ ✵ ✵ ✵ ✵ ✵

GIFTED COMMUNICATORS ♀ ☿

PLANETARY INFLUENCES
Ruling planet: Venus
Second decan: Personal planet is
Mercury

VIRTUES
Self-aware, inquisitive, motivated

VICES
Self-absorbed, narcissistic,
neglectful

CAREERS
Spiritual or political spokesperson,
writer, poet, musician, orator

SKILLS & APTITUDES
Abstract thinking, communication
skills, compassion

FAMOUS BIRTHS
Johannes Brahms (1833)
Pyotr Ilyich Tchaikovsky (1840)
Eva "Evita" Perón (1919)
Chiara Ferragni (1987)

COMPATIBLE WITH
August 6–10

Inherent in those born on this day is a profound mixture of inward-looking spirituality and externally-oriented concern with personal image. Thus while the former characteristic leads these people to recognize that life's most important truths and values are of the nonmaterialistic, intellectual and emotionally elevated variety, the latter endows them with an altogether more superficial desire to make the best possible impression on others. Yet this image-consciousness is not necessarily a negative quality, for once May 7 people have become aware of it, they may consciously influence others to achieve their ends. Indeed, as well as being deeply sensitive and often compassionate, these individuals are gifted communicators, with an outstanding ability to convey their strongly held convictions to others and thereby inspire them with their visions. Reflecting their skills and leanings, these people have the potential to excel in the artistic sphere, not only as writers, poets and composers, but also as spiritual or even political evangelists.

Despite their best intentions, however, those born on May 7 may have less-than-idyllic personal lives, for their interest in idealistic concepts and their desire to influence the wider world may leave them with little energy or attention to devote to those closest to them, a tendency that is particularly pronounced in the men born on this day. Indeed, it is ironic that, while they may devote enormous effort to winning allies when at work, they may unintentionally neglect the feelings of their partners, children and friends, despite the genuine affection that they feel for those closest to them.

MAY 8

♀ ☿   DRIVEN ARCHITECTS

Those born on this day harbor extremely strong convictions, which they will typically maintain with stubborn determination and strive to propagate as widely as possible. Although they are possessed of a highly developed sense of fair play, which may compel them to direct their efforts toward improving the lot of less fortunate individuals by serving, for example, as politicians, May 8 people generally feel a greater connection with the environment—be it with the natural world, or their immediate, perhaps man-made surroundings—a sympathy that is heightened by their profound innate appreciation of beauty. Hence they will often be found playing a leading role in preserving or improving landscapes, historically important buildings or their own homes. When in the grip of crusading zeal, they may put their ideas across forcefully, but since they instinctively understand the value of converting rather than alienating others, and are gifted and effective communicators with the persuasive talents of a salesperson, they usually prefer to be persuaded.

Despite the unwavering loyalty and affection that they manifest toward their friends, partners and families, those born on this day may be difficult to live with because of their high standards and ideals. Their aesthetic concern with their personal environment, may result in simmering resentment when those with whom they share their homes fail to fall in with their exacting requirements, particularly untidy teen-age children. Their energy and self-certainty instill in them a propensity to control the actions of their nearest and dearest rather than let them explore their own avenues independently.

PLANETARY INFLUENCES
Ruling planet: Venus
Second decan: Personal planet is Mercury

VIRTUES
Ambitious, moral, tenacious

VICES
Imposing, domineering, closed-minded

CAREERS
Historical preservation, landscape architect, salesperson, site developer

SKILLS & APTITUDES
Sense of justice and morality, aesthetic interests, effective communication skills

FAMOUS BIRTHS
Harry S. Truman (1884)
David Attenborough (1926)
Melissa Gilbert (1964)
Enrique Iglesias (1975)

COMPATIBLE WITH
August 6–10

MAY 9

Fiery Defenders ☿ ♀

Those born on this day can astonish those who do not know them well with their awesome flashes of temper, colorful pyrotechnical displays that are at variance with their generally steady and calm approach to life. Such tantrums are rarely gratuitous, however, instead being provoked by what May 9 people believe to be manifestations of perversity that hinder implemention of their progressive visions. For these are judgemental—almost magisterial—people, who feel compelled to adopt the champion's mantle when moved by examples of injustice or abuse, desiring to protect the downtrodden and reverse their misfortunes. And, in such instances, when faced with a humanitarian challenge, May 9 people typically draw deep on their prodigious resources of energy, determination and courage, thus making inspiring leaders. While such qualities suit them extremely well for careers in politics, the caring professions or the judiciary, their enormous sensitivity also endows them with outstanding artistic potential.

Because these people are overridingly possessed by highly developed instincts of moral rectitude, they generally find it hard to forgive the all-too-human failings of their nearest and dearest, expecting them to live up to the lofty ethical standards on which they themselves place such great value. When they experience inevitable disappointment within both their professional and personal relationships, their temperamental tendencies surge to the fore, a propensity that is especially marked if they were also born in the Chinese year of the dragon.

Planetary Influences
Ruling planet: Venus
Second decan: Personal planet is Mercury

Virtues
Compassionate, brave, committed

Vices
Irascible, temperamental, judgmental

Careers
Political leader, social worker, judge, lawyer, artist

Skills & Aptitudes
Progressive vision, drive to fight injustice, high energy levels

Famous Births
J.M. Barrie (1860)
Mike Wallace (1918)
Billy Joel (1949)
Rosario Dawson (1979)

Compatible With
August 6–10

MAY 10

♀ ☿   DEVOTED CRAFTERS

Many of those born on May 10 tend to be obsessive in exploring and promoting those concepts that fuel their imaginations and passions. Indeed, their capacity to become totally absorbed in pet projects can leave them with little time, energy or even interest to devote to unrelated people or projects. Without the unconditional tolerance and understanding of friends and family members, they are unlikely to experience any of the joys of personal interaction and close emotional support; this is especially the case for men born on this day, who often turn a blind eye to what they regard as the trivial, relatively unimportant chores and obligations of normal family relationships.

While there is no single captivating ideal or topic of interest that can impel May 10 individuals to sacrifice their personal lives in this manner, these sensitive people generally feel a strong affinity with the arts, and also with politics, both areas which allow scope for their great imaginative powers and ambitious urge to attain success.

Such qualities endow these people with the potential to make their mark on the world as far-seeing innovators, and when they are working toward fulfilling their innate promise, they are aided enormously by their vigor, their willingness to take a lone stand when necessary, their ability as gifted communicators to enlist the support of others, their capacity for logical thought and their outstanding tenacity. This combination of talents makes them particularly effective as influencers on social media sites.

PLANETARY INFLUENCES
Ruling planet: Venus
Second decan: Personal planet is
  Mercury

VIRTUES
Focused, ambitious, dynamic

VICES
Neglectful, obsessive,
unappreciative

CAREERS
Politician, campaign manager, art
director, visual artist

SKILLS & APTITUDES
Single-minded focus, imaginative
powers, logical thought,
communication

FAMOUS BIRTHS
Fred Astaire (1899)
Donovan (1946)
Bono (1960)
Kenan Thompson (1978)

COMPATIBLE WITH
August 6–10

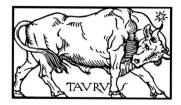

TAVRVS

MAY 11

LOYAL MAVERICKS   ♀ ♄

PLANETARY INFLUENCES
Ruling planet: Venus
Third decan: Personal planet is Saturn

VIRTUES
Innovative, determined, unorthodox

VICES
Isolated, alienating, radical

CAREERS
Judge, lawyer, politician, academic
or technical researcher

SKILLS & APTITUDES
Self-discipline, ability to think
and research independently, strong
imagination, powers of perception

FAMOUS BIRTHS
Irving Berlin (1888)
Salvador Dalí (1904)
Richard Feynman (1918)
Cory Monteith (1982)

COMPATIBLE WITH
August 6–10

Although exceptionally self-disciplined, those born on May 11 refuse to be constrained by others' narrow rules and regulations or ideas and ideals. Fiercely independent in both thought and deed, they also have a burning desire to discover the world's truths for themselves, an inherent compulsion that inevitably causes them to reject the mores of conventional beliefs and behavior patterns.

Their questing and imaginative intellectual qualities are typically supplemented by outstanding powers of perception, methodical attention to detail, true originality and stubborn tenacity when investigating or defining concepts that fascinate May 11 people. And, although they are naturally attracted to abstract ideas and are therefore suited to academic or technical research, these are sensitive individuals, whose interest in every aspect of the human condition endows them with feelings of considerable empathy, which may impel them to pursue careers in the judiciary or politics.

In their interpersonal relationships, their humanitarian concern and appreciation of individuality makes them remarkably tolerant of extreme or eccentric behavior. Coupled with their inherent gifts of intuition, protectiveness and loyalty, they make gifted parents, who encourage the natural enthusiasm and inquisitiveness of their children. They appreciate that a stable domestic life provides the best background for their more radical propensities. Their professional relationships, however, may be less harmonious, since they have a tendency to alienate more conventional souls.

MAY 12

♀ ♄   DEPENDABLE FRIENDS

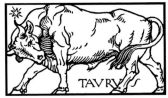

Those born on May 12 are valued by coworkers and family members alike for their dependability, for they have both a highly developed sense of responsibility and a protective desire to help those for whom they care by assuming their burdens. These are immensely capable individuals, who typically combine their urge to actively make progress with impressive intellectual gifts, including remarkable perspicacity, an unremitting ability for logical thought and unwavering tenacity.

Because they are direct and guileless, May 12 individuals tend to speak their minds bluntly, a characteristic that is not always advisable, however. Their steadfastness of purpose and independent outlook often propels those born on this day into leadership positions. These individuals are well equipped to succeed in virtually any career that they choose, but their marked orientation toward others may encourage them to work in the caring professions, while their overall sensitivity may furthermore bestow upon them great artistic talent.

Those who do not know May 12 people well may be surprised to find that lurking behind the somewhat serious face that they present to the world is an apparently uncharacteristically adventurous and hedonistic streak. For these are intellectually curious types, who are stimulated by contact with the different or unusual and enjoy new experiences and situations. They instinctively understand the importance of relaxation and, since they are gregarious individuals, like nothing better than to be hospitable to others and entertain them lavishly.

PLANETARY INFLUENCES
Ruling planet: Venus
Third decan: Personal planet is Saturn

VIRTUES
Supportive, deep-thinking, methodical

VICES
Blunt, hedonistic, overworked

CAREERS
Nurse, social worker, teacher, artist, musician

SKILLS & APTITUDES
Perspicacity and tenacity, high intelligence, direct form of communication, skills in hosting and hospitality

FAMOUS BIRTHS
Florence Nightingale (1820)
Katharine Hepburn (1907)
Tony Hawk (1968)
Domhnall Gleeson (1983)

COMPATIBLE WITH
August 11–16

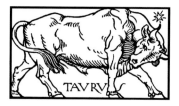

TAVRVS

MAY 13

✵ ✵ ✵ ✵ ✵ ✵ ✵ ✵ ✵ ✵ ✵ ✵ ✵ ✵

BREEZY CHARMERS   ♀ ♄

PLANETARY INFLUENCES
Ruling planet: Venus
Third decan: Personal planet is Saturn

VIRTUES
Charming, sensitive, intuitive

VICES
Restless, distracted, flighty

CAREERS
Human resources, project manager, entrepreneur, writer or artist

SKILLS & APTITUDES
Ability to think and act independently, discerning nature, people-oriented approach

FAMOUS BIRTHS
Bea Arthur (1926)
Stevie Wonder (1950)
Stephen Colbert (1964)
Robert Pattinson (1986)

COMPATIBLE WITH
August 11–16

In comparison to those who find it a struggle to attain their ideals, those born on May 13 appear to breeze through life, effortlessly notching up success after success, charming others in the process. And indeed, these are undeniably gifted people who are able to harmonize their often contradictory personal qualities to produce a remarkably effective holistic package. Thus while their great intellectual curiosity stimulates them to think and act independently, their enormous sensitivity and intuitive perspicacity makes them extremely receptive to the people and circumstances that surround them. Similarly, while many May 13 people manifest a profoundly serious sense of purpose when engaged in tasks that truly absorb them, their inherent earnestness is balanced by their infectious and enthusiastic enjoyment of life. Although their multitude of interests may lead them to consider a variety of careers in the professional spheres, their artistic aptitude marks them out for particular success in this realm.

Their skills and people-oriented approach generally make these people valued team members—both at work and within the family—and they typically display a remarkable level of affection and loyalty to their nearest and dearest, whose lives they seek to enrich while simultaneously assuming a supportive and protective role. Yet because May 13 individuals, and especially the men born on this day, respond so immediately to the stimulus of an exciting challenge, they may occasionally appear to be somewhat flighty, preferring to investigate an alluring new passion rather than sticking doggedly to a less attractive, but perhaps more critical, option.

MAY 14

♀ ♄   HUMANE VISIONARIES

TAVRVS

Although their enormous sensitivity bestows upon them the capacity to have deep feelings and compassion for those who are less fortunate, it is the realm of abstract ideas rather than of interpersonal relationships that really excites May 14 individuals. Thus while they may be found devising strategies for alleviating global human suffering, it is the excitement engendered by the challenge that stimulates them, rather than the end result of their labors.

Their marked—often extreme—powers of imagination instill in May 14 people an enthusiasm for exploring new concepts and techniques, a trait which is backed up extremely effectively by their great intellectual and intuitive perceptiveness, their steadfast commitment to the mastery of detail, and their obstinate refusal to concede defeat. Such qualities often indicate particular success in the realm of science, for example in information technology, or in the social sciences, although they also have an innate talent for such artistic pursuits as music, drama, literature and painting, too.

Such an overriding commitment to the world of ideas is usually the mark of the introvert and, while those born on May 14 may indeed sometimes appear to be solitary and obsessive types, their interest and concern for their coworkers, friends, partners and relations, combined with their sense of humor and healthy appreciation of pleasure and beauty typically give them strong interpersonal roots that ground them in the real world. Their knack for problem-solving, dependability and kindly attitude frequently encourage others to seek their advice.

PLANETARY INFLUENCES
Ruling planet: Venus
Third decan: Personal planet is Saturn

VIRTUES
Enthusiastic, determined, perceptive

VICES
Obstinate, isolated, stressed

CAREERS
IT consultant, anthropologist, town planner, community worker, painter, musician

SKILLS & APTITUDES
Abstract thinking, imagination, intuitive perceptiveness

FAMOUS BIRTHS
George Lucas (1944)
Cate Blanchett (1969)
Mark Zuckerberg (1984)
Miranda Cosgrove (1993)

COMPATIBLE WITH
August 11–16

MAY 15

✳ ✳ ✳ ✳ ✳ ✳ ✳ ✳ ✳ ✳ ✳ ✳ ✳ ✳

INTROSPECTIVE CREATIVES ♀ ♄

PLANETARY INFLUENCES
Ruling planet: Venus
Third decan: Personal planet is Saturn

VIRTUES
Sensitive, introspective, caring

VICES
Irresponsible, isolated, dreamy

CAREERS
Religious leader or academic, humanitarian, musician, painter

SKILLS & APTITUDES
Visionary powers, abstract thinking, imagination and creativity, open-minded attitude

FAMOUS BIRTHS
Eddy Arnold (1918)
Madeleine Albright (1937)
David Krumholtz (1978)
Andy Murray (1987)

COMPATIBLE WITH
August 11–16

Those born on this day are often perceived by others as being rather dreamy individuals who live in worlds of their own devising and therefore possess a somewhat otherworldly quality. And in many respects this somewhat superficial judgement is correct, for these are profoundly introspective beings, who not only have a near-irresistible urge to attain knowledge but, once they have accumulated sufficient information on subjects that excite their interest, to expand and develop it with unusual imagination and creativity.

Thus while their mental agility and independence, their open mindedness toward mystical concepts and their tenacity of purpose endow them with innovative potential, their steady and methodical approach provides them with the concrete means with which to support and validate their visions. Underlying all their actions is their enormous sensitivity, a defining characteristic which, in their professional lives, may manifest itself in areas where it can be employed to effect humanitarian progress, or in the artistic sphere, where their work can be shared with, and inspire, others.

Despite their often solitary interests and modi vivendi, the sensitivity of May 15 people is so all-encompassing that it propels them toward interpersonal contact, and is often manifested in unusual levels of empathy and compassion toward others, especially those closest to them. They are typically fiercely devoted to long-standing friends and families and particularly to their children. They are encouraged by the emotional support that they receive to share their talents with the wider world.

MAY 16

♀ ♄   FLAMBOYANT CHARACTERS

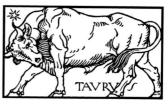

TAVRVS

May 16 individuals are often described as "flamboyant," for although they might not regard themselves as individualists, and especially not in terms of their attitude toward the predilections and foibles of others, they typically blaze a highly idiosyncratic and dynamic trail through life. They are larger-than-life characters, determined to impose their forceful wills upon people and circumstances and receive maximum possible attention and acclaim for their actions in the process. Despite these controlling and attention-seeking qualities that are such a vital part of their personal make-up, others thoroughly enjoy their company. Life is rarely dull when around them, for not only do they present awesome spectacles when in full flight, but their indomitable vigor and infectious joie de vivre draws others to them for the sense of fun—and sometimes danger—that they generate. Professionally, they will fare best when they can assume leadership or performing roles, and they are especially well equipped for careers in such artistic fields as acting or music-making, in which their talents will be appreciated by their audiences.

The direct approach favored by these people is fueled by their strength of purpose and orientation toward success, which usually takes the form of personal ambition. While they are generally loyal and affectionate to those who unquestioningly support them, they may brush aside, or even trample over, those who stand in their way. When impeded, they may express their frustration by means of spectacular outbursts of temper, a tendency which may, unless controlled, ultimately sabotage their success.

PLANETARY INFLUENCES
Ruling planet: Venus
Third decan: Personal planet is Saturn

VIRTUES
Passionate, dynamic, self-confident

VICES
Temperamental, intimidating, egotistical

CAREERS
Actor, comedian, musician, radio presenter

SKILLS & APTITUDES
Ambition, orientation for success, drive to be the center of attention, high levels of energy and creativity

FAMOUS BIRTHS
Liberace (1919)
Pierce Brosnan (1953)
Janet Jackson (1966)
Megan Fox (1986)

COMPATIBLE WITH
August 11–16

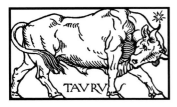

MAY 17

✳ ✳ ✳ ✳ ✳ ✳ ✳ ✳ ✳ ✳ ✳ ✳ ✳ ✳

TENACIOUS MISSIONARIES ♀ ♄

PLANETARY INFLUENCES
Ruling planet: Venus
Third decan: Personal planet is Saturn

VIRTUES
Ambitious, caring, determined

VICES
Judgmental, blunt, intolerant

CAREERS
Festival/event manager, travel consultant, art director, financial advisor

SKILLS & APTITUDES
Clear-sighted perception, people-oriented ambitions, original thinking, aesthetic sensitivity

FAMOUS BIRTHS
Bob Saget (1956)
Enya (1961)
Craig Ferguson (1962)
Tony Parker (1982)

COMPATIBLE WITH
August 17–22

Those born on May 17 are fueled by their fierce wish to see their ambitions realized: although these may involve personal betterment, they are above all concerned with the improvement of the lot of humanity as a whole. For these are not only perceptive people whose clear-sightedness helps them to readily identify faults and failings, but they are also individuals whose deep, people-oriented sensitivity bestows upon them the urge to work toward improving the lives of those less fortunate. Yet despite their prodigious energy, their capacity for original and logical thought, and their obstinate refusal to be diverted from their missions, many May 17 people seem doomed to failure. It may be that they have a tendency to set their sights too high, possibly recognizing that their aims are inherently unfeasible but nevertheless assuming that they can overcome any obstacles in their path through sheer determination and force of will.

Once they have developed a greater sense of realism, these people will thrive in those professions where their great practical skills and intellectual idealism can find best expression. The artistic sphere promises special potential for success, for those born on this day have a highly developed sense of the aesthetic, as well as enormous creativity. They may also find satisfaction in the world of finance or in tourism, where they can cater for the enjoyment of others. Within their personal relationships, these people typically show great commitment to those closest to them, perhaps in inherent recognition of the emotional rewards that result from a stable and supportive domestic life.

MAY 18

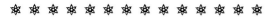

JUST ACTIVISTS

TAVRVS

Those born on May 18 favor a straightforward approach in everything that they do, possessed as they are by a driving urge to push onward rather than prevaricating or stagnating. They are blessed with an outstanding intellectual ability to cut incisively to the heart of an issue and then, employing their remarkable analytical powers, to build up their own strategy with which to achieve their aims. Because these are sensitive types who cannot bear to see injustice being done, and who are furthermore endowed with a keen sense of natural justice, their energies will often be directed toward the alleviation of suffering or the improvement of social systems. When convinced of their moral veracity in the face of a perceived abuse of power, those born on May 18 will not flinch from taking a brave stance and tenaciously persevering with their mission until the challenge has been overcome.

Individuals born on this day will flourish in any career in which they can attain tangible progress, but, given their latent humanitarian and often philosophical leanings, they will find special satisfaction when they can provide guidance to others. Despite their predilection for independence of thought and action, these are empathetic people who would rather not have to act in isolation, preferring instead to work as part of a harmonious and committed team, this being especially true in the case of women born on this day. Indeed, in both their professional and personal liaisons they typically exhibit great charm, consideration and loyalty, qualities that make them valued coworkers, friends and family members.

PLANETARY INFLUENCES
Ruling planets: Venus and Mercury
Third decan: Personal planet is Saturn
Second cusp: Taurus with Gemini
tendencies

VIRTUES
Steadfast, energetic, compassionate

VICES
Obstinate, closed-minded, stubborn

CAREERS
Judge, politician, mediator, ambassador or diplomat

SKILLS & APTITUDES
Straightforward approach, incisive and strategic thinking, analytical powers, inherent sense of justice

FAMOUS BIRTHS
Reggie Jackson (1946)
George Strait (1952)
Tina Fey (1970)
Jens Bergensten (1979)

COMPATIBLE WITH
August 17–22, September 26–28

MAY 19

✴ ✴ ✴ ✴ ✴ ✴ ✴ ✴ ✴ ✴ ✴ ✴ ✴ ✴

STEADFAST PROBLEM–SOLVERS   ♀ ☿ ♄

PLANETARY INFLUENCES
Ruling planets: Venus and Mercury
Third decan: Personal planet is Saturn
Second cusp: Taurus with Gemini
  tendencies

VIRTUES
Tactful, empathetic, calm

VICES
Suppressed, controlling, resentful

CAREERS
Politician, teacher, caregiver,
therapist, nurse, counselor

SKILLS & APTITUDES
Practical talents, ability to
implement realistic solutions,
pragmatic outlook

FAMOUS BIRTHS
Malcolm X (1925)
Andre the Giant (1946)
Grace Jones (1948)
Sam Smith (1992)

COMPATIBLE WITH
August 17–25, September 26–28

The steadfast kindness and dependability of those born on this day marks them out as people to whom others turn for support and encouragement in times of difficulty. When asked to advise upon problems, they typically muster their prodigiously practical talents to devise realistic and positive solutions and then devote their energies wholeheartedly toward implementation. Although they harbor extremely strong convictions, which are generally informed by their sense of natural justice, they pass on their opinions to others with a judicious use of tact, tailoring the manner in which they impart their ideas without ever compromising the essence of their beliefs. Such pragmatism, when combined with their humanitarian concern and idealism, suits those born on May 19 to a number of people-oriented careers, including politics, teaching and the caring professions, and, indeed, they will usually only find true satisfaction in work involving interpersonal contact.

These individuals will similarly assume a central role in their private lives, acting as rocks of stability and reliability around which their more flighty friends and relations flit back and forth, always returning for support. Two dangers are thus presented: that these people's sense of responsibility, protective urge and commitment to those nearest to them may sometimes cause them to suppress their own needs and desires in the interests of others; and that unless they are also able to pursue their personal interests their frustrated desire for independence may find a somewhat destructive outlet in the control of those around them.

MAY 20

♀ ☿ ♄   RELENTLESS EXPLORERS

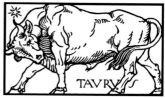

The apparently limitless energy of those born on May 20, and their appetite for savoring new intellectual or sensory experiences, arouses both awe and exhaustion in others. The awe is inspired by the variety of interests that fascinate them, and the exhaustion by the relentless pace with which they seek out and explore novel ideas and situations. Yet despite the speed with which they move from subject to subject, from place to place, or from person to person, the knowledge that they gain is rarely superficial, for their quick wits and intuition enable them to process information into a coherent and remarkably accurate précis. When they encounter an area that truly absorbs them, and the humanitarian, philosophical or artistic spheres are especially propitious for those born on this day, they manifest a highly developed capacity for detailed investigation and a single-minded tenacity for its development and implementation.

Despite their apparently ceaseless quest for stimulation, these people are typically steadfast, supportive and loyal in their personal relationships, although they may initially find it hard to commit themselves to a life partner. Not only is the welfare and happiness of their nearest and dearest of paramount importance to these caring individuals, but they are furthermore blessed with an endearing joie de vivre, which has an enlivening effect on those around them. In return, the ties that they form with their long-standing friends and family members provide a grounding and supportive framework from which to launch themselves on their voyages of discovery.

PLANETARY INFLUENCES
Ruling planets: Venus and Mercury
Third decan: Personal planet is Saturn
Second cusp: Taurus with Gemini tendencies

VIRTUES
Curious, practical, mercurial

VICES
Dissatisfied, inconstant, restless

CAREERS
Humanitarian, painter, musician, academic researcher or professor

SKILLS & APTITUDES
Practical and logical approach, energy, ability to absorb and process information quickly

FAMOUS BIRTHS
William Thornton (1759)
Jimmy Stewart (1908)
Cher (1946)
Matt Czuchry (1977)

COMPATIBLE WITH
August 17–25, September 26–28

♊ GEMINI

May 21 to June 21

RULING PLANET: *Mercury* ELEMENT: *Mutable air* SYMBOL: *Twins*
POLARITY: *Positive (masculine)* COLORS: *Red, yellow, orange*
PHYSICAL CORRESPONDENCE: *Lungs, shoulders, arms, hands*
STONES: *Beryl, garnet, citrine, amber, agate*
FLOWERS: *Verbena, balm, tansy, yarrow, orchid, myrtle*

The constellation of Gemini comprises the stars Castor and Pollux, and these brothers have popularly become associated with the zodiacal sign. The ancient Greeks told of the seduction of Leda by Zeus, who transformed himself into a swan for the purpose; Leda laid two eggs, one containing her children by her mortal husband Tyndareos, Kastor (Castor) and Clytemnestra, and the other her immortal offspring, Polydeuces (Pollux) and Helen. Castor was killed, and Pollux mourned his brother's death so deeply that Zeus raised his dead twin to immortality. The twin analogy is common to most traditions, though not all the characters are male, or even siblings. The ancient Egyptians envisaged the Gemini couple as a man and woman, while in Hindu belief the pair are lovers known as Maithuna.

The primary characteristic associated with Gemini is duality, symbolically represented by the opposition of masculinity and femininity, or mortality and divinity. The ambivalence, as well as its potential reconciliation and synthesis, is compounded by Gemini's planetary ruler, Mercury, who in various traditions was a hermaphroditic deity. As well as being blessed with mercurial minds and outstanding powers of communication, those born under this sign are intellectually diverse but occasionally indecisive and impulsive. The element of air confers the qualities of versatility and idealism, but also a potential lack of direction and restlessness.

MAY 21

☿ ♀ ENTHUSIASTIC VISIONARIES

Those born on this day can be characterized by their total commitment to whatever it is that excites their devotion and inspiration, be it their families, their hobbies, or their work. Blessed with tremendous physical and intellectual energy, these dynamic individuals typically throw themselves into the pursuit of their interests and ideological aims with boundless enthusiasm, tenaciously investigating, developing and implementing until they have achieved their purpose.

Since they have the potential to be stubborn, those born on this day may sometimes be regarded by others as obsessive and obstinate, yet because they are deeply practical and possess an ingenious turn of mind, their eventual success will often prove their doubters wrong. Their visionary and pragmatic tendencies augur particularly well for finance-related professions, as well as the realm of technical invention, but their great sensitivity also bestows upon May 21 people enormous aptitude for humanitarian work and artistic endeavors.

Although they may cut themselves off from society when engaging in what they may perceive to be their vocational labors, these people by no means prefer solitary lifestyles. Not only are they interested in other individuals, and experience great concern for their welfare, but they are gregarious and sensual types who enjoy relaxing with friends and family members and ensuring that everyone has a good time. One disadvantage of their generally guileless and affectionate approach toward others, however, is that they run the risk that are more manipulative people may take advantage of them.

PLANETARY INFLUENCES
Ruling planets: Mercury and Venus
First decan: Personal planet is Mercury
First cusp: Gemini with Taurean tendencies

VIRTUES
Attentive, determined, caring

VICES
Isolated, obsessive, obstinate

CAREERS
Financial advisor, engineer, humanitarian worker, artist

SKILLS & APTITUDES
Commitment in all areas, energy, genuine interest in others' welfare

FAMOUS BIRTHS
Alexander Pope (1688)
Henri Rousseau (1844)
Mr. T (1952)
Lisa Edelstein (1966)

COMPATIBLE WITH
August 21–22, September 21–25

MAY 22

❋ ❋ ❋ ❋ ❋ ❋ ❋ ❋ ❋ ❋ ❋ ❋

FLITTING POLYMATHS   ☿ ♀

PLANETARY INFLUENCES
Ruling planets: Mercury and Venus
First decan: Personal planet is
  Mercury
First cusp: Gemini with Taurean
  tendencies

VIRTUES
Inquisitive, pioneering, empathetic

VICES
Controlling, manipulative, bossy

CAREERS
Journalist, advertising consultant,
political leader, science professor

SKILLS & APTITUDES
Attention to detail, thirst for
knowledge, inspiring others

FAMOUS BIRTHS
Arthur Conan Doyle (1859)
Laurence Olivier (1907)
Naomi Campbell (1970)
Ginnifer Goodwin (1978)

COMPATIBLE WITH
August 21–22, September 21–25

Inherent in the behavior of those born on May 22 is an apparently paradoxical tendency to concentrate on one specific area of interest in meticulous detail, while flitting from fascination to fascination in an apparently superficial manner. Yet this dual propensity is not really so contradictory when one considers that these individuals have a profound urge to search for knowledge and thereby gain greater understanding.

Their compulsion to learn and investigate encompasses their tendency to gather a minutiae of information on subjects that truly arrest their attention and, when these are exhausted, to renew their quest for new areas of enlightenment. Their twin capacity to single-mindedly explore, as well as their abhorrence of intellectual stagnation, is an unusual and potentially extremely fulfilling combination. In addition to the artistic and scientific spheres, these people will find satisfaction in working in such arts-related business activities as journalism and advertising, as well as politics.

What motivates those born on May 22 is their desire to work for the improvement of humanity, be it by acting as inspirational innovators or by imparting the truths that they have learned in their own quests for illumination to guide the beliefs and actions of others. Whether within their professional or domestic relationships, these individuals effortlessly assume a leadership and mentoring role. Although this tendency makes them wise and effective parents and friends, it may also cause them to become overly controlling. In either event, their care and concern for their loved ones is never in doubt.

MAY 23

♀ ♀

MAGNETIC INTELLECTS

The vibrancy, enthusiastic outlook and great personal charm exuded by those born on May 23 make them popular characters who seem to effortlessly draw others to them. These bright individuals inspire affection and admiration in equal measure. A further potent ingredient that adds to their overall appeal is their orientation toward other people, a leaning inspired by their empathy, their genuine concern for the well-being of others, their natural gregariousness and, to some extent, their desire for approval.

In addition, their insatiable curiosity instills in May 23 people the urge to discover as much as they can of life's mysteries, and furthermore to pit their considerable skills and efforts against any challenges that they encounter. They typically combine their sharp wits with highly imaginative minds, as well as a redoubtable talent for practical action.

Their humanitarian bias, artistic sensibilities, acute intellectual powers, and urge to effect progress, equip them for a variety of careers, including those within the caring professions, the performing arts and also diplomacy. Whatever career they choose to pursue, however, they will usually only flourish if their work involves significant interpersonal contact.

Similarly, May 23 people will usually wish to be actively involved to the fullest extent in the lives of those closest to them and will have the outstanding ability both to enliven and provide close support to their personal relationships. They should, however, temper a certain compulsion to behave impulsively without having fully thought through the implications of their actions.

PLANETARY INFLUENCES
Ruling planets: Mercury and Venus
First decan: Personal planet is Mercury
First cusp: Gemini with Taurean tendencies

VIRTUES
Charming, caring, incisive

VICES
Impulsive, controlling, superficial

CAREERS
Nurse, actor, musician, diplomat

SKILLS & APTITUDES
Enthusiastic outlook on life, orientation toward other people, insatiable curiosity

FAMOUS BIRTHS
Drew Carey (1958)
Melissa McBride (1965)
Jewel (1974)
Apollo Robbins (1974)

COMPATIBLE WITH
August 22, September 24–26

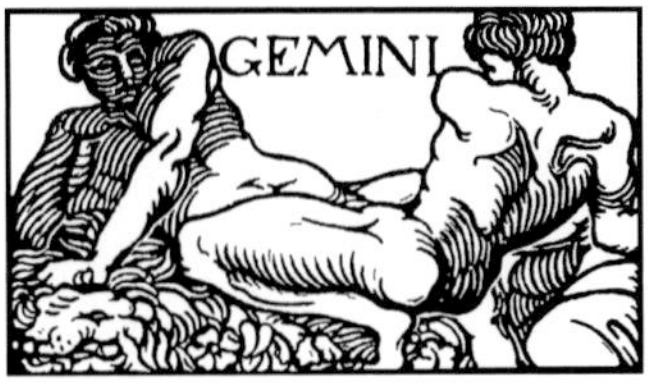

MAY 24

Persuasive Catalysts ☿

People born on May 24 can be compared to catalysts, for they have a gift for making things happen to others without being in any way affected themselves, whether this be done by changing the opinions of those around them or by spurring them into action.

Because they are blessed with incisive powers of thought and analysis, those born on this day typically approach any problem they encounter by first examining the diversity of issues associated with it, and then honing in on one specific area in which real improvements can be made.

Little stimulates these individuals more than an intellectual challenge to which they can apply their considerable energy and talents. These people possess the facility to communicate their ideas both verbally and in writing, giving them the ability to persuade and inspire others. Such loquacious and people-oriented qualities mark them out for careers as salespeople, politicians, teachers, or artists and performers.

Although it is the realm of abstract concepts that truly fascinates them, May 24 individuals are not content to lead solitary, contemplative lives, preferring instead to share their ideas with other people. But, they tend to seek an acquiescent audience rather than a open forum for debate, and may become impatient and frustrated if, despite their efforts, they fail to win converts to their cause. This somewhat controlling propensity also applies to their closest personal relationships—and particularly to their children if they are parents—for their strong sense of self-belief can lead them to expect, and often demand, unquestioning submission from their nearest and dearest.

Planetary Influences
Ruling planet: Mercury
First decan: Personal planet is Mercury

Virtues
Inspirational, resourceful, curious

Vices
Imposing, acerbic, controlling

Careers
Salesperson, politician, lawyer, teacher, performing artist

Skills & Aptitudes
Ability to spur into action, analytical problem-solving, verbal and written communication skills

Famous Births
Queen Victoria of Britain (1819)
Bob Dylan (1941)
John C. Reilly (1965)
Mark Ballas (1986)

Compatible With
September 24–27

MAY 25

☿   MORAL LEADERS

At the core of the personalities of May 25 individuals lies an intractable sense of honor, natural justice and decency, a deeply held moral code that underlies the majority of their personal convictions and actions. This is not to say that these people are intellectually rigid: to the contrary, they possess a mercurial turn of mind that leads them to embrace new ideas or innovations easily, albeit with the proviso that these do not conflict with their ethical or ideological beliefs.

Their sensitivity toward the suffering or misfortunes of others endows them not only with a great sense of compassion for the downtrodden, but also the desire to actively work toward the improvement of their lot: in the course of their struggle they typically draw upon their enormous energy and powerful communication skills. And, although they possess the courage to stand alone if necessary, their favored option is to inspire an equally determined and enthusiastic band of like-minded individuals. Such characteristics endow May 25 people with pronounced leadership potential, and they gain greatest satisfaction when blazing an artistic, political or humanitarian trail.

Within their personal lives, these people are oriented toward protecting and ensuring the happiness of their loved ones. Yet despite the indulgence and generosity that they typically display within their domestic relationships, their ethical convictions remain paramount. Should these be transgressed, they will experience deep hurt and disillusionment even to the point of abruptly withdrawing their affection and support from the offender, no matter how close the relationship.

PLANETARY INFLUENCES
Ruling planet: Mercury
First decan: Personal planet is Mercury

VIRTUES
Empathetic, charismatic, determined

VICES
Judgmental, impatient, controlling

CAREERS
Art teacher, charity organizer, motivational speaker

SKILLS & APTITUDES
Deep sense of honor and justice, openness to new ideas, sensitivity toward others' suffering

FAMOUS BIRTHS
Ralph Waldo Emerson (1803)
Sir Ian McKellan (1939)
Mike Meyers (1963)
Octavia Spencer (1970)

COMPATIBLE WITH
September 24–28

MAY 26

❀ ✱ ❀ ✱ ❀ ✱ ❀ ✱ ❀ ✱ ❀ ✱ ❀ ✱ ❀

INDEPENDENT ARTISTS ☿

GEMINI

PLANETARY INFLUENCES
Ruling planet: Mercury
First decan: Personal planet is
   Mercury

VIRTUES
Inspirational, dynamic,
independent

VICES
Hypocritical, imposing, impulsive

CAREERS
Theater or art director, business
entrepreneur, team manager,
academic department head

SKILLS & APTITUDES
Thirst for knowledge, firm
convictions, ability to lead

FAMOUS BIRTHS
John Wayne (1907)
Stevie Nicks (1948)
Lenny Kravitz (1964)
Helena Bonham Carter (1966)

COMPATIBLE WITH
September 24–28

....
....
....

Those born on May 26 may regard life as something of a struggle, particularly in their quest to find both intellectual and emotional fulfillment. It may seem somewhat paradoxical that it is their own talents, which they employ so effectively on others' behalf, that impede their own search for happiness. For inherent in these individuals are both firmly held ideological convictions and a restless urge to gain new knowledge and experience.

While having the potential to embrace new ideas, these people may also strive to impose or maintain their strong social ideals. These two characteristics can be remarkably efficacious when in harmony, but if imbalanced they may result in double standards and alternately impulsive and intolerant behavior. Nevertheless, the dynamism of those born on this day frequently inspires the admiration of others, and they may therefore assume leading roles in those professions that naturally attract them, such as the performing arts, with which they have a special affinity and where they may enjoy autonomy of action and influence over others.

Because intellectual and physical independence is of such fundamental importance to them, May 26 people will inherently resist submitting to another authority. Not only do they find it difficult to conform to corporate life, but they may also be reluctant to commit themselves to a single life partner. Within established personal relationships, however, they tend to reserve the freedom that they cherish for themselves exclusively, while at the same time expecting their nearest and dearest to conform to their expectations.

MAY 27

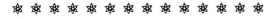

☿ CONFIDENT HUMANITARIANS

Although they are incisive and imaginative thinkers who possess the enviable capacity to easily absorb the intricacies of complex abstract theories, those born on this day are not really interested in pondering undisturbed in isolation; instead they feel compelled to share the fruits of their knowledge with the wider world. These people are fueled by the desire to be of benefit to humanity as a whole, and their favored approach is to take practical action to implement their progressive ideals. Although they are sympathetic to human suffering, they manage to remain somewhat emotionally detached, perhaps instinctively recognizing that too deep a level of emotional involvement would limit their ability to be of effective help.

These characteristics in particular equip May 27 people particularly well for the medical, teaching or diplomatic professions, as well as for those artistic realms where they can express themselves freely; the only vital requirement being that there should be an opportunity to guide or care for other people.

Their confidence, as well as the infectious optimism generated by their strength of purpose, endow these individuals with great magnetism, and they are generally well respected and greatly liked by those with whom their work brings them into contact. Yet their personal relationships may be less harmonious for a number of reasons, including the amount of time and attention that they devote to their work, their tendency to control the lives of those closest to them, and their strong self-belief, which makes it difficult for them to accept criticism.

PLANETARY INFLUENCES
Ruling planet: Mercury
First decan: Personal planet is Mercury

VIRTUES
Innovative, practical, dynamic

VICES
Dominating, impersonal, inaccessible

CAREERS
Doctor, teacher, diplomat, performing artist

SKILLS & APTITUDES
Imaginative thinking, ability to understand abstract concepts, practical approaches

FAMOUS BIRTHS
Henry Kissinger (1923)
Joseph Fiennes (1970)
Paul Bettany (1971)
Chris Colfer (1990)

COMPATIBLE WITH
September 25–29

MAY 28

✵ ✵ ✵ ✵ ✵ ✵ ✵ ✵ ✵ ✵ ✵ ✵ ✵

RADICAL THINKERS ☿

PLANETARY INFLUENCES
Ruling planet: Mercury
First decan: Personal planet is
Mercury

VIRTUES
Original, imaginative, tolerant

VICES
Defensive, destructive, isolated

CAREERS
Actor, theater director, author,
business entrepreneur

SKILLS & APTITUDES
Ability to envisage and initiate
progressive change, givers of loyal
support and respect in relationships

FAMOUS BIRTHS
Joseph Ignace Guillotin (1738)
Ian Fleming (1908)
Colbie Caillat (1985)
Carey Mulligan (1985)

COMPATIBLE WITH
September 25–29

Those born on May 28 are stimulated by the grand picture, by visions that are so progressive that others may find them radical and unrealistic. Yet because they are blessed with the ability to accept and investigate innovative ideas rather than reject them out of hand, the proposals that they advance rarely seem to be fantastic and unfeasible. In many ways those born on this day are ahead of their times, and, in retrospect, it will probably be their detractors who are proved wrong. Although they are able to communicate their ideals effectively to those who are sympathetic and like-minded, their words will fall on deaf ears when they preach to those who are less enlightened and adventurous.

Given the generally unenthusiastic reception to be expected for their enterprising proposals, people born on May 28 are likely to achieve greatest success when able to work apart from mainstream bodies in those areas where their personal flair and originality can be showcased. Thus, they can make very successful artists, writers or stage performers for example, or business entrepreneurs.

Because these people yearn to influence others and institute progress in their own, inimitable way, they have to learn to deal with the inevitable disappointment of having their most deeply cherished ideals disparaged by others. Some of those born on this day are able to cope with this by putting on a brave and defiant face, others by withdrawing into their own worlds. All, however, value the unquestioning respect, support and affection of their friends, partners and families, and usually reciprocate such loyalty in kind.

MAY 29

☿ GIVING CHARMERS

Others are drawn to May 29 people, attracted by their kindness, endearing charm and infectious joie de vivre, and in turn these gregarious individuals ensure that a good time is had by all. Not only are they fundamentally concerned with trying to bring happiness to others, but they believe in sharing their talents and, when they are blessed with it, good fortune. They therefore exhibit both hedonistic and altruistic tendencies, characteristics that are often incompatible in others, but which those born on this day manage to reconcile extremely effectively.

So determined are people born on May 29 to experience all that life has to offer that it may take them some time to alight on and settle into a fulfilling career, but once they have found their professional niche they will commit their prodigious energy and incisive analytical skills to the realization of their imaginative ideals. Because these are strongly people-oriented types, they will thrive in such diverse fields as politics, business and the arts.

In all their ventures, those born on May 29 typically seek to enlist approval and support from as many people as possible, and they are not above exploiting the power of their natural charisma. In both their professional and domestic lives they will therefore generally be surrounded by enthusiastic admirers, whom they will treat with generous affection and gentle humor. Exemplary friends and parents, these people may be less successful as partners, however, on account of their tendency to keep an open house, as well as to respond to new challenges: it is therefore of paramount importance that their partners should have a high tolerance level.

PLANETARY INFLUENCES
Ruling planet: Mercury
First decan: Personal planet is Mercury

VIRTUES
Magnetic, gregarious, altruistic

VICES
Unfocused, hedonistic, manipulative

CAREERS
Politician, project developer, film director, business manager

SKILLS & APTITUDES
Joie de vivre attitude, concern for the happiness of others, pleasure in exploring new ideas

FAMOUS BIRTHS
T.H. White (1906)
John F. Kennedy (1917)
Daniel Tosh (1975)
Laverne Cox (1984)

COMPATIBLE WITH
September 25–30

MAY 30

✸ ✸ ✸ ✸ ✸ ✸ ✸ ✸ ✸ ✸ ✸ ✸ ✸ ✸ ✸

JACKS OF ALL TRADES ☿

PLANETARY INFLUENCES
Ruling planet: Mercury
First decan: Personal planet is
Mercury

VIRTUES
Imaginative, innovative, polymathic

VICES
Skittish, unreliable, impulsive

CAREERS
Sportsperson, stockbroker, author,
blogger

SKILLS & APTITUDES
Thirst for knowledge, interest in
multiple areas, ability to inspire
others

FAMOUS BIRTHS
Peter Carl Fabergé (1846)
Wynonna Judd (1964)
Idina Menzel (1971)
CeeLo Green (1974)

COMPATIBLE WITH
September 26–30, October 1

Perhaps the defining personal characteristic inherent in those born on this day, and the one that informs and influences the majority of their actions, is their irresistible fascination with imaginative and innovatory concepts. Indeed, the adjective "mercurial" perfectly encapsulates the restless inquisitiveness of their intellectual approach, which leads them to search ceaselessly for knowledge and truth and makes them remarkably receptive and sympathetic to new ideas and proposals.

Although their curiosity and need for stimulation endow those born on this day with the potential to become gifted polymaths, it also carries the inherent risk that they may fail to settle on any interest long enough to develop it fully. Well able to inspire and direct the thoughts and actions of others by means of their enthusiasm, optimism and communication skills, some of those born on May 30 have a propensity to leave others to finalize the less intriguing aspects of their projects while they themselves move on to more alluring pastures, rarely completely getting to grips with the finer detail.

Professionally, May 30 people are suited to those areas in which they have the best chance of utilizing their talents and the least chance of becoming bored with the minutiae of working life. Finance-related careers, such as in stockbroking, are especially indicated, as are artistic and sporting pursuits. In their personal relationships, too, these people tend to shy away from sustained commitment and the constraints imposed by familial obligations; nevertheless they typically care deeply for their nearest and dearest.

MAY 31

☿   MERCURIAL INDEPENDENTS

Many of those who do not know them well can be bewildered by the apparent inconsistency of those born on this day: they can be enthusiastic about a new venture at one moment, and almost doctrinaire in their upholding of traditional values at the next. Similarly, their tendency to alternate between exuberant optimism and dark pessimism can make these people difficult to know and understand. Such seemingly conflicting patterns of behavior reflect their prodigious imaginative power, a gift that can have both positive and negative influences.

While their strong imagination endows May 31 people with enormous innovatory potential, it also bestows on them the ability to see all sides of an issue, thereby sometimes making them indecisive or reluctant to take potentially disastrous risks, instead opting for the safer, albeit more static, option. Yet once convinced of the veracity of a particular course of action, May 31 people will typically pursue it with directness and great capability, devising ingenuous means of overcoming any obstacles in their path, and gearing themselves toward influencing others by their work and vision.

Because they are independent in both thought and action, those born on this day fare best when unconstrained by the rules and regulations of others. They are especially attracted to artistic pursuits, but may also find fulfillment when engaged in humanitarian work. They are generous of their time and attention in both their professional and personal relationships, provided, that is, that they do not feel trapped or stifled by the demands of others, a propensity that is particularly pronounced in the men born on this day.

PLANETARY INFLUENCES
Ruling planet: Mercury
First decan: Personal planet is Mercury

VIRTUES
Individualistic, pragmatic, innovative

VICES
Jealous, authoritarian, capricious

CAREERS
Poet, author, marketing advisor, charity fundraiser,

SKILLS & APTITUDES
Imaginative powers, potential for innovation, ability to assess an issue fairly

FAMOUS BIRTHS
Walt Whitman (1819)
Clint Eastwood (1930)
Brooke Shields (1965)
Colin Farrell (1976)

COMPATIBLE WITH
September 27–30, October 1–2

JUNE 1

✵ ✵ ✵ ✵ ✵ ✵ ✵ ✵ ✵ ✵ ✵ ✵ ✵ ✵

ARDENT OBSERVERS ☿ ♀

PLANETARY INFLUENCES
Ruling planet: Mercury
Second decan: Personal planet is
Venus

VIRTUES
Inquisitive, progressive,
affectionate

VICES
Restless, superficial, guarded

CAREERS
Marketing or advertising
consultant, psychologist, detective

SKILLS & APTITUDES
Ability to understand abstract
concepts, strong inclination toward
understanding human behavior

FAMOUS BIRTHS
Marilyn Monroe (1926)
Morgan Freeman (1937)
Heidi Klum (1973)
Amy Schumer (1981)
Tom Holland (1996)

COMPATIBLE WITH
September 29–30, October 1–3

June 1 individuals possess the pronounced characteristic of mercurial inquisitiveness, which is manifested by their almost insatiable desire for intellectual stimulation and manifold interests. While their inherent curiosity endows them with a natural predilection for exploring abstract concepts and delving deeper in a truly innovative fashion, it may, however, equally prohibit them from concentrating on one topic alone.

Those born on this day have a remarkably low boredom threshold, as well as a horror of being stifled and stultified by petty details. These individuals are intrigued by human behavior, for observing other people and speculating about their characters and motivations provides them with an endless challenge. This orientation, when combined with an openness to change and progress, gives them the aptitude for such fields as marketing, advertising, the media and politics, or perhaps psychology or detective work.

Despite their almost compulsive interest in other people, however, those born on June 1 are often extremely private individuals, who guard their own personal lives jealously. It may be that they recognize the value of keeping the professional and domestic spheres in which they operate separate, or that they do not wish the personae that they have adopted with colleagues to be unmasked to reveal their "real" selves. Whether plagued by insecurity or not, they tend to resist committing themselves to a life partner, but once they are firmly enmeshed within bonds of family and friendship, these people typically enliven their personal liaisons, and make particularly affectionate and effective parents.

JUNE 2

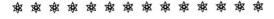

♀ ♀   FORMIDABLE TROUPERS

The lives of those born on June 2 rarely seem to run smoothly: no sooner has one hurdle been cleared, than another appears to impede the path of progress. Such is the frequency of these crises in their lives, that others often secretly wonder whether they have been manufactured—consciously or unconsciously—by the individuals themselves as a means of spicing up their daily routine.

It is indeed true that June 2 people thrive on challenge, relishing the opportunity to pit their skills against the difficult or unexpected, particularly if they were also born in the Chinese year of the monkey. These are quick-witted individuals, who can readily analyze the many facets inherent in a situation, more often than not devising an ingenious and effective course of action. And, because they enjoy sharing their considerable talents with others, they will frequently flourish in the artistic sphere—especially as performers—but also sometimes as scientific researchers or as corporate trouble-shooters; in any career, in fact, in which they are allowed autonomy of thought and action.

Their predilection for exposing themselves to new stimuli may, however, complicate their personal lives. Not only do they typically find it hard to take the plunge in committing themselves to a life partner, but they may also lack the capacity to stick with a relationship once it has lost its initial bloom of excitement. This is not to say that they do not possess profound feelings for their nearest and dearest, but rather that they may helplessly succumb to the irresistible lure of the unknown—or even the unattainable.

PLANETARY INFLUENCES
Ruling planet: Mercury
Second decan: Personal planet is Venus

VIRTUES
Flexible, courageous, intellectual

VICES
Trouble-seeking, compulsive, anxious

CAREERS
Scientific researcher, performing artist, quality controller

SKILLS & APTITUDES
Ability to overcome obstacles, analytical mindset, strategic thinking

FAMOUS BIRTHS
Thomas Hardy (1840)
Wayne Brady (1972)
Zachary Quinto (1977)
Justin Long (1978)
Awkwafina (1988)

COMPATIBLE WITH
September 30, October 1–3

JUNE 3

✳ ✳ ✳ ✳ ✳ ✳ ✳ ✳ ✳ ✳ ✳ ✳

FORCEFUL FREE-THINKERS ☿ ♀

Despite their marked independence of thought, June 3 people are not the types to distance themselves from the company of others in order to explore concepts that interest them, or to seek solitude. To the contrary, they feel a need to share their ideas with others, indeed, often to impose them on those around them.

June 3 people are intellectually restless, yet their strong urge to achieve tangible results by implementing the visions that inspire them gives them the ability to concentrate upon their chosen aims with single-minded dedication, thus giving their mercurial tendencies an outlet for resolving new problems. Such qualities, when supplemented by their impressive communicative talents, give these people the potential to succeed especially in such spheres as teaching, research and the performing arts.

Coupled with their predilection for putting across their occasionally idiosyncratic opinions—even in the face of a hostile audience—is these people's (often unconscious) desire to bask in the acclaim of others, a combination that is not easily reconciled. June 3 people sometimes alienate others and forfeit the goodwill and admiration that they seek to elicit. This reaction is usually due to the forceful and impatient manner in which they present their beliefs. While charming and benevolent when things are going their way, they may become negative and domineering when their path is blocked. This propensity is especially pronounced in confrontations with recalcitrant family members and friends.

JUNE 4

☿ ♀   LOGICAL PATHFINDERS

GEMINI

Those with June 4 birthdays are driven by their fascination with acquiring knowledge and then taking the learning process a step further, expanding upon the information they have garnered and developing new approaches in their own, original fashion. While their attention is primarily absorbed by the conceptual realm of ideas, they are people-oriented to the extent that they feel the urge to impart to others their enthusiasm for whatever it is that most excites them. Anxious to inform and guide their friends, family members and coworkers, they yearn to influence the world at large.

All June 4 individuals have great innovational potential, and although some are motivated in their work by humanitarian concerns and may perhaps become social workers or caregivers, others choose to apply their considerable intellectual talents to the realm of research. Most have a pronounced artistic streak that suits them admirably for careers as writers or actors if they are self-confident enough to capitalize on their creative capabilities. Although typically quite single-minded when inspired by a stimulating project, these people become easily bored when their intellects are restricted.

Whether unwittingly or consciously, many of those born on this day place their personal relationships in a subordinate position to their work. Their considerable charm, kindness and highly developed interpersonal skills draw others to them. Despite the great affection they genuinely feel for those closest to them, these people often may inadvertently hurt others when their profession rather than social commitments are regarded as paramount.

PLANETARY INFLUENCES
Ruling planet: Mercury
Second decan: Personal planet is Venus

VIRTUES
Determined, ingenious, charismatic

VICES
Closed-off, negligent, inconsiderate

CAREERS
Social worker, caregiver, medical researcher, actor

SKILLS & APTITUDES
Development of original ideas, communication skills, single-minded focus

FAMOUS BIRTHS
King George III of England (1738)
Angelina Jolie (1975)
Russell Brand (1975)
Brandon Jenner (1981)

COMPATIBLE WITH
October 1–5, December 18–19

JUNE 5

❋ ❋ ❋ ❋ ❋ ❋ ❋ ❋ ❋ ❋ ❋ ❋ ❋

VISIONARY GENIUSES ☿ ♀

PLANETARY INFLUENCES
Ruling planet: Mercury
Second decan: Personal planet is
Venus

VIRTUES
Steadfast, empathetic, far-sighted

VICES
Delicate, misunderstood, insecure

CAREERS
Poet, scientific researcher,
mathematical theorist, physicist

SKILLS & APTITUDES
Technical expertise, ability to focus,
imaginative powers

FAMOUS BIRTHS
Adam Smith (1723)
Pancho Villa (1878)
Mark Walburg (1971)
Pete Wentz (1979)

COMPATIBLE WITH
October 2–6, December 18–19

June 5 people have the capacity to generate such innovative ideas that others may regard them as either geniuses or crackpots. Their vision and soaring imaginative powers seem unlimited in scope, for these far-sighted individuals refuse to be fettered by conventional truths, recognizing that nothing can be taken for granted. Extremely perceptive, possessed of intellectual curiosity and apparently unlimited energy when it comes to developing and researching the topics that absorb them, those born on this day have the potential to flourish in a variety of professions.

The key to the success of individuals born on this day often lies simply in the extent to which they can communicate effectively with others. Despite their considerable verbal and literary skills, the task of explaining their idiosyncratic ideas often proves difficult. Both the artistic and scientific realms allow these people's talents to flourish: the first requires the suspension of belief, making their visions more likely to be acceptable, while the latter calls for rational enquiry and method, so that their theories may be proven unequivocally.

Those born on June 5 are hypersensitive within their personal relationships, for the numerous disappointments they experience due to the skepticism or ridicule of others undermine their self-confidence. They are needy and deeply appreciative of the unquestioning love and support of their close companions, while empathetic toward those who express their individuality. In this latter respect they make supportive, loving parents, who will typically encourage their children as well as delighting in the fresh approach children bring to life.

JUNE 6

♀ ♀   UNDERSTATED GEMS

Those born on June 6 hide their true nature behind deceptively ordinary and mild-mannered masks. They learn through bitter experience that the uninhibited expression of the sometimes radical visions that inspire them will not generally meet with widespread acceptance, so they present themselves in a deliberately conventional manner. These are, however, imaginative individuals, who disdain the ordinary in favor of the extraordinary: their mercurial intellects, inquisitiveness and flair for innovation typically lead them into uncharted realms.

Because they are sharp as well as attracted to the unorthodox, they have little difficulty in accepting new ideas and rising to intellectual challenges. In those professions where they can work independently toward their aims—artistic and outdoor pursuits are particularly well starred—they have the potential to startle and delight others with their originality and capacity for lateral thinking. If constrained by the strictures of large corporations, they will work diligently, but may harbor subversive feelings which could ultimately cause them to rebel.

Although they will often take a brave and solitary stand to promote their visions, those born on this day need to feel that others believe in them, particularly their nearest and dearest. Since so much of their time and energy must be devoted to persuading work colleagues of the potential success of their unusual approach, it is vital to their emotional health that they can count on the unquestioning support of those closest to them, a requirement that is even more pronounced if they were born in the Chinese year of the goat.

PLANETARY INFLUENCES
Ruling planet: Mercury
Second decan: Personal planet is Venus

VIRTUES
Original, adaptable, imaginative

VICES
Insecure, inhibited, suppressed

CAREERS
Visual artist, park ranger, sportsperson, special-projects developer

SKILLS & APTITUDES
Unorthodox perspectives, lateral thinking, diligent work ethic

FAMOUS BIRTHS
Diego Valazquez (1599)
Jason Isaacs (1963)
Paul Giamatti (1967)
Natalie Morales (1972)

COMPATIBLE WITH
October 3–7, December 18–20

JUNE 7

✵ ✵ ✵ ✵ ✵ ✵ ✵ ✵ ✵ ✵ ✵ ✵ ✵ ✵

POPULAR BRAINIACS ☿ ♀

PLANETARY INFLUENCES
Ruling planet: Mercury
Second decan: Personal planet is Venus

VIRTUES
Curious, tenacious, analytical

VICES
Restless, superficial, flighty

CAREERS
Social-media marketing or advertising executive, performing artist

SKILLS & APTITUDES
Single-minded focus, wide-ranging interests, self-confidence and originality

FAMOUS BIRTHS
Liam Neeson (1952)
Prince (1958)
Michael Cera (1988)
Iggy Azalea (1990)

COMPATIBLE WITH
October 4–8, December 21–23

June 7 individuals are, it sometimes seems, on a constant quest for ever more stimulation, seeking to experience novel sensations and to acquire new knowledge. Such is the depth of this urge that while they can demonstrate remarkably single-minded focus, concentration and analytical skills when absorbed by a stimulating task or concept, if bored or uninterested they tend to flit speedily from subject to subject in search of intellectual satisfaction.

Many of those born on this day profess a portfolio of wide-ranging interests, as well as many talents, and may find it hard to choose from among their options in making an initial career choice. Although they may be successful in a variety of professions, they will rarely gain true fulfillment unless they can follow their own creative path. Their creative talents and social inclinations provide for good personal interaction, thus suiting them well to the performing arts and such commercial activities as marketing or advertising.

Their pronounced originality, self-confidence and vigor endows these gregarious people with great powers of attraction, making them popular figures, and they enjoy the variety and fun inherent in a large circle of friends and acquaintances. Committing themselves to a single life partner does not come easily to June 7 people, who are often concerned that their independence of action will be thereby curtailed. It is not that they lack the capacity to be deeply affectionate, it is simply that these free-spirited individuals are afraid that the demands of partnership or marriage will ultimately stifle them.

JUNE 8

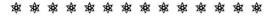

☿ ♀ REBELLIOUS LIVE WIRES

Those born on June 8 need to experience constant intellectual stimulation; being bored is their greatest fear and they typically go to enormous lengths to avoid any tedious situation. This strong aversion to anything that they perceive as being dull bestows upon them a tendency to make snap judgments as to the potential level of interest inherent in any person, project or pursuit they encounter, leading to either a speedy dismissal or an enthusiastic taking-up of the subject concerned. Their actions and interests are motivated by their formidable curiosity, their alertness and their desire to actively test themselves against challenges.

Their highly developed powers of analysis and their urge to effect progress make June 8 people especially well equipped for science-related careers, but artistic and design-related endeavors are also starred. Whatever profession they choose, however, it is of paramount importance that they should retain a degree of personal autonomy.

Within those personal relationships that are of their own making, those born on this day make charming, enlivening and loyal friends and partners. When they feel obligated to behave in a manner that is alien to their natures, or that their freedom of action is being limited by familial demands, however, their frustration can mount inexorably to the point of rebellion, a propensity that is especially marked when they are much younger than their parents or other authority figures. In such cases they may employ their incisive powers of perception in being cuttingly critical, thus incurring greater hurt than they perhaps intended.

PLANETARY INFLUENCES
Ruling planet: Mercury
Second decan: Personal planet is Venus

VIRTUES
Intelligent, enthusiastic, pioneering

VICES
Dismissing, rebellious, critical

CAREERS
Fashion designer, architect, scientific researcher

SKILLS & APTITUDES
Powers of analysis, intellectual talent and vigor, innovative inclinations

FAMOUS BIRTHS
Frank Lloyd Wright (1869)
Bonnie Tyler (1951)
Julianna Margulies (1966)
Kanye West (1977)

COMPATIBLE WITH
October 5–9, December 22–23

JUNE 9

✵ ✵ ✵ ✵ ✵ ✵ ✵ ✵ ✵ ✵ ✵ ✵ ✵ ✵

HANDS–ON PROGRESSIVES ☿ ♀

PLANETARY INFLUENCES
Ruling planet: Mercury
Second decan: Personal planet is
Venus

VIRTUES
Versatile, tenacious, curious

VICES
Judgmental, disapproving,
demanding

CAREERS
Software engineer, mechanical
engineer, arts producer

SKILLS & APTITUDES
Compulsion to discover new
concepts and ideas, progressive
inclinations, lively intelligence

FAMOUS BIRTHS
Les Paul (1915)
Michael J. Fox (1961)
Johnny Depp (1963)
Natalie Portman (1981)

COMPATIBLE WITH
October 6–10

Those born on June 9 remain true to their beliefs. Whatever form or orientation these beliefs take, these people will tenaciously maintain and propagate them as striking a profound chord with their inner selves. Together with this core characteristic, these individuals possess a restless, lively form of intelligence that bestows upon them the irresistible compulsion to explore any new and fascinating concept that presents itself. This urge to discover previously hidden or unknown areas of interest, as well as their marked fascination with the potential inherent in technology, endows them with a strong progressive inclination which, when developed, gives them the rare capacity to effect real advances.

Reflecting the multifaceted nature of their talents and inclinations, they may find satisfaction and success in a multitude of professions, ranging from the literary, musical or dramatic arts, to the more sober fields of medical research or computers, but they generally prefer active, hands-on involvement to managerial or administrative roles.

Their high personal standards and ambitious ideological aims may give June 9 people problems with interpersonal relationships. Because they are both highly discriminating with regard to choosing friends and partners, and also tend to give priority to their intellectual pursuits, they may inadvertently impose near-impossible demands on those closest to them. Futhermore, despite the quiet affection that they manifest toward those who offer them unconditional support, they may unwittingly fail to reciprocate the level of support that they themselves demand of others.

JUNE 10

☿ ♀ ROBUST COMMANDERS

GEMINI

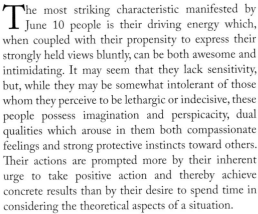

The most striking characteristic manifested by June 10 people is their driving energy which, when coupled with their propensity to express their strongly held views bluntly, can be both awesome and intimidating. It may seem that they lack sensitivity, but, while they may be somewhat intolerant of those whom they perceive to be lethargic or indecisive, these people possess imagination and perspicacity, dual qualities which arouse in them both compassionate feelings and strong protective instincts toward others. Their actions are prompted more by their inherent urge to take positive action and thereby achieve concrete results than by their desire to spend time in considering the theoretical aspects of a situation.

In most problematic situations June 10 people are blessed with the capacity to swiftly identify what needs to be done. Those born on this day will thrive in fields in which they can achieve tangible progress, and their vigor suits them particularly for such professions as the military or police forces, but also for theatrical careers.

The bright public personae assumed by many born on this day often hides a more negative, depressive facet of their personalities. It may be that the active lifestyles these people generally adopt is a conscious or unconscious strategy to seek an escape from the fears that haunt them during more introspective moments. And while they typically yearn for the comfort found in strong personal relationships, they may find it difficult to commit themselves to friends and partners, perhaps feeling that it would be dangerous to expose their emotional vulnerability.

PLANETARY INFLUENCES
Ruling planet: Mercury
Second decan: Personal planet is Venus

VIRTUES
Driven, inspirational, energetic

VICES
Closed-off, negative, depressive

CAREERS
Soldier, police chief, theatrical director

SKILLS & APTITUDES
Keen intellectual talents, prodigious energy, strong convictions, driving sense of purpose

FAMOUS BIRTHS
Prince Philip (1921)
Judy Garland (1922)
Elizabeth Hurley (1966)
Sasha Obama (2001)

COMPATIBLE WITH
October 7–11

JUNE 11

✳ ✳ ✳ ✳ ✳ ✳ ✳ ✳ ✳ ✳ ✳ ✳ ✳ ✳

FOCUSED LEARNERS
☿ ♄ ♅

PLANETARY INFLUENCES
Ruling planet: Mercury
Third decan: Personal planets are Saturn and Uranus

VIRTUES
Vigorous, focused, incisive

VICES
Stubborn, isolated, neglectful

CAREERS
Scientific researcher, graphic or visual artist, sportsperson

SKILLS & APTITUDES
Intellectual skills, ability to immerse themselves in one subject area, strong focus and sense of purpose

FAMOUS BIRTHS
Jacques Cousteau (1910)
Gene Wilder (1935)
Peter Dinklage (1969)
Shia LaBeouf (1986)

COMPATIBLE WITH
October 8–12

Although they share the same quality of restless curiosity with many of their Gemini fellows, the thirst for knowledge of those born on June 11 takes a less wide-ranging form, for once they have found a subject that truly absorbs them (and this may occur in childhood), they typically concentrate their attention and energy upon it almost exclusively. Indeed, they have an enviable facility totally to immerse themselves in their work, allowing nothing to distract them from their quest, their objective being to learn as much as they possibly can as a prelude to attempting a pioneering breakthrough.

Their strong focus, determination and energy give them the outstanding potential to achieve their goals, whether they be in the realms of scientific research, artistic innovation or sporting pursuits—all areas to which June 11 people are naturally attracted. They will flourish best when operating as independent agents, however, for they will usually feel unbearably stifled by the procedures and constraints of conventional organizations.

Although they possess great personal charm, and have a profound desire both to protect their loved ones and bring them fun and enjoyment, those born on this day may find it difficult to sustain a settled family life. It is not that they lack genuine care and concern for those closest to them, but rather that the lure of outside interests may prove irresistible, leading to a neglect of family affairs. This propensity is particularly marked in the case of June 11 men, especially those who are in any case not enamored of domestic chores and responsibilities.

JUNE 12

☿ ♄ ♅   ROLLING STONES

Those born on June 12 give the impression of being remarkably self-contained individuals, whose boundless energy, enthusiasm for embarking on unusual ventures, and quick intelligence bestow upon them the capacity not only to keep themselves occupied, but also to be pioneers in many aspects of their lives. They cannot bear inertia in any form—be it intellectual or physical—and will push themselves to their limits even during periods of so-called relaxation, filling their time away from work with hobbies, or devising entertainments for their friends and family members.

Their approach to challenges—indeed, to life itself—is typically characterized by a combination of optimism and curiosity, and while June 12 people may throw themselves wholeheartedly into the pursuit of projects that capture their interest, they rarely lose sight of the larger picture. And, although their outlook is informed by rational rather than intuitive observation, their sensitivity endows them with great empathy for those who are less able to help themselves.

Their quest to achieve progress, backed by their strong organizational powers, suits them to a wide range of professions, from outdoor, physical work to administrative jobs, whether corporate or humanitarian; they often make inspirational team leaders. They may lack patience, however, with coworkers or family members having less vigor and commitment than themselves, and in such cases have a propensity either to dismiss the objects of their irritation as hopeless causes, or to attempt to "improve" them by resorting to dictatorial tactics.

PLANETARY INFLUENCES
Ruling planet: Mercury
Third decan: Personal planets are Saturn and Uranus

VIRTUES
Perceptive, positive, dynamic

VICES
Impatient, dismissive, dictatorial

CAREERS
Construction worker, park ranger, corporate or humanitarian administrator

SKILLS & APTITUDES
Goal-oriented approach, single-minded focus, ability to push beyond personal limits

FAMOUS BIRTHS
David Rockefeller (1915)
George Bush (1924)
Anne Frank (1929)
Kendra Wilkinson (1985)

COMPATIBLE WITH
October 9–13

JUNE 13

✳ ✳ ✳ ✳ ✳ ✳ ✳ ✳ ✳ ✳ ✳ ✳ ✳ ✳

DREAMY FREETHINKERS ☿ ♄ ♅

June 13 individuals typically reject the conventional truths and behavioral norms accepted by less imaginative members of society, intuitively aware that there is more to life and human understanding than has yet been discovered. The desire to uncover hidden knowledge manifests itself in a pronounced otherworldly streak which may inspire some to explore the abstract realms of spirituality or metaphysics and others the boundaries of scientific exploration or artistic innovation.

In whichever field these people choose to make their professions—and their wide-ranging interests, openness to change, and strongly developed qualities of both perception and organization equips them well for many—those born on this day display a relish for confronting and overcoming challenges, as well as a refreshingly innovative approach that motivates others. Indeed, despite their predilection for testing their own limitations, those born on this day prefer to work as part of a team (naturally gravitating toward leadership) rather than in lonely solitude, especially if they are women.

In many respects, these individuals' quest to bring about progress is fueled by an often unconscious wish to benefit the human community as a whole, for the combination of their soaring imaginative powers and clear-sighted perspicacity cannot help but arouse profoundly empathetic feelings within them. In the personal sphere, they express this concern by striving to provide their loved ones with both emotional and material support, and enriching all their relationships with a sense of fun and magnanimous acceptance of others' foibles.

JUNE 14

GEMINI

♀ ♄ ♅   INCISIVE LEADERS

June 14 individuals have a strong urge to take charge, whether it be of those who surround them or of projects that demand active responses. This instinctive propensity for supervision stems from their impressive ability to swiftly sum up the inherent components and potential outcome of a given situation (the result of their all-encompassing perspicacity), then to incisively decide upon the best course to follow. Once they have settled upon their preferred strategy, these people will follow it with fierce tenacity, pragmatically amending minor details as necessary, but rarely conceding defeat.

Their confidence in their convictions is born of their strong self-belief, and it is this quality, as well as their aversion to standing idly on the sidelines, that endows the energetic people with June 14 birthdays with their enthusiasm for leadership. While this dynamic outlook may inspire less decisive individuals, others may be alienated by what they perceive to be the arrogant certainty and abrupt manner of those born on this day.

Although their single-mindedness and forcefulness augurs well for the successful attainment of their aims, their confrontational approach will almost inevitably cause havoc with their interpersonal relationships. They often cannot help but adopt a somewhat dictatorial approach. This predilection is therefore best confined to the workplace, where they typically become gifted corporate leaders with a special affinity for business, although they also have the potential to make outstanding contributions in whatever field they choose.

PLANETARY INFLUENCES
Ruling planet: Mercury
Third decan: Personal planets are Saturn and Uranus

VIRTUES
Energetic, direct, far-sighted

VICES
Blunt, disregarding, arrogant

CAREERS
Business manager, corporate leader, teacher, military leader

SKILLS & APTITUDES
Compulsion for direct action, prodigious energy, clear-cut opinions, leadership skills

FAMOUS BIRTHS
Harriet Beecher Stowe (1811)
Che Guevara (1928)
Donald Trump (1946)
Lucy Hale (1989)

COMPATIBLE WITH
January 6–8, October 11–15

JUNE 15

✳ ✳ ✳ ✳ ✳ ✳ ✳ ✳ ✳ ✳ ✳ ✳ ✳ ✳

GENEROUS TEAM–PLAYERS   ☿ ♄ ♅

PLANETARY INFLUENCES
Ruling planet: Mercury
Third decan: Personal planets are
   Saturn and Uranus

VIRTUES
Intuitive, perspicacious,
compassionate

VICES
Insecure, vain, vulnerable

CAREERS
Nurse, retailer, social worker,
marketing or advertising executive

SKILLS & APTITUDES
Interest in human condition,
aptitude for teamwork, desire to
please

FAMOUS BIRTHS
Jim Belushi (1954)
Helen Hunt (1963)
Courtney Cox (1964)
Neil Patrick Harris (1973)

COMPATIBLE WITH
January 6–8, October 12–16

Although those born on this day exhibit the same wide-ranging curiosity as others who share their mercurial star sign, this characteristic is manifested more by their intense interest in other people than by their attraction to abstract concepts. This is not to say that they are not inspired by intellectual or physical challenges—on the contrary, June 15 people are naturally oriented toward making active progress—but rather that they are motivated by human rather than technical or philosophical concerns.

Whether or not the professions that these people choose fall within the humanitarian field (and the medical and social work spheres are particularly well starred), these individuals will only thrive when they are surrounded by a closely knit team of coworkers, for interpersonal interaction is a fundamental requirement for their success and ultimate satisfaction. Many of those born on June 15 will find fulfillment in artistic careers, when their performances can bring enjoyment to others, thus also giving them the reciprocal acclaim that is vital to their self-esteem. Others will employ talents and inclinations to great effect in advertising, marketing or the retail trade.

Given their interest in others, it is not surprising that June 15 people are often found to be gregarious types, who place enormous value on the strong bonds that they forge with friends and family members and strive to ensure their well-being. One danger inherent in the good will radiated by these people, however, is that unscrupulous types may take advantage of their generosity.

JUNE 16

GEMINI

☿ ♄ ♅   GROUNDED EXPERIMENTERS

Those born on June 16 combine within their characters an unusual blend of adventurousness and caution, qualities born on the one hand of their great imaginative and innovative inclinations, and on the other of their perspicacity and astuteness. This conjunction generally means that they will take short-term risks in the interest of achieving their longer-term goals, and their willingness to be flexible without losing their sense of purpose, is a strategy that has the potential to bring them success.

In the world of business, for example, the combination of skills and talents in June 16 people may be manifested by backing an entrepreneurial endeavor with solid organizational support, or by judiciously speculating on the stock market to build a larger portfolio; while in the artistic and scientific realms it may be demonstrated by controlled experimentation. Yet despite the financial fruits that may be reaped by following this approach, June 16 people are motivated more by a profound desire to bring about progress.

These are serious and somewhat introverted people, who derive comfort and satisfaction from such nonmaterialistic pleasures as strong emotional relationships, or the beauty inherent in nature and the arts. They typically abide by a strongly humanitarian ethical code, which endows them with genuine concern for other people—especially those in need of help—and a innate horror of abuses of power. Thus while they are remarkably loyal and steadfastly affectionate to those closest to them, they find it hard to tolerate cynical or inconsiderate behavior.

PLANETARY INFLUENCES
Ruling planet: Mercury
Third decan: Personal planets are Saturn and Uranus

VIRTUES
Grounded, innovative, moral

VICES
Suppressed, stagnant, intolerant

CAREERS
Stockbroker, entrepreneur, playwright, scientist

SKILLS & APTITUDES
Ability to take risks while remaining pragmatic, capacity to foresee a range of possible scenarios

FAMOUS BIRTHS
Joan Van Ark (1946)
Tupac Shakur (1971)
John Cho (1972)
John Newman (1990)

COMPATIBLE WITH
January 6–8, October 13–17

JUNE 17

✻ ✻ ✻ ✻ ✻ ✻ ✻ ✻ ✻ ✻ ✻ ✻ ✻

EXTREME PARADOXES ☿ ♄ ♅

Many of the characteristics of those born on this day appear to be curiously paradoxical. Although they are geared toward benefiting human society and yearn to establish caring and committed personal relationships, they may have difficulty in becoming intimate with others; and while they possess highly developed organizational skills, their behavior may appear radical or impulsive in the extreme. When they are successful in reconciling these characteristics, June 17 people make remarkably effective agents of progress, but the task proves impossible for many.

Perhaps the primary motivation for those born on this day is their urge to realize the unusual visions that they have for improving human society; these may take the form of political or religious ideologies or of original forms of artistic endeavor. Although they make inspirational leaders when their often revolutionary ideas receive acceptance, other times they may find themselves plowing a lonely furrow.

Despite their considerable powers of persuasion, the forceful—often domineering—approach that these individuals adopt may meet with variable success, sometimes causing them to resort to more unorthodox—even unethical—methods. Because they may often experience disappointment in their professional ventures, June 17 people find profound solace in the unquestioning support and affection of their nearest and dearest, and reciprocate with loyalty and love the belief that their long-standing family members and friends show in them. Their tendency to distrust the motivations of more recent acquaintances, however, may hinder the development of new relationships.

JUNE 18

☿ ☽ ♄ ♅   POSITIVE ALLIES

Their great *joie de vivre*, their relish of new ideas, their typically positive and energetic approach to everything that they undertake, as well as the responsible attitude that they manifest toward their family members, friends and colleagues, all combine to make those born on June 18 attractive and popular personalities to whom others naturally gravitate. They are particularly valued for the generous encouragement and support that they offer to those closest to them, and for the enlivening and quirky sense of fun that they inject into their interpersonal relationships, a tendency that is redoubled if they were also born in the Chinese year of the horse.

June 18 people are imaginative individuals, whose restless curiosity can lead them to explore previously untapped areas, often with remarkably original results. They have the potential to make an especial mark in the performing arts, for which most have a natural affinity, but they may also blaze trails as scientific researchers or business entrepreneurs. Whatever career they choose, they prefer to work as part of a team rather than in an individual capacity, for they are greatly stimulated by personal contact.

Although their propensity to enjoy life to the fullest and their gregariousness may mean that those born on this day take some time to commit themselves to a life partner, once domestically settled they are typically deeply affectionate and considerate toward their loved ones. They usually make gifted parents, although they may find it hard to resist attempting to control their offsprings' lives, a tendency that may ultimately cause resentment.

PLANETARY INFLUENCES
Ruling planets: Mercury and Moon
Third decan: Personal planets are Saturn and Uranus
Second cusp: Gemini with Cancerian tendencies

VIRTUES
Adventurous, positive, loyal

VICES
Controlling, overprotective, flighty

CAREERS
Performing artist, scientific researcher, entrepreneur

SKILLS & APTITUDES
Energetic approach, supportiveness, aptitude for teamwork

FAMOUS BIRTHS
Anastasia Nikolaevna (1901)
Paul McCartney (1942)
Isabella Rossellini (1952)
Blake Shelton (1976)

COMPATIBLE WITH
October 15–19, July 23

JUNE 19

✺ ✺ ✺ ✺ ✺ ✺ ✺ ✺ ✺ ✺ ✺ ✺ ✺ ✺

STEADFAST GUIDES   ☿ ☽ ♄ ♅

PLANETARY INFLUENCES
Ruling planets: Mercury and Moon
Third decan: Personal planets are
  Saturn and Uranus
Second cusp: Gemini with Cancerian
  tendencies

VIRTUES
Progressive, strong, determined

VICES
Forceful, arrogant, dictatorial

CAREERS
Teacher, counselor, administrator

SKILLS & APTITUDES
Strategic thinking, evaluative skills,
incisive analytical talents, intuition

FAMOUS BIRTHS
Blaise Pascal (1623)
Paula Abdul (1962)
Zoe Saldana (1978)
Macklemore (1983)

COMPATIBLE WITH
January 9–10, October 16–20,
July 23–24

Perhaps the most outstanding characteristic of those people born on June 19 is their self-certainty—a quality that arouses both admiration and irritation in others: admiration because they are rarely beset by the feelings of doubt that often bedevil less focused types, and irritation on account of what may be seen as an arrogant unwillingness to compromise. Yet their steadfastness of purpose and single-minded determination in the pursuit of their visions is not the result of blinkered obstinacy, but rather of a profound confidence engendered by the knowledge that they have evaluated each alternative approach to the best of their ability and have arrived at their chosen strategy by means of logical deduction.

June 19 people are blessed with intellectual inquisitiveness, incisive analytical talents, and a pronounced intuitive streak—qualities which in such a combination endow them with a rare gift for understanding. Whatever their preferred career choice, they usually feel compelled to guide and improve the lives of others, and may thus find fulfillment as teachers, counselors or consultants.

Their desire to influence those around them is fueled by the best of intentions, but their typically forceful manner may not be well received by those whom they are seeking to assist. For, however selfless their motivations, others (especially their partners or children, and even more so if they are men) may resent the imposition of what they may regard as dictatorial or controlling tactics. Cultivating a more diplomatic, less upfront approach may therefore benefit June 19 people immensely.

JUNE 20

GEMINI

✶ ✶ ✶ ✶ ✶ ✶ ✶ ✶ ✶ ✶ ✶ ✶ ✶ ✶ ✶ ✶

☿ ☽ ♄ ♅   FLEXIBLE IDEALISTS

The dominant character trait of people born on June 20 is that of insatiable curiosity which, when coupled with their idealism and quick-thinking minds, results in a wide-ranging spectrum of interests and concerns. With their marked enthusiasm for exploring alternative angles and their willingness to instigate or accept change, they make excellent and inspiring members of a working team.

This outstanding ability to think on their feet and to adapt to shifting circumstances well equips June 20 people for careers in the fast-moving world of the investigative media, to which their searching intellectual qualities and stimulating ideas are ideally suited. Yet despite their outgoing and exuberant natures, people born on this day also possess a profound intuitive streak—a quality that endows them with unusual sensitivity in their relationships (especially if they are women) and which proves an invaluable asset when it comes to problem-solving at work.

Because they grasp intellectual concepts with enviable ease, there is an inevitable risk that June 20 people may become bored with a project once they have mastered it, and will feel tempted to move on to a new challenge. An awareness of this tendency, or the influence of a patient partner or vigilant parent, tempers this mercurial tendency and instills the discipline necessary to see a project through. Blessed with charming and magnetic personalities, June 20 people experience no difficulty in attracting others, while their lunar gift of empathy causes people to turn to them for emotional support as well as for their sparkling company.

PLANETARY INFLUENCES
Ruling planets: Mercury and Moon
Third decan: Personal planets are Saturn and Uranus
Second cusp: Gemini with Cancerian tendencies

VIRTUES
Open, incisive, insightful

VICES
Superficial, careless, self-doubting

CAREERS
Investigative journalist, private investigator, lawyer, consultant

SKILLS & APTITUDES
Adaptability, intuition, teamwork

FAMOUS BIRTHS
Errol Flynn (1909)
Lionel Richie (1949)
John Goodman (1952)
Nicole Kidman (1967)

COMPATIBLE WITH
January 9–10, October 17–22, July 24–25

JUNE 21

❋ ❋ ❋ ❋ ❋ ❋ ❋ ❋ ❋ ❋ ❋ ❋ ❋ ❋

ADVENTUROUS PERFORMERS ☿ ☽ ♄ ♅

PLANETARY INFLUENCES
Ruling planets: Mercury and Moon
Third decan: Personal planets are
Saturn and Uranus
Second cusp: Gemini with Cancerian
tendencies

VIRTUES
Adventurous, friendly, empathetic

VICES
Aloof, impatient, disrespectful

CAREERS
Sales executive, realtor, life coach

SKILLS & APTITUDES
Free-thinking, communication
skills, artistic inclinations

FAMOUS BIRTHS
Chris Pratt (1979)
Brandon Flowers (1981)
Prince William (1982)
Lana Del Rey (1985)

COMPATIBLE WITH
January 9–10, October 18–22,
July 25–26

Like most Geminis, the gregarious personalities and sociable natures of June 21 people mean that they do not enjoy solitude, instead finding stimulation and fulfillment in the company of others. They therefore relish lifestyles and careers that offer plenty of scope to satisfy their craving for variety, travel and human contact, as well as those in which their communication skills will be fully used—in the media or sales, for example.

June 21 people manifest their love of the arts from an early age, their artistic temperaments complemented by such curious and inquiring minds that they often feel compelled to attempt to seek out the truth or to stick by their principles doggedly, however unpopular their obstinacy makes them. Their enthusiasm and idealism make them inspirational—even revolutionary—leaders, yet these very qualities also generate such high standards that others find it hard to live up to them.

Thanks to their formidable analytical talents, people born on this day frequently prove successful in the financial sector, provided, that is, that they are given the liberty to engage their imaginative and creative powers to the fullest. Their independent attitudes provide these people with plenty of scope for adventure, thus making them compatible partners for like-minded Sagittarians. Their love of liberty may give more possessive people, like Scorpios and Pisceans, grounds for jealousy, however. Nevertheless, their lunar-influenced, intuitive qualities may temper any flighty tendencies or cerebral idealism with a rare level of sensitivity toward the feelings of others.

♋ CANCER

June 22 to July 22

RULING PLANET: *The Moon* ELEMENT: *Cardinal water* SYMBOL: *Crab*
POLARITY: *Negative (feminine)* STONES: *Pearl, moonstone, peridot*
PHYSICAL CORRESPONDENCE: *Stomach, breasts*
COLORS: *Cream, white, silver-blue, smoky gray*
FLOWERS: *Lily, lily of the valley, water lily, white rose*

Nearly every astrological tradition equates the constellation of Cancer with a crab. This near-universal identification can be explained by the movement of the Sun during the period of Cancer's ascendancy, for it appears to mimic the crustacean's distinctive sideways, scuttling movement on its southern descent. The Greco-Roman myth tells of how the mother goddess Hera (Juno) sent a crab to the aid of the nine-headed Hydra of Lerna in its struggle against Herakles (Hercules); Hera placed it in the heavens as a reward for its efforts. Cancer, known as the "gate of men," has enormous cosmic significance, for not only does the summer solstice (in the northern hemisphere) occur under this sign, but the universe came into being when the planets were aligned within this sign, and some hold that the world will end when a similar conjunction is effected.

Cancer is ruled by the Moon, the preserve of the goddess—the creator and destroyer—which regulates the ebb and flow of water, the habitat of the crab and the element that governs Cancer. The sign's dual lunar-watery influence confers loyalty, sensitivity, intuition and emotional receptiveness, as well as the procreative, nurturing and protective qualities associated with the feminine principle. Like the crab, those born under this sign are said to possess tenacity, but are also subject to the tendency to withdraw into their shells when threatened by others or inundated with emotion.

JUNE 22

HOPELESS ROMANTICS

PLANETARY INFLUENCES
Ruling planets: Moon and Mercury
First decan: Personal planet is Moon
First cusp: Cancer with Gemini
   tendencies

VIRTUES
Sensitive, romantic, imaginative

VICES
Disillusioned, depressed, maniacal

CAREERS
Novelist, musician, actor, designer,
match-maker

SKILLS & APTITUDES
Intellectual curiosity, commitment
to a vision, loyalty, creativity

FAMOUS BIRTHS
Meryl Streep (1949)
Cyndi Lauper (1953)
Dan Brown (1964)
Carson Daly (1973)

COMPATIBLE WITH
July 12–17, October 1–5

June 22 people are engaged in a constant search for their own personal idyll, be it an enduring romantic partnership, a perfect lifestyle, a Utopian environment or a combination of all three. These people yearn for personal happiness, an ideal state which ultimately depends on them winning a soul mate rather than professional success, for such is the value they place on strong emotional ties that they feel with the love and support of a partner they can weather any of life's storms or disappointments. It is not that other aspects of their lives lack significance in their eyes, just that finding true and lasting love is of paramount importance to their emotional well-being.

Some June 22 people will indeed be lucky in their search for happiness, but others will inevitably remain unsatisfied, their visions of a fantasy mate proving unrealistic, or the intensity of their emotions and demands frightening off potential partners unwilling to live up to the idealized personality projected upon them.

Thus while these individuals typically demonstrate profound affection and loyalty toward their friends and family members, reciprocating the support and comfort that this gives them, they may be doomed to disappointment in their love lives. However, such is their zestful enjoyment of the world and their enthusiasm for intellectual and sensory stimulation, that they will not stay down for long, and may find great consolation in their professional interests.

Their sensitivity suits June 22 individuals extremely well for careers within the arts. This creative arena is a sphere within which they can live out their personal fantasies as, for example, novelists, musicians or actors.

JUNE 23

♋ ☽ ☿   BEAUTY–SEEKERS

June 23 individuals yearn to make the world a beautiful place, not only in environmental terms but also by enriching the lives of others through artistic ventures and seeking to effect peace and harmony within human relationships. With this idealized vision blazing beaconlike before them, they typically devote their considerable practical and intellectual energies toward the attainment of their dreams, using their highly developed intuitive and mental perspicacity to identify areas requiring improvement and the remedial approaches that should be followed. Such is their interest in other people, and their concurrent desire to lighten their personal and professional workloads, that they cannot help but offer their assistance to coworkers, friends, family members or even to humanity as a whole.

Their innate skills and natural orientation suit June 23 people admirably to careers in which they can work with others in contributing toward human welfare—for example as nurses, doctors or social workers—or through artistic pursuits such as painting, the performing arts or poetry.

Unsurprisingly, those born on June 23 place enormous value on their own interpersonal relationships and treat their loved ones with great tenderness, consideration and affection. Finding and supporting unquestionably a life partner who will fulfill their desire for romance is one of their primary goals: once settled in such a close one-to-one liaison, these individuals will prove unwaveringly loyal, but run the concomitant risk of stifling the object of their affection with the jealous intensity of their love.

PLANETARY INFLUENCES
Ruling planets: Moon and Mercury
First decan: Personal planet is Moon
First cusp: Cancer with Gemini tendencies

VIRTUES
Intuitive, sensitive, helpful

VICES
Controlling, jealous, irritating

CAREERS
Nurse, doctor, social worker, landscape architect, painter, poet

SKILLS & APTITUDES
Practical and intellectual energies, intuition, ability to identify areas for improvement

FAMOUS BIRTHS
Alan Turing (1912)
Joss Whedon (1964)
Selma Blair (1972)
Jason Mraz (1977)

COMPATIBLE WITH
July 12–17, October 1–5

JUNE 24

❋ ❋ ❋ ❋ ❋ ❋ ❋ ❋ ❋ ❋ ❋ ❋ ❋

ELATED VISIONARIES ☽ ☿

PLANETARY INFLUENCES
Ruling planets: Moon and Mercury
First decan: Personal planet is Moon
First cusp: Cancer with Gemini
  tendencies

VIRTUES
Energetic, determined, realistic

VICES
Preoccupied, neglectful, withdrawn

CAREERS
Science or technical researcher,
management consultant,
sportsperson, musician

SKILLS & APTITUDES
Driven, humanitarian leanings,
innovative imagination

FAMOUS BIRTHS
Phil Harris (1904)
Mick Fleetwood (1947)
Mindy Kaling (1979)
Solange Knowles (1986)

COMPATIBLE WITH
July 12–17, October 1–5

Despite the quietly profound affection and unquestionable commitment that characterizes their approach to their nearest and dearest, the attention of June 24 people is typically less absorbed by their personal liaisons than by their professional activities, which frequently have a humanitarian slant. Although their sensitivity endows them with genuine empathy with those who are less fortunate than themselves, their compassion is manifested less by passive sympathy than by their urge to actively implement strategies to achieve progress. Because they are blessed with keen intellectual talents and innovative imaginations, their visions may be extremely original, although rarely unrealistic, for these are down-to-earth individuals who possess highly developed technical and practical skills. Despite the often inspirational effect that they have on others—who may elevate them to positions of leadership—these responsible people generally perform best when undistracted by the demands of others, although they recognize that they cannot always attain their aims single-handedly.

Professionally, June 24 individuals have a special aptitude for those fields in which they can combine their talent for analysis and theoretics with the opportunity to set the results of their research in motion. Careers as scientific or technical researchers and management consultants are thus especially highlighted, as are sporting and artistic pursuits (as hobbies if not professionally). Reflecting their vigor, those born on this day need periods of privacy in which to indulge in periods of inner reflection and to recharge their mental batteries.

JUNE 25

☽ ☿   ARTISTIC SPONGES

The personalities of those born on June 25 may be defined by two apparently contradictory characteristics: their sense of purpose in pursuit of lofty ideals, and their often vacillating or changeable behavior. Yet these seemingly conflicting tendencies are not really so paradoxical when one understands the nature of their enormous sensitivity which, when informed by their mercurial intellects, leads them to draw clear-sighted conclusions, and, when influenced by their highly developed intuitive powers, causes their hearts to rule their heads.

When they are successfully able to reconcile their mental and emotional responses, those born on this day have the ability to make remarkably effective instruments of progress, but, when these qualities are imbalanced, one or the other may manifest itself more strongly, or they may coexist uneasily, resulting in confusion or inconsistency of motivations.

In many respects, the realization of the potential of those born on June 25 depends upon the interests and concerns of those to whom they are emotionally closest, or whose opinion they most respect—for whatever reason. For, despite their original turn of mind and boundless imagination, these people are somewhat reliant on the encouragement and approval of others. This is a propensity that is especially pronounced if they were also born in the Chinese year of the rat.

Their well-developed sensitivity toward others' responses, as well as their natural affinity for artistic pursuits, augurs particularly well for their success as designers and commercial artists.

PLANETARY INFLUENCES
Ruling planets: Moon and Mercury
First decan: Personal planet is Moon
First cusp: Cancer with Gemini tendencies

VIRTUES
Visionary, intuitive, compassionate

VICES
Contradictory, indecisive, overwhelmed

CAREERS
Designer, commercial artist, childcare worker, author

SKILLS & APTITUDES
Sensitivity to others' responses and emotions, mercurial intellect, intuitive powers

FAMOUS BIRTHS
George Orwell (1903)
Jimmie Walker (1947)
Sonia Sotomayor (1954)
Ricky Gervais (1961)

COMPATIBLE WITH
July 12–17, October 1–5

JUNE 26

✦ ✦ ✦ ✦ ✦ ✦ ✦ ✦ ✦ ✦ ✦ ✦ ✦

PROTECTIVE SHIELDS ♋ ☽

PLANETARY INFLUENCES
Ruling planet: Moon
First decan: Personal planet is Moon

VIRTUES
Energetic, committed, self-confident

VICES
Overprotective, negative, restricting

CAREERS
Corporate executive, technician, researcher, writer, performing artist

SKILLS & APTITUDES
Aptitude for mentoring or leading roles, social orientation, strong sense of imagination, protective instincts

FAMOUS BIRTHS
Nick Offerman (1970)
Sean Hayes (1970)
Derek Jeter (1974)
Ariana Grande (1993)

COMPATIBLE WITH
July 18–22

D espite their strong ideological beliefs and often extremely imaginative inspirational vision, those born on this day are usually less geared toward the single-minded pursuit of intellectual goals than toward the people that surround them and the circumstances that impinge upon them.

June 26 people tend to be truly empathetic individuals, whose responsiveness to the feelings and situations of others arouses their highly developed protective instincts and their urge to guide and shield those for whom they feel concern. Although this tendency is especially pronounced with regard to their relations—and their children in particular if they are parents—they will generally also assume a mentoring role with regard to their work colleagues and choose careers that have a humanitarian slant. They will typically find fulfillment in those professions in which they can make an active and practical contribution toward the common good, and may employ their considerable organizational skills in such diverse functions as corporate executives, technicians and researchers, or writers and performers.

Whatever profession they pursue, these people will always be happiest when working as part of a team rather than as individuals and, within their personal lives, they similarly cherish the close bonds that characterize their liaisons with friends and family members. Their strong social orientation is perhaps their defining quality, but this may bring them both pleasure and pain for, inevitably, others will not always welcome their advice, perceiving it as an attempt to control their independence of action.

JUNE 27

♋ ☽   DEFENDERS OF THE WEAK

Perhaps the most marked characteristic inherent in those born on June 27 is their sense of responsibility toward others, be they family members and friends, work colleagues, or the larger community. For not only are these people blessed with highly developed intuitive responses, which inform their convictions and actions with a sense of justice, but they are also extremely strong-willed types who feel that they have a duty to guide others to follow the same uncompromisingly moral code to which they themselves adhere. The feelings of profound empathy that they experience toward the plight of the downtrodden and exploited arouse their fiercely protective instincts and instill in them a burning determination to bring about societal improvement. When thus inspired, little can shake their belief in the veracity of their cause or divert them from their mission.

Those born on this day may manifest such humanitarian concerns in a range of appropriate careers, including nursing, therapy or charitable organizations—even in the evangelical religious sphere—or they may choose to propagate their message in the less overt media offered by the arts.

Their relationships with those closest to them are similarly defined by their urge to protect and further the interests of those with whom they have forged deep emotional ties, but within their personal, as well as their professional, liaisons their well-meaning efforts may prove less than welcome. Part of the problem is that their often sternly uncompromising approach may be perceived—and resented—by others as an autocratic attempt to control and direct them.

PLANETARY INFLUENCES
Ruling planet: Moon
First decan: Personal planet is Moon

VIRTUES
Protective, progressive, responsible

VICES
Obstinate, close-minded, controlling

CAREERS
Nurse, therapist, charity organizer, religious leader, judge, writer

SKILLS & APTITUDES
Innate sense of justice, sense of obligation towards humanity, intuition, strong moral code

FAMOUS BIRTHS
Helen Keller (1880)
JJ Abrams (1966)
Khloe Kardashian (1984)
Matthew Lewis (1989)

COMPATIBLE WITH
July 18–22

JUNE 28

✳ ✳ ✳ ✳ ✳ ✳ ✳ ✳ ✳ ✳ ✳ ✳ ✳ ✳

FOLLOWERS OF THE HEART ♋ ☽

PLANETARY INFLUENCES
Ruling planet: Moon
First decan: Personal planet is Moon

VIRTUES
Empathetic, intuitive,
people-oriented

VICES
Pessimistic, impulsive,
contradictory

CAREERS
Nurse, caretaker, charity or
humanitarian organizer, teacher

SKILLS & APTITUDES
Intuitive and emotional response to
outside events, desire to implement
progress, people-oriented sensitivity

FAMOUS BIRTHS
King Henry VIII (1491)
Mel Brooks (1926)
John Cusack (1966)
Felicia Day (1979)

COMPATIBLE WITH
July 18–22

While June 28 individuals may at one moment present an extroverted and optimistic face, encouraging and entertaining others, at the next they may eschew company and withdraw into a bleakly pessimistic, introverted world of their own making. Such extreme tendencies are a result of their profoundly intuitive, and hence emotional, responses to the circumstances within which they find themselves, coupled with their innate intellectual capacity to rationalize the reasons behind their strong identification with those who excite their interest and empathy.

The actions and convictions of June 28 people are conditioned by the situations and individuals that—for whatever reason—exert a strong influence upon their imaginations and feelings. The combination of such people-oriented sensitivity with their urge to be instruments of progress naturally equips them with a propensity toward making careers in the caring professions or other humanitarian fields, although they may sometimes choose to utilize their talents in other fields where personal interaction is a key element.

Their often irresistible tendency to follow their hearts rather than their heads can lead June 28 people to misjudge the motivations or desires of other individuals. This can be especially the case when it comes to choosing a life partner. Yet once settled within a committed one-to-one relationship—as with long-standing friends and family members—they are typically steadfastly supportive and affectionate, for they sense the importance of profound emotional bonds in grounding their wilder inclinations within a stable framework.

JUNE 29

♋ ☽   ENIGMATIC SOCIALITES

To those who do not know them well, those born on June 29 present something of an enigma, for while their love of fun, quirky sense of humor and great imaginative powers place them in the "extroverted" category, their formidable organizational powers, steadfast—and often stubborn—tenacity, and tendency to keep their deeper emotions to themselves endow them also with introverted characteristics.

These are indeed complicated personalities, whose joie de vivre, particularly when in the company of others, often masks a profound need for periods of solitude in which June 29 people can explore the abstract world of concepts and dreams which exerts such a strong hold over them. When they are successful in reconciling the diverse facets of themselves, June 29 people can achieve considerable material success. Reflecting also their relish for interpersonal contact and their need for personal autonomy, they are, in many respects, best suited for careers in the fluid realm of arts and design.

Despite their social orientation, it can be difficult to get to know these people, for when they are in the company of casual acquaintances they generally hold back the essence of their real selves. This propensity toward privacy is the result of their great sensitivity, which may cause them to become beset with feelings of insecurity, and they typically hide their emotional vulnerability behind a misleading façade of bravado. Yet within their established relationships (ie. with those whom they have come to trust) those born on June 29 usually display enormous commitment, affection and loyalty.

PLANETARY INFLUENCES
Ruling planet: Moon
First decan: Personal planet is Moon

VIRTUES
Introspective, intuitive, practical

VICES
Pessimistic, closed-off, insecure

CAREERS
Fashion designer, visual artist, teacher, philosopher, author

SKILLS & APTITUDES
Imagination, organizational skills, abstract thought, interpersonal communication skills

FAMOUS BIRTHS
Slim Pickens (1919)
Gary Busey (1944)
Bret McKenzie (1976)
Nicole Scherzinger (1978)

COMPATIBLE WITH
July 18–22

JUNE 30

✳ ✳ ✳ ✳ ✳ ✳ ✳ ✳ ✳ ✳ ✳ ✳ ✳ ✳

PERFORMING CHAMELEONS   ♋ ☽

PLANETARY INFLUENCES

Ruling planet: Moon
First decan: Personal planet is Moon

VIRTUES

Optimistic, sensitive, imaginative

VICES

Insecure, unbalanced,
temperamental

CAREERS

Actor, musician, dancer, personal
assistant, comedian

SKILLS & APTITUDES

Ability to read others' emotions,
desire to please, practical skills,
aptitude for teamwork

FAMOUS BIRTHS

Rupert Graves (1963)
Mike Tyson (1966)
Lizzy Caplan (1982)
Michael Phelps (1985)

COMPATIBLE WITH

July 18–22

Those born on June 30 are extremely sensitive to the responses that they arouse in others, and will therefore tailor their verbal expressions and physical actions and reactions toward their audiences, hoping to receive the acceptance and acclaim that they desire. This predilection frequently stems as much from a sense of insecurity within themselves as from their innate ability to empathize with those around them, and bestows upon them a deep-rooted wish to please and thereby feel valued and loved. And, indeed, their intuitive perspicacity and inherent ability to anticipate the needs of those around them makes them popular figures, whose endearingly gratifying company is sought after by others, who furthermore appreciate the aura of optimism and fun that they exude.

Their orientation toward people, combined with their enormous sensitivity and highly developed practical skills, suits those born on this day extremely well to careers as artistic performers of all kinds (but they will usually flourish in spheres in which they can interact with their coworkers). The intellectual foresight and technical skills signified by this day also bode well for their professional success.

It is ironic that, despite their gregarious natures, their loyalty to their friends and family and their need for satisfying interpersonal relationships, these people may find it particularly hard to form enduring one-to-one liaisons. The problem lies in the very talent that draws others to them: their chameleonlike ability to reflect others' moods may cause them to suppress their own emotions and make their true selves difficult for others to know.

JULY 1

♋ ☽ ♂   GOOD SAMARITANS

Although many of the personal qualities manifested by July 1 people—their deep sensitivity, their capacity for profound thought and their propensity for introspection—may identify them as introverted types, they are also endowed with extroverted tendencies, as evidenced by their strong wish to please others and marked enjoyment of social occasions.

Despite their natural orientation toward exploring the realm of abstract themes, their innate priority is to understand every aspect of the human condition, a predilection that may lead them not only to explore such areas as spirituality and alternative philosophies, but also to actively immerse themselves in humanitarian work. For many, the defining quality that inspires their actions is an overwhelming empathy with others—especially those whom they perceive as having been forgotten or abused by society. Their inclinations and intuitive talents may lead them into careers devoted toward helping others or pushing society forward—for example as social workers, or as artists of all kinds.

To all their endeavors, be they of a professional or private nature, those born on this day bring their deeply empathetic and generous, but also imaginative and prescient, qualities. Yet despite—or perhaps because of—the prodigious emotional and physical energy that they typically devote to others, be they the disadvantaged or their friends and relations, July 1 people generally have a tendency to suppress their own emotional requirements, possibly as a result of a misplaced sense of insecurity. Indeed, it can appear is as if people born on this day need the recognition of others to validate their worth.

PLANETARY INFLUENCES
Ruling planets: Moon
Second decan: Personal planet is Mars

VIRTUES
Sensitive, just, intuitive

VICES
Sacrificing, suppressed, insecure

CAREERS
Social worker, human-rights activist, spiritual leader, charity worker, artist

SKILLS & APTITUDES
Imaginative talents, introspection, abstract thinking, intuiting the emotions of others

FAMOUS BIRTHS
Dan Aykroyd (1952)
Princess Diana (1961)
Missy Elliott (1971)
Liv Tyler (1977)

COMPATIBLE WITH
July 6–11

CANCER

JULY 2

✳ ✳ ✳ ✳ ✳ ✳ ✳ ✳ ✳ ✳ ✳ ✳ ✳ ✳

SELFLESS ALTRUISTS ♋ ☽ ♂

PLANETARY INFLUENCES
Ruling planets: Moon
Second decan: Personal planet is Mars

VIRTUES
Sensitive, empathetic, protective

VICES
Insecure, conflicted, destructive

CAREERS
Psychiatrist, psychologist, pharmacist, actor, author

SKILLS & APTITUDES
Incisive perception, sensitivity to others' needs, imaginative approach, practical skills and determination

FAMOUS BIRTHS
Hermann Hesse (1877)
Larry David (1947)
Ashley Tisdale (1985)
Lindsay Lohan (1986)

COMPATIBLE WITH
July 6–11

Despite their incisive clarity of vision when it comes to identifying perceived societal wrongs, and their marked determination to remedy any such abuses, those born on July 2 are generally less able to direct their considerable powers of perspicacity inward, toward analyzing and resolving the issues that often trouble their own psyches.

Yet this internal confusion stems from the same source as their extremely oriented talents: their extraordinary sensitivity, which renders them on the one hand responsive and empathetic to the needs of others and, on the other, overwhelmed by the conflicting emotional messages and urges that they, as well as those around them, generate. Since they furthermore tend to prioritize the demands of others over their own needs—in part a result of their innate tendency to favor the common over the personal good—they may unknowingly bury themselves in their careers as a means of escaping their own personal demons.

Indeed, when employed in professional situations—and their talents equip them especially well for psychiatry and similar branches of medicine (especially if they were also born in the Chinese year of the snake), as well as to the arts—their formidable practical skills, energetic determination and imaginative approach come to the fore, inspiring and motivating others. Within their personal lives, too, these individuals demonstrate a selfless concern for those closest to them, and they are also gifted home-makers. Yet while the love of those closest to them may temper their inherent feelings of insecurity, they will remain unfulfilled until they address their own deepest needs.

JULY 3

♋ ☽ ♂   SURVEYORS OF THE MIND

July 3 individuals have more of an intellectual than emotional sensitivity toward other people. This is not to say that these people are not moved by the plight of those in need, but rather that the feelings that arise in their hearts are filtered through their heads before being given expression.

Despite their intense interest in other people, their easy charm and their urge to effect progress, those born on this day may sometimes appear to others to be somewhat remote. In part, this may be because they have learned that if they expose their emotions, they are vulnerable to being hurt: but it also indicates that many of these remarkably perspicacious individuals prefer not to become actively involved with people or situations until they have observed and analyzed them and thereby built up a detailed store of information to give them command of all of the available facts. Such inclinations and talents, as well as their soaring imaginative powers, augur especially well for their success as artists, but also equip them admirably for careers as psychologists, psychiatrists and physicians.

Within their personal liaisons, July 3 people demonstrate their tireless involvement and loyalty toward those with whom they have formed deep emotional bonds. Their natural propensity for analyzing the human personality may, however, make it difficult for them to commit themselves to a life partner, for their perspicacity may lead them to envisage numerous potential problems in the relationship under consideration. Similarly, until they learn to couch their critical comments in more diplomatic terms, they may be misperceived by others as being censorious types.

PLANETARY INFLUENCES
Ruling planets: Moon
Second decan: Personal planet is Mars

VIRTUES
Intuitive, intellectual, sensitive

VICES
Isolated, passive, overly critical

CAREERS
Psychologist, psychiatrist, physician, graphic artist, author

SKILLS & APTITUDES
Intellectual interest in the human psyche, powers of observation and analysis, imagination

FAMOUS BIRTHS
Franz Kafka (1883)
Gloria Allred (1941)
Tom Cruise (1962)
Patrick Wilson (1973)

COMPATIBLE WITH
July 6–11

JULY 4

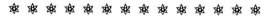

LOYAL SYMBIOTES   ♋ ☽ ♂

PLANETARY INFLUENCES
Ruling planets: Moon
Second decan: Personal planet is Mars

VIRTUES
Loyal, progressive, purposeful

VICES
Biased, closed-off, radical

CAREERS
Politician, doctor, police officer, soldier, artist, sportsperson

SKILLS & APTITUDES
Ability to embrace the identity of larger social groups, desire to effect progress, organizational skills, practical talents

FAMOUS BIRTHS
George Everest (1790)
Nathaniel Hawthorne (1804)
Geraldo Rivera (1943)
Malia Obama (1998)
Post Malone (1995)

COMPATIBLE WITH
July 6–11

....
....
....

Perhaps the most defining characteristic of July 4 people, and one that both inspires their intellectual actions and sustains their emotional needs, is their strong communal identification, be it with their families, their coworkers, their local community, their country—or indeed, with humanity as a whole. Their relationship with whatever societal group it is that especially absorbs their interest is a symbiotic one, for while their prodigious organizational skills, their fierce loyalty and their natural willingness to defend the wider interest all serve to benefit the common good, in return they receive a comforting sense of security by grounding themselves in the profound human bonds forged by shared concerns and goals.

The dreams and visions of July 4 people are therefore generally concerned with furthering human progress. Despite the fact that, initially, these ideals may appear to be unfeasibly radical to others, they will often prove to be startingly successful, especially when backed by their originators' practical talents, tenacity and determination.

Whatever career they choose, those born on this day will be happy surrounded by a like-minded team of colleagues working together toward a mutual aim. If not involved in politics, many will be found in such professions as medicine, the military or law-enforcement agencies; they may also direct their energies toward the arts, hoping to unite others in the pleasure that their skills may arouse. Ironically, given their human orientation, they are rather private individuals, preferring to keep their innermost emotions to themselves; opening up their hearts to potential partners may therefore initially prove difficult.

JULY 5

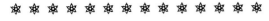

♋ ☽ ♂   SMART DESIGNERS

July 5 people are profoundly sensitive and intuitive types, who invest their inspirational visions with great emotional significance. Yet they are less oriented toward satisfying the demands of others than toward attaining their own emotional fulfillment—although they are nevertheless anxious to please those who surround them. It is this latter quest that typically informs many of the actions of July 5 people, who find it difficult to resist following the lure of a new and exciting person, subject or venture to which they may feel innately drawn as well as intellectually attracted.

When they alight upon a subject that truly absorbs their interest, those born on this day will typically explore it with acute perception, great energy and keen imagination and, when action is required, utilize their strong planning and organizational skills. While they have the potential to make gifted innovators in any sphere where they can follow their instincts unhindered by the restrictions of others, they are especially suited to the freedom offered by creative careers, perhaps in design.

The combination of their original approach, charm and energy makes them extremely magnetic and popular figures, who are able to, apparently effortlessly, attract hordes of admirers. But while they are outstanding performers and entertainers in the broader context of social circumstances, they may often shy away from committing themselves to one-to-one relationships, fearing, perhaps, that too intimate a relationship might prove stifling. Indeed, although their love for and loyalty to their friends and family members are never in doubt, they need freedom to pursue their personal dreams.

PLANETARY INFLUENCES
Ruling planets: Moon
Second decan: Personal planet is Mars

VIRTUES
Imaginative, sensitive, charming

VICES
Hedonistic, ungrounded, unsatisfied

CAREERS
Fashion designer, graphic artist, architect, comedian, entertainer

SKILLS & APTITUDES
Acute perception, energetic intellect, strong imagination, innovative inclinations, original approach, magnetic personality

FAMOUS BIRTHS
Paul Smith (1946)
Judge Joe Brown (1947)
Jenji Kohan (1969)
Paul DelVecchio (1980)

COMPATIBLE WITH
July 6–11

JULY 6

✵ ✵ ✵ ✵ ✵ ✵ ✵ ✵ ✵ ✵ ✵ ✵ ✵

BEACONS OF INSPIRATION   ♋ ☽ ♂

PLANETARY INFLUENCES
Ruling planets: Moon
Second decan: Personal planet is Mars

VIRTUES
Visionary, optimistic, charismatic

VICES
Obsessive, unrealistic,
closed-minded

CAREERS
International relations,
humanitarian, screenwriter, charity
organizer, musician

SKILLS & APTITUDES
Idyllic visions, single-minded focus,
energetic and optimistic approach,
natural affinity for the arts

FAMOUS BIRTHS
Geoffrey Rush (1951)
Kevin Hart (1979)
Eva Green (1980)

COMPATIBLE WITH
July 1–5

More than anything else, those born on this day yearn to realize their personal idyll, be it finding enduring love, the perfect career, a fulfilling lifestyle, or a Utopian humanitarian or spiritual vision. Whether their quest is motivated by a conscious or unconscious urge to achieve their ideal, it will nevertheless inform many of their actions and—despite the many setbacks and disappointments that they will inevitably experience—will usually remain a beacon of inspiration lighting their path through life.

July 6 individuals usually focus on a single vision. The vibrant optimism, infectious energy and dedicated enthusiasm with which they typically imbue the pursuit of this ideal may also fire the interest of others, especially if directed toward a global goal or if manifested in the realm of the arts to which, in any case, they have a natural affinity. And, when their magnetism, kindness and charm (born both of their strong wills and their desire to please others) are added to the equation, the sum of the components results in popular personalities who are both enthused and enthusing.

Because their enormous sensitivity toward those who surround them endows them with feelings of empathy and a sincere desire to lighten the lives of others, July 6 individuals make inherently loyal and affectionate friends, relations and especially parents. Forging a lasting one-on-one partnership that fully satisfies their emotional demands may prove difficult, however, unless they are prepared to compromise the often highly idealized standards that they have set for their soul mate.

JULY 7

♋ ☽ ♂   Dualistic Dreamers

Those born on this day are characterized by their somewhat dualistic natures, manifested on the one hand by their extraordinarily original dreams, and on the other by their fierce drive and determination. These are the type of individuals whose soaring imaginations will cause them to espouse what may appear to others to be utterly unrealistic and fanciful projects, and then to further confound their detractors by successfully implementing the very visions previously dismissed as being unfeasible. When their various personal qualities—including their idealism, energy and practicality—are in harmony with one another, they have the potential to effect truly remarkable innovations, and they should thus strive to retain their self-belief despite being inevitably subjected to the discouragement of less progressive minds. These are pragmatic people who draw on their sensitivity toward others to tailor their approach to the form that they expect to be best received by their audiences—their vision and vigor also proving inspirational.

Their career choices will depend, of course, on the specific areas of interest that motivate them as individuals, but they are usually naturally drawn to the sphere of artistic expression—be it as musicians, painters or actors—and may furthermore have the capacity to employ their intuition and energy extremely effectively within the business world. Despite their charisma, these are somewhat private people, who cherish the close bonds of kinship and friendship that define their relationships with their nearest and dearest, from whom they gain as much as they give in terms of emotional support.

Planetary Influences
Ruling planets: Moon
Second decan: Personal planet is Mars

Virtues
Imaginative, ambitious, intuitive

Vices
Uncompromising, defeatist, unrealistic

Careers
Musician, painter, actor, entrepreneur, project developer

Skills & Aptitudes
Capacity for highly original thinking, innovative mindset, determined drive to achieve goals, idealistic approach

Famous Births
Ringo Starr (1940)
Jim Gaffigan (1966)
Jorja Fox (1968)
Michelle Swan (1980)

Compatible With
July 1–5

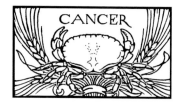

CANCER

JULY 8

✳ ✳ ✳ ✳ ✳ ✳ ✳ ✳ ✳ ✳ ✳ ✳ ✳ ✳

INDOMITABLE DYNAMOS

PLANETARY INFLUENCES
Ruling planets: Moon
Second decan: Personal planet is Mars

VIRTUES
Strong-willed, ambitious, pragmatic

VICES
Unappreciative, neglectful, ruthless

CAREERS
Project developer, lawyer, scientific researcher, media consultant, advertising agent

SKILLS & APTITUDES
Practical and technical abilities, realistic approach, organizational skills, strategic thinking

FAMOUS BIRTHS
John D. Rockefeller (1839)
Anjelica Huston (1951)
Kevin Bacon (1958)
Jaden Smith (1998)

COMPATIBLE WITH
July 1–5

....
....
....

Others generally admire those born on this day for their dynamism, fixity of purpose, prodigious energy and impressive practical skills, but the respect that they generate is of the awed, somewhat intimidated, variety rather than born of affection. For such is their strength of will, self-belief and uncompromising determination to achieve their aims that their tenacity can often take the form of ruthlessness. In many respects it is the organizational aspects of a task that interest them most: they have an overriding urge to realize their progressive visions by implementing a soundly supportive framework of actions, comparable to the setting in motion of a smoothly running machine. They may be found making their mark in any professional field where their imaginative visions can be imbued with the potential to achieve tangible results: their inclinations and talents equip them for commercial or scientific ventures as well as for those artistic pursuits which require detailed background research and development.

Their interpersonal relationships are typically characterized by their urge to direct the activities of those around them. Yet they usually combine the intellectual clarity of vision which informs the majority of their actions, with a sensitivity toward the feelings of others. Thus, although they have a propensity to take charge, they will rarely ride roughshod over others in their quest to achieve progress, possibly also instinctively recognizing that they will achieve more by enlisting the support of others. This pragmatic approach also stands them in good stead within their more intimate liaisons, particularly if they are men.

JULY 9

✳ ✳ ✳ ✳ ✳ ✳ ✳ ✳ ✳ ✳ ✳ ✳ ✳ ✳ ✳ ✳

♋ ☽ ♂　　ORIGINAL THEORISTS

CANCER

Their questing imagination and enthusiasm for thoroughly investigating the unusual and wide-ranging interests to which they are naturally attracted, bestow upon July 9 people the potential to blaze truly innovative trails through life. Indeed, such is their innate conviction that there is more to life than has yet been discovered that they are often irresistibly drawn to explore concepts that less open-minded types might dismiss as being fanciful or as having no future—pioneering scientific or artistic theories, for example, or even psychic phenomena, mysticism and spirituality. Despite the originality of the visions that inspire them, however, those born on this day are rarely unrealistic about the possibility of success, for they supplement their great intellectual and intuitive perspicacity with remarkably effective resourceful and practical skills. Add to this combination of personal qualities great optimism and energy, and the resulting individuals are attractive and popular people.

Although their actions may be motivated by the very personal visions that inspire them, they generally prefer to work toward their realization as part of a coordinated team rather than in solitary isolation. Not only are they stimulated by the company and ideas of others, but developing strong and supportive working relationships is of vital importance to their emotional equilibrium. Similarly, within their private lives, they appreciate and value the unquestioning love of those closest to them and they typically make caring and empathetic family members, especially if they were also born in the Chinese year of the monkey.

PLANETARY INFLUENCES
Ruling planets: Moon
Second decan: Personal planet is Mars

VIRTUES
Curious, intuitive, sensitive

VICES
Frustrated, temperamental, withdrawn

CAREERS
Scientific theorist, philosopher, literature professor, psychic, spiritual leader

SKILLS & APTITUDES
Powers of investigation, desire to delve into unexplored areas, original thinking, intuitive perspicacity

FAMOUS BIRTHS
Tom Hanks (1956)
Courtney Love (1964)
Fred Savage (1976)
Rebecca Sugar (1987)

COMPATIBLE WITH
July 1–5

JULY 10

TALENTED ANALYSTS

PLANETARY INFLUENCES
Ruling planets: Moon
Second decan: Personal planet is Mars

VIRTUES
Analytical, progressive, practical

VICES
Passive, isolated, overly cautious

CAREERS
Psychologist, psychiatrist, artist, writer, musician, athlete

SKILLS & APTITUDES
Powers of observation, interest in human psyche, research skills, powerful intellect

FAMOUS BIRTHS
Nikola Tesla (1856)
Marcel Proust (1871)
Sofia Vergara (1972)
Jessica Simpson (1980)

COMPATIBLE WITH
July 1–5

Those born on this day are vitally interested in all aspects of the human condition—ranging from the psyches of those who surround them to the behavior of humanity as a whole. Their forte is observation, rather than action, which is not to say that they lack strong opinions and ambitions, or the determination to implement these when they feel impelled to effect progress, it is rather that detailed information-gathering is a crucial prerequisite to the formulation and promotion of their strategies. In fact, their gentle, unassuming demeanor typically masks a keen and powerful intellect, the incisive expression of which may startle those who do not know them well and may have misjudged them as being passive and dull. But once they have secured the background data that they need for the best chance of success, these individuals will embark upon the quest to realize their visions with remarkable fixity of purpose and tenacity, drawing from their armory of talents upon their prodigious organizational skills.

July 10 people are naturally attracted to nonmaterialistic pursuits, and their inclinations and skills augur especially well for their success as insightful psychologists and psychiatrists, artists, writers and musicians, as well as dedicated athletes—in fact, in any field where a "corporate ethos" would not restrict their independence of thought and action. They are generally extremely discriminating in their choice of friends and life partners, but once they have committed their affections these sensitive and loyal individuals will stick to their nearest and dearest through thick and thin.

JULY 11

✷ ✷ ✷ ✷ ✷ ✷ ✷ ✷ ✷ ✷ ✷ ✷ ✷ ✷ ✷

♋ ☽ ♂   DRAMATIC PERFORMERS

Whether they are conscious of their overriding predilection or not, those born on this day are defined by the intensity of their interest in interpersonal relationships. Although their enthusiasm may be fired by abstract, intellectual concepts, or by personal ambition or vision, this will almost always involve the participation of others, be they friends, relations, coworkers or even audiences. July 11 individuals—who in any case have a natural affinity with the arts and will often make dramatic or musical pursuits their careers—are natural performers who not only relish the attention that is lavished upon them by others, but are also almost hypersensitive to the responses that they arouse. Since they are inherently charming and empathetic people who enjoy pleasing and entertaining others (both for reasons of human concern and because their confidence is boosted when they can bask in the goodwill that is thereby engendered), they will generally put the maximum possible effort into creating mutually rewarding liaisons, be they of the personal or professional variety.

Most July 11 people are innately geared toward achieving tangible success—in part a result of their driving energy and their urge to take practical action, and in part because of the acclaim that they will thus receive—and will often be found making their mark in the worlds of commercial enterprise, politics or sports. Within their private lives, too, they typically strive to bring happiness to their nearest and dearest, enlivening their relationships with their imagination and joie de vivre, but also offering more profound emotional support.

PLANETARY INFLUENCES
Ruling planets: Moon
Second decan: Personal planet is Mars

VIRTUES
Sensitive, optimistic, empathetic

VICES
Conceited, unfocused, insecure

CAREERS
Stage or film actor, musician, comedian, athlete, politician

SKILLS & APTITUDES
Abstract thinking, interpersonal interests, teamwork, charismatic appeal, practical approach

FAMOUS BIRTHS
John Quincy Adams (1767)
Giorgio Armani (1934)
Lisa Rinna (1963)
Lil Kim (1974)
Alessia Cara (1996)

COMPATIBLE WITH
July 1–5

JULY 12

DICHOTOMOUS PERSONALITIES ♋ ☽ ♃ ♆

PLANETARY INFLUENCES
Ruling planet: Moon
Third decan: Personal planets are Jupiter and Neptune

VIRTUES
Sensitive, intellectual, analytical

VICES
Controlling, manipulative, interfering

CAREERS
Politician, social worker, author, teacher, lawyer, HR representative

SKILLS & APTITUDES
Interpersonal skills, practical and analytical talents, ability to attune to others' emotions, leadership

FAMOUS BIRTHS
Henry David Thoreau (1817)
George Washington Carver (1864)
Kimberly Perry (1983)
Malala Yousafzai (1997)

COMPATIBLE WITH
June 22–25

There are two aspects to the personalities of those born on July 12: on the one hand they are "soft," profoundly empathetic and sympathetic individuals who are keenly attuned to the emotions exuded by others; and on the other hand they are "hard," having a compelling urge to direct the actions of those around them. Although these twin propensities may seem paradoxical, they are readily explained and reconciled by the strong orientation of these individuals toward others, which is typically manifested in a desire to set those around them on what they perceive to be the optimum path for achieving success. This instinct is the result of not only their inherent sensitivity but also their intellectual strengths—of clarity of vision, logical deduction, independence of thought and organizational powers. Their concern for others may be manifested at the personal, professional or even humanitarian level.

Because they naturally engender respect, July 12 people will often be elevated to positions of leadership, and their integrity and resistance to following the herd suits them for working autonomously. Apart from national and civic politics or social work, optimum careers include especially the artistic sphere, in which they may exert their benevolent influence on others. These people are typically sought after for their sound and carefully considered advice, particularly since they are rarely patronizing. And, within their personal relationships, their desire to protect and guide their nearest and dearest is even more pronounced: they are well aware that when differences have to be resolved confrontation or coercion is less effective than a more subtle and rational approach.

JULY 13

♋ ☽ ♃ ♆ LEADING ENTREPRENEURS

Their inherent preference to play an active part in life endows July 13 individuals with the irresistible urge to make progress and achieve the tangible targets that they typically set for themselves. And, when their highly developed intellectual and emotional perspicacity is added to this personal equation, it results in an outstanding capacity to recognize a potentially advantageous opportunity (whose merits may not be immediately obvious to less sensitive types), seize the moment and act incisively. To all their ventures—be they within their professional or their private lives—they bring their natural qualities of originality, inventiveness and vigor and, because they are so responsive to the emotions of others and are innately kind-hearted, also the desire to build supportive and close-knit teams to assist them in their endeavors. The same concern for other people naturally equips those born on this day for careers where they can work toward the welfare of humanity—as social scientists, perhaps—although their talents may suit them equally well to becoming commercial entrepreneurs or artists.

July 13 people's personal relationships are usually characterized by the deep affection and protectiveness that they manifest toward their nearest and dearest. The value that they place upon the emotional bonds that they form with others may stem from feelings of angst, or "otherness"—another result of their far-reaching perspicacity—which has the capacity to be enriching if positively channeled, but which may also cause them to become overly anxious with regard to what they perceive to be the fate that lies in store for them.

PLANETARY INFLUENCES
Ruling planet: Moon
Third decan: Personal planets are Jupiter and Neptune

VIRTUES
Kind-hearted, innovative, intuitive

VICES
Overloaded, depressive, angsty

CAREERS
Social scientist, entrepreneur, therapist, team manager, athlete

SKILLS & APTITUDES
Active approach to new challenges, ability to set and achieve goals, capacity to recognize advantageous opportunities, inventiveness

FAMOUS BIRTHS
Patrick Stewart (1940)
Harrison Ford (1942)
Cheech Marin (1946)
Deborah Cox (1974)

COMPATIBLE WITH
June 22–25

JULY 14

❊ ❊ ❊ ❊ ❊ ❊ ❊ ❊ ❊ ❊ ❊ ❊ ❊

VEHEMENT PROGRESSIVES ♋ ☽ ♃ ♆

Those born on this day have the enviable ability to attract the affection and admiration of others—even when, at moments of extreme passion, they may stridently attempt to communicate the humanitarian messages that are inspired by their profound empathy with the disadvantaged. Rather than being alienated by others for their vehement stance in such confrontational situations, they are often regarded with indulgence. Indulgence, however, is not usually the response that is sought, for these individuals are typically possessed of an urgent desire to bring about progress in human society, to harmonize interpersonal relationships and to right perceived wrongs, a compulsion that is the result of not only their all-encompassing sensitivity, but also their intellectual clarity and fixity of purpose. While these people will often be found in professions that are concerned with achieving humanitarian goals—as politicians or social campaigners, for instance—many will devote their talents to improving the quality of life of others by becoming artistic performers.

While their enormous empathy is perhaps their greatest quality, at the same time it is also one of their most pernicious attributes. For while they cannot help but offer sympathy and advice to those whom they intuitively sense are in need of assistance, they sometimes have an overriding tendency to suppress their own identities and needs when acting on behalf of others. They manifest this strong orientation toward others in all of their liaisons, particularly their personal relationships: when they find time for introspection, their optimistic veneer may be replaced by feelings of unspecific, yet overwhelming, sadness.

JULY 15

✻ ✻ ✻ ✻ ✻ ✻ ✻ ✻ ✻ ✻ ✻ ✻ ✻ ✻

♋ ☽ ♃ ♆   SENSITIVE IDEALISTS

July 15 people manage to combine their highly developed powers of imagination—which may often tend toward the mystical or the spiritual—with a more concrete awareness of their immediate surroundings, including not only their environment, but also the individuals who surround them as friends and kin, professional associates or even as part of a more global scenario. Both characteristics stem from their profound sensitivity, which typically manifests itself in the form of equal parts of intellectual perspicacity and as emotional empathy. Thus while those born on this day have the ability to arrive at astute impersonal analytical conclusions regarding a situation under consideration, their observations are given human depth by their intuitive ability to assess the input of, and the impact on, the people who are touched by it. In many respects this is a remarkable gift, which, when combined with their urge to effect progress, endows them with the potential to bring about considerable change for the good, enriching the lives of others.

Although July 15 people possess skills that are generally suited to the world of business and commerce, they typically lack the ruthlessness that is the mark of the tycoon. It is perhaps in the artistic realm that their talent to reach out and inspire others with their idiosyncratic and innovative views is most effective, especially if they are also men. And, while they appreciate the material fruits of their success as a means of generously providing for and indulging those closest to them, it is the dream of achieving perfection in the metaphysical sphere that underlies their more introspective visions.

PLANETARY INFLUENCES
Ruling planet: Moon
Third decan: Personal planets are Jupiter and Neptune

VIRTUES
Imaginative, empathetic, innovative

VICES
Unrealistic, overburdened, frustrated

CAREERS
Religious leader, team manager, international-relief organizer, actor

SKILLS & APTITUDES
Imagination, spiritual inclinations, sensitivity toward others, powers of observation

FAMOUS BIRTHS
Rembrandt (1606)
Gabriel Iglesias (1976)
Diane Kruger (1976)
Travis Fimmel (1979)

COMPATIBLE WITH
June 22–25

CANCER

JULY 16

✵ ✵ ✵ ✵ ✵ ✵ ✵ ✵ ✵ ✵ ✵ ✵ ✵ ✵

QUESTING CAMPAIGNERS ♋ ☽ ♃ ♆

PLANETARY INFLUENCES
Ruling planet: Moon
Third decan: Personal planets are Jupiter and Neptune

VIRTUES
Intuitive, progressive, idealistic

VICES
Discouraged, embittered, vulnerable

CAREERS
Social or religious campaigner, relief worker, author, painter, actor

SKILLS & APTITUDES
Desire to better others' lives, intellectual powers of perception and analysis, organizational skills

FAMOUS BIRTHS
Ida B. Wells (1862)
Jimmy Johnson (1943)
Will Ferrell (1967)
Corey Feldman (1971)

COMPATIBLE WITH
June 22–25

Those born on this day are on a constant quest to realize an ideal—be it to find their soul mate, to create the perfect work of art, or to implement a fault-less technical process or a revolutionary social system. Although their desire is primarily driven by their emotions, they typically marshal their highly developed intellectual powers of perception and analysis, as well as their formidable capacity for organization, in the pursuit of their aims. However personal the vision that fuels July 16 individuals, it rarely has a selfish purpose, for they combine their remarkable ability to identify abuses of power with their profound feelings of empathy for those suffering the ill-effects. Thus their yearning to employ their energies as significant agents for change is usually ultimately directed toward bringing improved circumstances and happiness to the lives of others. Their talents and inclinations suit them particularly to the arts—where they hope their innovative work will provide spiritual inspiration and solace to a wider audience—but they may also choose to help others by becoming social or religious campaigners.

Unfortunately, their Utopian ideals may doom them to disappointment, with the result that they will often adopt a façade of emotional robustness to protect their vulnerability and propensity for becoming depressed or frustrated by deeply felt setbacks. The emotional ties they form with those nearest to them are especially valued for the unquestioning support and belief that they offer. It may, however, take them some time to find a life partner—the result of their tendency to project a romantic ideal onto those who may not wish to be cast in such a role.

JULY 17

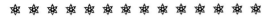

☉ ☽ ♃ ♆   MOTIVATED IMPROVERS

The steely ambition of those born on this day is often marked by the easy-going friendliness and sociability that characterize their approach to their interpersonal relationships. This latter quality may manifest itself in the realm of the arts—to which their great sensitivity renders them inherently sympathetic—or in the business or commercial world, to which their innovative ideas and practical skills suit them. Although some strong-willed July 17 individuals are motivated by the desire to achieve personal success and thereby win admiration and acclaim, others are more focused upon bringing about improvements for the societal group to which they have the closest affinity (their families or countries, for example). In all their endeavors they prefer to surround themselves with like-minded teams rather than acting as sole agents (despite their marked independence of thought and innovative individuality). When enlisting the assistance of other people, they typically make good use of their intuitive ability to pick up on their emotions and thus adjust their approach accordingly.

Although their professional fixity of purpose may lead July 17 people to adopt a somewhat manipulative stance toward their coworkers, within their personal lives they are generally relaxed and deeply affectionate toward their nearest and dearest—this is particularly true of the men born on this day. Indeed, it is when the pressure to achieve is off that their humor and talent to entertain come to the fore, for these individuals derive genuine pleasure from their ability to bring happiness to those they love with their joie de vivre and generosity.

PLANETARY INFLUENCES
Ruling planet: Moon
Third decan: Personal planets are Jupiter and Neptune

VIRTUES
Intuitive, tenacious, easy-going

VICES
Manipulative, calculating, pressured

CAREERS
Comedian, businessperson, salesperson, community organizer, advertiser, politician

SKILLS & APTITUDES
Sociability, artisitic inclinations, innovation, practical skills, intuition

FAMOUS BIRTHS
Donald Sutherland (1935)
David Hasselhoff (1952)
Jason Clarke (1969)
Luke Bryan (1976)

COMPATIBLE WITH
June 22–25

CANCER

JULY 18

✳ ✳ ✳ ✳ ✳ ✳ ✳ ✳ ✳ ✳ ✳ ✳ ✳

DEVOTED COMRADES   ♋ ☽ ♃ ♆

PLANETARY INFLUENCES
Ruling planet: Moon
Third decan: Personal planets are
Jupiter and Neptune

VIRTUES
Enthusiastic, friendly, empathetic

VICES
Dependent, suppressed, insecure

CAREERS
Athlete (particularly team sports),
soldier, political campaigner, actor,
community organizer

SKILLS & APTITUDES
Team-playing approach, empathetic
feelings for others, imaginative
powers

FAMOUS BIRTHS
William M. Thackeray (1811)
Nelson Mandela (1918)
Vin Diesel (1967)
Kristen Bell (1980)

COMPATIBLE WITH
June 26–30

The visions and goals that fuel the imaginations and actions of those born on July 18 are generally bound up with furthering the communal good rather than seeking personal success and recognition. The reasons for this approach are manifold, and include strong feelings of empathy with those who surround them—and with whom they typically come to identify—as well as their somewhat insecure need to ground themselves in the fraternal bonds of camaraderie that result from serving a common cause, and the recognition that they may thereby receive. Indeed, such is the overwhelming sensitivity and soaringly imaginative powers of these people that the uneasy sense of "otherness" that they often experience can lead them to seek the affection and solace that arise from manifesting solidarity with others in the pursuit of mutual interests. They may identify themselves with any of a number of societal groups—sporting, artistic or political associations, their families, their local communities, their nations or even humanity as a whole—but whichever one claims their loyalty will receive their exclusive devotion, often at the expense of their ability to be objective when it comes to a conflict of interest.

July 18 individuals will clearly be unhappy unless working as part of a close-knit team. Although they are blessed with remarkably independent and innovative intellectual gifts, their use of these is typically tempered by the boundaries set by the common consensus. They should therefore beware of becoming somewhat narrow-minded, of losing their appreciation of healthy expressions of individuality and should attempt to appreciate and embrace diversity.

JULY 19

CANCER

♋ ☽ ☉ ♃ ♆   SUBTLE BROADCASTERS

Others often admire July 19 individuals for their intellectual perspicacity and profound empathy, qualities that reflect their all-encompassing sensitivity to the circumstances and company that surrounds them, and upon which they draw when offering their carefully considered advice. Those born on this day typically not only care deeply for their nearest and dearest, seeking to ensure their happiness and success, but also are furthermore imbued with a more global desire to improve the lot of humanity. Although they are quick to identify social abuses or failings, and also to formulate strategies for humanitarian progress, they may be frustrated by their inability to communicate their visions to less imaginative people who are unwilling to accept the idea of change. Although July 19 people may prefer to act as politicians or social campaigners in their professional lives, they will often be more effective agents of progress when broadcasting their message through the more subtle medium of the arts to which, in any case, they are naturally drawn.

These are energetic individuals who need to keep their minds and bodies engaged in progressive activities. They may often display a talent for sporting pursuits, but their vigorous nature may equally be expressed in their mastery of artistic or technical pursuits. They bring to both their professional and personal liaisons their interest and concern for others—as well as a strong sense of humor—but may nevertheless appear to be somewhat solitary individuals, whose high ideals, profundity of thought and commitment to the visions that inspire them may be difficult for others to live up to or match.

PLANETARY INFLUENCES
Ruling planets: Moon and Sun
Third decan: Personal planets are Jupiter and Neptune
Second cusp: Leo tendencies

VIRTUES
Just, helpful, energetic

VICES
Radical, embittered, daunting

CAREERS
Politician, social campaigner, athlete, author, technical researcher

SKILLS & APTITUDES
Sense of justice, intellectual clear-sightedness, energetic approach, ability to formulate strategies

FAMOUS BIRTHS
Samuel Colt (1814)
Edgar Degas (1834)
Benedict Cumberbatch (1976)
Jared Padalecki (1982)

COMPATIBLE WITH
June 26–30, December 6–11

JULY 20

✴ ✴ ✴ ✴ ✴ ✴ ✴ ✴ ✴ ✴ ✴ ✴ ✴ ✴

ENERGETIC WANDERERS   ♋ ☽ ☉ ♃ ♆

PLANETARY INFLUENCES
Ruling planets: Moon and Sun
Third decan: Personal planets are Jupiter and Neptune
Second cusp: Leo tendencies

VIRTUES
Energetic, vibrant, cheerful

VICES
Superficial, unfocused, dissatisfied

CAREERS
Athlete, tour guide, game designer, actor, party planner, comedian

SKILLS & APTITUDES
Physical and intellectual energy, curiosity, desire for new experiences, ability to work as part of a team

FAMOUS BIRTHS
Carlos Santana (1947)
Sandra Oh (1971)
Gisele Bundchen (1980)
Julianne Hough (1988)

COMPATIBLE WITH
June 26–30, December 6–11

Perhaps the most striking personal feature of those born on July 20 is their energy which, like the water that is associated with their crustaceous natal sign, may meander in every direction, exploring the boundaries that contain it, or may surge irresistibly forward, rarely remaining static. Their vigor is not only of the physical variety (and many are sporting types, some even becoming professional athletes), but also defines their intellectual approach, which typically is questingly curious and constantly searching for knowledge and novel experiences. Unsurprisingly, the all-encompassing nature of their inquisitive perspicacity results in their espousal of a wide range of interests, as well as a profound empathy with others. Professionally, they will usually flourish in any field where they can combine their enjoyment of working as part of a team with their technical and practical talents, while at the same time retaining a certain autonomy of action by satisfying their need to stimulate their intellects. They are thus especially suited for the variety of opportunities that the creative or artistic sphere embraces.

Their natural exuberance and infectious optimism draws others to July 20 people, who relish taking the initiative and organizing group activities or entertaining social events. Their joie de vivre and highly developed sense of humor makes them popular with their coworkers and friends, who feel that they can be relied upon to provide loyal and constructive support during times of crisis. Similarly, they make concerned, but also enlivening, partners and parents, who care as much about the happiness of their loved ones as they do about their material success.

JULY 21

♋ ☽ ☉ ♃ ♆   CURIOUS EXHIBITIONISTS

The characters of those born on this day often pose something of an enigma to those who do not know them well, for at times they manifest the exhibitionist qualities that are the mark of the extrovert, and at others they reveal their more introverted capacity for profound and considered intellectual deliberation. There are often two pronounced sides to their characters: the side that enjoys observing other people and analyzing what makes them tick; and the side that utilizes this talent to provoke strong reactions from those who are being observed—in many cases, the more confrontational the better. Both propensities are born of their pronounced orientation toward others, a predilection that is less the product of a need to solicit the emotional support inherent in interpersonal liaisons than of the stimulation that they derive from surveying the complexities of human interaction. Such inclinations suit July 21 individuals admirably for research-based careers as psychologists or philosophers, but their great organizational skills, as well as their urge to exert a beneficial influence over others, also indicates potential success as teachers or artists.

Despite their intellectual independence and the somewhat clinical predilection for analyzing human behavior that often defines their professional relationships, those born on this day are typically extremely generous, loyal and supportive—even protective—when it comes to their nearest and dearest. Yet because they themselves adhere to a firm moral code (springing from their sense of natural justice), they find it hard to condone transgressions in others—even on the part of those closest to them.

PLANETARY INFLUENCES
Ruling planets: Moon and Sun
Third decan: Personal planets are Jupiter and Neptune
Second cusp: Leo tendencies

VIRTUES
Curious, determined, independent

VICES
Confrontational, overbearing, controlling

CAREERS
Psychologist, philosopher, teacher, playwright, therapist, counselor

SKILLS & APTITUDES
Intense interest in human nature, debating, organizational skills

FAMOUS BIRTHS
Ernest Hemingway (1899)
Cat Stevens (1948)
Robin Williams (1951)
Josh Hartnett (1978)

COMPATIBLE WITH
June 26–30, December 6–11

JULY 22

✻ ✻ ✻ ✻ ✻ ✻ ✻ ✻ ✻ ✻ ✻ ✻ ✻ ✻

ACTION–TAKERS   ♋ ☽ ☉ ♃ ♆

PLANETARY INFLUENCES
Ruling planets: Moon and Sun
Third decan: Personal planets are
   Jupiter and Neptune
Second cusp: Leo tendencies

VIRTUES
Visionary, active, caring

VICES
Conflicted, impatient, restless

CAREERS
Technical researcher, fashion
designer, graphic artist, inventor

SKILLS & APTITUDES
Predilection for active progress,
idealistic visions, innovative
thinking, intellectual perspicacity

FAMOUS BIRTHS
Willem Dafoe (1955)
David Spade (1964)
Selena Gomez (1992)
Prince George (2013)

COMPATIBLE WITH
June 26–30, December 6–11

The passive, emotionally-oriented, lunar forces and the active solar energies that govern the personalities of those born on this day stand in direct opposition to each other and may be difficult to reconcile. Thus while July 22 people possess great sensitivity and are fueled by often remarkably idealistic visions, they may unwittingly sabotage their efforts by their impatient tendency for taking immediate action without having fully thought through the potential consequences. Conversely, their strong compulsion to make direct progress may be hindered by the conflicting messages they intuitively receive. When, however, these qualities are in harmony, these individuals make remarkably effective instruments of innovation, drawing upon their intellectual perspicacity and energy in pursuing their single-minded quest to realize their ambitions. Their varied gifts give them the potential to succeed in a range of professions, but their inherent creativity makes them especially suited to those artistic or technical pursuits in which they can act as inspirational leaders of their fields.

Although these are empathetic types who cherish their close attachments to their friends and kin, they may find it hard to commit themselves to a life partner. For many, the problem lies with both their diversity of interests and their emotional restlessness, which are difficult to contain within a monogamous relationship. Those closest to them should therefore attempt to set flexible boundaries for their liaisons, within which July 22 people can maintain a certain freedom of action while simultaneously remaining securely anchored by bonds of affection.

♌ LEO

July 23 to August 22

RULING PLANET: *Sun* ELEMENT: *Fixed fire*
SYMBOL: *Lion* POLARITY: *Positive (masculine)*
PHYSICAL CORRESPONDENCE: *Spine, back, heart*
STONES: *Ruby, yellow topaz, tiger's eye, amber, cat's eye*
FLOWERS: *Sunflower, chamomile, marigold, celandine*
COLORS: *Golden yellow, orange*

The zodiacal sign of Leo governs the period when the Northern Hemisphere's summer is at its height, when the heat of the Sun is at its fiercest, and this manifestation of solar power is probably the reason why so many Middle Eastern astrological traditions equated the constellation with the lion, the king of beasts, whose golden mane was said by classical poets to resemble the rays of the Sun. The ancient Egyptians venerated the lion because the life-giving waters of the River Nile began to rise when the Sun was in Leo, while the ancient Greeks, Persians, and Hindu astrologers also unequivocally personified the constellation as a lion. The Babylonians, too, envisaged a leonine creature presiding over the sign, but in this case it was a lioness or dog, maybe because many of the powerful goddesses of the Mesopotamian tradition were strongly associated with these animals. Perhaps the most familiar and enduring myth associated with Leo is that of the slaying of the Nemean lion by the Greco-Roman hero Herakles (Hercules)—the first of his labors.

The combination of the related influences that cogovern Leo—the brightly burning Sun and element of fire that gives life but can also destroy, as well as the magnificent majesty of the lion—is therefore said to endow those born under this constellation with sunny natures, creative powers, exuberance, enthusiasm, energy, generosity, courage, and strength—all qualities that signify leadership potential. Conversely, however, the intellectual independence and pride that are further Leonine characteristics can result in egotism, vanity and self-indulgence.

JULY 23

✺ ✻ ✺ ✻ ✺ ✻ ✺ ✻ ✺ ✻ ✺ ✻ ✺ ✻

SUNNY SOCIALITES　　　⊙ ☽

PLANETARY INFLUENCES
Ruling planets: Sun and Moon
First decan: Personal planet is Sun
First cusp: Leo with Cancer
　　tendencies

VIRTUES
Likable, fun-loving, helpful

VICES
Authoritarian, willful, stubborn

CAREERS
Wedding planner, politician, actor

SKILLS & APTITUDES
Willingness to help others, strong
moral sense, team player

FAMOUS BIRTHS
Woody Harrelson (1961)
Slash (1965)
Alison Krauss (1971)
Daniel Radcliffe (1989)

COMPATIBLE WITH
April 21–25, June 18–19

....
....
....

Along with their sense of fun and enjoyment of the good things in life, the determinedly optimistic and cheerful face that July 23 people typically present to the world draws others to them and, indeed, they derive great stimulation from social interaction, being inherently curious about other people. These are not passive bystanders, however, for they prefer to be in the midst of their professional and social circles, contributing their strongly held opinions and exerting their influence over those around them. For despite their easy-going manner, those born on this day are often propelled by a strong desire to help others progress—be it professionally, materially or spiritually—and are prepared to devote their considerable energies to this cause. Inherently traditionalist, their intellectual beliefs and moral values will usually have been instilled in them in childhood and, once formed, will be adhered to with remarkable tenacity. Their strength of conviction, vigor and orientation toward others augurs especially well for their success as military or political leaders, but may also be effectively expressed within the varied realms encompassed by the arts.

Despite their being generous and loyal friends and relatives, who place great value upon the strong bonds of affection and support that characterize their relationships with their nearest and dearest, these people's strong wills and natural gregariousness may preclude them from forming close one-on-one relationships. They may also approach others with a sense of apprehension that they might be required to give more than they receive, thus stifling their inclination to become emotionally involved.

JULY 24

LEO

☉ ☽   DEPENDABLE NURTURERS

People born on July 24 are extroverts. Their enthusiastic espousal of the unusual, as well as the strong expression of their beliefs (often designed to attract others' attention) is testimony to that. Yet their personalities cannot be defined so simplistically, for underlying the self-confident veneer they typically adopt is a more reflective and sensitive core that enables them intuitively to absorb the finer details of a situation, or the intangible emotions transmitted by others. When these two sides to their characters exist in harmony, the resultant combination makes July 24 individuals formidably effective instruments of progress, who typically support their energetic quest for recognition with remarkable perspicacity, and often even empathy for those whose worth society generally discounts. When their protective instincts are aroused, those born on this day will bravely champion the cause of the downtrodden or abused, but in less extreme circumstances their ambitions are usually concerned with their personal desires: for fame, financial rewards and material comforts.

Thus, although July 24 people may pursue humanitarian careers, they may equally be found assiduously furthering their own interests as commercial entrepreneurs. Their talents suit them to a variety of professions, with the proviso that they must be allowed either to assume a leadership role, or else act as independent agents—as artists, for instance—if they are to flourish. Inevitably, their strong wills arouse similarly strong responses in others, but even when negative they will usually accept constructive criticism with grace. And, when assured of the love of those closest to them, they reciprocate such support with great generosity, loyalty and affection.

PLANETARY INFLUENCES
Ruling planets: Sun and Moon
First decan: Personal planet is Sun
First cusp: Leo with Cancer
tendencies

VIRTUES
Energetic, empathetic, sensitive

VICES
Argumentative, uncompromising, bull-headed

CAREERS
Entrepreneur, business consultant, company manager

SKILLS & APTITUDES
Champion of others, motivational skills, intuition

FAMOUS BIRTHS
Alexandre Dumas (1802)
Amelia Earhart (1898)
Barry Bonds (1964)
Anna Paquin (1982)
Elisabeth Moss (1982)

COMPATIBLE WITH
April 21–25, June 19–20

JULY 25

PURPOSEFUL DREAMERS ☉ ☽

Those born on this day are motivated by the desire to realize their remarkably progressive visions, ambitions which may be dismissed by others—rightly or wrongly—as being unfeasible fantasies, but from which July 25 individuals will rarely be dissuaded. Indeed, these people are typically defined by their driving determination to effect their dreams, and in the promotion of their convictions they draw upon their prodigious physical and intellectual vigor and clarity of purpose, as well as their capacity for brave persistence in the face of dissent. Many are motivated by purely personal aims—professional recognition, or the accumulation of monetary wealth—but such is their sensitivity toward others (even when working toward their self-aggrandizement) that their actions are conditioned by a strongly ethical code of conduct which prohibits them from making progress by taking unfair advantage of others. Some may make a humanitarian or ideological cause their mission; either way, they support their professional activities with both highly developed technical and organizational skills and a more intangible talent for inspiring and motivating others with the infectious nature of their dynamic enthusiasm.

Because they are often disappointed by the criticism of their detractors, July 25 people place enormous value on the support of those who believe in them, and they demonstrate their gratitude to those who profess unquestioning confidence in their ability to achieve their aims by rewarding them with their fierce and unwavering affection and devotion. They should, however, beware of accepting false praise: it may well bolster their confidence, temporarily, but will ultimately prove unhelpful.

JULY 26

LEO

❋ ❋ ❋ ❋ ❋ ❋ ❋ ❋ ❋ ❋ ❋ ❋ ❋

☉　　　ENERGETIC PRAGMATISTS

July 26 people have the potential to blaze a fiery trail through life, for their strong will-power, unusual independence of thought and action and predilection for idiosyncratic expressions of individuality mark them out as commanding and influential personalities. The success of those born on this day is largely determined by the responses that they arouse in others, who they will use to evaluate the effectiveness of their often radical theories through the responses that they elicit by their declarations. They may thus attract admiration or ridicule in equal measure, but since in many respects the primary motivating factor behind their actions is to draw attention to themselves, they typically accept the love or loathing that they provoke with equanimity, knowing that they have accomplished their aim of publicizing themselves or their beliefs. Natural performers, July 26 people are especially suited to careers in the arts, or else in such creative commercial professions as the media or advertising.

The energetic and extroverted face that these individuals present to the world often masks their deeper, more introspective side that enables them to plot a clearly delineated course through life, which they then follow with remarkable fixity of purpose and tenacity. Their professional and private personae may be so different as to seem schizophrenic—especially if they are women—for when out of the public spotlight they guard their privacy jealously and ground themselves in a closely knit circle of friends and family members, of whom they are fiercely protective and on whom they lavish enormous affection.

PLANETARY INFLUENCES
Ruling planet: Sun
First decan: Personal planet is Sun

VIRTUES
Perceptive, strategic, responsible

VICES
Confrontational, provocative, bossy

CAREERS
Radio host, actor, sports commentator

SKILLS & APTITUDES
Strongly influential, imagination, self-motivation

FAMOUS BIRTHS
George Bernard Shaw (1856)
Carl Jung (1875)
Mick Jagger (1943)
Sandra Bullock (1965)

COMPATIBLE WITH
April 21–25, June 21

JULY 27

✺ ✺ ✺ ✺ ✺ ✺ ✺ ✺ ✺ ✺ ✺ ✺ ✺

ZEALOUS GO–GETTERS ☉

PLANETARY INFLUENCES
Ruling planet: Sun
First decan: Personal planet is Sun

VIRTUES
Positive, progressive, energetic

VICES
Controlling, overprotective,
domineering

CAREERS
Analyst, CEO, marketing executive

SKILLS & APTITUDES
Leadership skills, enthusiasm,
determination

FAMOUS BIRTHS
Norman Lear (1922)
Bobbie Gentry (1944)
Peggy Fleming (1948)
Alex Rodriguez (1975)

COMPATIBLE WITH
April 17, April 26–30

Those born on this day are blessed with prodigious energy, passion and commitment, as well as highly developed practical and organizational skills—a formidably effective combination of characteristics that July 27 people utilize to the full. These are dynamic individuals who rarely do things by halves, throwing themselves into the active pursuit of their professional and private visions with single-minded determination and dedication, fueled by the desire to make tangible progress. Although their choice of career clearly depends upon their individual preferences, most will thrive in any profession in which they can work directly toward the achievement of their goals, supervising a well-ordered team and implementing their soundly considered promotional strategies in the process. Such inclinations and talents augur particularly well for their success as corporate players, but their natural flamboyance and creativity, adventurousness and vigor furthermore equip these individuals with outstanding artistic potential—and especially so if they were also born in the Chinese year of the dragon.

Within the domestic sphere, those born on July 27 will usually assume the role of the familial linch pin around whom others revolve. Typically extraordinarily affectionate toward their nearest and dearest, they do their utmost to safeguard the well-being and happiness of those closest to them—particularly their children—while at the same time injecting an enlivening sense of fun into their relationships. It is important, however, that they should judiciously moderate their desire to exert their benevolent influence over those to whom they are most strongly attached, and allow them to make, and thus learn from, their own mistakes.

JULY 28

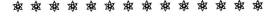

☉ COMPETITIVE CHALLENGE–SEEKERS

The personalities of July 28 people are defined by their competitiveness, a burning compulsion that may be manifested as either a personal or a professional ambition and that instills in them the urge to "win" at all costs. This dominating characteristic can be the result of a variety of causes, including these people's unwavering self-belief and concomitant wish to convince others of the veracity of their convictions. They also relish testing themselves against demanding challenges and like to enjoy the material rewards of success, including basking in the recognition and acclaim of others. And, when working toward their goal, those born on this day draw upon their considerable resources and talents, including their enormous physical and intellectual energy, their ability to formulate a formidable organizational and technical framework to support their driving quest, and, most significantly, their determined refusal to be deflected from their aims or to concede defeat. These people are thus admirably equipped for professions in which confrontational tactics play an important part, such as politics, the military and commercial enterprises, and also the sporting and artistic spheres.

Many July 28 people believe that the admiration their achievements arouse will be sufficient to provide the affection they crave from other people. However, this will rarely be the case, for their single-minded and combative approach is more likely to alienate those whom they are seeking to impress, who may perceive them as being selfishly lacking in consideration for the sensibilities of others. Thus, although they are genuinely emotionally attached to their nearest and dearest, they should realize that they may be regarded more ambivalently by the objects of their affection.

PLANETARY INFLUENCES
Ruling planet: Sun
First decan: Personal planet is Sun

VIRTUES
Multitalented, competitive, driven

VICES
Attention-seeking, combative, temperamental

CAREERS
Professional athlete, soldier, politician

SKILLS & APTITUDES
Dedication to career, determination, energy

FAMOUS BIRTHS
Beatrix Potter (1866)
Marcel Duchamp (1887)
Jacqueline Kennedy Onassis (1929)
Alexis Arquette (1969)

COMPATIBLE WITH
April 17–18, April 26–30

JULY 29

VIGILANT LEADERS ⊙

PLANETARY INFLUENCES
Ruling planet: Sun
First decan: Personal planet is Sun

VIRTUES
Protective, influential, tireless

VICES
Bossy, controlling, unfeeling

CAREERS
Social campaigner, government officer, events organizer

SKILLS & APTITUDES
Highly organized, focused on community, reliable

FAMOUS BIRTHS
George Bradshaw (1801)
Wil Wheaton (1972)
Tim Gunn (1953)
Martina McBride (1966)

COMPATIBLE WITH
April 18–19, April 26–30

In common with the majority of their leonine fellows, those born on July 29 are positive and energetic types, whose natural inclination is toward controlling the actions of those around them, a predilection that is redoubled if they were also born in the Chinese year of the dragon. Yet unlike many others born under the sign of Leo, their ambitions are directed less toward achieving personal success and acclaim (although they are not averse to receiving the applause of others) than toward furthering the interests of the social group with which they primarily identify—for example, their family, their local community, their country or even humanity as a whole. They may thus typically be found working as politicians or social campaigners—or even as athletes or artists—indeed, in any profession in which there is an inherent sense of team spirit. Within such environments those born on this day typically gravitate toward leadership positions, others deferring to their strong wills, clear-cut goals, and organizational talents, as well as to their gifts of motivation and inspiration.

Their willingness to protect and assume responsibility for those around them—and this is especially true if they are males—as well as the generosity and loyalty that these leonine characters display toward the members of their "pride," is generally reciprocated by the objects of their concern. Although their personal liaisons are similarly characterized by mutually profound feelings of affection, the overridingly communal orientation of July 29 people may leave them with little time to spare for their nearest and dearest—or indeed, for the pursuit of any independent individual interests.

JULY 30

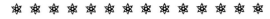

LEO

☉   PROSPEROUS ACHIEVERS

Those born on July 30 are firmly rooted in the physical world, their ambitions being primarily concerned with gaining personal status and monetary resources, or with making tangible progress of any kind, and their approach is typically of the extremely energetic variety. These individuals are blessed with the ability to think in a logical, linear fashion, and because they have a heightened sense of awareness of their surroundings, or of the inherent components of a proposal under consideration, they have the capacity to assess a situation astutely and devise a comprehensive strategy in response. They will then implement their plan with remarkable fixity of purpose and tenacity, utilizing their considerable organizational skills and gift for directing others in the process. Within their personal lives, too, they typically conduct their relationships with steadfast equanimity, displaying a profound concern for the physical and emotional well-being of their friends and family.

Their practical and interpersonal talents, when also combined with their strong goal orientation, equip July 30 people especially well for potentially glittering corporate careers in the financial and commercial realm, as well as for fame and acclaim in the sporting arena. Their highly developed sensuality also augurs well for their success as artists—painters, musicians, writers or actors, for example—although the majority of those born on this day will instead settle for surrounding themselves with objects of beauty (which, given their financial acumen, may often also represent lucrative investments).

PLANETARY INFLUENCES
Ruling planet: Sun
First decan: Personal planet is Sun

VIRTUES
Motivated, grounded, practical

VICES
Narrow-minded, attention-seeking, domineering

CAREERS
Accountant, corporate executive, media producer

SKILLS & APTITUDES
Ambitious nature, perceptiveness, attention to detail

FAMOUS BIRTHS
Emily Brontë (1818)
Henry Ford (1863)
Arnold Schwarzenegger (1947)
Delta Burke (1956)

COMPATIBLE WITH
April 19–20, April 26–30

JULY 31

✱ ✱ ✱ ✱ ✱ ✱ ✱ ✱ ✱ ✱ ✱ ✱ ✱ ✱

INQUISITIVE SCHOLARS ☉

PLANETARY INFLUENCES
Ruling planet: Sun
First decan: Personal planet is Sun

VIRTUES
Energetic, determined, focused

VICES
Undisciplined, workaholic, blinkered

CAREERS
Researcher, scientist, journalist

SKILLS & APTITUDES
Willingness to explore new ideas, dedication to work, creative thinking

FAMOUS BIRTHS
Milton Friedman (1912)
Wesley Snipes (1962)
J.K. Rowling (1965)
Dean Cain (1966)

COMPATIBLE WITH
April 26–30

The quest for discovery is extremely strong in many July 31 people. Although they are primarily fueled by an urge to further their own learning and understanding, any progress made by these individuals will usually also contribute significantly to the store of human knowledge since the topics that especially interest them are typically global in their scope—human psychology, for example, abstract political or economic theories, or even the as yet unrevealed secrets of the cosmos. Indeed, these are not the types to isolate themselves in the ivory towers of academia—they much prefer active modes of investigation, such as directing the activities of teams of researchers, and, once they have achieved a breakthrough, will rush to share their triumphs with the wider world (often with as much accompanying razzmatazz as possible). This highly developed concern for exploring every facet of human existence, combined with their extremely logical train of thought and their tenacity, suits those born on this day for investigative careers of all types—as academic researchers, scientists or journalists, for instance—but also as teachers, for they possess a powerful desire to utilize their findings to help others.

Despite the deep devotion and magnanimous tolerance that characterizes the nature of July 31 people's affection for those closest to them, they may not always enjoy the stable and magnanimous personal lives that they crave. Part of the problem may result from their tendency to throw themselves whole-heartedly into their work, which—despite their prodigious physical vigor—may leave them with little time to spare for their friends and families.

AUGUST 1

LEO

☉ ♃   PARADOXICAL PHILOSOPHERS

Those born on this day are self-sufficient types who present something of a paradox—even to their nearest and dearest. For on the one hand they can be empathetic toward the disadvantaged (responding to their natural sense of justice), yet on the other they will reserve their own right to privacy and autonomy. Their approach to life is underlined with two main personal qualities: their imaginative powers, which enable them to identify with others and be stimulated by their company; and their propensity to think logically. Ultimately it is the realm of abstract concepts—particularly artistic theories and expression—that most strongly interests them, and their frequent withdrawal into solitude is often necessitated by their predilection for intellectual exploration. Such is the value that they place on independence of thought and action that they are generally unsuited to working as cogs in the corporate wheel (unless they are themselves driving the mechanism). They are inherently better equipped for self-employment or for working in those professional areas where their research can be transformed into products—for example as scientists or writers.

Although August 1 people are not amenable to others' regulations (and even less so if they were born in the Chinese year of the dragon), they are disciplined when it comes to their own affairs—both personal and private—a tendency that results more from their desire to keep their lives running smoothly and efficiently than from any wish to exert control over others. Thus, despite the deep affection and magnanimous tolerance they display toward those closest to them, they will often conduct their relationships within strict boundaries, the limits of which they set for themselves.

PLANETARY INFLUENCES
Ruling planet: Sun
Second decan: Personal planet is Jupiter

VIRTUES
Imaginative, progressive, organized

VICES
Isolated, stubborn, disconnected

CAREERS
Writer, scientist, business owner

SKILLS & APTITUDES
Self-sufficiency, openness to new ideas, discipline

FAMOUS BIRTHS
Francis Scott Key (1779)
Herman Melville (1819)
Geoffrey Holder (1930)
Yves St. Laurent (1936)

COMPATIBLE WITH
May 1–5

AUGUST 2

✵ ✵ ✵ ✵ ✵ ✵ ✵ ✵ ✵ ✵ ✵ ✵ ✵ ✵

CANDID REALISTS ☉ ♃

PLANETARY INFLUENCES
Ruling planet: Sun
Second decan: Personal planet is Jupiter

VIRTUES
Intellectual, creative, loyal

VICES
Perfectionist, obsessive, pushy

CAREERS
Writer, entrepreneur, media or advertising executive

SKILLS & APTITUDES
Honesty, decision-making, capacity for hard work

FAMOUS BIRTHS
Carroll O'Connor (1924)
James Baldwin (1924)
Peter O'Toole (1932)
Wes Craven (1939)
Rose Tremain (1943)

COMPATIBLE WITH
January 17–19, May 1–5

The ambitions that motivate August 2 people are generally of the briskly progressive rather than the more nebulously idealistic type. These are straightforward people and their incisive clarity of vision makes it easy for them to identify their goals and then, aided by their directly logical approach and exceptional organizational abilities, work single-mindedly toward their realization. The nature of the aims that fire their enormous energy and determination inevitably vary according to their specific personal interests, but their great imaginative powers and sensuality typically propel them toward such artistic careers as acting, writing, painting or composing. Their intellectual curiosity furthermore promises potential success as scientists or even inventors. In all their professional endeavors they are rarely afraid to take a brave lone stand when convinced of the correctness of their convictions, and their self-knowledge and confidence is such that they will often prove their detractors wrong. Indeed, many August 2 people will eventually set up their own businesses rather than conform to a corporate ethos.

While their professional relationships are frequently characterized by confrontation—the result of a conflict between their driving urge to promote their ideas and the demurral of their colleagues or competitors—their personal liaisons are generally far more harmonious. August 2 people cherish the strongly supportive bonds they enjoy with their kith and kin, to whom they manifest their capacity for unwavering loyalty. Fiercely protective of those closest to them, they not only desire the physical and material well-being of their loved ones—especially their children if they are parents—but also their happiness.

AUGUST 3

✳ ✳ ✳ ✳ ✳ ✳ ✳ ✳ ✳ ✳ ✳ ✳ ✳

☉ ♃　　　　　　SPIRITED INNOVATORS

Those born on August 3 are energetic people, driven by their need for excitement, an overriding urge that can stem from many underlying psychological causes, including their low boredom thresholds, the stimulation they gain from pitting their talents against testing challenges, or even their yearning to receive the acclaim of others by succeeding in their ventures. This adventurous compulsion may inevitably lead them to behave impulsively, to seize an alluring opportunity before it vanishes into the past; but such is their ability to realistically assess the limits of their own potential that they will rarely embark upon a project that is utterly unfeasible (although it may often appear so to onlookers). And if they should fail, they will typically learn from their experience before moving on to address the next challenge that presents itself. Their personal bravery, vigor, self-discipline and single-minded determination to achieve their ambitions augurs especially well for their success in competitive situations, perhaps as business entrepreneurs, or wherever courage is essential, particularly in the emergency services. Whatever career they choose, however, it is vital that their freedom of action and thought remain largely unrestricted.

Although their professional activities may unavoidably generate confrontation and rivalry—particularly if they are men—in common with most of those born under the sign of Leo, their personal relationships are defined by the strong affection, loyalty and protectiveness they direct toward those closest to them. In all their interpersonal liaisons, however, they should beware of allowing their susceptibility to praise and flattery to lead to excessively egotistical feelings, which may isolate them from both others and reality.

PLANETARY INFLUENCES
Ruling planet: Sun
Second decan: Personal planet is Jupiter

VIRTUES
Focused, pioneering, courageous

VICES
Sensation-seeking, restless dissatisfied

CAREERS
Emergency-services worker, motivational speaker, freelance coach

SKILLS & APTITUDES
Self-belief, bold approach, drive

FAMOUS BIRTHS
Tony Bennett (1926)
Terry Wogan (1926)
Martin Sheen (1940)
Tom Brady (1977)

COMPATIBLE WITH
January 17–19, May 1–5

AUGUST 4

REBELLIOUS FREE-THINKERS ☉ ♃

PLANETARY INFLUENCES
Ruling planet: Sun
Second decan: Personal planet is Jupiter

VIRTUES
Intelligent, dynamic, persuasive

VICES
Controlling, domineering, unforgiving

CAREERS
Campaigner, politician, teacher

SKILLS & APTITUDES
Positive attitude, inspirational qualities, determination

FAMOUS BIRTHS
Percy Bysshe Shelley (1792)
Louis Armstrong (1901)
Billy Bob Thornton (1955)
Barack Obama (1961)
Meghan Markle (1981)

COMPATIBLE WITH
January 17–19, May 1–5

Those born on this day are strong-willed characters whose autonomy of thought and action is of the utmost importance to them. While they may seek to influence others, they claim the right of independence for themselves. Their need for freedom is as much the product of their constant quest for knowledge as of their incisive intellects, which lead them to gather as much information as possible before deciding upon a goal. But while their sense of justice may lead them to champion the disadvantaged as a whole—thus equipping them as campaigners or politicians—they may disregard the right of others to profess conflicting opinions, instead employing confrontational techniques in their quest to implement what they regard as being unquestionably the correct way forward. This propensity may occasionally lead them to behave somewhat perversely, rebelling against authority figures simply because of their strong antipathy for being restrained, as well as of their more general dislike of complacency and the unthinking acceptance of the status quo. They are probably most suited for artistic, educational or sporting careers, in which their inclinations and talents can best be used to inspire others.

So averse are August 4 people to submitting to the control of others that—even from childhood—they may reject entirely well-meaning attempts to assist them, fearing that more sinister, dominating motives lurk behind the helping hand, a propensity that can lead them to become rather isolated figures. When they channel their energies positively, they typically enliven their personal relationships greatly; those closest to them should be careful, however, never to restrain, or to appear to challenge, these people's independence.

AUGUST 5

LEO

✺ ✺ ✺ ✺ ✺ ✺ ✺ ✺ ✺ ✺ ✺ ✺ ✺ ✺

☉ ♃ CALCULATING DECISION-MAKERS

The focused approach and determination mani-fested by those born on this day instills in others a sense of awe, for once they have resolved upon their chosen course of action they will pursue it until their goal has been achieved with almost superhuman tenac-ity, compelled by their resolute sense of purpose. August 5 people rarely simply accept conventional truths, pre-ferring instead to independently investigate a subject thoroughly before evaluating the data they have col-lected and then making an informed decision as to how best to proceed. When engaged in assessment exercises they utilize their talent for clear-sighted analysis and their remarkable powers of perception, while the nature of their decision-making is characterized by their reli-ance on logical thought processes. Once satisfied with the soundness of their convictions, they promote their progressive aims and opinions by means of direct and energetic action. Inevitably, their fixity of purpose often arouses the antagonism of others, but these people are energized rather than discouraged by opposition and confrontation, which spurs them on still farther.

August 5 people have the potential to achieve suc-cess in any sphere that holds their interest, but their need to act autonomously suits them especially well for such artistic careers as movie-making or musician-ship, as well as to become scientific or social innovators. Their impressive self-discipline masks strong emotions which, if they are crossed in any way, may break free and explode in dramatic displays of temper. And, although their feelings of affection, generosity and protectiveness for those closest to them are similarly profound, the combination of their controlling and volatile tendencies may have an unsettling effect on those around them.

PLANETARY INFLUENCES
Ruling planet: Sun
Second decan: Personal planet is Jupiter

VIRTUES
Determined, logical, brave

VICES
Impatient, easily frustrated, short-tempered

CAREERS
Scientist, journalist, engineer

SKILLS & APTITUDES
Self-discipline, doggedness, generosity

FAMOUS BIRTHS
Guy de Maupassant (1850)
Neil Armstrong (1930)
Mark Strong (1963)
James Gunn (1970)

COMPATIBLE WITH
May 1–5

AUGUST 6

✳ ✳ ✳ ✳ ✳ ✳ ✳ ✳ ✳ ✳ ✳ ✳ ✳ ✳

DELIGHTFUL MORALISTS ☉ ♃

Blessed with great charm, the strong wills and convictions that occasionally emerge from behind the normally mild-mannered façade of those born on this day often surprise those who do not know them well. Yet despite their pragmatic recognition of the need to keep others on side, it is precisely these beliefs—arrived at after rigorous thought—that inform their actions and ambitions, in effect providing them with a blueprint to which they conduct their lives accordingly. And although their visions may also encompass short-term or minor goals, these individuals are generally concerned with the wider picture (especially if they were also born in the Chinese year of the dragon), with making global social, scientific or political improvements, for example, or with pushing the bounds of human endeavor forward as artists or athletes. Provided that they are allowed to retain decision-making powers and the fundamental autonomy that is so vital to them, their perceptive intellects, propensity for taking direct action and unwavering determination augurs well for their success in whatever professional field they choose to apply their considerable energies.

In their personal lives, too, August 6 individuals are often guided by their moral values, which instill in them an appreciation of the importance of secure bonds of friendship and kinship. Yet their overriding commitment to their work, when combined with their strong sense of responsibility for those closest to them, may cause those born on this day to overstretch themselves by attempting to devote equal time to their professional and private concerns. With their well-developed intellectual powers of perception and organization, they are also willing to compromise when necessary.

AUGUST 7

✻ ✻ ✻ ✻ ✻ ✻ ✻ ✻ ✻ ✻ ✻ ✻ ✻ ✻ ✻

☉ ♃   TRANSCENDENTAL PIONEERS

Those born on this day combine their curiosity with their urge to help others—whether individuals, or humanity as a whole. Innately predisposed toward investigating all data objectively before drawing their conclusions, these people are not content with accepting those conventional beliefs and societal norms that go unquestioned by less independently minded types, until they have satisfied themselves as to their veracity. This deep-rooted tendency to explore and test, on the one hand, may make August 7 people uncomfortable to work or live with, but on the other may yield startlingly innovative results, for once they have decided upon a course of action or a set of convictions they will promote it with all of the considerable personal resources available to them, including their intellectual and physical vigor, their highly developed practical skills and their obstinate tenacity. And although the frequently unconventional nature of their opinions may inevitably arouse antagonism in others, they possess the courage to press forward despite the personal consequences.

Yet although these individuals respond to challenge—and are stimulated by intellectual debate—their ultimate intention is not to act as devil's advocate simply for the sake of disrupting the status quo, but rather to embark on a personal journey of discovery. Their inclinations and talents suit them especially to careers in which they can express themselves freely, unrestricted by others. Because they are usually extrovert characters, they are often at the center of attention. Their sense of social responsibility is reflected in the protectiveness and deep affection that they offer their loved ones, while their unconventionality provides an invigorating element to their relationships.

PLANETARY INFLUENCES
Ruling planet: Sun
Second decan: Personal planet is Jupiter

VIRTUES
Perceptive, radical, determined

VICES
Confrontational, provocative, spiky

CAREERS
Actor, motivational speaker, drama teacher

SKILLS & APTITUDES
Open to challenges, communication skills, moral sense

FAMOUS BIRTHS
B.J. Thomas (1960)
David Duchovny (1960)
Michael Shannon (1974)
Charlize Theron (1975)

COMPATIBLE WITH
May 6–11

LEO

AUGUST 8

✳ ✳ ✳ ✳ ✳ ✳ ✳ ✳ ✳ ✳ ✳ ✳ ✳

RESTLESS REVOLUTIONARIES   ☉ ♃

PLANETARY INFLUENCES
Ruling planet: Sun
Second decan: Personal planet is
   Jupiter

VIRTUES
Strong-willed, vigorous, courageous

VICES
Overconfident, combative, obstinate

CAREERS
Political lobbyist, public speaker,
charity campaigner

SKILLS & APTITUDES
Effective leadership, technical skills,
capacity for experimentation

FAMOUS BIRTHS
Dustin Hoffman (1937)
David "The Edge" Howell
  Williams (1961)
J.C. Chasez (1976)
Drew Lachey (1976)

COMPATIBLE WITH
May 6–11

There are two especially pronounced sides to the characters of those born on this day: their desire for stimulation, which may take the form of intellectual exploration or of testing themselves against a variety of challenges; and their clarity of purpose, a quality which may be manifested in their pursuit of specifically goal-oriented projects or as a set of firmly defined intellectual or ethical values. And although these dual propensities might initially seem to be incompatible, they are in fact effectively reconciled within August 8 people's personalities, the latter providing a stable framework within which the former may be given its free expression. Thus, for example, if they pursue artistic or sporting careers (and these curious, imaginative and energetic people have a natural affinity for both), their experimental and innovative activities will typically be contained within the technical parameters of their chosen field. Similarly, whether or not they become political activists, their views and activities will be typically governed by a strong ethical code of whose veracity they will seek to convince others, regardless of the confrontation they may thereby engender.

Although their relish of competition and occasional combativeness may be directed toward others, these individuals are not really interested in scoring victories solely for the sake of winning, but rather are motivated by their urge to bring about progress or protect that which they hold dear. Indeed, they are devoted to their friends and family members, desiring above all to ensure their physical and emotional well-being, but also contributing their capacity for adding love and humor to their personal liaisons.

AUGUST 9

LEO

☉ ♃　　　RESPECTED ENCOURAGERS

The combination of their capacity for keenly incisive thought and strong orientation toward their fellow beings endows those born on this day with a fierce desire to help others to identify and then follow an optimum course through life. Blessed with powerfully perceptive skills, as well as the ability to marshal the information that they amass into a structured and constructive strategy for achieving progress, they have an apparently effortless talent both for analysis and for transforming the results of their researches into clear and direct plans of action. Those around them solicit their carefully considered advice, especially since they have a gift for communicating their genuine concern for others in an optimistic, kindly and encouraging manner. Natural leaders, these individuals are therefore well suited to professions in which they can devote themselves to guiding and benefiting others; careers as teachers, counselors or human resources specialists— are particularly well starred.

The personal relationships of those born on this day are similarly characterized by their profoundly protective attitude to those closest to them—especially their children, if they are parents. Desiring their emotional happiness as well as their material well-being, these individuals' typical approach (and one that is even more pronounced if they are women) is to gently steer their loved ones into what they perceive as being the best direction. Although this benevolent exertion of control is entirely unselfish, they should anticipate potential rebellion on the part of the subjects of their concern, who may resent such attempts to direct their actions.

PLANETARY INFLUENCES
Ruling planet: Sun
Second decan: Personal planet is Jupiter

VIRTUES
Positive, upbeat, inspirational

VICES
Bossy, interfering, domineering

CAREERS
Social worker, teacher, human-resources executive

SKILLS & APTITUDES
Interest in people, leadership ability, self-belief

FAMOUS BIRTHS
Philip Larkin (1922)
Sam Elliott (1944)
Whitney Houston (1963)
Anna Kendrick (1985)

COMPATIBLE WITH
May 6–11

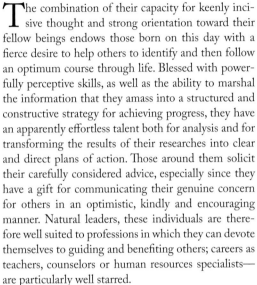

AUGUST 10

✻ ✻ ✻ ✻ ✻ ✻ ✻ ✻ ✻ ✻ ✻ ✻ ✻ ✻

POWERFUL COMMUNICATORS ☉ ♃

PLANETARY INFLUENCES
Ruling planet: Sun
Second decan: Personal planet is Jupiter

VIRTUES
Influential, articulate, self-assured

VICES
Intractable, doctrinaire, rigid

CAREERS
Social campaigner, fundraiser, speechwriter

SKILLS & APTITUDES
Strength of purpose, communication skills, ability to inspire

FAMOUS BIRTHS
Jimmy Dean (1928)
Betsey Johnson (1942)
Rosanna Arquette (1959)
Antonio Banderas (1960)

COMPATIBLE WITH
May 6–11

Possessed of firm opinions and strongly oriented toward others, August 10 individuals seek to communicate their ideas and beliefs to as wide an audience as possible by means of direct interpersonal action. It is their ability to think incisively and logically (especially if they are men), as well as their highly developed intellectual perspicacity, that leads them to form clear-cut and powerful views, which are usually of a positive and progressive nature and are intended to bring benefit to others—either in material or social terms, or in the less tangible emotional arena. And, once those born on this day have convinced themselves of the veracity of their beliefs, they typically seek to influence others accordingly. Indeed, these individuals are hard to ignore: possessed of remarkable self-assurance and a pronounced independent streak, they are unafraid of making a determined stand when promoting their visions—the main thing, as far as they are concerned, is that they should make their voices heard and thereby draw others' attention to what they have to say.

The specific issues that may move August 10 people vary according to the individual, but their natural sense of justice and desire to improve the lives of others have clear parallels in the realm of political or social campaigning. Their considerable creativity, when combined with their great communication skills, also augurs well for careers as writers, artists or actors. Their inherent optimism and infectious enthusiasm furthermore gives them the capacity to inspire others, as well as making them valued friends and relations. They should remember to make the time for periods of honest introspection, to objectively examine their motives and work consciously toward greater tolerance and cooperation.

AUGUST 11

✸ ✸ ✸ ✸ ✸ ✸ ✸ ✸ ✸ ✸ ✸ ✸ ✸ ✸

☉ ♂　　TIRELESS TRUTH-SEEKERS

Those born on August 11 have a desire to uncover essential truths and then communicate them to others, to enable humanity to progress—as individuals or as a whole. This overriding propensity usually takes the form of either long-term research into abstract, theoretical concepts, or the investigation of more immediate concerns. Thus on the one hand they may make careers within such academic disciplines as science or philosophy, for example, or on the other be found working as law-enforcement agents, journalists or critics. To whatever profession these tenacious individuals devote their energies, however, they typically contribute their talents of clear-sighted observation, their capacity for organized and logical thought, and their resourcefulness, courage and determination. And these last qualities are of particular importance, since their propensity to debunk conventional beliefs and expose hypocrisy will inevitably lead them into confrontation with those wishing to maintain the status quo.

Their marked autonomy suits these people best for working independently—at least while carrying out the research-based aspects of their work—although they recognize the importance of recruiting supporters when seeking to broadcast their conclusions, and employ their persuasive skills in doing so. Yet despite their general concern for others, their personal lives may be beset with difficulty, for their predilection for analyzing the motivations of others, and their tendency to criticize, can make even their nearest and dearest wary of incurring their censure. It is important that they moderate their propensity for brutal honesty, especially with their nearest and dearest, and develop greater tolerance of others' personal foibles and imperfections.

PLANETARY INFLUENCES
Ruling planet: Sun
Third decan: Personal planet is Mars

VIRTUES
Persistent, bold, incisive

VICES
Hurtful, tactless, bullying

CAREERS
Police officer, investigative journalist, forensic scientist

SKILLS & APTITUDES
Self-motivation, resilience, independence of mind

FAMOUS BIRTHS
Steve Wozniak (1950)
Hulk Hogan (1953)
Viola Davis (1965)
Chris Hemsworth (1983)

COMPATIBLE WITH
May 12–16

AUGUST 12

✻ ✻ ✻ ✻ ✻ ✻ ✻ ✻ ✻ ✻ ✻ ✻ ✻ ✻

SAGE COUNSELORS

☉ ♂

PLANETARY INFLUENCES
Ruling planet: Sun
Third decan: Personal planet is Mars

VIRTUES
Sensible, well-meaning, responsible

VICES
Biased, dogmatic, authoritarian

CAREERS
Laboratory technician, machinery operator, researcher

SKILLS & APTITUDES
Confidence, thoroughness, logical reasoning

FAMOUS BIRTHS
Buck Owens (1929)
Porter Wagoner (1930)
William Goldman (1931)
Casey Affleck (1975)

COMPATIBLE WITH
May 12–16

Like Janus, the Roman deity of doorways, those born on August 12 tend to simultaneously look forward and backward. Although their primary urge is to make progress by leading others, before striking out in a new direction they will examine and assess existing knowledge and conventions, retaining those concepts they regard as being valid and discarding those they consider to be false or inappropriate. In many respects they resemble historians or scientists (and some may devote their careers to these disciplines) in that they amass as much relevant information as possible, subject it to logical evaluation, and then reach their conclusions. When promoting their aims they draw deeply upon their reserves of resourcefulness, single-mindedness and tenacity, impressing others with their clarity of purpose. Although they are independently minded, their overriding purpose is to benefit humankind as a whole; their work may involve the smallest of details, but it is upon the wider picture that they are ultimately focused.

The knowledge that they have investigated every aspect of their beliefs endows August 12 people with unshakeable self-certainty, as well as the confidence to attempt to persuade others of the veracity of their views. Despite the potential professional success that such an uncompromising approach promises, however, it may arouse the resentment of the very people whom those born on this day are seeking to influence and guide—especially those closest to them—who may perceive August 12 individuals to be overly arrogant and authoritarian (especially if they were also born in the Chinese year of the ox). Developing greater patience, tolerance and pragmatism with regard to any expression of dissent will help them achieve their aims more effectively.

AUGUST 13

☉ ♂   FLAMBOYANT INQUISITIVES

LEO

Individuals born on this day are unconventional and guided by visions that are so unusual or ambitious—introducing a revolutionary invention or a novel social system, for example—that others may regard them as being fanciful, even ridiculous. Despite the mockery to which their detractors may subject them, August 13 people generally remain faithful to their beliefs. For not only are these of an inspirational variety, but their originators know that their visions have been investigated and tested before being revealed to the wider world. Indeed, the innovative theories advanced by those born on this day will typically be supported by sound evidence, for their imaginations are supplemented by analytical and organizational skills. Fueled by the desire to benefit others, these people are especially drawn to those political, scientific and artistic pursuits which enable them to make a tangible contribution to society.

Despite the courage of their convictions, and their optimism in the face of opposition from others, August 13 people are nevertheless sensitive types who must learn to develop effective self-defensive strategies with which to protect their sensibilities. While preferring to work as leaders of closely knit and highly motivated teams, they will more usually find themselves working in isolation (until the event of their recognition by others). They therefore place enormous value on receiving the unquestioning affection and support of their friends and relations, rewarding the belief of their loved ones with loyalty and generosity. They should always ensure that they do not cause themselves emotional damage by either promoting their aims at any cost in terms of interpersonal relationships or else suppressing the ambitions that are so vitally important to them.

PLANETARY INFLUENCES
Ruling planet: Sun
Third decan: Personal planet is Mars

VIRTUES
Original, practical, innovative

VICES
Critical, disconnected, needy

CAREERS
Science teacher, social campaigner, administrator

SKILLS & APTITUDES
Unconventional thinker, thorough approach, analytical skills

FAMOUS BIRTHS
Annie Oakley (1860)
Alfred Hitchcock (1899)
Lorna Simpson (1960)
Debi Mazar (1964)

COMPATIBLE WITH
May 12–16

AUGUST 14

OBSERVATIONAL COMEDIANS ☉ ♂

PLANETARY INFLUENCES
Ruling planet: Sun
Third decan: Personal planet is Mars

VIRTUES
Incisive, strong-willed, outgoing

VICES
Disconnected, solitary, insensitive

CAREERS
Journalist, documentary maker, drama teacher

SKILLS & APTITUDES
Sense of humor, good judge of character, surety of belief

FAMOUS BIRTHS
Steve Martin (1945)
Danielle Steel (1947)
Magic Johnson (1959)
Halle Berry (1968)

COMPATIBLE WITH
May 12–16

Those born on this day are interested in the workings of society and in the foibles of the human condition: their primary orientation is toward the people around them and the circumstances within which they live their lives. Blessed with clarity of vision and analytical talents, August 14 people have a gift for assessing not only the motivations of others, but also the influences and impulses that govern their behavior. Because they feel compelled to share their findings with as wide a public as possible, and possess a talent for expressing their conclusions in a direct (albeit sometimes brutally honest) fashion that is often made more palatable by the judicious use of humor, their observations are rarely ignored. In voicing their opinions they are generally fueled by the well-meaning intention of helping others to recognize their shortcomings and thereby to progress, although their success depends largely on how accurately they have assessed the receptiveness of their audience and how sensitively they present their views.

The professions to which those born on this day are especially suited are therefore those where they can exert an effective and positive influence by means of their social or political commentary: such literary fields as journalism, or dramatic or cinematic pursuits, for example. Yet ironically it is their very fascination with others' behavioral patterns that may preclude them from forming strong personal relationships, for others—and particularly those closest to them—will inevitably be uncomfortable with such close scrutiny. Although their talent for entertaining with the biting accuracy of their comments may bring short-term acclaim, in the long run it will make others wary of exposing their emotions to them.

AUGUST 15

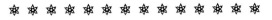

☉ ♂   COMMANDING IDEALISTS

Those born on this day are ambitious individuals, whose desire to realize their visions is the main factor underlying their actions. The nature of the dreams that inspire them varies according to their personal predilections and circumstances; some may yearn to achieve social recognition and material gains, while others may cherish less immediately selfish aims regarding the betterment of society as a whole. Whatever their guiding purpose in life, however, their approach is typically characterized by its extreme directness and refusal to be deflected from following the path of progress. They formulate their far-sighted strategies with the help of their strong talent for logical thought and practical organizational skills, which they put to good use in delegating details to, and orchestrating, others. These extroverted, confident people are above all oriented toward leadership, and will flourish in any profession where they have the freedom to not only implement plans of their own devising, but also take charge of a team.

Within their domestic lives, too, August 15 people assume a commanding role in their quest to ensure the happiness and well-being of their nearest and dearest. And although these pleasure-loving people demonstrate extreme magnanimity and open affection toward their loved ones, they generally expect the members of their pride to toe the line that they, the leonine leaders, have laid down, demanding the same high standards to which they themselves adhere—a tendency that is even more pronounced in women born on this day, or in those who were also born in the Chinese year of the dragon. They should try to develop a greater sense of empathy with others, and recognize that the right to personal autonomy is not their sole preserve.

PLANETARY INFLUENCES
Ruling planet: Sun
Third decan: Personal planet is Mars

VIRTUES
Tenacious, inspirational, influential

VICES
Authoritarian, unfeeling, bossy

CAREERS
Business manager, kindergarten teacher, sales team leader

SKILLS & APTITUDES
Self-confidence, leadership skills, adherence to high standards

FAMOUS BIRTHS
Napoleon Bonaparte (1769)
Julia Child (1912)
Ben Affleck (1972)
Jennifer Lawrence (1990)

COMPATIBLE WITH
May 12–16

AUGUST 16

✳ ✳ ✳ ✳ ✳ ✳ ✳ ✳ ✳ ✳ ✳ ✳ ✳ ✳

LIVELY PERFORMERS ☉ ♂

PLANETARY INFLUENCES
Ruling planet: Sun
Third decan: Personal planet is Mars

VIRTUES
Exuberant, extroverted,
level-headed

VICES
Confrontational, manipulative,
disconnected

CAREERS
Politician, teacher, motivational
speaker

SKILLS & APTITUDES
Ability to inspire, leadership skills,
strong presence

FAMOUS BIRTHS
Charles Bukowski (1920)
Kathie Lee Gifford (1953)
Madonna (1958)
Steve Carrel (1962)

COMPATIBLE WITH
May 12–16

No shrinking violets, August 16 people are driven by the compulsion to turn the spotlight upon themselves. It is sometimes difficult to tell what motivates these dynamic characters more: the urge to share their message or the means by which they draw others' attention to themselves. Certainly the majority of those born on this day are extroverts who bask in acclaim and are content even with a hostile reception—their main priority being to attract notice. Yet behind their often brash and confrontational façades lies a more serious self, an essential core that is often completely contrary to the personal image that they choose to project. In theatrical terms, it is as if these people are simultaneously actor and director, the former interpreting the commands of the latter and presenting them in the most attention-grabbing manner, while following an ambitious game plan with remarkable focus and tenacity. Indeed, some August 16 people will find professional success as performers or producers, although they are well equipped for any field—politics or teaching, for example—in which they can inspire and direct others.

The more profound ambitions of many of those born on this day are geared toward the attainment of happiness rather than material riches. They typically guard their private lives jealously, for this is the one arena in which they feel they can take off their masks and be themselves. Similarly, they value those who love them for what they actually are rather than what they seem to be, and in turn offer their nearest and dearest their fierce affection, protection and loyalty. In the interests of maintaining their emotional equilibrium they should ensure that they take the time to relax, to enjoy the simple pleasures of life, and remain grounded in reality.

AUGUST 17

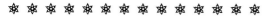

☉ ♂　ADMIRED EXHIBITIONISTS

LEO

Many of those born on this day are larger-than-life personalities, who attract the admiration of others by means of their flamboyance, dynamism and disregard for convention. These are independent types, whose great energy, imagination, determination not to be fettered by others' rules, and capacity for focusing on their goals bestow upon them outstanding potential for blazing their trails through life. They have a strong orientation toward other people and are usually unhappy unless they can test themselves and measure their success by the reactions that their behavior arouses in others. And, because they are the strong-willed professors of firm convictions, the responses that they engender will typically be extreme, either winning them devoted fans or creating implacable enemies. Convinced of the veracity of their views, these people prefer to recruit others to their cause and then control their actions: when their powerful influence fails, they are prepared to adopt confrontational tactics.

Their determination to live life on their own terms means that these people fare best when engaged in careers where they can carve out their own path or make an impact, and many will thus find success in the public eye, undaunted by pressure. Although they are protective and generous people, their personal relationships may occasionally be explosive: when, for example, loved ones fail to fall in with their wishes, or when their innate authoritarianism drives others (especially their children, if they are parents) to rebel. If they are to achieve success and enjoy fulfilling relationships, it is important that August 17 people should make the effort to listen to the opinions of others—especially if these are in conflict with their own firm views.

PLANETARY INFLUENCES
Ruling planet: Sun
Third decan: Personal planet is Mars

VIRTUES
Generous, confident, persuasive

VICES
Bull-headed, controlling, short-tempered

CAREERS
Police officer, political activist, office manager

SKILLS & APTITUDES
Forcefulness, influence, strength of purpose

FAMOUS BIRTHS
Davy Crockett (1786)
Mae West (1892)
Robert De Niro (1943)
Donnie Wahlberg (1969)

COMPATIBLE WITH
May 17–20

AUGUST 18

GENTLE TEACHERS ☉ ♂

PLANETARY INFLUENCES
Ruling planet: Sun
Third decan: Personal planet is Mars

VIRTUES
Far-sighted, progressive, benevolent

VICES
Needy, demanding, interfering

CAREERS
Social worker, probation officer, retail manager

SKILLS & APTITUDES
Logic, reasoning, self-belief

FAMOUS BIRTHS
Roman Polanski (1933)
Robert Redford (1936)
Patrick Swayze (1954)
Andy Samberg (1978)

COMPATIBLE WITH
May 17–20

The propensity for independence of thought and action professed by those born on this day gives them the potential to be masters of their chosen fields. Their conviction of belief and determination to improve the lives of others instills in them the urge to direct others. Many make inspirational leaders, whose genuine concern for those under their wing arouses loyalty and affection. Such inclinations and qualities, when also combined with their organizational powers and tenacity, augur well for their professional success—especially in the realms of law enforcement or social work, but also in the artistic world with which August 18 people have a strong affinity. Although many of those born on this day will have to work hard to realize their ambitions and will encounter many obstacles (including the resistance of others to their attempts to spread their powerful influence), they possess the resilience and resourcefulness—as well as the clarity of vision—to continue to promote their aims.

Because the emotional and professional fulfillment of the majority of August 18 people depends on their ability to persuade others, it follows that their relationships are of great significance to them. And despite the disappointment that they may experience when they fail to win professional allies, they typically retain their positive orientation toward others. The unquestioning support and love of those closest to them sustains their self-belief, and they reciprocate by manifesting profound protectiveness, generosity and tolerance toward their friends and family. These people should try to take regular breaks from their endeavors to spend time with their friends or family, to maintain an even balance between their professional and private concerns.

AUGUST 19

❋ ❋ ❋ ❋ ❋ ❋ ❋ ❋ ❋ ❋ ❋ ❋ ❋

☉ ☿ ♂   INSPIRED ACTIVISTS

LEO

Behind the deceptively easy and open façade that an August 19 person typically presents is an altogether more serious persona—one that has a definite agenda and will press ahead until this has been achieved. The visions that inspire them will often have been identified early—a desire to change society, for example, or a gap in the commercial market—but although these individuals will typically adhere to their convictions and ambitions, they are also realistic types, who recognize that innovation and change cannot be effected without careful preparation. Once their game plan has been set, they will devote their energies toward amassing an armory of information, expertise and contacts, and not until they feel that they are properly equipped and that the circumstances are right will they launch themselves on their mission. Such dedication, resourcefulness and fixity of purpose augurs well for their success in any profession that particularly holds their interest, provided, that is, that they can act without undue restriction.

Indeed, such is their outgoing nature, personal charm and talent for inspiring enthusiasm that others tend to follow wherever August 19 people lead. And in turn these individuals generally manifest great affection and concern for the well-being of those who place their trust in them. There is a risk, however, that the acclaim that they engender may go to their heads, and that they may become prey to delusions of invincibility; thus while they may be magnanimous to those who admire them, they may display enmity to those who—despite their efforts to enlist their support—nevertheless continue to express dissent. It is important that they do not lose sight of their core values, and that their close relationships are honest.

PLANETARY INFLUENCES
Ruling planets: Sun and Mercury
Third decan: Personal planet is Mars
Second cusp: Leo with Virgo
  tendencies

VIRTUES
Dynamic, focused, organized

VICES
Delusional, overconfident,
manipulative

CAREERS
Careers advisor, publicist,
advertising executive

SKILLS & APTITUDES
Generosity, organizational skills,
project-management skills

FAMOUS BIRTHS
Orville Wright (1871)
Coco Chanel (1883)
Bill Clinton (1945)
John Stamos (1963)

COMPATIBLE WITH
May 17–20

AUGUST 20

✳ ✳ ✳ ✳ ✳ ✳ ✳ ✳ ✳ ✳ ✳ ✳ ✳ ✳ ✳

BOLD WALLFLOWERS ☉ ☿ ♂

PLANETARY INFLUENCES
Ruling planets: Sun and Mercury
Third decan: Personal planet is Mars
Second cusp: Leo with Virgo
   tendencies

VIRTUES
Analytical, problem-solving,
sensible

VICES
Easily frustrated, resentful, needy

CAREERS
Academic researcher, counselor,
musician

SKILLS & APTITUDES
Thoroughness, dedication, concern
for others

FAMOUS BIRTHS
H.P. Lovecraft (1890)
Al Roker (1954)
Amy Adams (1974)
Andrew Garfield (1983)

COMPATIBLE WITH
January 3–5, May 17–20

....
....
....

Those born on August 20 are complex individuals who, despite their orientation toward others, may be difficult to understand. The reason for their elusiveness generally lies in their fiercely guarded private lives and in their need for periods of solitude where they may escape the demands made by other people, to be themselves and concentrate on the pursuits that interest them most. These people are blessed with logical minds and a clarity of vision that makes it easy for them to identify areas ripe for improvement and then formulate plans that they implement with determination and practical skills. Because the concepts that absorb the attention of these empathetic types are typically geared toward improving the lot of humanity, they are drawn toward guiding other people along what they perceive to be the best path, while others are in turn drawn to them by their aura of capability. They thus have the potential to make gifted academic researchers—especially in science—as well as counselors, but many also use their talents as artists, writers or musicians.

Their sense of social responsibility and concern for the well-being of those who surround them (tendencies that are especially pronounced if they are also women) means that August 20 individuals rarely ignore a cry for help and will work in the interests of others with unwavering dedication. The danger inherent in such an approach, however, is that they will neglect their own needs and may ultimately be left feeling resentful and unfulfilled. The mutual support to be found in strong and honest personal relationships is therefore extremely important to them. It is important that these individuals examine their priorities and try to work out exactly what it is that will bring them genuine happiness.

AUGUST 21

✸ ✸ ✸ ✸ ✸ ✸ ✸ ✸ ✸ ✸ ✸ ✸ ✸

☉ ☿ ♂ RESOURCEFUL COMPROMISERS

The public personae that August 21 people adopt are sometimes at odds with the personal core that they shield from the attention of others. For such is the originality of the visions that inspire them that many have learned through experience that others may be disturbed by their expression. Although those born on this day would clearly prefer not to have to compromise themselves, they are pragmatic and realistic enough to accept that such a course is necessary if they are to succeed in attaining their ambitions—and what innovative ambitions they are. Driven by the compulsion to effect tangible progress, these imaginative individuals utilize their prodigiously perceptive and rigorously logical intellectual skills in both identifying potential areas for improvement and then working with steadfast determination to implement their aims. Whatever profession they choose, they will generally be spurred by the desire to bring about positive global changes—be this in the artistic sphere with which most have a strong affinity, for example, or in the realms of science or government.

Their inward-looking preoccupation with their interests and aims means that August 21 individuals will typically flourish best when acting as independent operators unconstrained by the less daring imaginations of others, presenting their conclusions only when they are ready. Often somewhat solitary figures within their professional spheres, those born on this day place enormous value on the belief, love and loyalty demonstrated by those closest to them, and reciprocate such sentiments with profound dedication. They should beware of suppressing their deepest emotions in the interests of success, and should instead try to find effective ways of expressing the aspirations that inspire them.

PLANETARY INFLUENCES
Ruling planets: Sun and Mercury
Third decan: Personal planet is Mars
Second cusp: Leo with Virgo tendencies

VIRTUES
Imaginative, resourceful, pragmatic

VICES
Self-obsessed, demanding, blinkered

CAREERS
Political lobbyist, healthcare administrator, sports coach

SKILLS & APTITUDES
Independence of thought, strength of purpose, intelligence

FAMOUS BIRTHS
Count Basie (1904)
Wilt Chamberlain (1936)
Kenny Rogers (1938)
Usain Bolt (1986)

COMPATIBLE WITH
January 3–5, May 17–21

AUGUST 22

✳ ✳ ✳ ✳ ✳ ✳ ✳ ✳ ✳ ✳ ✳ ✳ ✳

PASSIONATE INNOVATORS ☉ ☿ ♂

PLANETARY INFLUENCES
Ruling planets: Sun and Mercury
Third decan: Personal planet is Mars
Second cusp: Leo with Virgo
  tendencies

VIRTUES
Practical, imaginative, determined

VICES
Self-destructive, bull-headed,
overbearing

CAREERS
Business leader, accountant, project
manager

SKILLS & APTITUDES
Forcefulness, ambition, drive

FAMOUS BIRTHS
John Lee Hooker (1917)
Ray Bradbury (1920)
Tori Amos (1963)
James Corden (1978)

COMPATIBLE WITH
January 3–5, May 17–21

Those born on this day are stimulated by the company of others, and because they are blessed with charm and an infectious optimism and vitality, others are effortlessly drawn to them. Yet they are rarely as uncomplicated and straightforward as their easy-going approach might suggest, for at the core of their personalities lies a strong-willed, opinionated kernel that fuels them with the urge to have their own way—sometimes regardless of the potential cost to others or, indeed, to themselves. The visions that motivate their actions are frequently grandiose ones, the product of their innate capacity to note the shortcomings of existing circumstances and then, assisted by their practical ability, to formulate resourceful and direct strategies for improvement. Such is their all-encompassing curiosity (and courage) that they are especially attracted to careers in the public service, although their inclinations and talents may lead them to become leaders and managers, inspiring others with their originality.

Many August 22 people are thus impelled to blaze a trail and direct the thoughts and actions of those who follow them. They manifest their leadership qualities in every sphere of their lives, both professional and personal. Because these pragmatic individuals understand the efficacy of persuading rather than forcing others to comply with their convictions, they generally employ their charismatic powers to enlist support. If obstructed, however, their natural combativeness comes to the fore and they will not hesitate to seek to impose their wishes by forceful methods. If they are not to become isolated, especially in terms of their private liaisons, it is vital that August 22 people take on board the opinions of others, and become willing to compromise if necessary.

♍ VIRGO

August 23 to September 22

RULING PLANET: *Mercury*   ELEMENT: *Mutable earth*
SYMBOL: *Virginal woman*   POLARITY: *Negative (feminine)*
PHYSICAL CORRESPONDENCE: *Intestines, abdomen, and spleen*
STONES: *Sapphire, amethyst, carnelian, peridot*   COLORS: *Indigo, navy blue*
FLOWERS: *Jasmine, wintergreen, sage, narcissus, cornflower*

The astrologies of most traditions identified the constellation of Virgo as a female figure who presided over the harvest season. The most ancient personifications of this divine woman, however, emphasized her fecundity and, by extension, the fruitfulness of the Earth. Like many other peoples, the ancient Egyptians depicted her (like Isis) holding an ear of corn; to the Romans she was Ceres, the goddess of corn; and to the Babylonians she was the grain goddess. Her virginal aspect was signified by the names that the Persians, Greeks, and Hindus gave her, all denoting a maiden or virgin. That an earth goddess should be so closely linked with a virginal deity may seem paradoxical, but in ancient tradition the universal Goddess was believed to encompass sexual inviolability and maturity (that is, motherhood), and thus simultaneously embodied both states. There are two Greco-Roman myths that tell of the creation of the constellation Virgo. Virgo is also associated with the Virgin Mary, the star-adorned "queen of heaven."

The personal characteristics bestowed by Virgo reflect apparently conflicting influences. The element of earth, as well as the constellation's ancient links with the mother goddess, endow Virgoans with stability, orderliness, conscientiousness, practical skills, and the potential to reap the fruits of material success. Virginal demureness is paralleled by modesty, idealism, and highly developed analytical capacities. The influence of the sign's ruling plant of Mercury denotes quick minds and intellectual curiosity. On the negative side, Virgoans are sometimes narrow-minded, overly critical, and unimaginative.

AUGUST 23

✺ ✺ ✺ ✺ ✺ ✺ ✺ ✺ ✺ ✺ ✺ ✺ ✺ ✺

DETERMINED ACHIEVERS ☿ ☉

PLANETARY INFLUENCES
Ruling planets: Mercury and Sun
First decan: Personal planet is
  Mercury
First cusp: Virgo with Leo tendencies

VIRTUES
Focused, objective, logical

VICES
Distracted, work-obsessed,
unreliable

CAREERS
Academic, lab technician,
researcher

SKILLS & APTITUDES
Self-reliance, team orientation,
resourcefulness

FAMOUS BIRTHS
William Ernest Henley (1849)
Vera Miles (1930)
River Phoenix (1970)
Kobe Bryant (1978)

COMPATIBLE WITH
May 19–20, December 22–25

The multihued strands that make up the complex fabric of the personalities of those born on August 23 may in many respects seem paradoxical. On the one hand, for example, these people are empathetic toward the plight of those in unfortunate circumstances, yet on the other their preoccupation with their personal goals can make them seem selfish and self-obsessed. Although some of these individuals are indeed exclusively focused on the exploration and ultimate attainment of the ambitions that drive them, the majority are able to accord their potentially conflicting characteristics by reconciling their interests with those of a wider social grouping. Endowed with strong perceptiveness, marked technical abilities and a remarkable level of flexibility, as well as resourcefulness and tenacity, August 23 people have the potential to achieve their visions, whatever form these may take: practical, humanitarian or academic. Despite their strong self-reliance and intellectual focus, their concern with others enables them to work as team players, provided, that is, that they retain the autonomy of thought and action that is so vital to them.

Their inherent kindness and desire to lend assistance to those in need makes these individuals valued and respected colleagues, friends and family members. Yet despite their orientation toward those who manifestly require support, the primary commitment of many August 23 individuals remains their fascination with the work or visions that absorb their interest. Thus although their affection and loyalty to their loved ones is never in doubt, they may inadvertently neglect less pressing—but equally important—aspects of their personal relationships when responding to the siren call of other preoccupations.

AUGUST 24

✳ ✳ ✳ ✳ ✳ ✳ ✳ ✳ ✳ ✳ ✳ ✳ ✳ ✳

☿ ☉   INTELLECTUAL EXPLORERS

Such is the all-encompassing nature of their intellectual curiosity that no detail is too small to escape the clear-sighted scrutiny of those born on this day. Possessed with an irresistible compulsion to understand every issue that excites their attention, they leave no stone unturned and no avenue unexplored in their quest to further their knowledge. Although this tendency is present in every activity they undertake, or with regard to every individual with whom they come into contact, most will channel their intellectual inquisitiveness into a specific professional interest—often academic. And August 24 people are naturally drawn to the endless possibilities for exploration and experimentation that are inherent in artistic pursuits—painting, writing and music, for example—and the products of their quests will frequently delight their audiences with their originality and vision. The realm of human relationships and social systems are similarly ever-changing subjects of fascination, and thus these individuals may make gifted and astute psychologists, therapists and commentators on human behavior—be this of an individual or a communal nature.

Despite their (often somewhat clinical) interest in others, those born on this day are frequently loners—especially if they were also born in the Chinese year of the snake—who prefer to observe others' activities rather than play an active part within them. Although their affection to those closest to them is never in doubt, these are not the sort of people whose relationships are characterized by unquestioning devotion, and their nearest and dearest may sometimes be wounded by the devastatingly critical—if accurate—expression of their observations, however well meant.

PLANETARY INFLUENCES
Ruling planets: Mercury and Sun
First decan: Personal planet is Mercury
First cusp: Virgo with Leo tendencies

VIRTUES
Original, innovative, observant

VICES
Aloof, solitary, critical of others

CAREERS
Psychologist, therapist, philosopher

SKILLS & APTITUDES
Inquisitive nature, propensity to learn, interest in others

FAMOUS BIRTHS
Jorge Luis Borges (1899)
Cal Ripken, Jr. (1960)
Dave Chappelle (1973)
Rupert Grint (1988)

COMPATIBLE WITH
May 19–20, December 22–25

AUGUST 25

SENSITIVE CAREGIVERS ☿ ☉

PLANETARY INFLUENCES
Ruling planets: Mercury and Sun
First decan: Personal planet is Mercury
First cusp: Virgo with Leo tendencies

VIRTUES
Perceptive, energetic, strategic

VICES
Impulsive, insecure, hypersensitive

CAREERS
Media producer, doctor, nonprofit organizer

SKILLS & APTITUDES
Emotional intelligence, leadership skills, determination

FAMOUS BIRTHS
Allan Pinkerton (1819)
Regis Philbin (1934)
Sean Connery (1930)
Gene Simmons (1949)
Claudia Schiffer (1970)
Blake Lively (1987)

COMPATIBLE WITH
May 19–20, December 22–25

Whether they are introverted or—as is often the case—extroverted types, August 25 people are strongly oriented toward other people. Their sensitivity to the feelings expressed by others compels them to respond actively and positively. This propensity may even cause August 25 individuals to make a career working for the benefit of people in distress—within the legal or political spheres, for example, or the social, medical or caring services. Impelled to offer their assistance, these people relish the challenge of pitting their intellects and talents against thorny problems, and are aided in their task by their imaginative yet logical thought processes, as well as their vigor and determination. When their individual preferences lean less toward altruistic professional pursuits, those born on this day nevertheless have the potential to exert a powerful influence over others as managers, team leaders, through the media or in any other role where they can summarize and express the conclusions of their observations in their own, inimitable "voice."

Despite the powerfully inspirational effect that their originality and humanitarian concern frequently has on others, and the acclaim that they may thereby generate, August 25 people are in many respects beset by insecurity. In this regard their enormous sensitivity may be as much a handicap as a blessing, firstly because the mass of data they pick up may have a confusing effect; and secondly because they may tend to measure their feelings of self-worth by means of the reactions they provoke in others. Rooting themselves in the grounding bonds of secure friendships and loving family relationships will help them gain a greater sense of confidence, perspective and priority.

AUGUST 26

✱ ✱ ✱ ✱ ✱ ✱ ✱ ✱ ✱ ✱ ✱ ✱ ✱ ✱

☿ ☉　ENTHUSIASTIC STRATEGISTS

Although the visions that inspire these people's actions may be soaringly ambitious ones, they are rarely fueled by the selfish desire for personal aggrandizement, but are instead more generally concerned with pushing forward the bounds of their experience and horizons. Endowed with markedly mercurial talents, such as intellectual curiosity and a predilection for testing conventional limits—whatever form these might take, be they academic, societal, technical or artistic—as well as the necessary supportive discipline and tenacity required to pursue their aims with remarkable concentration, August 26 individuals have the potential to devise and then implement original and effective strategies with which to benefit the wider world, within whatever professional sphere they choose to operate. Because they are geared toward making tangible progress rather than winning acclaim and glory, their goal orientation makes them committed team members who welcome the input of others just as their coworkers appreciate their fair and democratic manner.

Those born on this day typically demonstrate their interest and concern for those who surround them in both their professional and private relationships. And although their protective instincts are especially aroused by those who are experiencing difficulties—particularly if they were also born in the Chinese year of the goat—they treat most people with tolerance and respect for their individuality. Such qualities endear them especially to their nearest and dearest, who appreciate their willingness to offer advice and assistance without seeking to control and dominate their actions.

PLANETARY INFLUENCES
Ruling planets: Mercury and Sun
First decan: Personal planet is Mercury
First cusp: Virgo with Leo tendencies

VIRTUES
Independent, imaginative, innovative

VICES
Timid, easily embittered, unassertive

CAREERS
Tutor, counselor, charity worker

SKILLS & APTITUDES
Open to new experiences, respect for others, team-orientation

FAMOUS BIRTHS
Robert Walpole (1676)
Mother Teresa (1910)
Melissa McCarthy (1970)
Chris Pine (1980)

COMPATIBLE WITH
December 22–25

AUGUST 27

✵ ✵ ✵ ✵ ✵ ✵ ✵ ✵ ✵ ✵ ✵ ✵ ✵

BRILLIANT THINKERS   ☿

PLANETARY INFLUENCES
Ruling planet: Mercury
First decan: Personal planet is
Mercury

VIRTUES
Intelligent, tenacious, articulate

VICES
Perfectionist, insensitive, detached

CAREERS
Accountant, journalist, scientist

SKILLS & APTITUDES
Multitalented, approachable
personality, strong intellect

FAMOUS BIRTHS
Lyndon B. Johnson (1908)
Lester Young (1909)
Tom Ford (1961)
Aaron Paul (1979)

COMPATIBLE WITH
December 26–31

Rational and intellectual, as well as inventive and curious, those born on August 27 boast the capacity for genius. They are very practical and grounded—an earthy quality—and have the discipline to work hard to unusually high standards, often making them dazzling successes in their fields. They especially excel in careers in which their intellectual capacities, as well as their analytical and methodical gifts, can be utilized fully; they are particularly successful in the fields of science and medicine, financial planning and accountancy, or investigative journalism. Although keen lovers of the arts, they are nevertheless drawn to those practical and intellectual pursuits that satisfy their realistic and rational natures, qualities that make them refreshingly straightforward as friends and colleagues.

The powerful combination of incisive wit and fluent powers of communication possessed by August 27 people, as well as the analytical Virgoan approach, means that, as well as fascinating their audiences, they have the power to wound (even devastate) more sensitive people's feelings. They should therefore remember to choose their words with tact—this particularly applies to those born in the Chinese year of the rooster, who have a frequently irresistible tendency to speak their minds. Studious and diligent, people born on this day often find satisfaction by burying themselves in their work, but their shyness and modesty may mask a lack of self-confidence. Parents and partners should bolster August 27 people's self-esteem to allow their talents to flourish. In adult life, generous and appreciative partners, especially Leos, may similarly provide a stable relationship within which their gifts can thrive.

AUGUST 28

✳ ✳ ✳ ✳ ✳ ✳ ✳ ✳ ✳ ✳ ✳ ✳ ✳ ✳ ✳

☿ INVENTIVE NONCONFORMISTS

People born on August 28 are blessed with the potential for intellectual success because of their mental independence and creativity. Their search for knowledge and understanding often provides the driving force behind their actions. The desire to transcend the bounds of accepted wisdom in order to discover new insights means that these people have the originality and ability to excel in their careers, but their resistance to following the crowd can be taken too far and lead to isolation. Their birthdate indicates idealism, but this is counterbalanced by a practical and steady approach, thus producing a rare combination of imagination and groundedness. People born on this day are therefore especially suited to careers in academia—especially science—or in the literary arts, where their simultaneously creative and analytical talents, as well as their impressive articulacy, can be given full reign and can also benefit others.

Parents of August 28 children should encourage their interests from a young age—however quirky they may seem—for, if pursued, an enthusiasm conceived early on may lead to outstanding success in later life. In their relationships, too, people born on this day find happiness with people who value their creativity and single-mindedness, and who allow them the necessary freedom to grow and flourish: easy-going Leos, for example. They should also cherish their friendships and personal relationships (particularly if they are men) so that they receive the stable emotional support that will both add a rewarding dimension to their lives and provide a secure framework within which they can realize their full potential.

PLANETARY INFLUENCES
Ruling planet: Mercury
First decan: Personal planet is Mercury

VIRTUES
Creative, communicative, determined

VICES
Isolated, arrogant, self-absorbed

CAREERS
Acadmeic, project manager, literary editor

SKILLS & APTITUDES
Practical skills, focus, drive

FAMOUS BIRTHS
Johann Wolfgang von Goethe (1749)
Leo Tolstoy (1828)
Jack Black (1969)
Florence Welch (1986)

COMPATIBLE WITH
December 26–31

AUGUST 29

✤ ✤ ✤ ✤ ✤ ✤ ✤ ✤ ✤ ✤ ✤ ✤ ✤ ✤

ROMANTIC OPPORTUNISTS   ☿

PLANETARY INFLUENCES
Ruling planet: Mercury
First decan: Personal planet is
   Mercury

VIRTUES
Clever, wise, independent

VICES
Eccentric, intimidating, flaky

CAREERS
Graphic designer, IT specialist,
analyst

SKILLS & APTITUDES
Research skills, self-reliance,
organizational ability

FAMOUS BIRTHS
Oliver Wendell Holmes (1809)
Ingrid Bergman (1915)
Charlie Parker (1920)
Michael Jackson (1958)
Lea Michele (1986)

COMPATIBLE WITH
February 23–26, December 26–31

Two distinct sides may be perceived to the nature of August 29 people: on the one hand they are relentlessly drawn to abstract concepts and issues, while on the other they are somewhat romantic and idealistic individuals whose emotions may be less ordered. Yet these characteristics are neither discrete nor incompatible, stemming as they do from these individuals' all-encompassing curiosity and interest in exploring and experiencing all that life has to offer—and then sharing their ideas with others. In their intellectual pursuits their inquisitiveness and desire to make sense of the world can lead those born on this day to become talented analysts. They utilize their qualities of imagination, insight and technical or organizational skills to present the fruits of their researches in innovative and inspiring reinterpretations. Depending on their personal inclinations, their energies may be devoted to a variety of professional fields, but the technology, computing and design spheres, in which they can operate relatively unhindered, augur particularly well for their potential success.

Despite their typical desire to benefit others when it comes to their work, those born on this day may be somewhat solitary figures who are admired from afar. It may be that their radical aims or marked independence of mind intimidates others, or that they expect too much of their closest associates while at the same time jealously insisting on their own right to personal autonomy (a tendency that is especially pronounced if they are men). Thus while their affection for their nearest and dearest is considerable, those closest to them may have to be particularly indulgent and tolerant if their relationships are to flourish.

AUGUST 30

✳ ✳ ✳ ✳ ✳ ✳ ✳ ✳ ✳ ✳ ✳ ✳ ✳

☿   ATTENTIVE STRATEGISTS

In common with the majority of Virgoans, those born on August 30 are blessed with mercurial minds, a gift that not only bestows on them marked curiosity, but also the desire to impose order upon any area that impinges upon their lives. And these individuals are talented organizers, who put their analytical powers to use by identifying subjects with scope for improvement and then employing their logical intellects in formulating effective strategies to realize their perfectionist aims. Despite their recognition of the need to address every inherent detail—however small—in order to incorporate it into a smoothly running whole, those born on this day always retain a view of the wider picture, and this ability, as well as their capacity for self-discipline, augurs well for their success. Yet these are not usually unbendingly rigid types, for, being both pragmatic and geared toward achieving tangible results, they appreciate the need for adaptability and compromise when the occasion demands.

Their progressive inclinations and organizational skills endow those born on this day with the potential to succeed in any career that excites their interest, although commercial ventures, scientific pursuits (especially pharmacy and the medical field), sports and teaching may prove especially fruitful. As a result of the emphasis that they place upon building supportive frameworks, they gravitate toward forging close-knit teams, a propensity that applies as much to their private as to their professional lives. They do, however, prefer to play a leading role within their relationships and this may occasionally cause friction with those of their nearest and dearest—especially their children—who would prefer more personal freedom.

PLANETARY INFLUENCES
Ruling planet: Mercury
First decan: Personal planet is Mercury

VIRTUES
Inspiring, perceptive, ambitious

VICES
Authoritarian, demanding, overbearing

CAREERS
Pharmacist, doctor, entrepreneur

SKILLS & APTITUDES
Adaptable, willing to compromise, wide-ranging focus

FAMOUS BIRTHS
Mary Wollstonecraft Shelley (1797)
Roy Wilkins (1901)
Warren Buffet (1930)
Cameron Diaz (1972)

COMPATIBLE WITH
February 23–26, December 26–31

AUGUST 31

✴ ✴ ✴ ✴ ✴ ✴ ✴ ✴ ✴ ✴ ✴ ✴ ✴ ✴

ALLURING PRAGMATISTS ☿

PLANETARY INFLUENCES
Ruling planet: Mercury
First decan: Personal planet is Mercury

VIRTUES
Charismatic, focused, motivated

VICES
Controlling, intrusive, extreme

CAREERS
Entrepreneur, manager, company director

SKILLS & APTITUDES
Leadership, "can-do" attitude, pragmatism

FAMOUS BIRTHS
James Coburn (1928)
Van Morrison (1945)
Richard Gere (1949)
Chris Tucker (1971)

COMPATIBLE WITH
February 23–26, December 26–31

Others admire those born on this day for the apparently effortless way in which they carry out their endeavours with efficiency and charm. Indeed, although August 31 people are committed to achieving their professional goals, unless exasperated by inefficiency or lack of interest on the part of those with whom they are working, they typically manage to remain courteous and considerate in their dealings with colleagues. Such a balanced approach reflects both their pragmatic recognition of the benefits of making allies rather than foes and the empathy that is born of their perceptiveness (a quality that is even more pronounced if they are women). Yet their primary overall motivation is the achievement of their aims, to which they devote their independence of thought, highly developed organizational skills, technical expertise and tenacity, as well as their ability to inspire others. Friendships are also very important to these people.

The goals that fuel August 31 people's actions are typically progressive and directed toward benefiting the social group with which they are most closely identified—their coworkers, their community, or even humanity as a whole. They are well equipped to succeed in any number of professions, with the proviso that they should have influence and direct others. Yet they are also personally ambitious (not so much with regard to winning material rewards but more in terms of their individual development and fulfilment) and are, furthermore, vitally concerned with the well-being and happiness of their nearest and dearest, whose actions they have a propensity to control (albeit with the best of intentions).

SEPTEMBER 1

✴ ✴ ✴ ✴ ✴ ✴ ✴ ✴ ✴ ✴ ✴ ✴ ✴ ✴

☿ ♄　　ELOQUENT PERSUADERS

Their overriding ambition and single-minded focus in striving to achieve the visions that guide them are perhaps the most striking characteristics of those born on this day. The aims that propel them on their determinedly direct paths through life may be concerned with their personal betterment, or else with bringing about wide-ranging improvements for the benefit of others, but all their ventures are defined by their astuteness of perception, their enviable ability to formulate a practical progressive strategy, and their steadfast tenacity in implementing their plans of action. They also possess remarkable self-knowledge, a gift that endows them with the confidence to stand their ground in the face of adversity.

Yet because September 1 people are usually sensitive and blessed with immense personal appeal, when it comes to dealing with doubters, they typically prefer to charm them with regard to their visions, using their silver-tongued words, than to have to resort to the combative approach of which they are well capable. But they can at times get carried away, too.

The highly developed capacity of September 1 people verbally to influence others augurs especially well for their success in advertising, marketing, sales and retail careers, or as powerful writers, actors, singers or performers of any type. Their goal orientation and independence may, however, lead them to neglect their private lives—a tendency that is particularly pronounced in the men born on this day—despite the enormous value that they place on the support offered by the bonds of strong and honest emotional relationships.

PLANETARY INFLUENCES
Ruling planet: Mercury
Second decan: Personal planet is Saturn

VIRTUES
Organized, persuasive, engaged

VICES
Reckless, combative, pushy

CAREERS
Writer, actor, advertising executive

SKILLS & APTITUDES
Ambition, breadth of vision, excellent communication skills

FAMOUS BIRTHS
Ann Richards (1933)
Barry Gibb (1946)
Gloria Estefan (1957)
Zendaya Coleman (1996)

COMPATIBLE WITH
January 11–14

SEPTEMBER 2

✻ ✻ ✻ ✻ ✻ ✻ ✻ ✻ ✻ ✻ ✻ ✻ ✻

BLUNT PROBLEM–SOLVERS ☿ ♄

PLANETARY INFLUENCES
Ruling planet: Mercury
Second decan: Personal planet is
Saturn

VIRTUES
Straightforward, genuine,
self-disciplined

VICES
Detached, touchy, cold

CAREERS
Social worker, judge, lawyer

SKILLS & APTITUDES
Organizational skills, practical
approach, efficiency

FAMOUS BIRTHS
Robert Shapiro (1942)
Mark Harmon (1951)
Keanu Reeves (1964)
Salma Hayek (1966)

COMPATIBLE WITH
January 11–14

The straightforward face that September 2 people present to the world is no façade: with those born on this day, what you see is what you get—a direct and focused personalized package of determination and energy. Such is their urgent desire to realize their ambitions as efficiently as possible that these individuals have no patience with subterfuge or prevarication, regarding game-playing or indecision as irritating obstacles on the path to success. And indeed, when obstructed in any way, these usually controlled people may explode with frustration, the uncharacteristically violent expression of their seething annoyance startling those who have not experienced it before. Yet despite such occasional flare-ups they are otherwise organized, practical and disciplined in the pursuit of their goals. While the concerns and interest manifested by those born on this day may vary according to the individual, a common feature is their progressive nature and their wish to exert a beneficial influence on others—in the public services, perhaps, or as administrators.

These people are scrupulously fair in their dealings with others—a quality that results from their critical discernment and their empathy with those who are unhappy or the victims of perceived abuses. And in such instances, as in all their endeavors, their independence of thought and predilection for devising remedial strategies come to the fore. Yet in devoting themselves to resolving the problems of others, September 2 people may neglect their own needs. Furthermore, despite their profound—if understated—affection for those closest to them, unless they are in real trouble they may expect the same level of self-reliance to be demonstrated by their nearest and dearest as they exhibit themselves.

SEPTEMBER 3

✦ ✦ ✦ ✦ ✦ ✦ ✦ ✦ ✦ ✦ ✦ ✦ ✦

☿ ♄   BALANCED PEACEKEEPERS

Those born on this day are remarkably determined individuals, a quality that those who do not know them well may not recognize until particular situations arise in which they demonstrate their readiness to adopt combative methods. Generally, however, they prefer a conciliatory and affable manner, believing that more will be achieved by communication than by confrontation: this personal style, however effective, may lead others to misjudge their strength of purpose. Blessed with mercurial and independent minds, a highly developed sense of natural justice and empathy for the downtrodden, and enormous technical and organizational talents, September 3 people are especially interested in finding practical solutions to the problems that beset humanity. They may thus gravitate toward professions where they can help others to make tangible progress, or at least live their lives more happily, and careers as engineers, scientific researchers, artists and in sports are particularly well starred.

Those born on this day bring to all their endeavors their astute perceptiveness, tolerance, patience and tenacity, as well as their desire to set everything—or everyone—that they encounter on a smoothly running path. This propensity is especially pronounced within their personal lives (and even more so if they are women), and their friends and family members appreciate the support and understanding that they readily offer. Yet despite their typically quiet and understated manner, these people are no pushovers, a caveat that applies as much to their private as to their professional liaisons.

PLANETARY INFLUENCES
Ruling planet: Mercury
Second decan: Personal planet is Saturn

VIRTUES
Driven, clever, thoughtful

VICES
Misleading, reticent, opaque

CAREERS
Civil engineer, artist, sports coach

SKILLS & APTITUDES
Advocacy, administrative skills, ability to conciliate

FAMOUS BIRTHS
Charles H. Houston (1895)
Kitty Carlisle (1914)
Al Jardine (1942)
Shaun White (1986)

COMPATIBLE WITH
January 11–14

SEPTEMBER 4

✵ ✵ ✵ ✵ ✵ ✵ ✵ ✵ ✵ ✵ ✵ ✵ ✵ ✵

PUZZLING PERSONALITIES ☿ ♄

Those born on this day may present something of an enigma to those who don't know them well. On the one hand they are gifted problem-solvers who are stimulated by challenge—be it physical or intellectual—yet on the other are impatient when forced to deal with the petty details that form part of the routine of business practices. The answer to this apparent conundrum of character lies in their mercurial minds, which give them a relish for new experiences. Indeed, when frustrated by circumstances outside their control, these usually pragmatic and self-disciplined types are prone to explode in startling displays of temper. Generally, however, September 4 individuals are good-natured people, who make cooperative—sometimes inspirational—team members, with the provision that they are able to retain autonomy of thought and action. They are, moreover, rarely ambitious for personal glory, being instead motivated by the desire to realize more impersonal progressive aims.

Because their skills usually assume more of an intellectual than a technical aspect, and in view of their innate urge to achieve tangible results through their own vigorous and focused efforts, these individuals are frequently best suited for acting as independent agents of change. Their talents and inclinations equip them for potential success in a wide variety of professions, but the freedom inherent in artistic and academic pursuits may prove especially attractive to September 4 individuals. They retain a similarly independent stance within their personal relationships, and, although they have a deep affection for those closest to them, they are not interested in embroiling themselves in the minutiae of domestic life.

SEPTEMBER 5

✹ ✹ ✹ ✹ ✹ ✹ ✹ ✹ ✹ ✹ ✹ ✹ ✹ ✹

☿ ♄   IDEALISTIC DAYDREAMERS

These magnetic people are fueled by a desire to realize their own idiosyncratic visions of Utopia, yet while their dreams are highly individual, they rarely encompass selfish ambitions alone, instead being concerned with building a happier and more enlightened world for others. In common with the majority of those born under the planet of Mercury, these are inquisitive and perceptive types, who have little difficulty in quickly and astutely identifying areas that are ripe for improvement, and who are furthermore fired with the burning determination to be the agents of change. Despite the practical skills that they bring to their missions, in their righteous enthusiasm to set the world to rights they may fail to assess realistically their chance of success and thereby inadvertently sabotage their best efforts. The form that their ambitions take will vary according to the September 5 individual, but most will espouse professions that enable them to exert their influence over others in some positive way: possibly as social campaigners, for example, but more likely as artistic performers who can impart their messages in inspirational fashion.

Their pronounced concern about the welfare of others permeates every aspect of their lives, and, in turn, others are drawn to them because of their easy charm, infectious optimism and enormous generosity. These are individuals who like to encourage those around them, and—particularly if they were also born in the Chinese year of the dog—they usually expend tremendous energy in bolstering the confidence of those of whom they are fond. Occasionally, however, their magnanimity may cause them to neglect their own emotional needs.

PLANETARY INFLUENCES
Ruling planet: Mercury
Second decan: Personal planet is Saturn

VIRTUES
Empathetic, generous, imaginative

VICES
Weak, neglectful, unrealistic

CAREERS
Social campaigner, motivational speaker, copywriter

SKILLS & APTITUDES
Practical skills, ambition, vision

FAMOUS BIRTHS
King Louis XIV of France (1638)
Johann Christian Bach (1735)
Jesse James (1847)
Freddy Mercury (1946)

COMPATIBLE WITH
January 11–14, December 4–6

VIRGO

SEPTEMBER 6

✷ ✷ ✷ ✷ ✷ ✷ ✷ ✷ ✷ ✷ ✷ ✷ ✷ ✷

HEADSTRONG PROGRESSIVES   ☿ ♄

PLANETARY INFLUENCES
Ruling planet: Mercury
Second decan: Personal planet is
Saturn

VIRTUES
Organized, adventurous, brave

VICES
Highly strung, remote,
noncommittal

CAREERS
Attorney, judge, surgeon

SKILLS & APTITUDES
Sense of justice, focus,
administrative skills

FAMOUS BIRTHS
John Dalton (1766)
Jeff Foxworthy (1958)
Macy Gray (1969)
Idris Elba (1972)

COMPATIBLE WITH
January 15–19, December 4–7

September 6 people are complex characters whom others may find difficult to get to know well, or understand. On the one hand their natural sense of justice gives them sensitivity—particularly toward the less fortunate—and concern for the well-being of others, yet on the other, these are also strong-willed types whose force of conviction and independence of mind often belies their mild, somewhat stoic, manner. However, their desire for intellectual autonomy and their orientation toward others are not necessarily incompatible—indeed, those born on this day may combine these traits to great effect in their professional lives as doctors, lawyers or social campaigners, for example. For above all these individuals are compelled by the urge to bring about progressive advances that will benefit the wider world (they are usually unconcerned with attaining personal gains), especially if they were also born in the Chinese year of the dragon. And, when engaged upon their quest, they draw upon their considerable resources of energy, determination and integrity, as well as their strong organizational talents.

Despite their interest in others and generally reluctantly assumed leadership qualities, September 6 people may sometimes appear to be somewhat solitary figures, who prefer to follow their inquisitive instincts independently rather than allow themselves to be bound by the ties inherent in human relationships, perhaps fearing that to do so would compromise their need for freedom. As is the case with their liaisons with family and friends, when they eventually commit themselves to equal one-on-one partnerships, they typically demonstrate their innate capacity to be loyal, affectionate and supportive.

SEPTEMBER 7

✹ ✹ ✹ ✹ ✹ ✹ ✹ ✹ ✹ ✹ ✹ ✹ ✹ ✹

☿ ♄　　PROSPEROUS ADMINISTRATORS

Those born on this day are tenacious individuals whose actions are primarily motivated by a desire to push the bounds of human knowledge and endeavour forward. This is not to say that they do not welcome the acclaim or financial rewards that their actions may reap—to the contrary—but rather that their questing natures and intellectual dynamism are more compelling factors in their behaviour than is mere personal ambition. And should they find themselves masters of their fields (which is often very likely, given their independent drive and strength of purpose), they will rarely bask in the glory that others reflect on them, but harness the support thereby garnered toward the attainment of their aims. For as well as being blessed with the highly developed qualities of perspicacity and resourcefulness, enabling skills and innately pragmatic approach equips them as naturally gifted leaders.

September 7 people gravitate toward any profession (and their multifaceted skills equip them admirably for many) where they can achieve tangible results and exert their progressive influence over others. Since they also demand complete autonomy, in many respects they are particularly well suited to those academic, artistic, literary or musical careers where they can work relatively unhindered. Although they demand the same level of freedom within their personal relationships, they may paradoxically seek to control their nearest and dearest—albeit with the best of intentions—a predilection that may arouse the resentment of their loved ones, especially, if they are parents, within their children.

PLANETARY INFLUENCES
Ruling planet: Mercury
Second decan: Personal planet is Saturn

VIRTUES
Energetic, determined, ambitious

VICES
Hypersensitive, impatient, controlling

CAREERS
Social-media promoter, police officer, teacher

SKILLS & APTITUDES
Leadership skills, dynamism, self-motivation

FAMOUS BIRTHS
Queen Elizabeth I of England (1533)
J.P. Morgan, Jr. (1867)
Sonny Rollins (1930)
Buddy Holly (1936)

COMPATIBLE WITH
January 15–19

SEPTEMBER 8

✻ ✻ ✻ ✻ ✻ ✻ ✻ ✻ ✻ ✻ ✻ ✻ ✻ ✻

OPINIONATED VOICES ☿ ♄

Their remarkable strength of conviction and fierce determination to set others on the path that they regard as being the correct one endow those born on this day with pronounced leadership potential. They are usually respected (although not necessarily regarded with affection) for both their dynamism and their fixity of purpose. While these individuals may be fueled by the desire to maintain or protect the status quo, they may be equally fired by the urge to implement change. Either way, they will have first evaluated the existing situation thoroughly, drawing upon their capacity for objective analysis in the process, and then utilized their organizational skills either to bring about improvement by modification, or to formulate an alternative. Once they have decided upon their course of action, they will promote it with uncompromising forcefulness, often demonstrating their powerful talent for communication in their quest to convince others. Such inclinations have a clear parallel with the political sphere, and many of those born on this day may become career politicians; others choosing to spread their message through other channels.

Despite their perspicacity, clarity of vision and persistence—qualities which augur well for their professional success—when it comes to their intellectual interests many of those born on this day may experience troubled personal relationships, particularly if they are men. The problem is that others may not concur with their opinions and can become alienated by, and resistant to, their often stubborn attempts to persuade them otherwise; bitter confrontation is usually inevitable.

SEPTEMBER 9

✵ ✵ ✵ ✵ ✵ ✵ ✵ ✵ ✵ ✵ ✵ ✵ ✵ ✵

☿ ♄   BENEVOLENT CHAMPIONS

Those born on September 9 are serious people who are not only absorbed by abstract concepts but also feel a strong sense of responsibility toward those around them. Like the majority of Virgoans, their birthright includes an independent turn of mind, with the result that they have a predilection both for intellectual exploration and for innovation. Having examined an issue from all angles with incisive judgement, they will typically draw an original conclusion as to the best course of action and then dip deep into their reserves of resourcefulness and organizational skills to promote their aims tenaciously. These are sensitive individuals who will seek to enlist the support of others; their determination should not be underestimated, however, and they will battle on alone if necessary. Such is their concern with the well-being of others that their inclinations and talents may lead them into pursuing humanitarian careers, or at least those where their work can be of wider benefit—as scientific researchers or educators, for example.

Despite their interest in others, September 9 people may appear solitary. They will participate in team or social pursuits but still seem to stand apart from the crowd. This may be partly explained by their innate preference for independent observation, but may also be a product of their sensitivity which may, in some instances, cause them to be beset by feelings of insecurity (a tendency which is even more pronounced if they are women). Receiving the unconditional love and support of their nearest and dearest is of great importance to them, and they reciprocate such emotional bolstering with quiet but unwavering loyalty.

PLANETARY INFLUENCES
Ruling planet: Mercury
Second decan: Personal planet is Saturn

VIRTUES
Progressive, inquisitive, nurturing

VICES
Solitary, workaholic, unbalanced

CAREERS
Humanitarian, philanthropist, research scientist

SKILLS & APTITUDES
Concern for others, progressive outlook, drive

FAMOUS BIRTHS
Leo Tolstoy (1828)
Otis Redding (1941)
Michael Keaton (1951)
Hugh Grant (1960)

COMPATIBLE WITH
January 15–19

SEPTEMBER 10

✳ ✳ ✳ ✳ ✳ ✳ ✳ ✳ ✳ ✳ ✳ ✳ ✳ ✳

STEADY FACILITATORS ☿ ♄

PLANETARY INFLUENCES
Ruling planet: Mercury
Second decan: Personal planet is Saturn

VIRTUES
Orderly, practical, patient

VICES
Tense, blinkered, thin-skinned

CAREERS
Administrator, social worker, teacher

SKILLS & APTITUDES
Reliability, team-orientation, efficiency

FAMOUS BIRTHS
Robert Wise (1914)
Arnold Palmer (1929)
Bill O'Reilly (1949)
Colin Firth (1960)

COMPATIBLE WITH
January 15–19

The aura that surrounds September 10 people is that of capability, and indeed these are focused, resourceful and thoughtful individuals who prefer steering a steady and controlled path through life rather than acting impulsively. Motivated by the urge to bring order and implement progress where before there was chaos and unproductiveness, their attention is drawn to those subjects and situations where they adjudge improvements, thereby hoping that through their efforts they will make a real contribution to the welfare of others. Their typical approach is to make an objective and realistic assessment of the existing scenario, and then, utilizing their practical and organizational talents, construct a strategy designed to facilitate advancement through the support of a stable, supportive system. Their dealings with others are similarly characterized by their predilection for creating and directing effective interpersonal frameworks, and they thus make responsible team captains who, as well as being goal-oriented, manifest genuine concern for those under their aegis.

Although those born on this day favor a sensible and considered approach, this does not mean that they are dull and unimaginative individuals—far from it: being intellectually inquisitive types, they are fascinated by unusual and innovative topics and people, and even if they do not make a career of exploring such subjects—as writers, artists or academics, for instance—they will still be attracted to boldly individualistic characters. Indeed, being defined by mutual tolerance and respect, any relationships that they may form with such polar opposites will often be remarkably successful.

SEPTEMBER 11

☿ ♄

SILVER-TONGUED CARERS

Those born on this day share their celebration with an anniversary that often overshadows it. Yet their stars augur well for them, nevertheless. They have the ability to think clearly and independently. The empathy of many September 11 people is aroused by the plight of the disadvantaged, resulting in a fraternal feeling that instills in them the determination to improve their circumstances by whatever means they can. And, indeed, they have many talents at their disposal, including their pronounced gift for communication—both verbal and literary—and their highly developed organizational skills, as well as the courage of their convictions, which compels them to battle on, even in the face of stiff opposition. Such inclinations and talents augur especially well for their potential success as politicians, lawyers or social campaigners, although many September 11 individuals may choose to exert their influence by less direct—though no less powerful—artistic means, as writers, for example, a propensity that is even more marked if they were also born in the Chinese year of the goat.

Their urge to help those around them may take a somewhat radical form, but may equally be manifested in the defense of existing social systems. For in many respects those born on this day are traditionalists, whose love of order may lead them to lend their support to tried-and-tested conventions. Certainly, September 11 people believe in the virtues of stable familial relationships for the mutual support that they offer, and typically make concerned friends, partners and parents, although their forceful opinions and moral rectitude may cause conflict with their children.

PLANETARY INFLUENCES
Ruling planet: Mercury
Second decan: Personal planet is Saturn

VIRTUES
Perceptive, observant, strategic

VICES
Stubborn, overbearing, combative

CAREERS
Lawyer, social campaigner, journalist

SKILLS & APTITUDES
Communication skills, strong moral sense, empathy

FAMOUS BIRTHS
D.H. Lawrence (1885)
Bear Bryant (1913)
Harry Connick, Jr. (1967)
Taraji Henson (1970)

COMPATIBLE WITH
January 15–19

SEPTEMBER 12

✴ ✴ ✴ ✴ ✴ ✴ ✴ ✴ ✴ ✴ ✴ ✴ ✴ ✴

SOLITARY THINKERS   ☿ ♀

PLANETARY INFLUENCES
Ruling planet: Mercury
Third decan: Personal planet is Venus

VIRTUES
Independent, communicative, inspiring

VICES
Withdrawn, opinionated, unyielding

CAREERS
Motivational speaker, therapist, self-help author

SKILLS & APTITUDES
Intelligence, thinking outside the box, determination

FAMOUS BIRTHS
Jesse Owens (1913)
George Jones (1931)
Barry White (1944)
Emmy Rossum (1986)

COMPATIBLE WITH
January 1–5

....
....
....

Never the types to indulge in subterfuge, manipulation or power games, those born on this day are straightforward and direct, their primary motivation being to attain their aims and to do so as effectively as possible. Stimulated by their quest for knowledge and, being of an independent turn of mind, they prefer to seek out facts for themselves and then draw their own conclusions rather than unquestioningly to accept conventional truths. Their intellectual approach is typically characterized by their incisive ability to grasp abstract concepts, their perceptiveness and their capacity to marshal their findings into logically constructed strategies for progress. And, once these have been reached, they will not only adhere to their conclusions with single-minded tenacity, but also seek to persuade others of their veracity—often with considerable success, since September 12 people have a marked facility with words, and because others cannot help but respect their sincerity. Their social concern and desire to instruct and thereby assist others suits them particularly well to careers as educators, for example, or in the public service.

Despite their genuine urge to exert their influence over those around them—or society as a whole—these are somewhat solitary individuals, who have a strong need for periods of privacy in which they can be alone with their thoughts, undisturbed by the demands of others. Yet they are also loyal and supportive friends, partners and family members, who, moreover, respect the individuality of their nearest and dearest and will rarely attempt to impose their opinions on those closest to them if this would be hurtful.

SEPTEMBER 13

✳ ✳ ✳ ✳ ✳ ✳ ✳ ✳ ✳ ✳ ✳ ✳ ✳ ✳

☿ ♀   SANGUINE SCHOLARS

Those born on September 13 are remarkably self-sufficient individuals who, despite their somewhat abstract interest in humanity as a global entity, may appear to others to be remote, even standoffish figures. This is not an entirely fair assessment, however, for these people are sensitive and may be deeply moved by their strong feelings of empathy with those who are miserable or in trouble. It is just that they would prefer to be able to pursue their intellectual interests (and thereby contribute to human knowledge) undisturbed by the trivia of everyday existence. In many respects, those born on this day may often be characterized as workaholics and, although otherwise generally positive and good-humored, grow restless and tetchy if circumstances prevent them from immersing themselves in a particularly absorbing undertaking. Blessed with keen concentration and application, they will rarely abandon a project or problem until they have completed or solved it to their own satisfaction.

These individuals will thrive in any professional field where they are both constantly challenged and allowed total autonomy; their problem-solving talents make them suited to scientific or business careers, although their original and imaginative approach also augurs well for writing and design. And, if they do work as part of a team, they are only happy if they can direct others; hard task-masters, they lead by example and expect the same level of dedication and goal-orientation from others as they themselves demonstrate. This is also true of their personal relationships (even more so if they are men), within which they have a tendency to claim their own right of freedom while seeking to control the lives of those closest to them.

PLANETARY INFLUENCES
Ruling planet: Mercury
Third decan: Personal planet is Venus

VIRTUES
Original, determined, driven

VICES
Aloof, combative, prickly

CAREERS
Business analyst, laboratory researcher, designer

SKILLS & APTITUDES
Self-motivation, tenacity, focus

FAMOUS BIRTHS
Milton S. Hershey (1857)
Roald Dahl (1916)
Tyler Perry (1969)
Stella McCartney (1971)
Fiona Apple (1977)

COMPATIBLE WITH
January 1–5

SEPTEMBER 14

✳ ✳ ✳ ✳ ✳ ✳ ✳ ✳ ✳ ✳ ✳ ✳ ✳ ✳

ASTUTE ORGANIZERS ☿ ♀

Perhaps the primary preoccupation of those born on this day is with bringing order to any system (or person) that they suspect is not realizing its maximum potential. Possessed of an acutely critical eye—the result of both their incisive intellects and their observant natures—they find it easy to identify areas in which the component parts are imbalanced or deficient in some way. Because their urge to plan, organize, control and thereby institute and maintain smoothly running and effective programs is so strong—and even more so if they were born in the Chinese year of the ox—they are able to take charge of situations quickly, work out optimum strategies for success and then direct the actions of others. September 14 individuals are thus natural leaders who pursue their goals with a determined sense of purpose (and expect others to do the same), and will flourish in any career where they can harmonize discord and bring about tangible results—the scientific, political and legal professions are particularly well starred, as are city planning and the building trades.

Yet these individuals are not totally geared toward intellectual or professional pursuits: to the contrary, they innately understand the importance of counter-balancing the pressures of work with a full personal life. Many of them are somewhat sensuous types, who appreciate beauty in all its manifold forms and possess a lively sense of fun. Responsible friends and family members (and totally devoted, if at times con-trolling, parents), they are also good conversational-ists and sociable types, who enjoy surrounding them-selves with people and hosting well-organized social entertainments.

SEPTEMBER 15

✤ ✤ ✤ ✤ ✤ ✤ ✤ ✤ ✤ ✤ ✤ ✤ ✤ ✤

☿ ♀　　　UNSTOPPABLE VISIONARIES

In many respects those born on this day can be characterized as specialists, for they are drawn to a single area of interest (their choice often having been made in childhood) and seek to become masters of their field. The subjects that typically fascinate September 15 individuals are those where the scope for exploration is boundless and where their quest for discovery can therefore lead them into previously uncharted territories. Even though they are intellectually curious, these are rarely restless or roving types. Once they have alighted upon a topic that absorbs their attention they will devote their energies exclusively to its study, probing, testing and amassing a wealth of information. Their inclinations and simultaneously imaginative and organized methods suit September 15 people for a variety of professions, from scientific research to the arts. They are gifted directors of others, who never lose sight of the wider picture or, indeed, surrender their own inherent requirement for autonomy of thought and action.

Others admire their technical expertise, as well as their determination and clarity of vision, but may be somewhat intimidated by their refusal to compromise their convictions or integrity. Although they may appear to be somewhat solitary figures, they are by no means solely oriented to their work, for they value the strong emotional bonds that they form with their family and friends. As sensual individuals, they are moved by music, the beauty of art and the flavors of gourmet cuisine. And it is primarily in order to indulge such tastes, as well to support their families, that those born on this day appreciate the material rewards that their professional success brings them.

PLANETARY INFLUENCES
Ruling planet: Mercury
Third decan: Personal planet is Venus

VIRTUES
Responsive, loyal, affectionate

VICES
Perfectionist, critical, avaricious

CAREERS
Director, company manager, researcher

SKILLS & APTITUDES
Dedication to work, open-mindedness, leadership potential

FAMOUS BIRTHS
William H. Taft (1857)
Agatha Christie (1890)
Margaret Keane (1927)
Tommy Lee Jones (1946)

COMPATIBLE WITH
January 1–5, December 24–26

SEPTEMBER 16

UNCONVENTIONAL IMAGINARIES ☿ ♀

PLANETARY INFLUENCES
Ruling planet: Mercury
Third decan: Personal planet is Venus

VIRTUES
Optimistic, adventurous, positive

VICES
Superficial, restless, easily bored

CAREERS
Artist, architect, interior designer

SKILLS & APTITUDES
Energy, independence, originality

FAMOUS BIRTHS
King Henry V (1387)
Lauren Bacall (1924)
B.B. King (1925)
David Copperfield (1954)

COMPATIBLE WITH
January 1–5, December 24–26

Exuberant and energetic, positive and progressive, September 16 people are physical and intellectual live-wires who are fueled by the urge to push the boundaries of human knowledge forward and thereby blaze an innovatory trail to light the way for others. Their questing compulsion is in part due to their humanitarian principles and desire to assist others, but is also the result of their mercurial inquisitiveness and relish for discovering and experiencing novel concepts and situations. Their urge to make progress is a forceful one, and once they have settled upon a subject that absorbs their interest (and this may not be immediately evident, given their wide range of interests), they will typically harness their considerable vigor and talents—including their originality, objectiveness and organizational skills—in their tenacious drive to effect a breakthrough. Achieving concrete results is of great importance to them—as is receiving recognition for their efforts—and they are therefore particularly suited to financial planning, scientific or artistic pursuits, or manufacturing trades where they can not only demonstrate the fruits of their labors, but also inspire or benefit others and make a name for themselves.

Although their intellectual independence and refusal to be bound by convention augurs well for their ability to work autonomously, those born on this day are strongly oriented toward others, wishing both to share their knowledge and to derive pleasure from the stimulation of social interaction. The same is true of their personal liaisons, where they assume mentoring roles (especially if they are women), and enliven their relationships with an infectious joie de vivre.

SEPTEMBER 17

✶ ✶ ✶ ✶ ✶ ✶ ✶ ✶ ✶ ✶ ✶ ✶ ✶ ✶

☿ ♀   DETERMINED ACHIEVERS

Such is their focus and drive that those born on this day frequently appear to be powerfully single-minded individuals who will allow nothing or no one to stand in the way of their progress. In many respects this assessment is an accurate one, for these people are not only remarkably goal oriented, but they also combine their capacity for concentration, logical thought and intellectual and physical vigor with their somewhat stubborn tenacity to generate an almost irresistible force. Yet the personalities of those born on this day are not as straightforward as they may appear on superficial examination, for as well as being linear thinkers, their intellectual curiosity also endows them with the ability to think laterally, while they are also blessed with sensitivity and perceptiveness, qualities that make them extremely empathetic toward others. The combination of their humanitarian instincts and organizational talents may lead them to pursue professions where they can assist or enlighten others, possibly through creative endeavors. They also make gifted and generous team leaders.

Similar feelings of concern and responsibility for the well-being of others characterize their relationships with their nearest and dearest, toward whom September 17 people typically assume a protective stance. Although they rarely express their emotions openly, they demonstrate their affection for those closest to them through nurturing and practical action. Although initially shy, many are lively companions, who are stimulated by artistic pursuits (to which some choose to devote their careers) and also have an infectious sense of fun.

PLANETARY INFLUENCES
Ruling planet: Mercury
Third decan: Personal planet is Venus

VIRTUES
Decisive, progressive, forceful

VICES
Private, easily frustrated, touchy

CAREERS
Philanthropist, therapist, entrepreneur

SKILLS & APTITUDES
Drive, proactive outlook, determination

FAMOUS BIRTHS
Hank Williams (1923)
John Ritter (1948)
Cassandra "Elvira" Peterson (1951)
Baz Luhrmann (1962)

COMPATIBLE WITH
January 6–10, December 24–26

SEPTEMBER 18

✵ ✵ ✵ ✵ ✵ ✵ ✵ ✵ ✵ ✵ ✵ ✵ ✵

INGENIOUS CREATIVES   ☿ ♀

PLANETARY INFLUENCES
Ruling planet: Mercury
Third decan: Personal planet is Venus

VIRTUES
Sensitive, artistic, charismatic

VICES
Isolated, opaque, remote

CAREERS
Scientist, writer, musician

SKILLS & APTITUDES
Creativity, originality, capacity for
hard work

FAMOUS BIRTHS
Greta Garbo (1905)
Bob Dylan (1933)
Ben Carson (1951)
Lance Armstrong (1971)

COMPATIBLE WITH
January 6–10

Those born on this day are private and introspective individuals, who nevertheless sometimes emerge from their self-imposed solitude to share the fruits of their labors with others. The planets that govern their day of birth exert a particularly powerful influence on their psyches, Mercury endowing them with a strong urge for intellectual exploration and discovery, and Venus blessing them with profound sensuality and an appreciation of beauty. And when these two inclinations achieve their highest level of harmonious interaction, September 18 people have the potential to initiate truly innovative and inspirational advances that others will admire and that may even influence generations to come. Their natural affinity with all things artistic augurs especially well for their success as writers, musicians or artists, while their equally strong attraction to the acquisition of technical knowledge suits them also for scientific pursuits and the digital realm. Although the focus of their professional endeavors fully absorbs their attention, their ultimate aims are typically to benefit humanity as a whole.

It is this dual propensity to help others advance while at the same time concentrating upon the concepts that fascinate them that may cause September 18 people's personal lives to be troubled. Because they exude empathetic concern, and are attractive and interesting individuals, others are drawn to them. Yet in many respects the interest that they show in other individuals assumes a somewhat abstract rather than direct form and they therefore shy away from having to assume responsibility for the happiness of others, particularly if this would mean having to divert their attention from their intellectual quests.

SEPTEMBER 19

✧ ✧ ✧ ✧ ✧ ✧ ✧ ✧ ✧ ✧ ✧ ✧ ✧ ✧

☿ ♀   MAGNETIC DYNAMOS

September 19 individuals are vitally interested in everything that crosses their paths, their mercurial minds latching onto every novel concept that presents itself. Their keen eye for beauty and warm sensuality endow them with a more aesthetic—and frequently also rather earthy—disposition. They are not content to sit quietly on the sidelines of the game of life, instead they throw themselves enthusiastically into the stimulating pursuit of new experiences, indulging their taste for the unusual and original (and particularly so if they were also born in the Chinese year of the horse). Yet despite their versatile interests, those born on this day are rarely flighty types, for they are also gripped by the desire to transcend the superficial and move into more serious, progressive realms, thereby hoping to add to their own lexicon of knowledge and to benefit the wider world by means of their efforts. Innately humanitarian, as well as being blessed with the potential to make a significant impact as ingenious scientists or artists working in a variety of areas, these are the multitalented individuals who will flourish in any profession they choose, provided that their attention and interest are constantly occupied.

A similar combination of concern for others, sociability and joie de vivre characterizes their interpersonal relationships, and their dynamic and lively personalities in turn typically draw others into their magnetic orbit. Despite their gregariousness, however, September 19 people manage to devote special attention to those closest to them, maintaining easy and relaxed relationships, while at the same time protecting their own interests.

PLANETARY INFLUENCES
Ruling planets: Mercury and Venus
Third decan: Personal planet is Venus
Second cusp: Virgo with Libran tendencies

VIRTUES
Lively, enthusiastic, sensual

VICES
Unfocused, superficial, vain

CAREERS
Academic, researcher, artist

SKILLS & APTITUDES
Refined taste, interest in others, positive personality

FAMOUS BIRTHS
William Golding (1911)
"Mama" Cass Elliot (1941)
Jeremy Irons (1948)
Jimmy Fallon (1974)

COMPATIBLE WITH
January 6–10

SEPTEMBER 20

✳ ✳ ✳ ✳ ✳ ✳ ✳ ✳ ✳ ✳ ✳ ✳ ✳

SELF–ASSURED SOCIAL BUTTERFLIES ☿ ♀

PLANETARY INFLUENCES
Ruling planets: Mercury and Venus
Third decan: Personal planet is Venus
Second cusp: Virgo with Libran
  tendencies

VIRTUES
Independent, sociable, resourceful

VICES
Manipulative, domineering,
overconfident

CAREERS
Politician, actor, social-media
executive

SKILLS & APTITUDES
Persuasiveness, team-orientation,
capacity to innovate

FAMOUS BIRTHS
Upton Sinclair (1878)
Sophia Loren (1934)
George R. R. Martin (1948)
Gary Coleman (1968)

COMPATIBLE WITH
January 6–10

....
....
....

Those born on this day generally possess two defining characteristics: an almost irresistible urge to take control of situations and people; and a desire the win the genuine affection and admiration of those around them. Their perceptive and mercurial dispositions propel them to seek the best way to organize both themselves and others. Although the visions that fuel their actions are frequently highly individualistic, their concerns are usually intended to benefit or inform a wider audience, and they favour teamwork over individual action. While they feel compelled to exert their benevolent influence over others, they seek to do so by employing persuasive rather than coercive methods, thereby hoping to inspire others to cooperate enthusiastically in the pursuit of a common mission. They are endowed with the potential to attain success in a variety of professions, but many often have a special attraction to the innovative possibilities inherent in the arts or the media.

Their wish to build harmonious relationships with others pervades every aspect of the lives of those born on this day, and reflects their urge to achieve their aims as smoothly and quickly as possible, as well as their innate—and sometimes unacknowledged—desire to win the love and respect of those with whom they come in contact. However, their self-assurance and their confidence in the veracity of their convictions may cause the resentment of others (particularly those closest to them) for what may be perceived to be a manipulative approach, no matter how charmingly it is presented.

SEPTEMBER 21

✳ ✳ ✳ ✳ ✳ ✳ ✳ ✳ ✳ ✳ ✳ ✳ ✳ ✳ ✳ ✳

☿ ♀   QUIRKY CREATIVES

T he stellar influences that govern those born on this day endow September 21 people with an unusual combination of characteristics and tendencies. On the one hand these intellectually progressive people are fascinated with the unusual and innovative, and are therefore drawn to the exploration of novel subjects at which more conventional types might balk. On the other hand they are sensuous types, who possess a highly developed aesthetic sense, as well as receptiveness to others. Not only do they feel compelled to seek out new experiences, but their appreciation of the potency of artistic media as powerful means of expression gives them the potential to make their highly original mark on the world as writers, composers, artists or movie-makers. They are aided in their quest to realize their extremely original ambitions by their strong practical and organizational skills, qualities that also equip them well for more technical or administrative careers.

Although their overriding preoccupation with their private visions inevitably sets September 21 people apart from the crowd, their ultimate aim is to share their discoveries or viewpoints with others. This concern often takes a spiritual or intellectual slant, so that while they may communicate their ideas simply, their messages are often extremely profound, (and even more so if they were born in the Chinese year of the pig). Nevertheless, they are frequently misunderstood, causing them either to withdraw further into their solitary world or to become discouraged or depressed. The unconditional love and support of those closest to them is therefore of great importance in bolstering their self-confidence.

PLANETARY INFLUENCES
Ruling planets: Mercury and Venus
Third decan: Personal planet is Venus
Second cusp: Virgo with Libran
    tendencies

VIRTUES
Original, innovative, artistic

VICES
Self-conscious, downbeat,
withdrawn

CAREERS
Writer, musician, administrator

SKILLS & APTITUDES
Creativity, vision, boldness

FAMOUS BIRTHS
H.G. Wells (1866)
Leonard Cohen (1934)
Stephen King (1947)
Bill Murray (1950)

COMPATIBLE WITH
January 6–10, May 21–22

SEPTEMBER 22

Academic Trailblazers ☿ ♀

Planetary Influences
Ruling planets: Mercury and Venus
Third decan: Personal planet is Venus
Second cusp: Virgo with Libran tendencies

Virtues
Clever, innovative, progressive

Vices
Defensive, uncompromising, combative

Careers
Academic, researcher, emergency medical worker

Skills & Aptitudes
Determination, self-belief, dedication to work

Famous Births
David Coverdale (1951)
Scott Baio (1961)
Joan Jett (1961)
Billie Piper (1982)

Compatible With
January 6–10, May 21–22

Those born on September 22 are typically motivated by two fundamental desires: to satisfy their intellectual thirst for stimulation and exploration; and to devote their energy to helping others. They may often combine these dual inclinations to form a single, remarkably progressive, vision, which they will promote with fierce determination.

Blessed with deeply perceptive and mercurial intellects, September 22 individuals are particularly adept at identifying social abuses, and devising imaginative and effective strategies with which to redress the situation. Not only are they drawn to innovative concepts and theories, but they also have a highly developed sense of justice that often compels them to work for the common good. Clearly suited to scientific, public service or humanitarian work, they may also seek to inform and enlighten others by means of writing or research—for example, by blogging on a subject that is close to their heart.

Despite their general concern for the welfare of others, their typically forthright manner and uncompromising promotion of their beliefs will inevitably alienate some people: those born on this day will therefore often be reluctantly forced to assume a confrontational stance in their desire to achieve their visions. They therefore rely on the unquestioning support of personal relationships, and they reciprocate the affection of those closest to them wholeheartedly, especially if they are women. It is important that they make a conscious effort to nurture close relationships to counterbalance the hostile and obstructive responses they will inevitably face at work.

♎ LIBRA

September 23 to October 22

RULING PLANET: *Venus* ELEMENT: *Cardinal air*
SYMBOL: *Scales* POLARITY: *Positive (masculine)* COLORS: *Pink, blue, lavender*
PHYSICAL CORRESPONDENCE: *Kidneys*
STONES: *Quartz, opal, jade, emerald, sapphire*
FLOWERS: *Rose, pansy, foxglove, daisy, hydrangea*

The balance or scales that represent the zodiacal sign of Libra are universal to the various astrological traditions: the Persians, Babylonians, and Hindus all gave it names that signify scales. The only notable exception was the symbol used by the ancient Greek astrologers, to whom Libra was Zugos, "the yoke." The constellation's association with a balance (or a primitive yoke with which oxen were harnessed) is explained by the fact that Libra dominates the period when night and day are of approximately equal length. Yet the image of the scales also has a more spiritual significance, for this instrument is symbolically related to ancient Egyptian lore, in which a balance was used in Osiris's hall of judgment to weigh the hearts of the recently deceased against the feather of Ma'at, the goddess of truth. Some scholars postulate that the ancient Egyptian hieroglyphic that symbolized Libra—which resembles the sign's modern sigil—represents the Sun (embodying masculinity) setting over the Earth (signifying femininity), an analogy compatible with both the postmortem weighing of souls and the balancing of opposing principles.

The Romans sometimes considered their deity of metal-working and measurement, Vulcan, to be present in this constellation, and his consort Venus (known as the morning star) is the planetary ruler of Libra. She endows those born under this sign with charm, a love of beauty, and a desire to bring harmony, while the element of air that further exerts its influence over Libra signifies intellectual affinities, as well as a desire for freedom. The zodiacal scales signify a strong sense of natural justice and steady psychological equilibrium, but may equally imply flightiness and emotional or intellectual indecisiveness.

SEPTEMBER 23

✿ ✿ ✿ ✿ ✿ ✿ ✿ ✿ ✿ ✿ ✿ ✿ ✿ ✿ ✿

EMPATHETIC CHARMERS   ☿ ♀

PLANETARY INFLUENCES
Ruling planets: Mercury and Venus
First decan: Personal planet is Venus
First cusp: Libra with Virgo
tendencies

VIRTUES
Resourceful, compassionate,
multitalented

VICES
Timid, sensitive, self-sacrificing

CAREERS
Novelist, screenplay writer, painter

SKILLS & APTITUDES
Respectfulness, stability, honesty

FAMOUS BIRTHS
Mickey Rooney (1920)
John Coltrane (1926)
Ray Charles (1930)
Bruce Springsteen (1949)

COMPATIBLE WITH
January 20–22, May 21–22

....
....
....

Others are drawn to September 23 individuals for a variety of reasons, including their unassuming personal charm, genuine kindness, integrity and reliability. Despite the potentially conflicting qualities that are bestowed by the planets that rule their day of birth—sensory indulgence and intellectual inquisitiveness—they are generally able to reconcile these characteristics, with the result that they are not only balanced, but also versatile. Thus while they are inspired by progressive visions, and typically display considerable energy and resourcefulness in pursuing them, their ambition is rarely at the expense of others. Those born on this day usually enjoy harmonious and mutually respectful working relationships, and many may choose to devote their careers to the service of others, perhaps—and particularly if they are women—within the caring professions.

September 23 people are also blessed with a sensitive appreciation of beauty, a gift that endows them with a profound affinity for the myriad forms of subtle expression encompassed by the artistic realm, and some may therefore choose to share their talents with a wider audience as writers, artists, movie-makers or, particularly well-starred for this date, musicians—both amateur and professional. Their pronounced empathy with, and orientation toward, other people characterizes all of their interpersonal relationships, and in turn they are regarded with deep affection by everyone with whom they come into contact. Their desire to please is genuine, and they typically treat others, especially those closest to them, with consideration, generosity and loyalty.

SEPTEMBER 24

✻ ✻ ✻ ✻ ✻ ✻ ✻ ✻ ✻ ✻ ✻ ✻ ✻

☿ ♀   INQUISITIVE LOVERS

LIBRA

For those born on September 24, the balance that symbolizes their astrological sign of Libra often appears weighted in favor of Venus, for not only are these people sensual and pleasure-loving, they also have a deep desire to love and be loved. Yet the presence of Mercury at the other end of their personality scale endows them with keenly curious intellectual qualities, adding a progressive and inquiring streak to their natures. While the dispositions of those born on this day vary from one individual to another, these two astrological influences generally combine to create people who are not only considerate, sensitive and empathetic, but are also oriented toward helping others through their resourceful and imaginative efforts. Some may be inclined to devote their careers to social, humanitarian or political issues, while other September 24 people may harness their affinity for all things artistic to their quest for enlightening or entertaining others, a propensity that is doubly pronounced if they were also born in the Chinese year of the goat.

The liaisons formed by those born on this day—be they professional or personal—are typically defined by these individuals' intuitive ability to detect unhappiness in others, and their urge to relieve such feelings of distress through positive and supportive gestures. Despite their sociability and concern for others' well-being, they do, however, have an inherent need both for periods of solitude, in which they can indulge in the pursuits that particularly interest them, and for intellectual and sensory stimulation. Unless these needs are fully respected by those closest to them, they may sometimes result in discord within their most intimate relationships.

PLANETARY INFLUENCES
Ruling planets: Mercury and Venus
First decan: Personal planet is Venus
First cusp: Libra with Virgo tendencies

VIRTUES
Empathetic, versatile, loving

VICES
Self-absorbed, noncommittal, detached

CAREERS
Artist, philosopher, news anchor

SKILLS & APTITUDES
Adventurousness, inventiveness, motivational skills

FAMOUS BIRTHS
F. Scott Fitzgerald (1896)
Fats Navarro (1923)
Jim Henson (1936)
Linda McCartney (1941)

COMPATIBLE WITH
January 20–25, May 21–27

LIBRA

SEPTEMBER 25

❋ ❋ ❋ ❋ ❋ ❋ ❋ ❋ ❋ ❋ ❋ ❋

PLANETARY INFLUENCES
Ruling planets: Mercury and Venus
First decan: Personal planet is Venus
First cusp: Libra with Virgo
tendencies

VIRTUES
Progressive, self-sufficient,
straightforward

VICES
Critical, belittling, blunt

CAREERS
News reporter, charity worker,
political campaigner

SKILLS & APTITUDES
Honesty, articulacy, analytical skills

FAMOUS BIRTHS
William Faulkner (1897)
Barbara Walters (1931)
Christopher Reeve (1952)
Will Smith (1968)

COMPATIBLE WITH
January 20–28, May 22–29

....
....
....

September 25 people are complex individuals whose primary personal characteristics can be somewhat contradictory. Their sympathetic and empathetic qualities lead them to identify with others, while their keen perception and independence of mind may cause them to stand apart from the crowd, noting and criticizing everything they observe. Ultimately, however, those born on this day often have noble aims, although their methods may not always make this clear.

People born on this day usually enjoy exploring their intellectual interests, be they scientific theories, modes of artistic expression, or societal structures and conventions, as well as sharing their knowledge with a wider audience. And because these are honest people who are not afraid of articulating the truth—however uncomfortable—and who possess an innate sense of natural justice, they have the potential to make effective political and social campaigners, although many may choose to communicate their ideas by means of journalism or artistic media.

In many respects their humanitarian orientation generally assumes a rather abstract form (especially if they are men), a tendency which, when combined with their need for personal autonomy of thought and action, may cause difficulties within their interpersonal relationships. For despite their genuine affection for those closest to them, and their relish for the comforts of domestic life, their judgemental propensities and need for independence may result in emotional isolation.

SEPTEMBER 26

✲ ✲ ✲ ✲ ✲ ✲ ✲ ✲ ✲ ✲ ✲ ✲ ✲ ✲

☿ ♀   IMPASSIONED PERFECTIONISTS

LIBRA

Others often regard September 26 individuals as perfectionists, whose tenacity in their desire to achieve their elevated visions is the subject of awed—if somewhat baffled—admiration. And indeed, when enthralled by an inspirational ambition, the determination, self-discipline and absorption manifested by those born on this day can become obsessive. Since they are also blessed with great imagination and an uncompromisingly logical turn of mind, their career potential is therefore of the highest order.

Many September 26 people are attracted by the progressive opportunities inherent in science and (especially) the arts, but all desire to make a positive contribution to humanity by means of their discoveries or guiding influence, prompting some to academic careers, and others to mentoring or recruitment.

Despite their intellectual independence and fascination—indeed, compulsion—for experimentation, the love and support those closest to them is of profound value to those born on this day, who innately recognize the importance of maintaining a grounding emotional counterbalance to their cerebral interests. Typically affectionate and loyal to those who believe in them, as well as interesting and enlivening companions, they may nevertheless unwittingly neglect their emotional needs, or those of their loved ones, when their attention is irresistibly occupied by a work-related challenge (a tendency that is even more pronounced if they are men). For those September 26 people for whom work becomes overly important, it may be sensible to develop recreational interests, particularly sociable ones—for example, joining a choir.

PLANETARY INFLUENCES
Ruling planets: Mercury and Venus
First decan: Personal planet is Venus
First cusp: Libra with Virgo
tendencies

VIRTUES
Resourceful, scholarly, ambitious

VICES
Compulsive, obsessive, neurotic

CAREERS
Tutor, academic researcher,
recruitment consultant

SKILLS & APTITUDES
Imagination, drive, attention to
detail

FAMOUS BIRTHS
T.S. Eliot (1888)
George Gershwin (1898)
Olivia Newton-John (1948)
Serena Williams (1981)

COMPATIBLE WITH
January 21–30, May 18–20,
May 23–30

LIBRA

SEPTEMBER 27

✿ ✿ ✿ ✿ ✿ ✿ ✿ ✿ ✿ ✿ ✿ ✿ ✿ ✿

INSPIRING LEADERS ♀

PLANETARY INFLUENCES
Ruling planet: Venus
First decan: Personal planet is Venus

VIRTUES
Perceptive, fearless, determined

VICES
Outspoken, perfectionist, demanding

CAREERS
Graphic designer, lobbyist, motivational speaker

SKILLS & APTITUDES
Ability to inspire others, self-motivation, sense of justice

FAMOUS BIRTHS
Samuel Adams (1722)
Jayne Meadows (1926)
Don Cornelius (1936)
Avril Lavigne (1984)

COMPATIBLE WITH
January 22–31, May 18–20, May 24–31

Those born on this day are determined and vigorous individuals who are driven by their ambitions, however obstacle-strewn the path to success. Indeed, in many respects they are stimulated by adversity, leading others to wonder why they so often appear to focus on difficult and demanding aims instead of opting for those that offer an easier route to success. There are no easy answers to this question, for these are complex people, whose motivations vary. Imbued with a strong sense of fairness, which causes them to seek to reverse social injustices, many feel compelled to engage in a personal struggle of strength by testing their abilities against the most unpromising of challenges. Yet because these are objective and realistic types, their aims are rarely unfeasible, and September 27 people's courage, tenacity and perfectionism augur well for their attainment.

Despite their pronounced individualistic stance, their critical and progressive faculties are usually oriented toward humanitarian aims, and they may therefore choose to employ their talents as either political, social or legal campaigners, or else artistic, technical or design pioneers whose efforts are intended to inspire or enhance others' lives. In terms of their interpersonal liaisons, they operate well as team captains (but not as small and unquestioning cogs in a larger social wheel) and they prefer to lead by example, demanding the same level of commitment from others as they themselves demonstrate. Despite their profound concern and affection for their loved ones, their judgemental and perfectionist tendencies may make for explosive personal relationships.

SEPTEMBER 28

✸ ✸ ✸ ✸ ✸ ✸ ✸ ✸ ✸ ✸ ✸ ✸ ✸ ✸ ✸

♀ ALLURING ROMANTICS

LIBRA

September 28 people are particularly susceptible to the potent influence of the planet of Venus that governs their day of birth, and, like the eponymous Roman goddess of love, many seek fulfillment through affairs of the heart, indulgence of the senses, or the pursuit of beauty in all its forms. They are also, however, imaginative and empathetic types who wish to bring progress and harmony to the world, even while they have a special affinity with the less tangible spiritual and artistic concerns that arouse strong emotional responses in them. Their intellectual independence and compulsion to explore the world of emotions and senses cause those born on this day to place a far greater value on nonmaterialistic achievements than on those that offer rewards of wealth and status. The hard-nosed realm of commerce is therefore anathema to them, and they will generally flourish only when they can satisfy their natural inclinations and inspire others in the process, as artists, writers, designers or actors, for example, or even as athletes.

Others are drawn to these magnetic people for the aura that they exude, and they in turn are not only stimulated by personal interaction, but manifest a concern for the happiness of those with whom they come into contact. Yet ironically their relationships with their nearest and dearest may not be of the smoothest, for despite their love for those closest to them, their innate nonconformity and urge to further their personal progress by means of individual experience precludes their capacity to sacrifice their independence to the altar of familial harmony. Their romantic idealism may furthermore set an impossibly high standard for their partners.

PLANETARY INFLUENCES
Ruling planet: Venus
First decan: Personal planet is Venus

VIRTUES
Individualistic, artistic, idealistic

VICES
Critical, hard to please, unrealistic

CAREERS
Artist, interior designer, retail buyer

SKILLS & APTITUDES
Creativity, progressiveness, adventurousness

FAMOUS BIRTHS
Ed Sullivan (1902)
Brigitte Bardot (1934)
Janeane Garofalo (1964)
Hilary Duff (1987)

COMPATIBLE WITH
January 24–31, February 1, May 18–20, May 25–31

SEPTEMBER 29

✳ ✳ ✳ ✳ ✳ ✳ ✳ ✳ ✳ ✳ ✳ ✳ ✳ ✳

INGENIOUS INFLUENCERS ♀

PLANETARY INFLUENCES
Ruling planet: Venus
First decan: Personal planet is Venus

VIRTUES
Perceptive, practical, inspirational

VICES
Unsatisfied, imbalanced, unsettled

CAREERS
Artist, sculptor, writer

SKILLS & APTITUDES
Motivational qualities, leadership skills, flexibility

FAMOUS BIRTHS
Miguel de Cervantes (1547)
Gene Autry (1907)
Jerry Lee Lewis (1935)
Kevin Durant (1988)

COMPATIBLE WITH
January 27–31, February 1–3, May 27–31, June 1

There are often two distinct sides to the characters of those born this day, for on the one hand they have a predilection for bringing about harmonious solutions to unbalanced situations and circumstances through orderly systems, yet on the other they are highly imaginative, sensitive and idealistic individuals, whose instinctive responses may create the same chaos within their personal lives as they devote their professional energies to trying to resolve. Maintaining their intellectual and emotional balance may therefore be a constant struggle, for September 29 people possess a strong sense of social responsibility and often feel compelled to suppress their own needs in order to concentrate their efforts on helping others. These are thus multifaceted people, who promote their ideas with determination, yet never lose their sensitivity and feelings of empathy toward others.

The combination of their tenacity and originality, along with their positive orientation toward others, endows September 29 people with the ability to inspire others, whether in the pursuit of a tangible common quest or in the more intangible arena of artistry, with which in any case they have a strong affinity. Yet many find that personal happiness is an elusive commodity—perhaps because their active concern with the well-being of others may obscure their recognition of what is most important for their own emotional fulfillment. Thus, while they manifest both genuine affection and loyalty to their nearest and dearest, their tendency to sublimate selfish desires in favor of more altruistic behavior (a trait that is especially pronounced in the women born on this day) may leave them feeling dissatisfied, restless or frustrated.

SEPTEMBER 30

✳ ✳ ✳ ✳ ✳ ✳ ✳ ✳ ✳ ✳ ✳ ✳ ✳

♀   SENSITIVE MORALISTS

LIBRA

Those born on this day are focused individuals, who can perhaps best be characterized as champions of the truth, for they have an acute eye for identifying what they believe to be social or intellectual wrongs. They are driven by the desire to convince others of the veracity of their judgements and thereby effect change. Because they are especially sensitive to social injustice, and are extraordinarily empathetic toward the victims of such abuse, September 30 people are strongly drawn to those professions where they can devote their energy and talents to rectifying the situation. And in working toward their humanitarian aims they typically utilize their organizational skills, uncompromisingly logical intellectual approach and meticulous attention to detail in building dynamic force for progress. Because they recognize that their efforts will often be met with opposition, they strive to create a veritable armory of weapons, which they employ with courage and resourcefulness. There is a danger, however, that their heightened sense of justice may lead them to employ an overly aggressive approach toward those—especially their nearest and dearest—whose behavior does not live up to their high moral standards.

Their inclinations clearly suit these individuals for careers where they can make tangible advances, for example as social campaigners, lawyers or members of the caring professions. But those born on this day also have a sensual affinity with the beauty inherent in the arts, and many will therefore seek both to help others and to provide inspiration through literature, music, or visual forms of artistic expression.

PLANETARY INFLUENCES
Ruling planet: Venus
First decan: Personal planet is Venus

VIRTUES
Fair, focused, compassionate

VICES
Judgmental, critical, intolerant

CAREERS
Lawyer, analyst, nurse

SKILLS & APTITUDES
Organizational skills, precision, protectiveness

FAMOUS BIRTHS
Hans Geiger (1882)
Truman Capote (1924)
Elie Wiesel (1928)
Martina Higgins (1980)

COMPATIBLE WITH
January 28–31, February 1–3, May 29–31, June 1–3

LIBRA

PLANETARY INFLUENCES
Ruling planet: Venus
Second decan: Personal planet is Saturn

VIRTUES
Original, loyal, disciplined

VICES
Perfectionist, obsessive, highly strung

CAREERS
Biologist, architect, civil engineer

SKILLS & APTITUDES
Dedication, responsibility, groundedness

FAMOUS BIRTHS
James Whitmore (1921)
Jimmy Carter (1924)
Julie Andrews (1935)
Zach Galifianakis (1969)

COMPATIBLE WITH
February 1–4, May 30–31, June 1–4, June 22–25

OCTOBER 1

✸ ✸ ✸ ✸ ✸ ✸ ✸ ✸ ✸ ✸ ✸ ✸ ✸ ✸

INVENTIVE REFORMERS   ♀ ♄

Those born on this day are focused individuals, the majority of whom are unquestionably ambitious. However, their goals rarely have to do with personal glory or self-aggrandizement (although most appreciate the security and comfort that comes with the attainment of financial rewards), being instead concerned with the achievement of more intellectually significant matters. By working toward their inspirational visions, they hope to not only satisfy their desire to progress as far as possible as individuals, but also to leave a lasting legacy that will benefit their peers and, perhaps, even future generations.

Some October 1 people may thus seek to aid human advancement by devoting their energies to political or humanitarian pursuits; some will capitalize on their precision and natural aptitude for the innovative possibilities offered by the scientific or technical fields; and some will be attracted to exploring and pushing forward the more subtle boundaries of artistic expression, with which all of those born on this day have a strong affinity. To all these endeavors they bring their dedication, tenacity and no-nonsense approach to getting the job done.

October 1 people may find themselves elevated to leadership positions, but while they will discharge their responsibilities to others with integrity, they may nevertheless resent being distracted from their work. A similar duality often prevails in their personal relationships, for although they draw strength from the affection they receive from their loved ones, their preoccupation with intellectual concerns may preclude their ability to reciprocate in kind.

OCTOBER 2

✳ ✳ ✳ ✳ ✳ ✳ ✳ ✳ ✳ ✳ ✳ ✳ ✳ ✳ ✳

♀ ♄

LOVABLE EXTROVERTS

LIBRA

The infectiously invigorating aura of vitality and joie de vivre of those born on October 2 attracts others to them, and these gregarious, pleasure-loving types in turn relish the stimulation of social interaction. Whatever career they choose to pursue, their strong orientation toward others invariably plays an integral part—whether it be in the nature of their work (often in the service industries or sales) or in the interpersonal professional relationships that they form. In all their ventures, their favored approach is typically a direct one aimed at attaining their goals as swiftly and effectively as possible. Because they have a propensity for making instant decisions and then promoting them with determination, October 2 people have little patience with those who manifest uncertainty or prevaricate, and will seek to influence them to adopt the course that they believe to be the correct one. Their self-certainty and predilection for action thus endows them with leadership potential (which is doubly pronounced if they were also born in the Chinese year of the dragon).

Despite their genuinely well-intentioned desire to guide others—and particularly those closest to them—those born on this day may have difficulty persuading others of the veracity of their viewpoints. The problem frequently stems from their propensity to analyze every issue that holds their attention in black-and-white terms—a tendency that may lead them to ignore the subtleties in between. And, since they are straightforwardly direct and have the courage of their convictions, the unvarnishedly honest expression of their beliefs may alienate the very individuals whom they are trying to help.

PLANETARY INFLUENCES
Ruling planet: Venus
Second decan: Personal planet is Saturn

VIRTUES
Gregarious, intelligent, determined

VICES
Confrontational, self-sabotaging, blinkered

CAREERS
Salesperson, trainer, principal

SKILLS & APTITUDES
Goal orientation, strength of will, leadership skills

FAMOUS BIRTHS
Mahatma Gandhi (1869)
Groucho Marx (1890)
Sting (1951)
Kelly Ripa (1970)

COMPATIBLE WITH
February 2–5, May 31, June 1–5, June 22–25

OCTOBER 3

✲ ✲ ✲ ✲ ✲ ✲ ✲ ✲ ✲ ✲ ✲ ✲ ✲ ✲

INSPIRATIONAL PROBLEM–SOLVERS   ♀ ♄

PLANETARY INFLUENCES

Ruling planet: Venus
Second decan: Personal planet is
Saturn

VIRTUES

Strong-willed, focused, practical

VICES

Highly strung, hard to please,
critical

CAREERS

Artist, inspirational speaker,
research scientist

SKILLS & APTITUDES

Logical mindset, problem-solving
abilities, attention to detail

FAMOUS BIRTHS

Chubby Checker (1941)
Stevie Ray Vaughan (1954)
Gwen Stefani (1969)
Kevin Richardson (1972)

COMPATIBLE WITH

February 3–7, June 1–6,
June 22–25

The streak of perfectionism that is manifested by the majority of those born under the astrological sign of Libra is particularly pronounced in October 3 individuals, who are constantly striving to achieve the very best—both in terms of their personal activities and within the more global realm of human endeavor. Blessed with incisive perspicacity, a direct and logical intellectual approach, as well as remarkable resourcefulness in overcoming obstacles, these are people who find it easy to identify areas that are flawed or ripe for improvement and then to formulate imaginative and straightforward strategies to bring about progress. Their natural inclinations and talents equip them for professions where they can benefit others by initiating tangible advances, giving them the potential to make particularly innovative scientists or engineers, inspirational and ground-breaking artists or, indeed, pioneering figures in such socially oriented realms as government.

While October 3 people are to be admired for their energy and dedication, others may wonder why they are so unwilling to delegate tasks to others or to take satisfaction from their own achievements. The answer lies in both their active natures and their predilection for critical evaluation, which they apply as objectively to themselves as to others. Their desire to exert a benevolent influence on the lives of those around them pervades all their interpersonal relationships, although the importance they accord their work may result in them spending less quality time with their family and friends than they would under ideal circumstances (especially if they are men).

OCTOBER 4

✳ ✳ ✳ ✳ ✳ ✳ ✳ ✳ ✳ ✳ ✳ ✳ ✳ ✳ ✳

♀ ♄   BALANCED PROTECTORS

LIBRA

Not only do most October 4 individuals seem remarkably at ease with themselves, but they also have a pronounced gift for getting along harmoniously with other people. In many respects their relaxed attitude to life is the product of their astutely perceptive way of looking at the world, which endows them with a strong sense of realism as to the nature of what is possible and what is simply unfeasible. This is not to say that they do not harbor firm opinions or inspirational visions and, when convinced that these are ultimately attainable, work toward their realization with clear-sighted determination, but rather that they instinctively prefer not to waste their energy trying to effect impossible changes. For this reason they are often drawn to professions where they can not only achieve tangible goals but also make a significant and positive contribution to the lives of others. Thus careers are indicated as social workers, doctors, lawyers or judges, for example, or as engineers or scientists.

Those born on this day manifest their genuine interest for others within all their interpersonal relationships, and the subjects of their concern in turn appreciate their good-humored and tolerant acceptance of human quirks and foibles and respect their integrity. And, since October 4 people are also sensual types who are blessed with an infectious sense of fun, they have a talent for enlivening even their most serious ventures. A similar combination of invigorating joie de vivre and steady and benevolent protectiveness characterizes their more personal liaisons, especially if they are men or if they were also born in the Chinese year of the dog.

PLANETARY INFLUENCES
Ruling planet: Venus
Second decan: Personal planet is Saturn

VIRTUES
Level-headed, gregarious, ambitious

VICES
Easily distracted, overextended, disconnected

CAREERS
Lawyer, pediatrician, judge

SKILLS & APTITUDES
Social skills, energy, realism

FAMOUS BIRTHS
Charlton Heston (1924)
Anne Rice (1941)
Susan Sarandon (1946)
M. Ward (1973)

COMPATIBLE WITH
February 4–9, June 3–7, June 22–25

OCTOBER 5

✴ ✴ ✴ ✴ ✴ ✴ ✴ ✴ ✴ ✴ ✴ ✴ ✴ ✴

EMPATHETIC DEFENDERS ♀ ♄

PLANETARY INFLUENCES
Ruling planet: Venus
Second decan: Personal planet is
   Saturn

VIRTUES
Sensitive, optimistic, admirable

VICES
Self-righteous, impatient,
temperamental

CAREERS
Actor, musician, activist

SKILLS & APTITUDES
Resourcefulness, supportiveness,
leadership skills

FAMOUS BIRTHS
Robert Goddard (1882)
Clive Barker (1952)
Neil deGrasse Tyson (1958)
Kate Winslet (1975)

COMPATIBLE WITH
February 5–9, June 4–8,
June 22–25

Two predominant characteristics influence those born on this day: their highly developed sense of justice and their sensuality. Some may thus feel compelled to devote their professional energies to reversing perceived social or moral abuses—perhaps as social campaigners or judges—while others may make successful careers within such artistic specialties as drama or music. Yet in whatever field they choose, they will typically display both a marked humanitarian concern and a predilection for sensory indulgence, thus making them not only deeply empathetic and supportive to those in need, but also charming, sociable and fun-loving. Despite their independence of thought, those born on this day are natural team leaders rather than solitary operators, who are blessed with an impressive talent for motivating others in the determined pursuit of a common cause, and are admired by others for these qualities.

Ideally, many would prefer to explore their intellectual or artistic interests without distraction, but such is the importance that they attach to the just treatment of others that, in this imperfect world, their sense of ethical responsibility often propels them to assume a champion's mantle and vigorously defend those who they believe to be victims of injustice. In such instances they draw upon their courage and resourcefulness (frequently surprising others with their vehement forcefulness), but, when carried away with the urgency of their mission, they may nevertheless sabotage their own efforts by failing to adopt a more pragmatic and diplomatic approach. It goes without saying that October 5 people are loyal, loving and lively friends and family members, and particularly gifted parents.

OCTOBER 6

✳ ✳ ✳ ✳ ✳ ✳ ✳ ✳ ✳ ✳ ✳ ✳ ✳ ✳ ✳

♀ ♄   VERSATILE ADVENTURERS

LIBRA

Perhaps the defining characteristic of those born on October 6 is their zest for living—the urge to savor and be stimulated by the multitude of experiences and sensations that life has to offer. Their strong exploratory predilection is evident in everything they encounter or undertake, and whenever a novel person, situation or intellectual concept enters their personal orbit they will typically waste little time in enthusiastically garnering as much information as they can about it—their task assisted by their intuition, as well as their talent for swift analysis and judgement. Although their need to satisfy their intellectual curiosity is a compulsive one, October 6 people are rarely motivated by selfish urges, for their empathetic identification with others fills them with the desire to benefit those around them—and even humanity as a global entity—by means of their discoveries.

These multitalented and resourceful people will flourish in a variety of professions—provided, that is, that they can retain autonomy of thought and action—but they are especially well suited for careers where they can satisfy their progressive urges and influence others. Blessed with pioneering potential, the engineering, building and scientific realms have a fascinating allure for those born on this day, but perhaps the field that offers them the greatest opportunity for experimentation and expression is art and design, with which these undoubted sensualists have a naturally strong affinity. Interesting, positive and enlivening companions, partners and family members, October 6 individuals value the grounding bonds of kinship as a counterbalance to their somewhat restless intellectual tendencies.

PLANETARY INFLUENCES
Ruling planet: Venus
Second decan: Personal planet is Saturn

VIRTUES
Optimistic, progressive, enthusiastic

VICES
Flighty, frenzied, unsettled

CAREERS
Architect, web designer, retail manager

SKILLS & APTITUDES
Inventiveness, commitment, self-motivation

FAMOUS BIRTHS
George Westinghouse (1846)
Fannie Lou Hamer (1917)
Amy Jo Johnson (1970)
Ioan Gruffudd (1973)

COMPATIBLE WITH
February 6–10, June 5–9

OCTOBER 7

✳ ✳ ✳ ✳ ✳ ✳ ✳ ✳ ✳ ✳ ✳ ✳ ✳ ✳

ASSERTIVE GO–GETTERS   ♀ ♄

PLANETARY INFLUENCES
Ruling planet: Venus
Second decan: Personal planet is
  Saturn

VIRTUES
Alluring, engaging, assertive

VICES
Self-righteous, combative,
opinionated

CAREERS
Preacher, builder, entrepreneur

SKILLS & APTITUDES
Focus, determination, self-belief

FAMOUS BIRTHS
Amiri Baraka (1934)
Oliver North (1943)
Yo-Yo Ma (1955)
Toni Braxton (1967)

COMPATIBLE WITH
February 8–11, June 6–10,
December 1–3

Those born on this day are vigorous and strongly opinionated, and people who come into contact with them are impressed by their determined promotion of the ideals that motivate them (whether they agree or disagree). Indeed, October 7 people often engender love and loathing in equal measure and—although they are sensitive and apparently intuitively pick up the emotions exuded by others—they seem to accept the extremes of reactions that they provoke with equanimity, perhaps strengthened by their acceptance that progress cannot be achieved without alienating the more conventional upholders of the status quo. Thus while they would prefer to win allies rather than to make enemies, their strength of belief endows them with the courage to battle when necessary for the realization of their visions. Their profound orientation toward others and their all-encompassing curiosity typically compels those born on this day to strive to effect the advances they believe are justified.

The nature of their progressive urge varies according to the October 7 individual, and while many will choose to channel their energies in the furtherance of social or spiritual ideals, others will try to exert their influence on others through technical, creative or artistic pursuits. And, despite their radical messages, all employ their considerable personal charm, humor and ingenious and imaginative powers in the propagation of their aims. Within their personal relationships (which they often prefer to keep strictly separate from their intellectual or professional work), such gentler qualities come to the fore, especially with regard to those who arouse their protective instincts—their closest friends, partners and children in particular.

OCTOBER 8

✳ ✳ ✳ ✳ ✳ ✳ ✳ ✳ ✳ ✳ ✳ ✳ ✳ ✳

♀ ♄   WHIMSICAL ROMANTICISTS

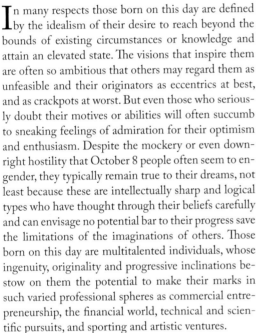

In many respects those born on this day are defined by the idealism of their desire to reach beyond the bounds of existing circumstances or knowledge and attain an elevated state. The visions that inspire them are often so ambitious that others may regard them as unfeasible and their originators as eccentrics at best, and as crackpots at worst. But even those who seriously doubt their motives or abilities will often succumb to sneaking feelings of admiration for their optimism and enthusiasm. Despite the mockery or even downright hostility that October 8 people often seem to engender, they typically remain true to their dreams, not least because these are intellectually sharp and logical types who have thought through their beliefs carefully and can envisage no potential bar to their progress save the limitations of the imaginations of others. Those born on this day are multitalented individuals, whose ingenuity, originality and progressive inclinations bestow on them the potential to make their marks in such varied professional spheres as commercial entrepreneurship, the financial world, technical and scientific pursuits, and sporting and artistic ventures.

Despite their great charm, the combination of their innate perfectionism and unceasing compulsion to attain their soaring visions may cause those born on this day to be somewhat demanding and remote with regard to their personal relationships, not only in their intellectual pursuits, but also when searching for a romantic idyll. Their ideal soul mate may prove elusive, with the result that October 8 people—and even more so if they are men—may find it hard to commit themselves to a potential life partner.

PLANETARY INFLUENCES
Ruling planet: Venus
Second decan: Personal planet is Saturn

VIRTUES
Optimistic, idealistic, clever

VICES
Scatterbrained, unrealistic, vague

CAREERS
Careers advisor, retail manager, writer

SKILLS & APTITUDES
Enthusiasm, imagination, self-belief

FAMOUS BIRTHS
Chevy Chase (1943)
R.L. Stine (1943)
Sigourney Weaver (1949)
Matt Damon (1970)

COMPATIBLE WITH
February 9–41, June 7–11, December 1–3

LIBRA

OCTOBER 9

✻ ✻ ✻ ✻ ✻ ✻ ✻ ✻ ✻ ✻ ✻ ✻ ✻ ✻

PERCEPTIVE OBSERVERS　　♀ ♄

PLANETARY INFLUENCES
Ruling planet: Venus
Second decan: Personal planet is
Saturn

VIRTUES
Mindful, sensitive, problem-solving

VICES
Critical, judgmental, dismissive

CAREERS
Psychiatrist, academic, school
counselor

SKILLS & APTITUDES
Observational skills, energy,
practical approach

FAMOUS BIRTHS
Bruce Catton (1899)
John Lennon (1940)
Sharon Osbourne (1952)
Tony Shalhoub (1953)
Guillermo del Toro (1964)
Bella Hadid (1996)

COMPATIBLE WITH
February 10–14, June 8–12,
December 1–3

Those born on October 9 are observant people, and little escapes their attention, particularly in the realm of human behavior and social systems, with which they are often strongly fascinated. Blessed with good powers of perception—both intellectual and intuitive—as well as a logically progressive mindset, these people are talented analysts who possess not only the ability to identify the nub of problems but also the ingenuity to devise strategies for improvement. Once they have determined the optimum method for effecting the advances they deem necessary, they will promote it with zeal and tenacity. Such a focused and determined approach augurs well for their potential success in whichever professional field holds their interest, but since the majority are oriented toward enlightening those around them, many will choose to direct their energies toward helping others—perhaps in mentoring roles as academics, psychiatrists, judges, social workers or even spiritual guides, or in those spheres where they can inspire by example, for instance as athletes or artists.

Although the independently minded individuals born on this day are natural leaders whose strength of conviction enables them to push bravely forward regardless of the opposition that their determined stance may provoke, they do not relish conflict for conflict's sake. They would far prefer to make friends rather than foes (especially if they are women). Their goodwill toward others is evident within all of their interpersonal relationships—particularly with regard to their nearest and dearest—although their tendency to criticize and direct, albeit with the best of motivations, may not always be taken in the spirit that it is intended.

OCTOBER 10

♀ ♄ METHODICAL ORGANIZERS

Those born on this day are sensible individuals who typically abhor disorder, regarding chaos as a hindrance to the progress that they are so intent on achieving. Indeed, blessed as they are with logical and perceptive intellects, they are able to identify the existing flaws in any situation they encounter and suggest constructive solutions. They positively itch to actively throw themselves into the absorbing task of bringing order and harmony to unproductive or otherwise unsatisfactory situations. In many respects they take as much pleasure in instituting and maintaining effectively functioning systems as they do in reaping the rewards of their labors, a predilection that is more pronounced if they were also born in the Chinese year of the rooster. Their inclinations and talents suit them to a wide variety of careers, and their no-nonsense, hands-on approach, self-discipline and realistic clarity of purpose augurs especially well for their success as supervisors, team leaders and business executives.

Many October 10 people display the same love of order within their personal lives, running smoothly functioning households and giving steady support—both emotional and financial—to their loved ones. Yet beneath the rational and balanced exterior they present to the wider world lies a more sensual and emotional core that not only endows those born on this day with a relish for indulging in the good things in life but also makes them susceptible to romance of all kinds. Thus when these two sides to their personalities are in harmony, others are drawn to them for their charming, as well as their reliable, qualities.

PLANETARY INFLUENCES
Ruling planet: Venus
Second decan: Personal planet is Saturn

VIRTUES
Perceptive, rational, practical

VICES
Repressed, negative, workaholic

CAREERS
CEO, manager, marketing executive

SKILLS & APTITUDES
Discipline, coordination, organizational skills

FAMOUS BIRTHS
David Lee Roth (1955)
Tanya Tucker (1958)
Brett Favre (1969)
Mario Lopez (1973)

COMPATIBLE WITH
February 10–14, June 9–13, December 1–3

LIBRA

PLANETARY INFLUENCES
Ruling planet: Venus
Second decan: Personal planet is Saturn

VIRTUES
Empathetic, intellectual, gentle

VICES
Extreme, self-indulgent, unyielding

CAREERS
Musician, charity worker, activist

SKILLS & APTITUDES
Concern for others, diligence, professionalism

FAMOUS BIRTHS
Eleanor Roosevelt (1884)
Elmore Leonard (1925)
Joan Cusack (1962)
Jane Krakowski (1968)

COMPATIBLE WITH
February 11–16, June 10–14

Those born on this day are positive individuals, who in many respects may be characterized as social idealists, for they are fueled by their desire to effect not only their own emotional happiness, but also that of others—be it those with whom they come into contact, wider communal groupings, or humanity as a global entity. Indeed, these twin aims are often inextricably linked, for such is the strong sense of natural justice possessed by these people, and their profound empathy with those whom they believe are being unfairly treated, that even if their own circumstances are harmonious they may nevertheless feel compelled to campaign on the behalf of the less fortunate. A similarly benevolent concern for others defines their personal and professional relationships, yet although they generally favor conciliation and cooperation over aggression and confrontation, their urge to reverse perceived injustices should not be underestimated (although it frequently is by those who misjudge their easy-going approach for weakness of will).

Balancing their altruism and clear-sighted perspicacity are the markedly more self-indulgent personal characteristics possessed by October 11 individuals. Their highly developed response to emotional and sensual stimuli bestows on them the tendency to immerse themselves with willing abandon in the pleasures of the senses. Given such extreme inclinations, those born on this day have the potential to flourish across a wide spectrum of professions—as writers, musicians, athletes, philanthropists or social reformers, for example.

OCTOBER 12

✳ ✳ ✳ ✳ ✳ ✳ ✳ ✳ ✳ ✳ ✳ ✳ ✳ ✳ ✳

♀ ♅ ☿　　MULTIFACETED INDEPENDENTS

LIBRA

The influences that govern October 12 endow those born on this day with complex characters: on the one hand pleasure-loving and sensual, these individuals are also independent, intellectually curious and resourceful types who demand autonomy while being simultaneously oriented toward others. Such a combination of personal characteristics may manifest in various ways, depending on the individual. Some may sublimate their self-indulgent side in their dedication to serving their communities in an imaginative yet traditional fashion; while others may appear to be more maverick, nonconformist types, who forge their own, inimitable paths through life. All, however, cherish the inherent desire—and, indeed, possess the potential—to lead or inspire others by example. Whatever career those born on this day choose to pursue, their ultimate aim is to make a concrete contribution to the advancement of humanity (perhaps as educators, or maybe as visionary researchers or academics) by instituting truly pioneering innovations.

Despite their prerequisite for independence, the actions of those born on this day are fueled by their selfless, humanitarian concern with improving the welfare of others. That is not to say that they do not appreciate the acclaim and rewards that may accompany their own success—to the contrary, they long to receive the recognition of their peers, and they welcome the security and comfort that money can buy—but rather that their goals are generally of the globally beneficial rather than personally ambitious variety. And, as long as their need for freedom is respected, they are generous and affectionate to those closest to them.

PLANETARY INFLUENCES
Ruling planet: Venus
Third decan: Personal planets are Uranus and Mercury

VIRTUES
Inquisitive, imaginative, organized

VICES
Attention-seeking, argumentative, eccentric

CAREERS
Technician, scientific researcher, academic

SKILLS & APTITUDES
Selflessness, innovativeness, ambition

FAMOUS BIRTHS
Jean Nidetch (1923)
Dick Gregory (1932)
Luciano Pavarotti (1935)
Hugh Jackman (1968)

COMPATIBLE WITH
February 11–16, June 11–15

OCTOBER 13

✳ ✳ ✳ ✳ ✳ ✳ ✳ ✳ ✳ ✳ ✳ ✳ ✳ ✳ ✳

CONFRONTATIONAL PROGRESSIVES ♀ ♅ ☿

PLANETARY INFLUENCES
Ruling planet: Venus
Third decan: Personal planets are Uranus and Mercury

VIRTUES
Focused, courageous, resourceful

VICES
Belligerent, unrealistic, demanding

CAREERS
Political activist, marketing manager, public-relations executive

SKILLS & APTITUDES
Focus, ambition, strategic planning

FAMOUS BIRTHS
Art Tatum (1910)
Sammy Hagar (1947)
Jerry Rice (1962)
Ashanti (1980)

COMPATIBLE WITH
February 12–17, June 12–17

....
....
....

Their strength of conviction and total focus on the attainment of their ideals inevitably arouses strong and unambiguous responses to those born on this day. Indeed, October 13 people recognize that their clear-cut visions and uncompromisingly direct methods have a tendency to shock the generally apathetic out of their lethargy. In many cases, however, they are naturally combative types who enjoy the cut and thrust of confrontational debate, not least because they secretly relish drawing the spotlight upon themselves. Apart from any attention-seeking motivations, these are intellectually progressive individuals, who possess strong feelings of social responsibility. Not only are they critical types who cannot help but identify perceived societal failings or injustices, but also their logical turn of mind endows them with the propensity to formulate practical strategies with which they can bring about positive advances for the benefit of others. Natural leaders, their strong communication skills suit October 13 people especially well for advertising and marketing careers, although they may equally excel as ground-breaking, if controversial, politicians.

Despite their typically well-intentioned humanitarian orientation, the concern that those born on this day manifest toward others often assumes an abstract rather than a personal form. Thus, although their fierce affection, support and ambition for their nearest and dearest is never in doubt, their innate perfectionism and personal standards may cause them to make near-impossible demands upon those closest to them, without consideration for personal predilections or talents, a tendency that is even more pronounced if they were also born in the Chinese year of the rooster.

OCTOBER 14

✳ ✳ ✳ ✳ ✳ ✳ ✳ ✳ ✳ ✳ ✳ ✳ ✳ ✳

♀ ⛢ ☿   INQUISITIVE INDIVIDUALISTS

LIBRA

The personalities of many of those born on this day typically manifest a curious combination of a marked propensity for excessive behavior and a striving for order and harmony. While some October 14 people are able to maintain their personal equilibrium—albeit with a struggle—others are not, particularly when such behavioral extremes are more pronounced. Blessed with enormous intellectual curiosity, which endows them with a strong sense of adventure—and these individuals are keen travelers—those born on this day are undoubtedly independently minded. Yet they also appreciate the importance of remaining grounded within the social conventions that bind society together, and therefore recognize the need to moderate, or at least channel, their more questing tendencies and self-indulgent cravings.

When they are successful, October 14 people have the potential to make imaginative and inspirational leaders, perhaps most obviously as social or political figureheads, but also as gifted and original teachers, painters, actors or designers.

To all their endeavors they bring their enthusiasm, good humor and unusual perspective on the world, making them attractive individuals who are popular with others. In turn October 14 people often identify strongly with the social group with which they have the strongest affinity, and they will work hard to promote or protect its interests. Although their preferred approach is to be easy-going, tolerant and noncombative, their readiness to protect those closest to them from any threat should not be underestimated.

PLANETARY INFLUENCES
Ruling planet: Venus
Third decan: Personal planets are Uranus and Mercury

VIRTUES
Receptive, imaginative, adventurous

VICES
Unbalanced, selfish, unrealistic

CAREERS
Schoolteacher, designer, healthcare worker

SKILLS & APTITUDES
Concern for others, inspirational qualities, leadership skills

FAMOUS BIRTHS
Dwight D. Eisenhower (1890)
e e cummings (1894)
Ralph Lauren (1939)
Usher (1978)

COMPATIBLE WITH
February 13–18, June 13–17

LIBRA

OCTOBER 15

✻ ✻ ✻ ✻ ✻ ✻ ✻ ✻ ✻ ✻ ✻ ✻ ✻ ✻

SOCIABLE NONCONFORMISTS ♀ ♅ ☿

PLANETARY INFLUENCES
Ruling planet: Venus
Third decan: Personal planets are
Uranus and Mercury

VIRTUES
Intelligent, orderly, organized

VICES
Jealous, headstrong, stubborn

CAREERS
Business owner, manager, event
coordinator

SKILLS & APTITUDES
Structured approach, attention to
detail, efficiency

FAMOUS BIRTHS
Friedrich Nietzsche (1844)
P.G. Wodehouse (1881)
Penny Marshall (1942)
Tito Jackson (1953)

COMPATIBLE WITH
February 14–18, June 14–18

Although October 15 individuals possess resolutely independent wills and cannot bear to be constrained in any way, they are also sociable types who are strongly connected to all those around them. Thus even though they are strong individualists, they are also socially concerned and responsible people whose actions are often motivated by their desire to make a significant contribution to the world, or to redress instances of injustice. Indeed, their mercurial minds and highly developed powers of perception and analysis, along with their relish of discovery and novelty, bestow upon them the potential to become pioneers in their specific field of interest, while their predilection for creating orderly and efficient systems gives them the ability to capitalize on their innovative visions by supporting them with soundly structured operational frameworks. Their natural talents, progressive inclinations and positive orientation toward others equip them admirably for a wide variety of careers, but they need to be able to retain autonomy of thought and action as well as interacting with others.

Despite their deep-rooted (but frequently rather abstract) concern for other people, the relationships that those born on this day form with others may sometimes be tempestuous, for although their affection for those closest to them is profound, their need for freedom is so strong that any perceived attempts to tie them down or make them conform to societal norms may arouse negative feelings of resistance (especially if they are men). As long as their nearest and dearest understand their innate desire for independence, however, they typically prove enlivening and generous partners and friends.

OCTOBER 16

✻ ✻ ✻ ✻ ✻ ✻ ✻ ✻ ✻ ✻ ✻ ✻ ✻

♀ ⛢ ☿   BLUNT OBSERVERS

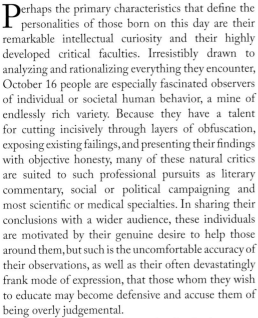

LIBRA

Perhaps the primary characteristics that define the personalities of those born on this day are their remarkable intellectual curiosity and their highly developed critical faculties. Irresistibly drawn to analyzing and rationalizing everything they encounter, October 16 people are especially fascinated observers of individual or societal human behavior, a mine of endlessly rich variety. Because they have a talent for cutting incisively through layers of obfuscation, exposing existing failings, and presenting their findings with objective honesty, many of these natural critics are suited to such professional pursuits as literary commentary, social or political campaigning and most scientific or medical specialties. In sharing their conclusions with a wider audience, these individuals are motivated by their genuine desire to help those around them, but such is the uncomfortable accuracy of their observations, as well as their often devastatingly frank mode of expression, that those whom they wish to educate may become defensive and accuse them of being overly judgemental.

Others admire those born on this day for their stimulating wit, integrity and independence of mind, but often choose to do so from a distance, safely removed from the line of fire. And unless those closest to them have extra thick skins or are extremely forgiving, the dual propensity of October 16 people to criticize others while reserving the right to behave as they wish can make them difficult to live with. But despite their tendency to speak their minds, their intentions are rarely malicious, and beneath their tough exterior lies a generous and affectionate heart.

PLANETARY INFLUENCES
Ruling planet: Venus
Third decan: Personal planets are Uranus and Mercury

VIRTUES
Helpful, perceptive, knowledgeable

VICES
Belittling, critical, bruising

CAREERS
Psychiatrist, literary critic, political analyst

SKILLS & APTITUDES
Attention to detail, articulacy, principled

FAMOUS BIRTHS
Oscar Wilde (1854)
Angela Lansbury (1925)
Suzanne Somers (1946)
John Mayer (1977)

COMPATIBLE WITH
February 15–18, June 15–19

....

....

....

OCTOBER 17

✳ ✳ ✳ ✳ ✳ ✳ ✳ ✳ ✳ ✳ ✳ ✳ ✳ ✳

INQUISITIVE THINKERS   ♀ ♅ ☿

Inherent in the characters of those born on this day is a mixture of conflicting qualities. On the one hand, they're perfectionists who seek to improve upon existing circumstances, and on the other, sensation-seekers who are stimulated by the lure of the new. Depending on their personal make-up, these essential characteristics may be in equilibrium or may combine to produce either staunch and judgmental traditionalists or intellectually and physically reckless types. Common to all, however, will be their strength of conviction and desire to influence others. Blessed with powerfully perceptive and analytical minds, those born on this day are rarely willing to accept the conventions of others without question, but instead feel compelled to think through and reach their own conclusions. And, once convinced, they will defend or promote their viewpoints with vigorous tenacity.

The combination of their social orientation and independence of thought fuels those born on this day with the urge to lead by example, particularly at work. Thus although they may derive great personal satisfaction from their career pursuits, their ultimate intention is to further the advancement of humanity. Many are therefore suited to educational careers, while others may seek to communicate their findings by means of more subtle artistic expression, or by effecting scientific or technical innovations. Yet despite their profound desire to enlighten and instruct those around them—especially those closest to them, whose affection is so vital to their emotional balance—their nearest and dearest may either feel neglected as a result of their more global concern with others, or become the undeserving victims of their critical pronouncements.

OCTOBER 18

✳ ✳ ✳ ✳ ✳ ✳ ✳ ✳ ✳ ✳ ✳ ✳ ✳ ✳

♀ ♅ ☿   Versatile Ambiverts

LIBRA

Self-reliant and yet socially aware, October 18 individuals typically have two prerequisites for their personal happiness: freedom to explore intellectual issues, and stimulation and opportunity to pursue the shared goals inherent in their interpersonal activities. These are on the one hand essentially selfish and, on the other, more altruistic urges, and their innate attraction to both may result in a finely balanced variety of interests or cause them to favor one or the other. Whatever their personal inclinations, however, all have analytical, progressive and resourceful qualities, as well as a highly developed sense of responsibility for safeguarding the common good and promoting the happiness of others. In the most serendipitous of professional circumstances, October 18 people will flourish in those careers where, while working toward advancing the welfare of others, they are allowed the autonomy of thought and action that is so vital to them.

When thus harnessed to their social orientation, their intellectual versatility and imaginative talents augur well for their success as teachers, although many may choose to impart their messages by developing more overtly creative means of expression—as artists, writers, actors or musicians, for example. In all their endeavors, however individualistic, their genuine benevolence and obvious sincerity engenders the respect and affection of others, while their easy-going, humorous wit draws people to them. There is a danger, however, that those born on this day may give more than they receive—particularly if they are also women—and that they may therefore become overburdened by the demands of others.

PLANETARY INFLUENCES
Ruling planet: Venus
Third decan: Personal planets are Uranus and Mercury

VIRTUES
Affectionate, balanced, inspiring

VICES
Overwhelmed, vain, selfish

CAREERS
Caregiver, self-help author, emergency medical worker

SKILLS & APTITUDES
Resourcefulness, motivational skills, open-mindedness

FAMOUS BIRTHS
Chuck Berry (1926)
Peter Boyle (1935)
Jean-Claude Van Damme (1960)
Zac Efron (1987)

COMPATIBLE WITH
February 16–18, June 17–21

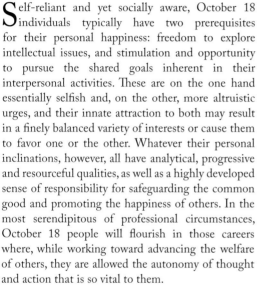

OCTOBER 19

✳ ✳ ✳ ✳ ✳ ✳ ✳ ✳ ✳ ✳ ✳ ✳ ✳ ✳

TENACIOUS WARRIORS   ♀ ♇ ♅ ☿

The influences that govern their day of birth endow October 19 people with a complex set of personal characteristics which they may spend their lives struggling to reconcile. Although they are sensual individuals who seek to find happiness in the simpler things in life, such as beauty or personal relationships, they are also inquisitive, reluctant to accept conventional truths without having first analyzed them to their own satisfaction. Simultaneously peace-loving yet prepared to fight for the causes in which they believe, they often feel torn between defending the status quo and battling to reverse injustices or promote their visions. Perhaps the single most striking quality manifested by those born on this day, however, is their desire to benefit the social group with which they most strongly identify by means of their independent discoveries or actions. Energetic and determined individuals who do not shrink from taking a contrary stance if they believe it to be right, they are natural leaders and innovators, whose talents and inclinations equip them admirably as scientists and artistic pioneers.

Despite their social orientation and propensity for acting on behalf of the greater good, October 19 people may appear to be somewhat solitary figures. This is in part a result of their jealously upheld prerequisite for personal autonomy, and the inevitable product of their uncompromisingly direct approach, which may at best intimidate, and at worst incur the enmity of those who feel themselves threatened. Yet when they are fortunate enough to enjoy unquestioning tolerance and love, their softer, profoundly protective, affectionate and generous side emerges, particularly if they were also born in the Chinese year of the ox.

OCTOBER 20

✻ ✻ ✻ ✻ ✻ ✻ ✻ ✻ ✻ ✻ ✻ ✻ ✻ ✻

♀ ♇ ⛢ ☿   ARTISTIC TRAILBLAZERS

LIBRA

There are typically two sides to the personalities of October 20 people: their artistry, evident in their aesthetic appreciation, sensuality and creativity; and their harder, more judgmental qualities. Those born on this day accommodate both propensities within their daily lives, perhaps indulging their artistic tastes in relaxing pastimes and pursuing more conventional careers or, if they are especially talented, earning their livings as professional artists, writers, designers or architects. Whatever career they choose, however, their highly developed visual and analytic powers generally play an important part in their success, as do their objective and independent turn of mind and their desire to make a significant contribution to humanity. Such personal characteristics and inclinations equip these people for a wide range of professions, from scientific research to politics and social campaigning, or from sporting activities to business and commerce.

Despite their twin enthusiasms for sensory and intellectually stimulating exploration, those born on this day are rarely maverick types who give themselves completely over to self-indulgent activities; on the contrary, they possess remarkable discipline, especially when engaged in promoting the common good. Possessed of strong convictions formed jointly by their capacity for logical analysis and their progressive imaginations, these otherwise easy-going individuals can display tremendous determination—even obstinacy—when called upon to defend or promote their beliefs, and will resort to combative tactics if necessary. However, they are interesting and invigorating companions, who display genuine concern for, and enormous magnanimity toward, their nearest and dearest.

PLANETARY INFLUENCES
Ruling planet: Venus and Pluto
Third decan: Personal planets are Uranus and Mercury
Second cusp: Libra with Scorpio tendencies

VIRTUES
Expressive, creative, sensitive

VICES
Flighty, combative, noncommital

CAREERS
Surveyor, business owner, digital designer

SKILLS & APTITUDES
Self-discipline, objectiveness, logical approach

FAMOUS BIRTHS
Bela Lugosi (1884)
Joyce Brothers (1928)
Mickey Mantle (1931)
Tom Petty (1953)

COMPATIBLE WITH
February 17–18, June 19–21

Planetary Influences
Ruling planet: Venus and Pluto
Third decan: Personal planets are Uranus and Mercury
Second cusp: Libra with Scorpio tendencies

Virtues
Idealistic, charming, thoughtful

Vices
Vain, self-obsessed, negative

Careers
Activist, motivational speaker, engineer

Skills & Aptitudes
Creativity, intuition, drive

Famous Births
Alfred Nobel (1833)
"Dizzy" Gillespie (1917)
Carrie Fisher (1956)
Jeremy Miller (1976)
Doja Cat (1995)

Compatible With
June 20–21

OCTOBER 21

Charismatic Defenders ♀ ♇ ♅ ☿

Others admire those born on this day for their charisma, as well as their physical and intellectual vigor, and are drawn into their personal orbit by their charming nature and infectious joie de vivre. Indeed, in an ideal world October 21 people would like nothing more than to indulge their sensual and pleasure-loving propensities, sharing their enjoyment of such entertainment with like-minded individuals. But since they are perceptive and critical types who wish to make a contribution to society, they recognize the unfeasibility of such an agreeable scenario. Because they are so concerned with effecting the well-being of others on the one hand and have such a strong affinity with artistic pursuits on the other, many of these people will combine these two interests to make careers as inspirational writers, artists, musicians and actors. Others may prefer to capitalize upon their analytical skills and progressive inclinations within the realms of science or commerce as long as their need for personal autonomy of thought and action is not compromised, a prerequisite that is especially important if they were also born in the Chinese year of the horse.

Yet despite their undoubted ability to sublimate their more selfish desires in favor of what they perceive to be the common good, they remain profoundly emotionally oriented individuals whose desire to attain their romantic ideals cannot be completely suppressed (nor, indeed, should it be). This propensity may find an outlet in social or artistic idealism, but is more often directed toward their nearest and dearest—and particularly their partners—who may find it difficult to live up to the idealized qualities that are projected upon them.

OCTOBER 22

✱ ✱ ✱ ✱ ✱ ✱ ✱ ✱ ✱ ✱ ✱ ✱ ✱ ✱ ✱

♀ ♇ ♅ ☿   BENEVOLENT ECCENTRICS

LIBRA

Those born on this day are blessed with a charismatic presence that draws all eyes to them, and although they are not averse to basking in the attention of others, they would prefer to be admired for their capabilities rather than for more superficial reasons. And, indeed, October 22 people possess a veritable treasure chest of talents and positive qualities, including their intelligent thoughtfulness, which endows them with the ability to discriminate between right and wrong, and their profound empathy with those whose circumstances are less than happy, as well as their urge to defend or promote the interests of those with whom they identify. Although they are imaginative and independent individuals who are irresistibly attracted to seeking out and exploring novel experiences, their ultimate aim is to combine their personal predilections with their desire to assist the emotional or circumstantial advancement of others.

Despite their orientation toward others, however, October 22 individuals remain resolute individualists who never lose sight of their emotional ideals, a propensity that may make them difficult to live with, in that they may become overly preoccupied with their dreams or else make unfeasible demands of their nearest and dearest. Especially perfectionist when it comes to the regulation of their own lives, they typically set their visionary sights high, and will work toward their attainment with prodigious determination. Best suited to careers where they can pursue their innovative aims freely, those born on this day will therefore especially flourish as artists working in a variety of specialties; or, with their powerful sense of justice, careers in the legal or social spheres.

PLANETARY INFLUENCES
Ruling planet: Venus and Pluto
Third decan: Personal planets are Uranus and Mercury
Second cusp: Libra with Scorpio tendencies

VIRTUES
Imaginative, sensitive, empathetic

VICES
Demanding, strict, unforgiving

CAREERS
Judge, police officer, beautician

SKILLS & APTITUDES
Multitasking, focus, sense of justice

FAMOUS BIRTHS
Franz Liszt (1811)
Christopher Lloyd (1938)
Deepak Chopra (1947)
Jeff Goldblum (1952)

COMPATIBLE WITH
June 20–21

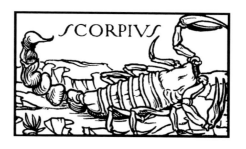

♏ SCORPIO

October 23 to November 21

RULING PLANET: *Pluto* ELEMENT: *Fixed water*
SYMBOL: *Scorpion* POLARITY: *Negative (feminine)* COLORS: *Red, maroon*
PHYSICAL CORRESPONDENCE: *Genitals, bladder*
STONES: *Topaz, agate, ruby, garnet, carnelian, amber*
FLOWERS: *Heather, thistle, geranium, chrysanthemum*

With the exception of the ancient Egyptian zodiac, which depicted a scarab presiding over this sign, most astrological traditions have seen a scorpion's form in this constellation. The cultural myths associated with Scorpio are primarily concerned with protection and aggression: for example, in Greco-Roman lore a scorpion was sent by Apollo to punish Orion for his vanity: the constellation of Orion sets when Scorpio rises. Sacred to the god of war, Ares (Mars), the scorpion—and the characteristics it confers on those born under its sign—was said to mirror the deity's disposition, in particular his martial, combative qualities. Scorpio's association with destruction is further underlined by the ancient Egyptians' belief that Osiris died when the Sun was in Scorpio, while the Celtic festival of Samhain (Hallowe'en) was also celebrated when this constellation was dominant. Following the discovery of the planet Pluto (named after the Roman god of the underworld, the counterpart of the Greek Hades) in 1930, rulership of Scorpio was shared by Pluto and Mars. Yet Scorpio's connotations are not all negative: the "regenerated Scorpio" is personified by the mighty eagle and heralds rebirth.

The personal characteristics of this sign are complex: the disciplined aggression of Mars, as well as his potent sexuality, are counterbalanced by the emotional depth signified by the element of water. Scorpio people have Plutonian, jealous natures and destructive powers. Conversely, however, they are blessed with subtlety, creative imaginations, and outstanding potential to attain spiritual enlightenment, transformation, and regeneration.

OCTOBER 23

✵ ✵ ✵ ✵ ✵ ✵ ✵ ✵ ✵ ✵ ✵ ✵ ✵ ✵

♇ ♀ ♂   CHAOTIC VANGUARDS

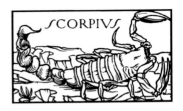

Others frequently admire October 23 people for their intellectual and physical energy, as well as their ability to make quick decisions and stick by them with remarkable determination. But some secretly wonder why these people appear to make life so difficult for themselves, for they seem to create a maelstrom around them whatever they do. Part of the answer to this conundrum may lie in these individuals' inherent zest for stimulation. Easily bored, they are naturally drawn to demanding or difficult situations in which they can test their courage and talents. Blessed with clarity of vision and balanced objectivity, they have the imagination and resourcefulness to devise and implement strategies for improvement that are ambitious, even radical. Given such a dynamic combination, those born on this day manifest clear innovatory and leadership potential, propensities that are further underlined by their sense of fairness and humanitarian concern with helping and directing others.

October 23 people are suited to any professional activity where they can make tangible—even ground-breaking—advances, so they may be found working effectively as artists or athletes, or equally as pioneering business entrepreneurs or social campaigners. Retaining their autonomy is important to them, and they typically prefer to captain a committed team rather than to act as independent agents. A similar feeling of interest and connection characterizes their relationships with those closest to them, although, however well-meaning their intentions, their tendency to assume a commanding and controlling role within their circle may cause those who would prefer to follow their own path through life to become resentful.

PLANETARY INFLUENCES
Ruling planets: Pluto and Venus
First decan: Personal planet is Mars
First cusp: Scorpio with Libran tendencies

VIRTUES
Rational, objective, progressive

VICES
Demanding, controlling, domineering

CAREERS
Corporate manager, politician, art instructor

SKILLS & APTITUDES
Comfortable in leadership roles, self-motivated, fair-minded

FAMOUS BIRTHS
Johnny Carson (1925)
"Weird" Al Yankovic (1959)
Nancy Grace (1959)
Ryan Reynolds (1976)

COMPATIBLE WITH
April 21–23, December 22–25

/CORPIV/

OCTOBER 24

✤ ✤ ✤ ✤ ✤ ✤ ✤ ✤ ✤ ✤ ✤ ✤ ✤ ✤ ✤

DISCIPLINED TRENDSETTERS   ♇ ♀ ♂

PLANETARY INFLUENCES
Ruling planets: Pluto and Venus
First decan: Personal planet is Mars
First cusp: Scorpio with Libran
   tendencies

VIRTUES
Innovative, imaginative, organized

VICES
Unrealistic, judgmental,
uncompromising

CAREERS
Financial adviser, administrative
assistant, mechanic/engineer

SKILLS & APTITUDES
Organizational abilities, dedication
to tasks, self-discipline

FAMOUS BIRTHS
J.P. Richardson,
"The Big Bopper" (1930)
Bill Wyman (1936)
Kevin Kline (1947)
Drake (1986)

COMPATIBLE WITH
April 21–23, December 22–25

Those born on this day possess two pronounced—and apparently contradictory—sets of personal characteristics: those related to their perfectionism and those stemming from their adventurous, somewhat radical, persona. And while it is true that some October 24 people may tend toward one or other of these extremes, others reconcile them by backing up their highly original and ambitious visions with their more grounded qualities: meticulous attention to detail, self-discipline and strong organizational talents.

These are energetic types, fueled by the compulsion to effect concrete and progressive advances with which they hope to find satisfaction and to benefit others. Although independently minded, their strong social orientation leads them to seek to enlist the support of others in their cause. Because their preferred approach is hands-on, they set themselves—as well as those around them—prodigiously high standards. They typically lead by example, however, demonstrating extraordinary dedication and focus in the process.

The careers that attract those born on this day vary depending on the individual, but their technical and practical talents, as well as their desire for autonomy suit them well for both mechanical and administrative pursuits. Despite the admiration that their commitment and imagination arouses in others, these very qualities—particularly when combined with their judgmental and perfectionist tendencies—may make them difficult to live with. They sometimes neglect the needs of those closest to them when preoccupied with their work (a propensity that is doubly pronounced in October 24 men) and they may seek to direct or "improve" the behavior of their loved ones.

OCTOBER 25

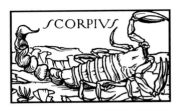

✳ ✳ ✳ ✳ ✳ ✳ ✳ ✳ ✳ ✳ ✳ ✳ ✳ ✳ ✳

♇ ♀ ♂　　　AMBITIOUS QUIBBLERS

Those born on this day are forceful and determined individuals whose actions are fueled by their urge to give expression to the visions that inspire them—that is, to translate their dreams into reality. Critically observant, imaginative and yet also extremely practical, they have a talent for incisively identifying perceived failings and then formulating remedial strategies, which they promote with unwavering tenacity and vigor. And because October 25 people are vitally interested in, and highly responsive to, everything that enters their personal orbit, this driving compulsion may be manifested in a wide range of areas or professions. Thus they may be seized by the desire to replace an unsatisfactory existing social or political system with a more fair and enlightened one; to develop a scientific or technical theory or instrument; to fill a gap in the commercial market; to make a company more productive; or to impart their messages to others by means of an inspirational artistic body of work. Inherent in all their aims and preferred methods is their innate perfectionism, as well as their predilection for directing the opinions or controlling the actions of others.

It perhaps goes without saying that those born on this day are socially responsible individuals who possess a burning desire to set others on what they believe to be the right path, or otherwise make a positive contribution to humanity. It is also clear, however, that their extremely critical, judgmental tendencies endow them with a profound sense of self-belief that may cause them to refute the validity of alternative viewpoints. So although they are reliable, protective, generous and affectionate friends and family members, they are typically intolerant of those who deviate from their wishes.

PLANETARY INFLUENCES
Ruling planets: Pluto and Venus
First decan: Personal planet is Mars
First cusp: Scorpio with Libran tendencies

VIRTUES
Perceptive, organized, progressive

VICES
Uncompromising, perfectionist, stubborn

CAREERS
Politician, scientist, artist

SKILLS & APTITUDES
Critical thinkers, champions of humanity, reliable

FAMOUS BIRTHS
Pablo Picasso (1881)
Marion Ross (1928)
Bob Knight (1940)
Katy Perry (1984)

COMPATIBLE WITH
April 21–23, December 22–25

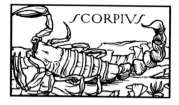

OCTOBER 26

✿ ✿ ✿ ✿ ✿ ✿ ✿ ✿ ✿ ✿ ✿ ✿ ✿ ✿

INFLUENTIAL MENTORS ♇ ♂

PLANETARY INFLUENCES
Ruling planet: Pluto
First decan: Personal planet is Mars

VIRTUES
Commanding, focused, coordinated

VICES
Controlling, opinionated, repressive

CAREERS
Accountant, campaign coordinator, senior manager

SKILLS & APTITUDES
Leadership skills, dedication to work, event planning

FAMOUS BIRTHS
Leon Trotsky (1879)
Pat Sajak (1946)
Hillary Clinton (1947)
Keith Urban (1967)

COMPATIBLE WITH
December 22–25

Perhaps the most prominent personal characteristic manifested by October 26 people is their compulsion to organize others. They harbor a conviction that concerted communal endeavors are more effective in achieving progress than the efforts of lone agents of change. With their ability to focus upon distant goals while at the same time addressing more immediate concerns, these are gifted leaders, whose decisiveness and dedication arouse respect (if not always affection). These are people who can be found planning local or political events and serving on committees, always involved in community affairs or blogging and campaigning in support of causes. They are admirably suited to careers as national or civic politicians, business executives, accountants or bankers.

Their desire to mold those around them applies as much to their personal relationships as to their professional lives, and they will typically do their utmost to persuade their kith and kin of the veracity of their viewpoints—a task usually undertaken with enthusiasm and logic rather than by passionate or combative means. Because they are natural pragmatists they will accept the demurrals of those who do not share their beliefs, but will nevertheless impress their disapproval upon others. When they and those closest to them are in agreement, their endearingly affectionate and generous qualities come to the fore.

To avoid becoming isolated, it is important that October 26 people remember that personal expression is important and does not necessarily need to be suppressed for the common good. They should allow people around them to assert their individuality.

OCTOBER 27

♇ ♂ WHIMSICAL ENTHUSIASTS

Such is the passion with which they express their emotions, and their active and immediate response to anyone or anything that they encounter, that the majority of October 27 people are impossible to ignore. Although unquestionably attention-seekers, their compulsion to attract others to them is rarely fueled by self-serving motivations or vanity but instead results from their almost irresistible urge to express their feelings and opinions freely and to influence or direct those around them.

While their convictions and actions are essentially emotion driven, October 27 people have considerable intellectual talents and practical skills at their disposal with which to work toward the realization of their goals. Thus despite their tendency to react somewhat impulsively to emotional stimuli—especially those concerned with morality or spirituality—once their interest has been aroused they manifest imagination, resourcefulness and organizational powers in support of their ambitions.

Those born on this day are perfectionists, but this quality is usually of the idealistic rather than the technical variety. Blessed with great communication skills, they will thrive in careers where they can impart their visions to others, maybe as journalists or teachers, but especially as writers, musicians and actors—professions in which their emotions and innovative dreams can simultaneously be given free rein and inspire their audiences. They are admired for their driving energy and pioneering turn of mind, but it is these very characteristics that can make them demanding—but lively and fun—colleagues, friends and family members.

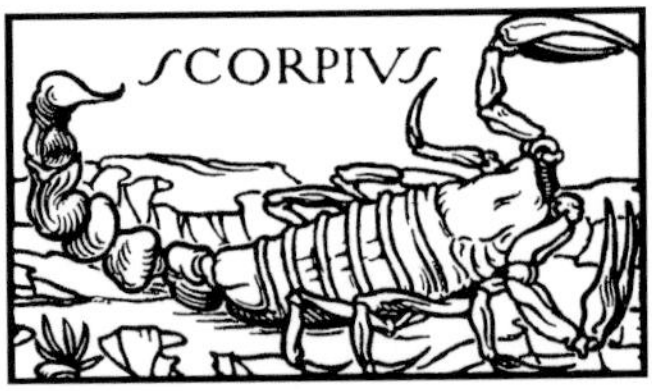

PLANETARY INFLUENCES
Ruling planet: Pluto
First decan: Personal planet is Mars

VIRTUES
Imaginative, rational, practical

VICES
Temperamental, impatient, overbearing

CAREERS
Reporter, professor, motivational speaker

SKILLS & APTITUDES
Social, inspiring, resourceful

FAMOUS BIRTHS
Theodore Roosevelt (1858)
Ruby Dee (1922)
Sylvia Plath (1932)
John Cleese (1939)
Aron Ralston (1975)

COMPATIBLE WITH
December 26–31

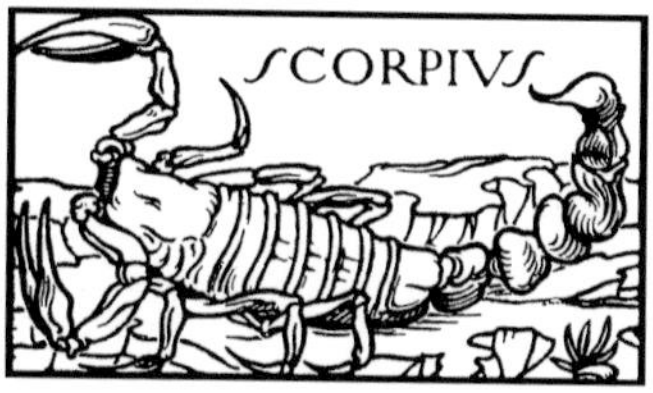

OCTOBER 28

INQUISITIVE RATIONALISTS

♇ ♂

PLANETARY INFLUENCES
Ruling planet: Pluto
First decan: Personal planet is Mars

VIRTUES
Ingenious, logical, creative

VICES
Workaholic, emotionally reserved, obsessive

CAREERS
Research scientist, engineer, IT specialist

SKILLS & APTITUDES
Sense of purpose, progressive mindset, focused

FAMOUS BIRTHS
Charlie Daniels (1936)
Bill Gates (1955)
Julia Roberts (1967)
Ben Harper (1969)
Joaquin Phoenix (1974)

COMPATIBLE WITH
December 26–31

Their work is of all-consuming importance to many of those ambitious individuals born on this day. Yet their ambition is rarely of the type to demand personal glory or spectacular financial rewards, but is instead the natural product of their perfectionism. October 28 individuals are inquisitive types who are determined to use the fruits of their discoveries to move forward into uncharted waters.

Fascinated with deconstruction and reconstruction, the meticulous attention to detail and logical turn of mind give October 28 people remarkable potential to make pioneering contributions to the world. Because they are extremely tenacious and focused, they are typically absorbed in their endeavors—indeed, when others regard them as having reached the pinnacle of their success, they will remain unsatisfied, believing that their task remains uncompleted and that progress can still be made.

Their independent inclinations endow those born on this day with the capacity to break new ground in any area that excites their interest, particularly in the realms of science and technology. Although they are fueled by their desire to benefit others, and are firm but fair leaders, their concern is often of the more abstract, humanitarian variety rather than emotionally based. Their propensity to immerse themselves in their intellectual or professional interests make them rather solitary figures, whose love and loyalty is genuine: however, those closest to them may not always realize this, since they are not given to expressing their affection openly.

OCTOBER 29

✳ ✳ ✳ ✳ ✳ ✳ ✳ ✳ ✳ ✳ ✳ ✳ ✳ ✳

♇ ♂   CALCULATED LEADERS

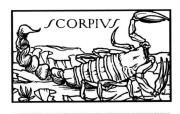

SCORPIUS

Although they possess highly independent minds and a relish for innovation, the combination of their pronounced sense of social responsibility and compulsion to organize and synchronize the actions of others makes October 29 people natural leaders. Indeed, such are their clarity of vision, logistical talents and resourcefulness, that in many respects those born on this day can be described as highly accomplished tacticians and strategists. This is not to say that they lack charisma—to the contrary, others respond instinctively to their aura of authority and strength of purpose—but rather that they prefer to research their subject rather than dashing impulsively forward with guns blazing. And just as the chess master appreciates the element of surprise, October 29 individuals are somewhat secretive types, who may keep even those closest to them in the dark regarding their true intentions.

Their progressive predilections, along with their pragmatic way of looking at the world, augur well for the success of these people in any professional sphere that they choose, although many will feel themselves drawn to those political, military or commercial pursuits where they can harness the efforts of others to promote their goals. Admired by their colleagues for their rationality, tenacity and loyalty, a completely different side to their characters emerges when they relax with their nearest and dearest (and they prefer to keep their professional and private lives separate), a side that includes their passionate affection, their fierce protectiveness, and their sensuality and love of pleasure.

PLANETARY INFLUENCES
Ruling planet: Pluto
First decan: Personal planet is Mars

VIRTUES
Independent, intellectual, skillfull

VICES
Secretive, authoritarian, high-handed

CAREERS
Politician, marketing executive, soldier

SKILLS & APTITUDES
Strategic thinking, persuasive powers, tenacity

FAMOUS BIRTHS
Bob Ross (1942)
Richard Dreyfuss (1947)
Randy Jackson (1961)
Winona Ryder (1971)

COMPATIBLE WITH
December 26–31

OCTOBER 30

✽ ✽ ✽ ✽ ✽ ✽ ✽ ✽ ✽ ✽ ✽ ✽ ✽ ✽

GENEROUS GOOD SAMARITANS   ♇ ♂

PLANETARY INFLUENCES
Ruling planet: Pluto
First decan: Personal planet is Mars

VIRTUES
Forward-thinking, responsible, organized

VICES
Demanding, repressed, lacking emotional balance

CAREERS
Nurse, pediatrician, caregiver

SKILLS & APTITUDES
Sensitivity to others, teamwork, dedication to goals

FAMOUS BIRTHS
John Adams (1735)
Ezra Pound (1885)
Henry Winkler (1945)
Nastia Liukin (1989)

COMPATIBLE WITH
December 26–31

October 30 people tend to immerse themselves in projects and issues that affect their communities, often volunteering to participate in, or organize, school, club or fundraising activities. Because these are active types who prefer to take charge of situations rather than stand idly by, they typically throw themselves wholeheartedly into the pursuit of common goals, in the process enlisting the support of those around them and directing their cohorts with imagination and confidence. Possessing logical and progressive intellects, those born on this day understand innately that most ventures need to be supported by meticulous preparation: thus they pay special attention to even the most mundane issues of research and organization. They are friendly, sociable and straightforward people who enjoy being with others and are rarely given to solitary pursuits. Given their socially oriented inclinations and interpersonal skills, October 30 people are particularly suited to teaching, the medical field and the service industries.

These individuals are generally unhappy when working as independent operators, far preferring to surround themselves with a supportive team of like-minded people—a predilection that applies as much to their personal as to their professional lives. Their communal commitment is total, and therefore they not only have a tendency to suppress what they may regard as selfish desires, but also to demand the same level of dedication from their colleagues, kith or kin, regardless of their personal inclinations. They come into their own as parents, devoting endless energy to encouraging their children's growth and interests.

OCTOBER 31

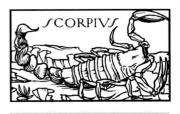

✵ ✵ ✵ ✵ ✵ ✵ ✵ ✵ ✵ ✵ ✵ ✵ ✵ ✵

♇ ♂   SELF–MOTIVATED LEADERS

The perfectionist tendencies of October 31 people are stimulated by challenging situations of all kinds, for they are not only blessed with incisive clarity of vision but also possess the courage and integrity necessary to stand firm when promoting their strongly held beliefs. Many of those self-reliant individuals born on this day gravitate toward demanding scenarios that offer the opportunity to test themselves, a personal predilection that stems less from sensation-seeking motives, than from their desire to place themselves at the service of others.

Underpinning the actions of October 31 people therefore are dual propensities for self-sacrifice and confrontation, both of which arise from their profound concern for and interest in the welfare of those with whom they most strongly identify—their friends and families, workmates, compatriots, or even humanity as a whole. To all their endeavors they bring their direct and logical turn of mind, their organizational skills, and the determination to realize their visions.

Their orientation toward others and their idealistic inclinations suit October 31 people to any profession where they can work toward the common good. Natural pioneers and leaders, their strength of purpose and commitment is respected by others, although those closest to them in particular may feel reluctant or, indeed, unable, to meet their standards. In their urge to lead by example, they run the risk of alienating those about whom they care the most, who may feel that their individual needs are being disregarded. This is especially noticeable when October 31 people embark on an Internet (blog or petition) crusade.

PLANETARY INFLUENCES
Ruling planet: Pluto
First decan: Personal planet is Mars

VIRTUES
Perceptive, rational, determined

VICES
Quarrelsome, single-minded, intolerant

CAREERS
Humanitarian activist, social worker, local-government officer

SKILLS & APTITUDES
Leadership skills, ability to rely on own resources, organizational skills

FAMOUS BIRTHS
John Keats (1795)
Ethel Waters (1896)
Dan Rather (1931)
John Candy (1950

COMPATIBLE WITH
December 26–31

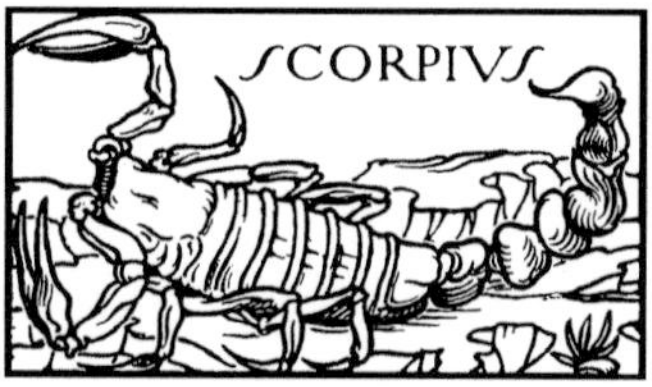

NOVEMBER 1

INTELLECTUAL EXPLORERS ♇ ♃ ♆

PLANETARY INFLUENCES
Ruling planet: Pluto
Second decan: Personal planets are Jupiter and Neptune

VIRTUES
Energetic, inspirational, dynamic

VICES
Impulsive, restless, anxious

CAREERS
Entrepreneur, digital designer or consultant, inventor

SKILLS & APTITUDES
Strong self-motivation, resourcefulness, thoughtfulness

FAMOUS BIRTHS
Lyle Lovett (1957)
Jenny McCarthy (1972)
Tim Cook (1960)
Anthony Kiedis (1962)
Penn Badgley (1986)

COMPATIBLE WITH
January 1–5, March 4–7

Those born on this day have an absolute dread of inactivity and intellectual boredom. Typically "doers" rather than thinkers, their intellectual talents are of the progressive rather than the quietly reflective kind. Especially stimulated by pioneering—even radical—concepts, November 1 individuals throw themselves into the exploration and development of new ideas with single-minded enthusiasm, using ingenuity and resourcefulness to realize their goals. Because they are blessed with remarkable self-assurance and fearlessness in the face of adversity or opposition, these natural leaders refuse to be bound by convention and have the capacity to perform especially well in a wide range of professional areas, particularly artistic, inventive or scientific fields or as business entrepreneurs where independence of thought is an asset.

Because their urge to effect progress is so strong, and their *modi operandi* so vigorous, those born on this day have a tendency (especially notable if they were born in the Chinese year of the dragon) to focus on their aims regardless of personal consequences—to themselves or those around them. This approach can be detrimental to maintaining stable emotional relationships. Yet despite this caveat, November 1 people are naturally predisposed toward grounding themselves in the strong and affectionate ties of kith-and kinship and make loyal and stimulating friends and relations. They will benefit from remembering to make time for honest introspection on a regular basis, as well as avoiding unnecessary confrontations.

NOVEMBER 2

✳ ✳ ✳ ✳ ✳ ✳ ✳ ✳ ✳ ✳ ✳ ✳ ✳ ✳

♇ ♃ ♆   CHARISMATIC REFORMISTS

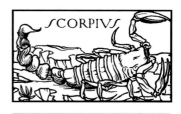
SCORPIUS

The combination of their natural predilection for taking action and their keen interest in promoting the welfare of those around them (a concern that often takes a more abstract, humanitarian form) endows those born on this day with real leadership potential. Incisive and progressive thinkers, November 2 people can identify the faults and flaws in various situations and devise solutions. Despite their willingness to adopt a combative stance if they believe that confrontation is the only available option—a policy that applies particularly when they defend humanitarian or ideological issues—their personal charm and benevolent intentions usually elicit an affectionate, if not always acquiescent, reaction from others.

Their strong and positive orientation toward other people, as well as their undoubted interpersonal talents, equip those born on this day admirably for careers as politicians or social campaigners, although some may be drawn to pursuing such artistic modes of expression as acting as a means of exerting their influence over a wider audience.

Their goodwill and desire to assist others to advance is evident in all areas of their lives, and generally makes November 2 people popular figures. Their irresistible urge to offer even unsolicited advice and support and innate belief that their viewpoints are morally correct may, however, cause them to unwittingly arouse the resentment of those who would prefer to be allowed to forge their own path through life, especially their nearest and dearest.

PLANETARY INFLUENCES
Ruling planet: Pluto
Second decan: Personal planets are Jupiter and Neptune

VIRTUES
Logical, genuine, good-natured

VICES
Meddlesome, opinionated, combative

CAREERS
Politician, political campaigner, stage actor

SKILLS & APTITUDES
Powers of persuaion, tenacity, willingness to help others

FAMOUS BIRTHS
Marie Antoinette (1755)
Warren G. Harding (1865)
Burt Lancaster (1913)
David Schwimmer (1966)

COMPATIBLE WITH
January 1–5, March 4–7

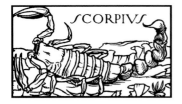

NOVEMBER 3

✴ ✴ ✴ ✴ ✴ ✴ ✴ ✴ ✴ ✴ ✴ ✴

ENTHUSIASTIC SELF-STARTERS ♇ ♃ ♆

PLANETARY INFLUENCES
Ruling planet: Pluto
Second decan: Personal planets are
Jupiter and Neptune

VIRTUES
Purposeful, organized, resourceful

VICES
Uncompromising, self-obsessed,
interfering

CAREERS
Teacher, musician, administrator

SKILLS & APTITUDES
Self-motivation, determination to
succeed, independence

FAMOUS BIRTHS
Charles Bronson (1921)
Anna Wintour (1949)
Roseanne Barr (1952)
Dennis Miller (1953)
Dylan Moran (1971)

COMPATIBLE WITH
January 1–5, March 4–7

Perhaps the most pronounced characteristic of November 3 personalities is that of driving ambition. And because they possess a straightforward turn of mind and a remarkable talent for organization, many will have formulated their life plans as early as childhood. The nature of their goals will vary from one person to another: some may be concerned primarily with personal betterment (in terms of their social or financial status, for example); while others may seek to make a contribution to the world.

Whatever their underlying motivations, November 3 individuals will always reveal their progressive instincts, as well as the mental and physical vigor, courage and tenacity to promote their aims regardless of the consequences (to themselves or others). These characteristics that are especially notable in those born in the Chinese year of the dragon. Indeed, they relish testing their skills and stamina against demanding challenges.

Despite the overriding importance that they place on the attainment of their self-set goals—a prerequisite that may cause them to act independently of the common consensus—November 3 people generally prefer to elicit the support of allies rather than the enmity of foes. They are often drawn to professions that provide an effective forum in which to exert their influence on those around them—as educators or entertainers, for instance. However, their forceful and uncompromising approach may have an alienating effect on those around them.

NOVEMBER 4

✳ ✳ ✳ ✳ ✳ ✳ ✳ ✳ ✳ ✳ ✳ ✳ ✳ ✳

♇ ♃ ♆ CHARMING COMMUNICATORS

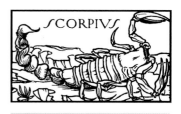

SCORPIVS

The conjunction of their logical minds and independence of thought endows those born on this day with perceptive and progressive intellects that give them the ability both to pinpoint areas ripe for improvement and to formulate strategies for advancement. Fueled by the urge to share the conclusions that result from their analytical and conceptual skills, November 4 people are not content to keep their opinions to themselves. They always try to enlighten others and help them to advance. They show their communication skills in every area of their lives, and such is their talent for putting their messages across that people will rarely be left in the dark. Indeed, many of those born on this day are drawn to careers where they can reach the widest possible public—as actors or performers on stage and screen; writers, journalists and artists, or as politicians or social reformers. And because their typical approach is based on a mixture of strong convictions laced with a dash of humor, others generally respond positively to them, even if their viewpoints are sometimes not very palatable.

Indeed, such is the respect and affection that November 4 individuals engender that they may often find themselves elevated to positions of leadership—somewhat to their surprise (although not necessarily their displeasure)—and because they are socially responsible types they will discharge their duties with integrity. Yet in many respects these people would prefer to be left to their own devices in order to pursue their intellectual interests free from the demands of others and to enjoy the enriching pleasures of domestic life and fulfilling interpersonal relationships, from which they derive such support and satisfaction.

PLANETARY INFLUENCES
Ruling planet: Pluto
Second decan: Personal planets are Jupiter and Neptune

VIRTUES
Charming, objective, clear-sighted

VICES
Opinionated, immoderate, interfering

CAREERS
Actor, poet, artist

SKILLS & APTITUDES
Communication skills, tirelessness, dedication

FAMOUS BIRTHS
Will Rogers (1879)
Walter Cronkite (1916)
Laura Bush (1946)
Matthew McConaughey (1969)

COMPATIBLE WITH
January 1–5, March 4–7

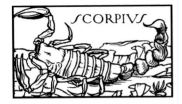

NOVEMBER 5

✳ ✳ ✳ ✳ ✳ ✳ ✳ ✳ ✳ ✳ ✳ ✳ ✳

WELL-ROUNDED ACADEMICS ♇ ♃ ♆

PLANETARY INFLUENCES
Ruling planet: Pluto
Second decan: Personal planets are Jupiter and Neptune

VIRTUES
Intellectual, socially concerned, analytical

VICES
Easily frustrated, tending to spread themselves too thin, tactless

CAREERS
Business manager, journalist, social scientist

SKILLS & APTITUDES
Influential charisma, creativity, innovation skills

FAMOUS BIRTHS
Vivien Leigh (1913)
Ike Turner (1931)
Art Garfunkel (1941)
Bryan Adams (1959)

COMPATIBLE WITH
January 1–5, March 4–7

Those born on this day have two pronounced sides to their personalities: their feeling of connection with the people around them; and their individual interests, which they like to pursue undisturbed by the demands of others. The influence of these two tendencies may cause November 5 people to feel torn between their desire to help others—whether this be at the familial, communal, or global level—and their more selfish urge to shut themselves away to be able to concentrate on pursuits they love. Many, however, are fortunate enough to be able to reconcile these predilections, often by choosing careers where they can retain their autonomy while sharing their findings with a broader audience, thereby making a positive contribution to the lives of others. The scientific and business realms, as well as such artistic specialties as writing and acting can thus be said to provide ideal professional arenas for their inclinations and skills.

November 5 individuals are intellectually curious and progressive types, who prefer to seek out knowledge for themselves rather than to be spoon-fed with it. Drawing on their highly developed powers of perception to amass a fund of information, they have the capacity to identify existing failings or abuses and then prepare logical and realistic proposals with which to bring about advancement; they thus possess real leadership ability. Yet although the honest expression of their criticism may be inherently uncomfortable to those who wish to maintain the status quo, these people's evident goodwill and earnest desire to bring about tangible advances usually make them subjects of admiration and especially valued friends, partners and parents.

NOVEMBER 6

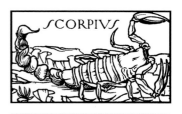
SCORPIVS

✸ ✸ ✸ ✸ ✸ ✸ ✸ ✸ ✸ ✸ ✸ ✸ ✸ ✸

♇ ♃ ♆ Dynamic Positive Thinkers

Such is their active, positive outlook on life that it often seems to others that November 6 people are blessed with limitless supplies of energy and optimism. These "can-do" individuals typically refuse to be dissuaded from pushing their interests to their ultimate conclusions, brushing aside objections in their determination to achieve their goals. Possessing not only great perceptiveness when it comes to identifying areas in which action is called for, but also logical and straightforward minds, as well as highly developed practical and technical talents, those born on this day manifest remarkable strength of conviction, self-belief and tenacity when working toward the aims that are so ambitious that others might brand them as unfeasible. Yet, despite the skepticism they engender, the engaging enthusiasm and galvanizing vigor of November 6 people generally arouse indulgent affection rather than concerted opposition.

These individuals will thrive in any profession where their imaginative and progressive qualities are not suppressed; if they are employed within corporate structures, for example, they will do best when given the freedom to plan policy. Naturally inspirational leaders, many are perhaps happiest working as scientists and artists of various types, simultaneously effecting innovations and exerting their influence directly over their publics. And, although they are stimulated by personal challenge, these are deeply humanitarian people who wish to benefit others through their efforts. Enlivening and generous companions, their concern for the well-being of those around them is evident in both their personal and professional relationships, particularly for the women born on this day.

PLANETARY INFLUENCES
Ruling planet: Pluto
Second decan: Personal planets are Jupiter and Neptune

VIRTUES
Inventive, practical, level-headed

VICES
Inflexible, insensitive, closed-minded

CAREERS
Marketing executive, administrator, business leader

SKILLS & APTITUDES
Idealistic, progressive, forward-looking

FAMOUS BIRTHS
Sally Field (1946)
Glenn Frey (1948)
Pat Tillman (1976)
Emma Stone (1988)

COMPATIBLE WITH
January 6–10, March 8–10

NOVEMBER 7

✿ ✿ ✿ ✿ ✿ ✿ ✿ ✿ ✿ ✿ ✿ ✿ ✿

Charismatic Movers & Shakers ♇ ♃ ♆

Planetary Influences
Ruling planet: Pluto
Second decan: Personal planets are Jupiter and Neptune

Virtues
Inquisitive, enthusiastic, positive

Vices
Overly ambitious, neglectful of others, demanding

Careers
Athlete, nonprofit coordinator, instructor

Skills & Aptitudes
Focus, practical skills, willingness to take responsibility

Famous Births
Marie Curie (1867)
Albert Camus (1913)
Billy Graham (1918)
Christopher Knight (1957)
Lorde (1996)

Compatible With
January 6–10, March 8–10

Those physically and mentally active individuals born on this day are extremely responsive to challenge, stimulated not by combative instincts (although they will take a confrontational stance to defend their strongly held convictions) but by their desire to break through the existing limits of human knowledge or experience. These are curious and progressive types, who relish the opportunity to test their skills and stamina against demanding (in the eyes of others, even hopeless) challenges. Acutely perceptive, rigorously logical and ingenious in their intellectual approach, and endowed with highly developed organizational and practical skills, November 7 people have the potential and talent to become pioneers in their professions. They are also blessed with the magnetic charisma necessary to enlist the support and direct the actions of those around them. And although they are personally excited by their career ambitions or private interests, their innate humanitarianism and sense of social responsibility bestows on them the desire to work toward goals that they believe will be of concrete benefit to the wider world.

The nature of the careers chosen by November 7 people will vary. Some may seek to bring about social changes, some to advance scientific knowledge, while others will be drawn to the artistic or sporting spheres. All will lead by example, expecting a high level of commitment from others. (Those born in the Chinese year of the rooster are especially single-minded in pursuit of their goals.) Although they are generally magnanimous and affectionate friends and family members, those closest to them may have difficulty living up to their expectations.

NOVEMBER 8

✳ ✳ ✳ ✳ ✳ ✳ ✳ ✳ ✳ ✳ ✳ ✳ ✳ ✳

♇ ♃ ♆   INVENTIVE ECCENTRICS

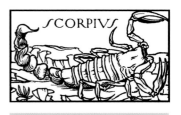

SCORPIVS

November 8 individuals are blessed with extraordinary vitality—a quality manifested by their physical vigor, but also (and perhaps especially) by their remarkably imaginative and progressive minds. They are attracted by subjects so unusual that other, less receptive, people may reject them as too radical or threatening to the status quo.

Yet although those born on this day have original and curious turns of mind, their interests are rarely flighty or superficial. They support their search for knowledge with meticulous attention to detail. Their powers of concentration and courage pursuing their quests augur well for their success (although winning the recognition of their peers may take some time).

A happy domestic life and the support of those closest to them are important to grounding November 8 people in emotional equilibrium. They are generous, tolerant and invigorating friends and family members, although they may at times be moody. This tendency can lead to them becoming cut off from others, so they should take extra care not to isolate themselves from friends and particularly family members.

Personally stimulated by intellectual discovery, November 8 people will flourish in any profession where they can meet their altruistic needs and retain autonomy of thought and action. Given the nature of their talents and inclinations, they have marked potential to become inspiring artists, writers, musicians, actors, or pioneering scientists, digital innovators and engineers.

PLANETARY INFLUENCES
Ruling planet: Pluto
Second decan: Personal planets are Jupiter and Neptune

VIRTUES
Optimistic, energetic, resourceful

VICES
Unfocused, hypersensitive, moody

CAREERS
Engineer, journalist, scientist

SKILLS & APTITUDES
Imagination, thirst for knowledge, innovation skills

FAMOUS BIRTHS
Bram Stoker (1847)
Margaret Mitchell (1900)
Gordon Ramsay (1966)
Tara Reid (1975)

COMPATIBLE WITH
January 6–10, March 8–10

NOVEMBER 9

❋ ❋ ❋ ❋ ❋ ❋ ❋ ❋ ❋ ❋ ❋ ❋ ❋ ❋

RESTLESS GROUNDBREAKERS ♇ ♃ ♆

PLANETARY INFLUENCES
Ruling planet: Pluto
Second decan: Personal planets are
Jupiter and Neptune

VIRTUES
Enthusiastic, vibrant, socially
responsible

VICES
Easily bored, restless, tending to be
dissatisfied

CAREERS
Tour guide, computer engineer,
interior designer

SKILLS & APTITUDES
Enthusiasm, talents in several
spheres, desire to help

FAMOUS BIRTHS
Spiro Agnew (1918)
Carl Sagan (1952)
Ryan Murphy (1965
Nick Lachey (1973)

COMPATIBLE WITH
January 6–10, March 8–10

....
....
....

Those born on this day are not the types to sit on the sidelines of life watching the world pass them by, which is not to say that they are not observant people—to the contrary, they are extremely perceptive, especially with regard to human behavior—it is simply that they prefer to do rather than view. Possessing a dread of inactivity, November 9 people feel compelled to involve themselves fully in every area of their lives—professional and personal, intellectual, emotional and sensual—so as to satisfy their need for growth and to contribute to the lives of those around them. Extremely responsive to stimuli of all kinds, they are often blazing a pioneering trail and directing those who follow in their wake. Yet while they manifest a keen, impulsive interest in any subject they encounter, their fascination is rarely superficial, for they will explore it to its fullest extent and uncover hidden truths. Such is the wide variety of subjects that excite their attention that they have the potential to make significant contributions across the full professional spectrum, but they are especially drawn to the limitless possibilities inherent in art and design.

Although they are strong-willed and self-indulgent types (and even more so if they were also born in the Chinese year of the horse), those born on this day are profoundly oriented toward those around them. Others enjoy their enlivening companionship, and appreciate their kindness and generosity, characteristics that are particularly pronounced in their dealings with their nearest and dearest, or with those whom November 9 people believe have been dealt a raw deal in life. As well as being natural leaders, they are also instinctive humanitarians who will dip deep into their pockets to help the victims of misfortune or social abuses.

NOVEMBER 10

✳ ✳ ✳ ✳ ✳ ✳ ✳ ✳ ✳ ✳ ✳ ✳ ✳ ✳

♇ ♃ ♆   GIFTED CREATIVES

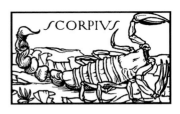

Those born on this day are highly creative individuals with the imagination, skills and focus to make a substantial contribution to the world and an unforgettable impression on everyone they encounter. Empathetic and benevolent, they are concerned with helping humanity as a whole to progress via spiritual, intellectual or material means. However, they are also introspective, and have a profound need to satisfy their desires to explore, assimilate, experiment and grow. They are often perfectionists, who set themselves high standards and are reluctant to share their findings with others until they are sure of the value of their conclusions. Inquisitiveness, ingenuity and resourcefulness mark their efforts in professions that call for independent research and development. Academia, science and the arts may attract them, as these fields also offer intermittent solitude.

Although their genuine goodwill and affection for their close associates is undoubtable, their absorption with their work may limit the attention they pay to emotional needs—a tendency that men born on this day display the most. They may even become dismissive or intolerant of those who do not share their interests and beliefs.

If they are not to become isolated and depressed, it is important that November 10 individuals pay particular attention to sharing their thoughts and feelings to those around them. While they are honest and caring, they can sometimes come across as intense and off-putting. They should take time to relax and nurture social skills and relationships carefully.

PLANETARY INFLUENCES
Ruling planet: Pluto
Second decan: Personal planets are Jupiter and Neptune

VIRTUES
Dedicated, meticulous, inquisitive

VICES
Obsessive, secretive, unbalanced

CAREERS
Professor, historian, laboratory technician

SKILLS & APTITUDES
Ingenuity, attention to detail, independence

FAMOUS BIRTHS
Martin Luther (1483)
Richard Burton (1925)
Sinbad (1956)
Miranda Lambert (1983)

COMPATIBLE WITH
January 6–10, March 8–10

NOVEMBER 11

✵ ✵ ✵ ✵ ✵ ✵ ✵ ✵ ✵ ✵ ✵ ✵ ✵ ✵

VERSATILE BENEFACTORS　　　♇ ♃ ♆

November 11 individuals are complex personalities who have the capacity to surprise those around them through hidden sides of their characters. Indeed, those born on this day may themselves be unsure about the exact nature of their convictions and what they want from life. Although their multitude of interests and powerfully instinctive responses to concepts, situations and other people are undoubted strengths, they may also have a confusing effect. On the one hand these people are active, straightforward and progressive types who yearn to advance toward tangible goals, while on the other they are also profound—sometimes even darkly pessimistic—thinkers, whose propensity for deep deliberation may restrict their progress. When they are able to reconcile these conflicting propensities they have the potential to do well in their careers and form lasting relationships. The nature of their chosen careers will vary from individual to individual: some may prefer work in hands-on positions in building or technical fields; others may have their interest fired by writing or research—all, however, will manifest extraordinary determination, imagination and humanitarian concern in pursuit of their professional goals.

Their desire to serve others underlies virtually everything undertaken by those born on this day. Even though they are innately independent operators, they are fueled by their compulsion to assist, direct or at least positively inspire others by example. Their colleagues typically respect them greatly, but many may feel that they do not know them fully and, indeed, November 11 people often prefer to keep their professional and private lives separate, cherishing the domestic sphere as a haven in which they can relax and be themselves.

NOVEMBER 12

❋ ❋ ❋ ❋ ❋ ❋ ❋ ❋ ❋ ❋ ❋ ❋ ❋ ❋

♇ ☽   DYNAMIC IDEALISTS

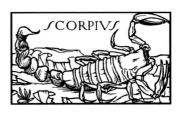
ſCORPIVſ

Others admire those born on this day for the energy, sense of purpose and transforming touch that they display in their professional ventures, but in many respects the self-assured image that November 12 people project is consciously manufactured, to conceal the emotional turmoil beneath. For these are complex individuals who are torn between their desire to achieve perfection (particularly in terms of their career goals) and their internal battle with the strong and sometimes confusing emotions that beset them. While on the one hand they are imaginative, straightforward and positive types, on the other they may innately feel that they will never attain the soaring visions that drive them, and they sometimes give way to feelings of frustration or even despair. And because their goals are ambitious, and they themselves so demanding, they will often only be reached after a great internally and externally oriented personal struggle.

The natural inclinations of those born on this day suit them for a wide variety of careers, but their idealistic urges will often find a particularly rewarding outlet in the realms of the arts or science, and although their audiences may venerate their achievements they will rarely be aware of the amount of hard work and worry—maybe even self-doubt—that underpin them. Given to concealing their problems from those around them, November 12 people are nevertheless extremely empathetic to the unhappiness or misfortune of others and will do their utmost to lend their practical support to those in need. Yet, despite their special concern for the well-being of their nearest and dearest, they may still need to occasionally withdraw from their loved ones in order to address their personal demons.

PLANETARY INFLUENCES
Ruling planet: Pluto
Third decan: Personal planet is Moon

VIRTUES
Visionary, clever, organized

VICES
Insecure, fearful, detached

CAREERS
Director, psychologist, musician

SKILLS & APTITUDES
Self-motivation, sincerity, direct focus on others

FAMOUS BIRTHS
Grace Kelly (1929)
Neil Young (1945)
Tonya Harding (1970)
Ryan Gosling (1980

COMPATIBLE WITH
January 11–14

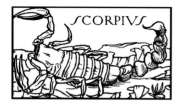

NOVEMBER 13

✳ ✳ ✳ ✳ ✳ ✳ ✳ ✳ ✳ ✳ ✳ ✳ ✳

INSIGHTFUL INFLUENCERS   ♇ ☽

Perhaps the primary characteristics manifested by November 13 people are their interest in people and their strong wills, qualities that inform their predilection for observing and opining the mores and workings of human society. Indeed, in many respects those born on this day could be compared to chemists because of their ability to absorb all manner of data, subject it to rigorous analysis and process it before transmitting it into the public arena in a converted or crystallized configuration. With their heightened powers of perception, they have the enviable capacity to draw upon their intuitive as well as their objective talents when assessing the world or people around them, yet once they have arrived at their opinions after careful deliberation they will typically adhere to them with remarkable tenacity, even in the face of opposition. Just as their interest is aroused by virtually everything they encounter, so they may be found working in a variety of professions, although they may be especially drawn to scientific or technical pursuits, as well as to those concerned with informing or enlightening their peers—such as teachers, journalists, or even as spiritual or political leaders.

Such is their urge to exert their progressive influence over those around them that November 13 people will often gravitate toward leadership or pioneering roles: in turn, they are respected by others for their strength of conviction and charismatic presence. Although strongly socially oriented, they may overlook the more personal—though no less important—needs of their nearest and dearest in their quests to assist the wider human community to advance (a tendency that is even more pronounced in the men who share this birthday).

NOVEMBER 14

✳ ✳ ✳ ✳ ✳ ✳ ✳ ✳ ✳ ✳ ✳ ✳ ✳

♇ ☽ PERCEPTIVE PROGRESSIVES

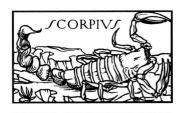

SCORPIVS

Those born on this day are serious individuals with a strong desire to understand those concepts, circumstances or people who excite their interest, a predilection that stems from not only their innate curiosity but also their urge to apply their skills in the effective service of others. Indeed, their sense of social responsibility is so essential to their natures that it will typically have been evident from childhood, manifested, for example, by their empathy with other people's unhappiness and their endearing attempts to "make it better". This deep-rooted wish to assist others remains a guiding principle throughout their lives (especially if they were also born in the Chinese year of the rooster), and although they are stimulated as individuals by learning, honing their expertise and refining their views, their ultimate purpose is make themselves agents of progress. November 14 people thus have a natural affinity with those professional realms that are concerned with benevolently directing, illuminating or otherwise making a positive contribution to those around them, and have the potential to become outstanding social workers, nurses, doctors and therapists.

Those born on this day place enormous value on the tight bonds that they form with their friends, partners and children, and draw real emotional support and strength from the unquestioning affection of their loved ones. Despite their tolerance and generosity, they frown upon any instances of selfish or thoughtless behavior and will not hesitate to make their displeasure known. Inherent in their magnanimous approach, however, lies a danger that either they may neglect their own personal needs, or their goodwill may be exploited by more unscrupulous types.

PLANETARY INFLUENCES
Ruling planet: Pluto
Third decan: Personal planet is Moon

VIRTUES
Enlightened, humanitarian, compassionate

VICES
Unbalanced, moody, self-critical

CAREERS
Nurse, therapist, pediatrician

SKILLS & APTITUDES
Drawn to others, benevolent nature, gentle personality

FAMOUS BIRTHS
Claude Monet (1840)
Prince Charles (1948)
Condoleezza Rice (1954)
Josh Duhamel (1972)

COMPATIBLE WITH
January 11–14

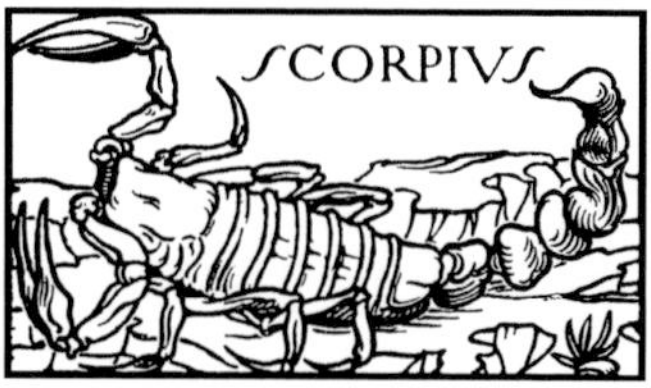

NOVEMBER 15

CONVICTED CONFORMISTS ♇ ☽

PLANETARY INFLUENCES
Ruling planet: Pluto
Third decan: Personal planet is Moon

VIRTUES
Strong, charitable, progressive

VICES
Indecisive, anxious, weak

CAREERS
Medical researcher, research analyst, curator

SKILLS & APTITUDES
Positive nature, willing to serve others, protectiveness

FAMOUS BIRTHS
Felix Frankfurter (1882)
Georgia O'Keefe (1887)
Marianne Moore (1887)
Sam Waterson (1940)
Lily Aldridge (1985)

COMPATIBLE WITH
January 11–14

Inner conflict is often an inevitable fact of life for those people born on November 15; indeed, however calm and competent the face that they present to the world, underneath their typically composed façade lie personalities that are in turmoil. The main problem these individuals have is in reconciling their desire to devote themselves single-mindedly to the service of others (especially their colleagues or compatriots) with their personal integrity, individual convictions or emotional needs. When these interests coincide and they are able to accomplish this, they frequently become highly respected pillars of strength, who inspire, reassure and protect those with whom they identify most strongly—perhaps as civic or national politicians. Yet all too often they will initially dutifully espouse the party line, believing that social conformity is the best way in which to serve the common interest: subsequently, since they are perceptive types, they will become uncomfortably aware of its inherent failings and abuses, and incur profound feelings of doubt. In such circumstances they may reluctantly feel it necessary to rebel and oppose the system in order to remain true to themselves.

Underlying all their actions is their compulsion to make a positive contribution to those around them—even humanity as a wider entity—and some may therefore chose careers within the spheres of scientific or artistic research and development, in which their progressive urge can be fulfilled and expressed without the need to compromise their convictions. Loving and generous friends and relations, they furthermore enjoy the simple pleasures of life and thus make enlivening as well as supportive companions.

NOVEMBER 16

✼ ✼ ✼ ✼ ✼ ✼ ✼ ✼ ✼ ✼ ✼ ✼ ✼

♇ ☽   INVESTED RINGLEADERS

SCORPIVS

Those born on this day combine active and inquiring minds with a profound urge to understand how things work and the insight to promote their ideas to the common good. As children or young adults, their innate sense of connection to those around them may not be immediately apparent, and as their personalities form, they often challenge the status quo. But once they reach conclusions that satisfy their minds, they will not only remain true to them, but seek to convince others of their worth.

Those born on this day are especially suited for leadership roles in which they can exert influence over others. They will frequently gravitate toward such professions as politics, activism and teaching, although they may also be drawn to more artistic activities, in which they may find that they can inspire a broader audience.

Those around them generally respect their strength of purpose (even when they do not agree with their forthright opinions or methods) and, in fact, November 16 individuals should try to use tact and tolerance in enlisting support for their aims—especially with regard to their nearest associates, whose love and support is important to their emotional well-being.

It is important that November 16 people remember to keep a sense of proportion and perspective. They should not get so carried away with their own interests and projects that they forget to take account of the needs of those around them. They should also remember that others are entitled to their own opinions, and those opinions might be as valid, or more so, than their own.

PLANETARY INFLUENCES
Ruling planet: Pluto
Third decan: Personal planet is Moon

VIRTUES
Charismatic, inquisitive, strong-willed

VICES
Biased, close-minded, intolerant

CAREERS
Teacher, life coach, college professor

SKILLS & APTITUDES
Connection with others, originality of perspective, leadership skills

FAMOUS BIRTHS
Tiberius (42 BC)
George S. Kaufman (1889)
Diana Krall (1964)
Maggie Gyllenhaal (1977)

COMPATIBLE WITH
January 11–14

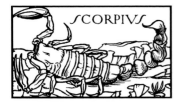

SCORPIVS

NOVEMBER 17

❋ ❋ ❋ ❋ ❋ ❋ ❋ ❋ ❋ ❋ ❋ ❋ ❋

LIBERATED FREETHINKERS ♇ ☽

PLANETARY INFLUENCES
Ruling planet: Pluto
Third decan: Personal planet is Moon

VIRTUES
Keen, rational, fair-minded

VICES
Authoritarian, intimidating, critical

CAREERS
Web designer, marketing executive, software engineer

SKILLS & APTITUDES
Expressive communication skills, magnetic personality, autonomous self-reliance

FAMOUS BIRTHS
Rock Hudson (1925)
Martin Scorsese (1942)
Danny DeVito (1944)
Rachel McAdams (1978)

COMPATIBLE WITH
January 15–19

Their perspicacity, sense of justice and orientation to the social group with which they identify most strongly endow those born on this day with the potential to make a real contribution to the world. Yet despite their benevolent urge to help others, November 17 people are autonomous: their independence of mind often causes them to stand apart even from those whose welfare they have at heart. Gifted social commentators, they use their observations to expose wrong-doings or failings and work toward correcting them. They deliver their messages with unerring accuracy and a sense of humor that fosters co-operation rather than alienation.

Those born on this day are admirably equipped to excel in any profession in which they can retain their prerequisite for freedom of thought and expression while simultaneously working toward a concrete goal, and high-tech pursuits like web or app design, computer game coding and virtual reality are particularly well starred.

Others admire their personal magnetism, ready wit and enviable ability to elicit the cooperation of those around them, but may nevertheless feel that they do not know the essence of November 17 individuals' personalities. And, indeed, these people guard their privacy jealously (a propensity that is even more pronounced in the men born on this day) and will only open up fully to those whom they trust implicitly. Their relationships with their nearest and dearest are thus of vital importance to them as emotional havens of unquestioning affection and security.

NOVEMBER 18

✳ ✳ ✳ ✳ ✳ ✳ ✳ ✳ ✳ ✳ ✳ ✳ ✳

♇ ☽   BELOVED MERRYMAKERS

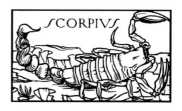

Others enjoy the company of people born on this day, who enliven any gathering with their vitality, humor and goodwill. November 18 people are in turn stimulated by those around them—not least because they enjoy being the center of attention. Beneath the cheerful face that they present to the world, however, confusion and self-doubt abound. These intuitive people are receptive to any unhappy "vibes" that emanate from others, and susceptible to the unsettling influence of their emotional responses. Thus they may feel directionless, a tendency that is pernicious to active individuals whose ultimate fulfillment is bound up with their desire to achieve progress (on behalf of themselves, as well as others). This is why, in their search for fulfillment, they are so strongly oriented to others, and also why they make empathetic friends, colleagues and companions, for in sublimating their own needs to those of others they are often able to clarify their thoughts and feelings.

The conjunction of their sensitivity with their yearning to effect their own individual growth and life goals augurs particularly well for the potential success of November 18 people as artists, musicians and writers—even as spiritual guides—as well as innovators in a variety of fields, including science and technology. While they assume positive and charismatic personae when engaged in their professional endeavors, it is within their personal liaisons that their insecurity is most apparent, and they therefore place enormous value on receiving the support and affection of their loved ones (and even more so if they were also born in the Chinese year of the goat), who know and accept them as they are and thus bolster their self-esteem.

PLANETARY INFLUENCES
Ruling planet: Pluto
Third decan: Personal planet is Moon

VIRTUES
Intuitive, dependable, considerate

VICES
Easily overwhelmed, indecisive, prone to depression

CAREERS
Musician, counselor, spiritual guide

SKILLS & APTITUDES
Empathy with others, progressive tendencies, sociability

FAMOUS BIRTHS
Al Shepard (1923)
Susan Sullivan (1943)
Kevin Nealon (1953)
Owen Wilson (1968)

COMPATIBLE WITH
January 15–19

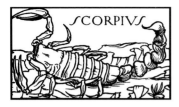

NOVEMBER 19

✤ ✤ ✤ ✤ ✤ ✤ ✤ ✤ ✤ ✤ ✤ ✤ ✤

HUMANITARIAN ENTHUSIASTS ♇ ♃ ☽

PLANETARY INFLUENCES
Ruling planets: Pluto and Jupiter
Third decan: Personal planet is Moon
Second cusp: Scorpio with Sagittarian
   tendencies

VIRTUES
Socially oriented, confident,
dynamic

VICES
Undisciplined, controlling,
authoritative

CAREERS
Public speaker, teacher, engineer

SKILLS & APTITUDES
Strong intellect, likable nature,
interest in others

FAMOUS BIRTHS
Tommy Dorsey (1905)
Larry King (1933)
Meg Ryan (1961)
Jodie Foster (1962)

COMPATIBLE WITH
January 15–19

Those born on this day are vigorous individuals who are naturally enthusiastic participants in life; rarely content to assume a passive role, they instead itch to play a vital part in every activity that excites their interest and they hope to make a significant contribution to the world. Both perceptive and intuitive, November 19 people are stimulated by addressing the various issues inherent in human society, be it within their immediate circle, their local communities, or even on a humanitarian level. Whatever profession they choose to pursue—and their progressive intellects and the technical expertise suit them to many, including scientific and creative pursuits—their ultimate purpose is to direct the actions of those around them to ways of benefiting the common good. In any event natural leaders, many will be drawn to pursuing high-flying careers.

Those born on this day are self-assured people, whose confidence stems from their strength of purpose in promoting the convictions in which they believe. As a result they attract admirers and detractors in equal measure but, such is their belief in the veracity of their viewpoints and their corresponding urge to implement them that they accept both reactions with equanimity (as long as they can proceed unhindered). As committed to involving themselves as fully as possible in the lives of their nearest and dearest as they are dedicated to their professional interests, November 19 people are generally concerned and affectionate friends and relations, but nevertheless have a tendency—which is especially marked in the women born on this day—to seek to regulate the actions of those closest to them, a propensity that may not always be welcome.

NOVEMBER 20

✶ ✶ ✶ ✶ ✶ ✶ ✶ ✶ ✶ ✶ ✶ ✶ ✶ ✶ ✶

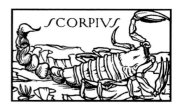

♇ ♃ ☽ INFLUENTIAL GAME–CHANGERS

Among the primary personal characteristics of those born on this day are their active and progressive minds, plus a deep desire to promote the interests of those to whom they feel most strongly connected—families, friends or the human community. Quick-thinking and intuitive, they readily identify faults in existing concepts, systems or behavioral patterns, and produce clear-cut remedial strategies.

November 20 people often have a tendency to show marked impatience with those who impede their progress, dismissing expressions of dissent with harsh words or, if provoked, even spectacular displays of temper (especially those who were born in the Chinese year of the dragon). However, their usual approach is to be self-controlled and disciplined, and they would rather use their (considerable) powers of charm and persuasion than coerce others into doing what they want.

The careers to which those born on this day are most attracted include politics, scientific and technical pursuits, commercial ventures, city planning and environmental issues. All throw themselves wholeheartedly into these ventures while nurturing their personal relationships as well.

Their tendency to be on a short fuse, however, means that November 20 people sometimes aim higher than is good for them. It's not a question of ability: they possess plenty of talents. It is more that if they get too wrapped up in their goals, problems or ambitions, they can simply lose their sense of perspective and either fly off the handle or lose control of the entire situation. Balance is the key.

PLANETARY INFLUENCES
Ruling planets: Pluto and Jupiter
Third decan: Personal planet is Moon
Second cusp: Scorpio with Sagittarian tendencies

VIRTUES
Perceptive, influential, intuitive

VICES
Impatient, short-tempered, aggressive

CAREERS
Politician, environmental planner, charity worker

SKILLS & APTITUDES
Disciplined nature, intelligence, problem-solving ability

FAMOUS BIRTHS
Edwin Hubble (1889)
Robert F. Kennedy (1925)
Veronica Hamel (1943)
Dominique Dawes (1976)

COMPATIBLE WITH
January 15–19

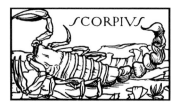

NOVEMBER 21

✳ ✳ ✳ ✳ ✳ ✳ ✳ ✳ ✳ ✳ ✳ ✳ ✳ ✳ ✳ ✳

CHEERFUL HELPERS   ♇ ♃ ☽

PLANETARY INFLUENCES
Ruling planets: Pluto and Jupiter
Third decan: Personal planet is Moon
Second cusp: Scorpio with Sagittarian
tendencies

VIRTUES
Generous, energetic, supportive

VICES
Easily frustrated, lacking in
perspective, obsessive

CAREERS
Sculptor, art curator, writer

SKILLS & APTITUDES
Caring personality, hard-working
dedication, creativity

FAMOUS BIRTHS
Voltaire (1694)
Harold Ramis (1944)
Goldie Hawn (1945)
Michael Strahan (1971)

COMPATIBLE WITH
January 15–19

....

....

....

Good-natured, with an infectious sense of fun, eager to please others, November 21 individuals are usually regarded with affection—not only by those closest to them, but by their colleagues and casual acquaintances. Beneath the sunny exterior that they present to the world, however, lie hidden depths. Their emotional responses to the people around them are at least as influential as their intellectual concerns. And it is partly because they are highly attuned to unhappiness that they make such empathetic and generous companions. Their concern for others does not preclude the pursuit of their personal interests and visions, but most November 21 people will choose careers where they can combine their internal and external orientations by generating concepts or products (particularly within the realm of artistry) that they envisage will help society progress: inspirational oeuvres of literary, artistic, musical or dramatic work, for example, or maybe pioneering technical advances.

Such is the importance that many of those born on this day place on their emotional happiness (which is inextricably bound up with that of those around them) that even when they fulfill their professional potential and are applauded for their work they will rarely be genuinely happy unless they can share their success with a close-knit circle of family and friends. For not only do they value the strong bonds that they form with their nearest and dearest for the strengthening love and support that they receive while working for the benefit of others, but their personal relationships are perhaps the only part of their lives in which they feel they can relax, be themselves and share their worries and visions with those who understand them best.

SAGITTARIUS

November 22 to December 21

RULING PLANET: *Jupiter* ELEMENT: *Mutable fire*
SYMBOL: *Centaur/archer* POLARITY: *Positive (masculine)*
PHYSICAL CORRESPONDENCE: *Liver, hips and thighs*
STONES: *Garnet, turquoise, amethyst, citrine, topaz* COLORS: *Blue and purple*
FLOWERS: *Wallflower, dandelion, narcissus, lime flower, carnation*

The name "Sagittarius" is derived from the Latin word *sagitta*, "arrow", and the archer is traditionally associated with this sign. Although the hybrid centaur—half man and half horse—is often portrayed as this zodiacal archer, some scholars believe instead that they represent scorpion-men. The majority of astrological traditions have identified this constellation with an archer, the ancient Greeks, for example, calling it Toxotes ("the archer"), and Hindu astrologers, Dhanus ("the bow"). The myth that specifically explains the origins of the constellation of Sagittarius tells of the centaur Chiron of Magnesia, mentor of Achilles, Pholus and Jason. After his accidental wounding by Herakle's (Hercules') poisoned arrow he was said to have bestowed his immortality upon Prometheus, and in recognition of his noble gesture was raised to the heavens by Zeus (Jupiter).

Paralleling the hybrid nature of the centaur, Sagittarians are said to possess the impetuous animal power of the horse and the intellectual capacity of humanity, along with the aspirational qualities signified by the arrow. Under the influence of the element of fire, Sagittarians often display restlessness and emotional warmth, while the sign's ruling planet, Jupiter, bestows joviality, versatility and a sense of honor. There is risk, however, that material concerns may prevail over intellectual wisdom, and that passion, impulsive enthusiasm and impatience may hinder a focused approach.

SAGITTARIUS

NOVEMBER 22

✳ ✳ ✳ ✳ ✳ ✳ ✳ ✳ ✳ ✳ ✳ ✳ ✳ ✳ ✳

CONCEPTUAL INNOVATORS   ♃ ♇

B lessed with both physical and intellectual vigor, those born on this day seek to combine their goals in life with the general good. Their desire to move ever onward and upward is influenced less by the craving for personal aggrandizement than by their desire to implement idealistic programs. Astute, inquisitive and perceptive, they work to replace existing systems with more effective alternatives, or to pioneer new concepts. And because they tend to be perfectionists, they set themselves (and others) high standards. Energetic, determined and given to directing others along what they perceive to be the best path, November 22 people lead by example and are not afraid to adopt combative methods if they believe these to be necessary. They are thus sometimes seen as interfering or downright bossy, though they rarely bear grudges and usually win the affection of their colleagues and friends.

Their inclinations and talents equip those born on this day admirably for a wide range of careers, with the proviso that they can retain the autonomy of thought and deed that is so vital to them while simultaneously exerting their powerful influence on their coworkers, audiences or publics (prerequisites that are especially pertinent if they were also born in the Chinese year of the dragon). They may thus be found working in management or supervisory positions. In all their actions and ventures their essential humanitarianism and concern for those whose welfare they have most strongly at heart—particularly their nearest and dearest—shines through. As strong-willed as they are energetic, their urge to direct everyone around them may, however, arouse the resentment of those who value their individuality as much as they themselves do.

NOVEMBER 23

✳ ✳ ✳ ✳ ✳ ✳ ✳ ✳ ✳ ✳ ✳ ✳ ✳

♃ ♇   VIRTUOUS UPHOLDERS

There are often two distinct sides to the November 23 personality: one that is inspired by original visions that can make a significant contribution to society; and another, more pugnacious, side that seems inevitably to involve them in confrontational situations. Yet those born on this day do not enjoy conflict for conflict's sake, but are prepared to challenge views or methods that they regard as wrong or ineffectual. These are essentially fair-minded individuals, whose passions are especially aroused by any instances of perceived societal abuses, and who are consequently naturally inclined toward designing and actively advancing pioneering remedial solutions. Because they are also blessed with rational intellectual powers, as well as considerable practical expertise, their proposed strategies are typically carefully thought through from every angle; even so, the upholders of the status quo may regard them as being unfeasibly radical, and it is thus that feelings of mutual antagonism arise.

November 23 people have the potential to make their mark within many professional pursuits, but will perhaps be happiest—and most successful—when working within those spheres where the realization of their soaring fantasies is not constrained by the objections of less imaginative individuals: the many specialties encompassed by new technology and creative ventures are thus especially well starred. Because their professional relationships are so often characterized by argument, these individuals deeply value the unquestioning love and belief of their nearest and dearest, and return their support with profound affection, loyalty and generosity.

PLANETARY INFLUENCES
Ruling planets: Jupiter and Pluto
First decan: Personal planet is Jupiter
First cusp: Sagittarius with Scorpio
   tendencies

VIRTUES
Independent, courageous, clever

VICES
Argumentative, pushy, aggressive

CAREERS
Lawyer, coder, sports coach

SKILLS & APTITUDES
Articulacy, intelligence, strength of will

FAMOUS BIRTHS
Billy the Kid (1859)
Boris Karloff (1887)
Harpo Marx (1888)
Miley Cyrus (1992)

COMPATIBLE WITH
March 18–23

NOVEMBER 24

✿ ✿ ✿ ✿ ✿ ✿ ✿ ✿ ✿ ✿ ✿ ✿ ✿ ✿

GIFTED CAREGIVERS   ♃ ♇

PLANETARY INFLUENCES
Ruling planets: Jupiter and Pluto
First decan: Personal planet is Jupiter
First cusp: Sagittarius with Scorpio
  tendencies

VIRTUES
Creative, artistic, tolerant

VICES
Critical, impatient, disconnected

CAREERS
Social worker, dramatist, local
politician

SKILLS & APTITUDES
Inclusivity, supportiveness,
intellectual curiosity

FAMOUS BIRTHS
Percy Sutton (1920)
Billy Connolly (1942)
Nia Vardalos (1962)
Katherine Heigl (1978)

COMPATIBLE WITH
March 19–24

Those born on this day are deeply interested in, and orientated toward, the people around them. They try to improve conditions for them, whether family members, neighbors, or the wider society. They may find satisfaction in working as politicians, humanitarians, parents, or members of the caring professions. When their independent and sensual traits predominate, their career goals often center on creativity, leading them to become artists, writers, musicians or actors. Inspiring, enlightening and bringing pleasure to others is appealing, but they are also stimulated by the chance to expand their emotional and intellectual horizons through these artistic media. The approbation this brings is welcome, but not essential to their innate sense of self-worth.

November 24 people surprise those who do not know them well by their strength of conviction in promoting the causes they espouse. Underlying their tolerant approach toward others is an emotional core that causes them to react strongly to social abuses and faults. Although their potential to make loving, supportive and protective friends, partners and parents is second to none, they will criticize thoughtlessness or wrongdoing sharply. Those who value their fine qualities will make allowances for their occasional displays of impatience, which are not intended to wound.

Deeply affectionate and supportive friends and relations who are vitally concerned with, and protective of, those closest to them, they sometimes seek to suppress any behavior that deviates from the societal norm, believing that they are acting in their loved ones' ultimate best interests.

NOVEMBER 25

✳ ✳ ✳ ✳ ✳ ✳ ✳ ✳ ✳ ✳ ✳ ✳ ✳ ✳

♃ ♇   CONSERVATIVE REFORMERS

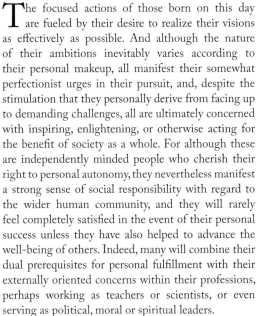

The focused actions of those born on this day are fueled by their desire to realize their visions as effectively as possible. And although the nature of their ambitions inevitably varies according to their personal makeup, all manifest their somewhat perfectionist urges in their pursuit, and, despite the stimulation that they personally derive from facing up to demanding challenges, all are ultimately concerned with inspiring, enlightening, or otherwise acting for the benefit of society as a whole. For although these are independently minded people who cherish their right to personal autonomy, they nevertheless manifest a strong sense of social responsibility with regard to the wider human community, and they will rarely feel completely satisfied in the event of their personal success unless they have also helped to advance the well-being of others. Indeed, many will combine their dual prerequisites for personal fulfillment with their externally oriented concerns within their professions, perhaps working as teachers or scientists, or even serving as political, moral or spiritual leaders.

November 25 people are blessed with astute, rational and perceptive minds, and are naturally attracted to the exploration of novel concepts. Yet despite their intellectual appreciation of the new and original, they prefer to build upon or reform existing beliefs or systems, exploring, assessing and then amending them as they believe necessary rather than espousing radically innovative causes. To some extent they are thus upholders of tradition and continuity (a propensity that is especially pronounced in the women who share this birthday) and may regard those who appear to disrupt the status quo with disapproval.

PLANETARY INFLUENCES
Ruling planets: Jupiter and Pluto
First decan: Personal planet is Jupiter
First cusp: Sagittarius with Scorpio tendencies

VIRTUES
Efficient, public-spirited, progressive

VICES
Intolerant, overdemanding, suppressive

CAREERS
Teacher, community leader, scientific researcher

SKILLS & APTITUDES
Self-discipline, practicality, supportiveness

FAMOUS BIRTHS
Andrew Carnegie (1835)
John F. Kennedy, Jr. (1960)
Ben Stein (1944)
Christina Applegate (1971)

COMPATIBLE WITH
March 22–25

NOVEMBER 26

✴ ✴ ✴ ✴ ✴ ✴ ✴ ✴ ✴ ✴ ✴ ✴

PRODIGIOUS DAYDREAMERS ♃

PLANETARY INFLUENCES
Ruling planet: Jupiter
First decan: Personal planet is Jupiter

VIRTUES
Focused, determined, visionary

VICES
Commitment-phobic, workaholic, obsessive

CAREERS
Academic researcher, musician, technician

SKILLS & APTITUDES
Experimentation, innovation, drive

FAMOUS BIRTHS
Charles Schulz (1922)
Tina Turner (1939)
Peter Facinelli (1973)
Rita Ora (1990)

COMPATIBLE WITH
March 23–26

November 26 people are determined and free-thinking individualists, who are absorbed by discovery and experimentation and feel compelled to set examples to others. They are prodigiously organized and practical types, who manifest great technical expertise when engaged in their work, yet are also blessed with extremely active imaginations. They may thus become fixated on realizing visions that are so unusual or ambitious that those around them sometimes question whether they are actually achievable. These individuals, however, are rarely troubled by feelings of doubt when in thrall to a fascinating challenge, for since they are astute assessors of both their own abilities and the potential chances of success, they envisage no obstacles to their progress beyond those imposed by the closed minds of others. Perfectionist, tenacious and determined, they concentrate on their aims to the exclusion of all else.

These people will thrive in any career where they can pursue their quests for knowledge and innovation unhindered by outside constraints. Naturally drawn to the possibilities for advancement offered by academic research of all kinds, as well as science and the arts, those born on this day have the potential to make truly outstanding contributions to humanity. Others admire their originality and independent minds, but these very strengths may prohibit November 26 people from maintaining enduring life partnerships in particular, for they often secretly fear that by committing them-selves to another person their freedom of thought and action may be restricted (a propensity that is even more pronounced in the men born on this day). Despite this caveat, however, they typically make enlivening, loyal and affectionate friends and family members.

NOVEMBER 27

✳ ✳ ✳ ✳ ✳ ✳ ✳ ✳ ✳ ✳ ✳ ✳ ✳ ✳

♃ STRONG–WILLED NURTURERS

Those born on this day are complex people who are fiercely individualistic. On the one hand they react negatively to any perceived attempts to limit their autonomy, and on the other, they are positively oriented to those around them. Some November 27 people are able to successfully reconcile these two sides within their careers, for example by working independently and then sharing the fruits of their labors with a wider audience. These are mentally active and technically minded people with the potential to research, develop and then pioneer advances that could enlighten, inspire or otherwise assist others. In many respects their concern for those around them is the result of their sense of justice and instinctive dislike of authoritarianism, as well as their more emotional response to the plight of those who are unhappy or suffering. Although stimulated by the pursuit of their interests, the motivations underlying their work often stem from their desire to lighten the lives of others. They may become politicians, carers, artists or scientists.

Their relationships—both professional and personal—with those around them are typically characterized by mutual respect and goodwill; but they will not hesitate to make their feelings forcefully known if they detect any transgressions. Predisposed toward forming and maintaining open and relaxed relationships with their nearest and dearest—provided, that is, that their loved ones understand and accommodate their need for a certain level of freedom, a prerequisite that is all the more important if they were also born in the Chinese year of the tiger—November 27 people make deeply supportive, generous and enlivening partners and companions, and especially gifted parents.

PLANETARY INFLUENCES
Ruling planet: Jupiter
First decan: Personal planet is Jupiter

VIRTUES
Community-spirited, independent, practical

VICES
Rebellious, overly forceful, judgmental

CAREERS
Scientific researcher, community leader, systems analyst

SKILLS & APTITUDES
Independent mindset, social orientation, technical skills

FAMOUS BIRTHS
Bruce Lee (1940)
Jimi Hendrix (1942)
Bill Nye (1955)
Jaleel White (1976)

COMPATIBLE WITH
March 24–27,

NOVEMBER 28

✳ ✳ ✳ ✳ ✳ ✳ ✳ ✳ ✳ ✳ ✳ ✳ ✳ ✳

OBSERVANT REALISTS   ♐

PLANETARY INFLUENCES
Ruling planet: Jupiter
First decan: Personal planet is Jupiter

VIRTUES
Intuitive, fair-minded, astute

VICES
Outspoken, critical, intimidating

CAREERS
Journalist, social campaigner, market analyst

SKILLS & APTITUDES
Analytical skills, interest in human behavior, social awareness

FAMOUS BIRTHS
Berry Gordy (1929)
Randy Newman (1943)
Jon Stewart (1962)
Karen Gillan (1987)

COMPATIBLE WITH
March 26–27

Those born on this day are astute and critical observers, not only of others, but of group dynamics as a whole. Blessed with sensitive powers of intuition, they test their conclusions analytically before sharing them with a wider audience. Their independence of mind fosters skepticism in the face of prejudice and convention. Because they have an innate sense of fairness, November 28 people are natural debunkers, but their intentions are not destructive. They rarely offer criticisms without proposing viable alternatives attuned to the needs of those around them.

Their interest in the workings of society and in human behavior suit November 28 individuals especially well for careers as social reformers, politicians, psychologists, careers advisors and journalists. Professions in the artistic or scientific spheres may also attract them, especially as venues for personal and social enlightenment.

Given their critical propensity, the people with whom they live and work tend to admire and respect them but inevitably feel uncomfortable lest they become the next target of their censure. This is an unfortunate (if understandable) reaction, since November 28 people are ultimately motivated by the most well-meaning of intentions and, furthermore, crave the affection and security that result from profound bonds of friend- and kinship. Because November 28 people can be uncompromisingly frank, despising as they do all expressions of hypocrisy, they can run the risk of alienating others, including those to whom they are close.

NOVEMBER 29

✳ ✳ ✳ ✳ ✳ ✳ ✳ ✳ ✳ ✳ ✳ ✳ ✳

♃   RESOURCEFUL RATIONALISTS

Those born on this day are dynamic individuals, stimulated by challenge. Even during periods of relaxation they remain busy, perhaps pursuing sporting activities or adding to their knowledge by reading and observation. Imbued with the desire to move forward in terms of personal growth, career goals, or the common good, they are "can-do" types, who can assess a given situation and formulate innovative strategies. They are also pragmatic realists, who will rarely focus their energies on a venture unless they believe it stands a good chance of success. They also expect others to fall in with their views and may become impatient if the beliefs they espouse are slow to gain acceptance.

November 29 individuals are usually drawn to careers that can satisfy their pioneering and progressive urges and make a contribution to others. Despite their independence of mind, they have a strong sense of social responsibility and may gravitate toward political or scientific ventures, teaching, or humanitarian causes. A similarly profound concern for the well-being of their loved ones defines their personal relationships, and they in turn are deeply valued for their enlivening influence and loyalty. However, their tendency to direct those closest to them may not always be taken in the spirit in which it was intended.

In the interests of retaining the goodwill of others and protecting themselves from disappointment, these individuals should recognize that not everyone will share their enthusiasms. A more tolerant attitude to expressions of dissent will help them to enlist cooperation and to form lasting friendships.

PLANETARY INFLUENCES
Ruling planet: Jupiter
First decan: Personal planet is Jupiter

VIRTUES
Positive, independent, ambitious

VICES
Domineering, impatient, intolerant

CAREERS
Athlete, architect, surveyor, social campaigner

SKILLS & APTITUDES
Progressive impulses, social responsibility, energizing abilities

FAMOUS BIRTHS
Louisa May Alcott (1832)
C.S. Lewis (1898)
Joel Coen (1954)
Howie Mandel (1955)

COMPATIBLE WITH
March 26–28

NOVEMBER 30

✳ ✳ ✳ ✳ ✳ ✳ ✳ ✳ ✳ ✳ ✳ ✳ ✳

STRATEGIC DEFENDERS   4

PLANETARY INFLUENCES
Ruling planet: Jupiter
First decan: Personal planet is Jupiter

VIRTUES
Congenial, astute, determined

VICES
Secretive, abrupt, bossy

CAREERS
Project director, politician, journalist

SKILLS & APTITUDES
Analytical mindset, single-minded focus, organizational skills

FAMOUS BIRTHS
Mark Twain (1835)
Winston Churchill (1874)
Ridley Scott (1937)
Chrissy Teigen (1985)

COMPATIBLE WITH
March 27–30

The typically mild-mannered and good-humored face that those born on this day present to the world often masks an incisive mind that is hard at work analyzing people and circumstances. These astute individuals often harbor a plan for life whose ambition would surprise those who take their rather laid-back image at face value. This is not to say that these people are not genuinely charming and benevolent, but they understand the importance of reserve until they are ready to act. Perfectionist by nature, they use their resources to maximize their potential for success. For some November 30 people, disapproval or dissent on the part of others frequently has the effect of spurring them on along their chosen path with renewed vigor and determination. All are self-motivated, in any case, and will prove themselves tireless.

Organizational skills, boldness, determination and a talent for communication make those born on November 30 natural leaders. Often concerned with helping others to advance, they may defend or promote political, social or national interests. Or, on a more pragmatic level, they may make a good office manager, foreman, project manager or team leader in almost any setting.

The preparation, self-control, and fixity of purpose of many November 30 people usually elicits the admiration of others, but may become detrimental in their personal lives. This is especially likely if those closest to them resent their propensity for taking charge, or friends see them as unfeeling.

DECEMBER 1

✳ ✳ ✳ ✳ ✳ ✳ ✳ ✳ ✳ ✳ ✳ ✳ ✳ ✳

♃ ♂   GOOD-NATURED FREE SPIRITS

Those born on December 1 are extremely energetic individuals fueled by a driving ambition, yet such is their charm and their astute use of humor that others are seduced into applauding actions that they might otherwise consider ruthless. Some have a clear idea as to what they are aiming for in life: perhaps the achievement of excellence, the acclaim of their peers and concomitant financial rewards; others may be less focused, but nevertheless feel the urge to manifest their individuality unfettered by the constraints of opinion. All express themselves freely and will react particularly badly to any perceived attempts to restrict their autonomy of thought and action.

While December 1 people will defend or promote the freedom they cherish so greatly, sometimes to the point of defiance, these are not individuals who generally employ combative strategies for the sake of confrontation: they prefer to win others over by the sheer force of their personalities.

December 1 people will flourish in any profession where they can act independently and make an original contribution. They can work well as part of a team, but they are better suited to being leaders than followers. Given their predilections, they have the potential to make outstanding performers and entertainers, particularly in the sporting or artistic fields. Others admire their driving energy and good humor, and those born on this day revel in the attention they excite, yet also take real pleasure in pleasing those around them. Indeed, they are also genuinely concerned and affectionate friends and relations, valued for their enlivening company and optimistic, "can-do" attitude.

PLANETARY INFLUENCES
Ruling planet: Jupiter
Second decan: Personal planet is Mars

VIRTUES
Charismatic, sociable, freethinking

VICES
Eccentric, rebellious, extreme

CAREERS
Standup performer, actor, athlete

SKILLS & APTITUDES
Expressiveness, energizing qualities, trailblazing potential

FAMOUS BIRTHS
Lou Rawls (1936)
Richard Pryor (1940)
Bette Midler (1945)
Sarah Silverman (1970)
Zoë Kravitz (1988)

COMPATIBLE WITH
March 25–30, October 7–10

....
....
....

DECEMBER 2

PROLIFIC VISIONARIES ♃ ♂

PLANETARY INFLUENCES
Ruling planet: Jupiter
Second decan: Personal planet is Mars

VIRTUES
Socially responsible, empathetic, driven

VICES
Short-tempered, overcommitted, unbalanced

CAREERS
Artist, scientific researcher, lawyer

SKILLS & APTITUDES
Social responsibility, resourcefulness, independence

FAMOUS BIRTHS
Gianni Versace (1946)
Stone Phillips (1954)
Lucy Liu (1968)
Britney Spears (1981)
Charlie Puth (1991)

COMPATIBLE WITH
March 30–31, October 7–10

Many of those born on this day feel torn between their desire to forge their own path through life and their profound sense of responsibility for others—be they their families, friends, colleagues, or even the fellowship of humanity. Blessed with imaginative, innovative and curious minds, on the one hand these vigorous people feel compelled to pursue the interests they love, while on the other their fair-mindedness and empathy with those whom they perceive to be victims of injustice urges them to champion the oppressed. When these tendencies are imbalanced, December 2 people may experience frustration. They have quick tempers when crossed, particularly if they were also born in the Chinese year of the dragon. If they can reconcile their need for independence with their concern for promoting the welfare of others, they have the potential not only to attain personal satisfaction, but to make contributions to society, perhaps as pioneering scientists or inspirational artists.

Those around them respect the strength of character of December 2 people and may often elevate them to positions of leadership—a responsibility that those born on this day may view ambivalently. Although they have an enviable gift for organization and motivation and would far rather command than obey, they may feel that their leadership duties preclude them from pursuing their own ambitions. A similarly ambiguous attitude characterizes their relationships with their nearest and dearest (which is even more pronounced in the women who share this birthdate), for while they manifest deep affection and protectiveness for their loved ones, they may sometimes feel stifled by their (often self-imposed) duties of caretaking.

DECEMBER 3

✳ ✳ ✳ ✳ ✳ ✳ ✳ ✳ ✳ ✳ ✳ ✳ ✳ ✳

♃ ♂ INQUISITIVE INVESTIGATORS

Intricate systems and abstract concepts exert tremendous fascination upon December 3 people. Blessed with investigative and progressive minds, their attention is irresistibly drawn to complex issues, identifying flaws and then formulating solutions. Despite the unusual—even radical—ideas they typically espouse, and the ambitious nature of their visions, these are rational and meticulous types who prefer not to make their theories public until they are convinced of their feasibility; their proposals can thus rarely be likened to castles built on shifting sand, as the have the most stable of foundations. Add to this solid basis their organizational and technical skills, as well as their tenacity, and the result is an effective instrument of progress. Indeed, December 3 people show pioneering promise, and will excel in those fields where they can combine their innovative inclinations and practical expertise and thus lead by example—perhaps as scientists or engineers, or else within the more fluid realms of artistry and athletics.

While others respect their vigor, focus and drive, they may feel that these individuals have thrown up an invisible shield around them, making it difficult (if not impossible) to penetrate to the core of their personalities. And it is true that those born on this day prefer to keep their emotions private—sometimes even concealing them from their nearest and dearest—perhaps believing that their expression would distract from intellectual pursuits. Many of their visions are driven by the desire to assist society, and they make caring, responsible and generous friends and family members, even when their professional interests take a higher priority.

PLANETARY INFLUENCES
Ruling planet: Jupiter
Second decan: Personal planet is Mars

VIRTUES
Progressive, clear-sighted, precise

VICES
Emotionally detached, obsessive, undemonstrative

CAREERS
Scientific researcher, lawyer, sports coach

SKILLS & APTITUDES
Meticulousness, determination, practical skills

FAMOUS BIRTHS
Ozzy Osbourne (1948)
Julianne Moore (1960)
Brendan Fraser (1968)
Amanda Seyfried (1985)

COMPATIBLE WITH
March 25–31, April 1,
October 7–10

DECEMBER 4

✴ ✴ ✴ ✴ ✴ ✴ ✴ ✴ ✴ ✴ ✴ ✴ ✴ ✴

WELL–INTENTIONED REBELS   ♃ ♂

PLANETARY INFLUENCES
Ruling planet: Jupiter
Second decan: Personal planet is Mars

VIRTUES
Freethinking, courageous, determined

VICES
Domineering, easily frustrated, rash

CAREERS
Politician, entrepreneur, social campaigner

SKILLS & APTITUDES
Inclusivity, supportiveness, intellectual curiosity

FAMOUS BIRTHS
Dennis Wilson (1944)
Jeff Bridges (1949)
Jay-Z (1969)
Tyra Banks (1973)

COMPATIBLE WITH
March 26–31, April 1–2,
September 4–6

It is a curious dichotomy of December 4 people's characters that although they cherish their individuality, they feel compelled to impose their own convictions upon those around them. Often lacking self-awareness, they see no contradiction in seeking to control the thoughts and actions of others while at the same time reserving their own right to autonomy. But their pushiness usually stems from the best of intentions. Those born on this day are thoughtful and socially responsible, their guiding visions generally concerned with advancing the greater good rather than any more selfish ambitions. Their sense of natural justice and balanced objectivity in particular propel them toward activities that are intended to bring about a more enlightened or better regulated society, and they may hence often be found promoting a clear-cut set of ideological or political beliefs, either as politicians or social campaigners, or else through the more subtle, but no less effective media encompassed by the artistic disciplines.

December 4 people back their strongly held opinions and ambitions with resourcefulness, energy and vigor, and—since they are additionally practical and organized types—with carefully devised and impeccably executed plans of action. Stimulated by challenge, they relish taking risks and facing obstacles squarely—a strategy that often has remarkable results but which may equally cause them to explode with frustration when they find their progress blocked. Others regard their determined and confrontational approach with awe, but sometimes prefer to give them a wide berth lest they find themselves in the firing line. Those closest to them see the gentler, more affectionate side to their characters.

DECEMBER 5

✹ ✹ ✹ ✹ ✹ ✹ ✹ ✹ ✹ ✹ ✹ ✹ ✹ ✹

♃ ♂   PURPOSEFUL ACADEMICS

Being actively engaged in a potentially rewarding endeavor is a prerequisite for the happiness of those born on this day. Both intellectually and physically energetic, with a deep-rooted need to stimulate their minds and bodies in the pursuit of progress and knowledge, their attention is quickly captured by the pioneering possibilities inherent in challenging concepts or situations. Indeed, they respond to ideas and visions that would be dismissed by more conservative and cautious individuals. Yet such are their powers of imagination, and their optimistic approach to the most daunting tasks, that December 5 people rarely allow themselves to be dissuaded from an exciting new venture. This sometimes leads them to make serious errors of judgment, but may equally result in remarkable innovations—and those around them admire their indomitable spirit and enthusiasm. They are regarded with affection and tolerance by their coworkers, friends and relations (feelings that they reciprocate), but in many respects their primary concern is with their intellectual ambitions.

The majority of those born on this day are concerned with making a real contribution to those with whom they identify, whether their families, compatriots or even humanity as a whole, and may be drawn to political or social pursuits. They supplement their clarity of purpose by drawing upon their resourcefulness, technical and organizational skills. They will thrive in any career where their interest remains actively engaged, but perhaps will derive the greatest satisfaction as artists, writers, digital coders and designers, musicians or movie-makers.

PLANETARY INFLUENCES
Ruling planet: Jupiter
Second decan: Personal planet is Mars

VIRTUES
Imaginative, positive, resourceful

VICES
Emotionally disconnected, inflexible, dismissive

CAREERS
Entrepreneur, digital designer, musician

SKILLS & APTITUDES
Innovative mindset, dogged determination, positive focus

FAMOUS BIRTHS
Martin Van Buren (1782)
Walt Disney (1901)
Little Richard (1935)
Margaret Cho (1968)

COMPATIBLE WITH
March 28–31, April 1–3, September 5–6

DECEMBER 6

✳ ✳ ✳ ✳ ✳ ✳ ✳ ✳ ✳ ✳ ✳ ✳ ✳ ✳

CONNOISSEURS OF REASON   ♃ ♂

PLANETARY INFLUENCES
Ruling planet: Jupiter
Second decan: Personal planet is Mars

VIRTUES
Perceptive, meticulous, committed

VICES
Critical, bossy, stubborn

CAREERS
Market analyst, project manager, movie director

SKILLS & APTITUDES
Analytical mindset, organizational skills, leadership qualities

FAMOUS BIRTHS
Ira Gershwin (1896)
Steven Wright (1955)
Judd Apatow (1967)
Noel Clarke (1975)

COMPATIBLE WITH
March 29–31, April 1–5,
July 19–22, September 5–6

....

....

....

Perhaps the primary characteristics manifested by those born on this day are their perceptive and rational ways of looking at the world. In many respects they may be compared to scientists (which, indeed, many may decide to become), for they assume a clinical approach to collecting data, assessing it objectively, and identifying areas in need of improvement or change before formulating plans. This talent for impartial evaluation is not only applicable to the scientific sphere, but may also be employed to great effect in many other professions, including those related to commerce, as well as to political, sporting and even artistic ventures, in which imaginative reinterpretations of existing conventions can have startlingly successful results.

Because they are themselves convinced of the veracity of their convictions, having submitted them to exhaustive examination before reaching their conclusions, December 6 individuals typically seek to enlist the support of those around them in their promotion, and, as gifted organizers, have the potential to spearhead highly motivated and smoothly operating teams.

Others regard their solid commitment to their often unusual—even radical—causes with awed admiration. Yet since the ultimate goal of those born on this day is to achieve concrete results, and because they are sometimes coercive (particularly so for the men born on this day), they may not always inspire affection—even if their aims are good. Their preoccupation with their own interests, along with their habit of pointing out failings on the part of others, may lead them to stand apart from those around them, a tendency that may not always augur well for domestic harmony.

DECEMBER 7

✻ ✻ ✻ ✻ ✻ ✻ ✻ ✻ ✻ ✻ ✻ ✻ ✻ ✻

♃ ♂   UNIQUE VISIONARIES

December 7 people are especially notable for daring to be different, a propensity that is due not to attention-seeking (although this usually inevitably follows) but to their great originality and enjoyment of adventurous forays into the unknown. These individuals seek knowledge and experience beyond society's conventional norms, a predisposition that is influenced by their ability to absorb and assess information and to uncover truths that are as yet obscure.

With the Sagittarian qualities of intellectual curiosity and an original turn of mind, they possess pioneering—even leadership—potential. Maintaining their freedom of thought and action is vital to their well-being: they feel intellectually and emotionally stifled if forced to conform to others' mores. They are well suited to professions in which they can act independently, including science and the arts.

Despite their tendency to stand apart from the crowd, those born on this day are not true loners, for they feel a strong sense of responsibility for those around them, a propensity that is even more pronounced in the women born on this day. Their questing outlook on the world instills tolerance, but they will stand up for their strongest convictions—humanitarian principles, for instance. While their inherent restlessness leads them to investigate new issues, people and places with great enthusiasm, they are reliable and loyal people and are devoted to their friends, partners and families, who in turn cherish them for their benevolent and affectionate qualities.

PLANETARY INFLUENCES
Ruling planet: Jupiter
Second decan: Personal planet is Mars

VIRTUES
Individualistic, freethinking, tolerant

VICES
Restless, nonconformist, isolated

CAREERS
Scientific researcher, academic, experimental artist

SKILLS & APTITUDES
Originality of thought, questing curiosity, independent instincts

FAMOUS BIRTHS
Noam Chomsky (1928)
Ellen Burstyn (1932)
Larry Bird (1956)
Sara Bareilles (1979)

COMPATIBLE WITH
March 30–31, April 1–7,
July 19–22, September 6

DECEMBER 8

✳ ✳ ✳ ✳ ✳ ✳ ✳ ✳ ✳ ✳ ✳ ✳ ✳ ✳

DELICATE ROMANTICS   ♃ ♂

PLANETARY INFLUENCES
Ruling planet: Jupiter
Second decan: Personal planet is Mars

VIRTUES
Idealistic, enthusiastic, inspirational

VICES
Dissatisfied, demotivated, unfocused

CAREERS
Musician, nonprofit worker, community activist

SKILLS & APTITUDES
Total dedication, infectious enthusiasm, positive focus

FAMOUS BIRTHS
Eli Whitney (1765)
Jim Morrison (1943)
Teri Hatcher (1964)
Sinead O'Connor (1966)

COMPATIBLE WITH
March 31, April 1–9,
July 19–22

....
....
....

December 8 individuals are passionate people, driven by their compulsion to live life to the full. Extraordinarily active in every respect, they often show intense emotional and sensual responses, throwing themselves wholeheartedly into any new venture or relationship that promises stimulation. Indeed, these individuals may be characterized as true idealists, engaged in a constant quest to realize their visions of perfection—intellectual, spiritual or emotional. In their search for their personal Utopia, they manifest boundless enthusiasm, determination and vigor, often inspiring others with their drive and infectious optimism.

The motives of December 8 individuals are rarely selfish, however. These people have a deep-rooted desire to bring happiness to others, and many will capitalize upon their artistic affinities to become professional writers, musicians, artists and performers.

Perhaps inevitably, given their high expectations, December 8 people may never feel that they have attained their elusive goals, even when others applaud them. They may spur themselves on to even greater efforts (especially if they were born in the Chinese year of the horse), or else sink into deep depression, when disappointed with themselves or the results of their efforts. It is important that their confidence be bolstered by understanding friends and relations, whose support helps to safeguard their emotional well-being. They should try to retain a realistic perspective on their chances for success, and, while not giving up on their dreams, remember that some goals are unlikely to be achievable.

DECEMBER 9

✳ ✳ ✳ ✳ ✳ ✳ ✳ ✳ ✳ ✳ ✳ ✳ ✳ ✳

♃ ♂   ENLIGHTENED MOTIVATORS

Whether or not they present a physically dashing figure to the world, those born on this day are gripped by the most original and ambitious of visions—dreams in which they envisage themselves making a substantial and inspirational contribution to the greater good. Blessed with soaringly imaginative minds (which are as much influenced by their emotional orientation to others as by their more abstract, intellectual propensities), as well as the more rational capacity to identify faults or failings in existing systems or concepts, December 9 people possess true pioneering potential.

Utilizing both their intuition and their clear-sighted perspicacity, those born on December 9 have an innate ability to identify what is lacking or wrong in the lives of those around them, and a concomitant urge to remedy the situation, if it is within their power to help. And in pursuing their ambitions they draw upon their prodigious vigor, organizational and technical skills, along with their unwavering fixity of purpose. The nature of their aims varies: some will advance within the political or scientific spheres, while others choose such artistic media as music, literature, drama, fashion or interior design.

Active concern also characterizes the interpersonal relationships of December 9 individuals, with colleagues, family and the larger community. They do their utmost to safeguard the emotional and physical well-being of others. Inherent in such an involved approach, however, is the tendency to control, and others may reject or resent their advice.

PLANETARY INFLUENCES
Ruling planet: Jupiter
Second decan: Personal planet is Mars

VIRTUES
Socially concerned, imaginative, analytical

VICES
Fault-finding, controlling, intolerant

CAREERS
Social worker, local politician, teacher

SKILLS & APTITUDES
Leadership skills, self-confidence, progressive proclivities

FAMOUS BIRTHS
John Milton (1608)
Judi Dench (1934)
Beau Bridges (1941)
Simon Helberg (1980)

COMPATIBLE WITH
April 1–10, July 19–22,

....
....
....

DECEMBER 10

✳ ✳ ✳ ✳ ✳ ✳ ✳ ✳ ✳ ✳ ✳ ✳ ✳ ✳

SOFT–SPOKEN SAVANTS   ♃ ♂

PLANETARY INFLUENCES
Ruling planet: Jupiter
Second decan: Personal planet is Mars

VIRTUES
Progressive, selfless, idealistic

VICES
Overly demanding, insensitive,
emotionally closed

CAREERS
Social worker, artistic director, local
politician

SKILLS & APTITUDES
Self-discipline, unwavering focus,
leadership potential

FAMOUS BIRTHS
Emily Dickinson (1830)
Kenneth Branagh (1960)
Bobby Flay (1964)
Raven Symone (1985)

COMPATIBLE WITH
April 2–11, July 19–22

The quiet and generally controlled demeanor that characterizes those born on this day often masks their steadily burning determination to realize their ideals. Deep thinkers, December 10 individuals tend to be concerned with furthering human knowledge—exploring abstract, academic or spiritual concepts, instituting scientific or artistic advances, or reforming social systems. Blessed with objective and balanced intellects, they are able to make informed and soundly reasoned assessments when approaching major decisions and formulate effective plans. Indeed, their organizational skills are second to none, and they may seek careers as event managers, in politics or in other forms of community service. Others are attracted to the opportunities inherent in the academic world.

Since their endeavors are intended to result in benefits for the greater good, rather than simply to satisfy selfish ambitions, and because of their initiative and focus, those born on this day make gifted leaders. They may well be demanding, but never expect more from others than they themselves give, a propensity that is redoubled if they were also born in the Chinese year of the rat. Sometimes accused of insensitivity, they are actively concerned with the welfare of their friends, families and coworkers, but do not often express themselves. Others generally admire and respect their selfless motivations and drive, but even their nearest associates may feel excluded from sharing their inner worlds of emotions and dreams, which they tend to keep hidden (particularly if they are men) beneath their disciplined exterior.

DECEMBER 11

✳ ✳ ✳ ✳ ✳ ✳ ✳ ✳ ✳ ✳ ✳ ✳ ✳ ✳ ✳

♃ ♂   CONFLICTED QUIBBLERS

Those born on this day often feel torn between their strong sense of social responsibility and their equally profound desire to attain happiness by indulging in their personal interests. These dual propensities can create conflict in the realm of family life. While they derive pleasure from the company of their loved ones, they are apt to be controlling. December 11 people are often drawn to professional pursuits that challenge their intellectual qualities and are concerned with improving the lives of those around them. Many are interested in systems of social regulation and feel inclined to act as the champions of the downtrodden, perhaps as humanitarian activists or politicians. Others seek to make scientific advances intended to help humanity, or to work in medical or emergency services or as mechanics or engineers.

Whatever professions they pursue, all December 11 individuals are notable for their energy and dedication to their causes. Innate perfectionists, they demand as high a level of commitment from those around them as they themselves demonstrate, and do not easily tolerate errors or poor judgment. This level of intensity may produce remarkable results but may also backfire or have an intellectually and physically exhausting effect on everyone involved. And, despite their profound affection and concern for the well-being of those closest to them (as well as the value they in turn place on receiving their unquestioning emotional support), their elevated standards and sometimes overly active promotion of the behavioral and ethical principles that they espouse may arouse the resentment of those whose interests they have most strongly at heart.

PLANETARY INFLUENCES
Ruling planet: Jupiter
Second decan: Personal planet is Mars

VIRTUES
Committed, progressive, public-spirited

VICES
Controlling, overly intense, demanding

CAREERS
Social activist, scientific researcher, paramedic

SKILLS & APTITUDES
Social orientation, indefatigable focus, drive

FAMOUS BIRTHS
Brenda Lee (1944)
Nikki Sixx (1958)
Mo'Nique (1967)
Jermaine Jackson (1954)

COMPATIBLE WITH
April 3–13, July 19–22

DECEMBER 12

❊ ❊ ❊ ❊ ❊ ❊ ❊ ❊ ❊ ❊ ❊ ❊ ❊ ❊

SOCIAL COMMUNICATORS ♃ ☉

PLANETARY INFLUENCES
Ruling planet: Jupiter
Third decan: Personal planet is Sun

VIRTUES
Fair-minded, determined, charismatic

VICES
Attention-seeking, reckless, outrageous

CAREERS
Teacher, advertising executive, stage performer

SKILLS & APTITUDES
Communication skills, risk-taking tendencies, self-confidence

FAMOUS BIRTHS
Gustave Flaubert (1821)
Frank Sinatra (1915)
Bob Barker (1923)
Mayim Bialik (1975)

COMPATIBLE WITH
April 4–14

Perhaps the most obvious trait of December 12 people is their tendency to express their emotions and convictions in the public arena. Generally, they are not seeking notice for its own sake, but in the belief that they have an important message to impart to the world—one that will help people to progress. Highly perceptive in terms of both intellect and intuition, their profound sense of justice causes them to react strongly to social abuses. Their attempts to redress these are pursued with vigor and unwavering determination—even (or especially) in the face of opposition.

December 12 people make effective and popular teachers and are often successful in the fields of marketing and sales, especially when they are promoting novel or technological products. Their outgoing personalities help them in people-centered jobs.

Although the causes that inspire December 12 people vary, all feel compelled to share them with the world through their talent for communication, which is even more pronounced if they were born in the Chinese year of the horse. Whether they employ verbal, literary, visual or musical media, their ability to hold the attention of their audiences—either by shocking or delighting—augurs well for their success. Many are aware that by opening such conduits for discussion they will excite negative as well as positive reactions, but believe that the potential benefits outweigh the risks, or sometimes simply cannot keep silent. The real danger, however, is that they may forfeit their privacy—and that of others whose love and support is vital to their emotional well-being.

DECEMBER 13

✳ ✳ ✳ ✳ ✳ ✳ ✳ ✳ ✳ ✳ ✳ ✳ ✳ ✳

♃ ☉　　　GROUNDED DELEGATES

Simultaneously curious and perfectionistic, those born on this day have the potential to initiate advances notable not only for their originality, but based upon solid foundations. Their innovations utilize their highly developed powers of perception to identify gaps in knowledge and endeavor. Innately vigorous and capable of deep concentration, they seek to fill these gaps, or rectify faults that they have pinpointed.

To all their ventures, December 13 people bring confidence, resourcefulness and tenacity, along with meticulous attention to detail. They will thrive in any profession where their exploratory and active needs can be fulfilled, but many require a structured working environment and are especially drawn to the fields of accountancy, engineering, actuarial work, science, the law, police work or civil service.

December 13 people are instinctive humanitarians, whose natural sense of justice and empathy for those in unfortunate circumstances arouse protective responses in them. Their interpersonal relationships—whether with coworkers, friends, partners or children—are also characterized by genuine interest and concern, especially in the women born on this day, although they do not tend to show their feelings openly. Dependable individuals, they usually offer carefully considered advice based on astute observations, but their desire for involvement is such that their benevolent intentions may be misinterpreted by independent loved ones as attempts to mold or control them.

PLANETARY INFLUENCES
Ruling planet: Jupiter
Third decan: Personal planet is Sun

VIRTUES
Tenacious, astute, reliable

VICES
Interfering, unemotional, overinvolved

CAREERS
Accountant, forensic lawyer, scientific researcher

SKILLS & APTITUDES
Social responsibility, appetite for problem-solving, focus on detail

FAMOUS BIRTHS
Dick van Dyke (1925)
Ted Nugent (1948)
Jamie Foxx (1967)
Taylor Swift (1989)

COMPATIBLE WITH
April 5–18

DECEMBER 14

✳ ✳ ✳ ✳ ✳ ✳ ✳ ✳ ✳ ✳ ✳ ✳ ✳ ✳ ✳

EARNEST REVOLUTIONARIES   ♃ ☉

Others cannot help but admire the aura of energy, capability and efficiency exuded by those born on this day, December 14 people are active types who cannot bear to stand idle when there are things to do and progress to be made. Blessed with rational and yet imaginative intellects, mental and physical vigor, and strong organizational skills, they approach all their endeavors with enthusiasm and determination. Their decisiveness makes them natural leaders, and they have a talent for directing others with a firm but benevolent hand, frequently balancing their high expectations with a dash of humor. They will thrive in any profession where they are allowed the freedom of action to work toward their objectives unhindered by others' constraints (which is not to say that are not rigorously disciplined—to the contrary) and they are therefore especially suited to careers where research and development play an integral part—within the academic, manufacturing or pharmaceutical spheres, for example.

Although they are sociable people who display enormous goodwill toward those around them, in many respects those born on this day are self-contained and self-reliant types whose potential for fulfillment lies in their individual quests for discovery and progress. Thus although others frequently turn to them for advice and support—and are never turned away—they may feel torn between their sense of social responsibility and their profound desire to pursue their personal interests undisturbed by the demands of those around them. It is important therefore that their friends and relations respect their need for privacy and space, and that they in turn try to find a happy medium between their internal and external orientations.

DECEMBER 15

✳ ✳ ✳ ✳ ✳ ✳ ✳ ✳ ✳ ✳ ✳ ✳ ✳ ✳

♃ ☉   PERSUASIVE CHARISMATICS

Those born on this day are complex personalities: on the one hand optimistic, vital and filled with benevolent feelings for those around them, and on the other possessing somewhat uncompromising, controlling and dictatorial tendencies. Blessed both with intellectual clarity—which enables them to pinpoint perceived faults and failings—and extremely logical minds, they devise straightforward plans of action. Mentally and physically active, they do not isolate themselves in a personal vacuum, but prefer to lead from the front, enlisting the support of like-minded individuals and motivating them with the help of their great personal charm. Indeed, others are attracted to these natural leaders on account of their invigorating enthusiasm, "can-do" attitude and no-nonsense approach.

Many of those born on this day have the ability to develop real expertise in the fields that interest them, including business, new technology and corporate management. Whatever career they choose, however, their ultimate objective is concerned with enlightening, educating or making their mark on a broader public. Their intentions toward others are thus of the most positive variety, but they should nevertheless beware of seeking to control those around them at any cost, however justified they feel themselves to be. This is particularly pertinent within their personal relationships, for by trying to direct the thoughts and actions of their loved ones they may inadvertently be suppressing their need for individual autonomy, and they may lose their receptiveness to other ideas and perspectives.

PLANETARY INFLUENCES
Ruling planet: Jupiter
Third decan: Personal planet is Sun

VIRTUES
Clear-thinking, progressive, ambitious

VICES
Controlling, uncompromising, impatient

CAREERS
IT worker, teacher, social campaigner

SKILLS & APTITUDES
Motivational skills, practical outlook, analytical instincts

FAMOUS BIRTHS
Gustave Eiffel (1832)
Tim Conway (1933)
Adam Brody (1979)
Michelle Dockery (1981)

COMPATIBLE WITH
April 8–20

DECEMBER 16

✳ ✳ ✳ ✳ ✳ ✳ ✳ ✳ ✳ ✳ ✳ ✳ ✳ ✳

FANCIFUL INNOVATORS   ♃ ☉

SAGITTARIUS

PLANETARY INFLUENCES
Ruling planet: Jupiter
Third decan: Personal planet is Sun

VIRTUES
Tenacious, imaginative, objective

VICES
Isolated, radical, obsessive

CAREERS
Academic, scientific researcher, writer

SKILLS & APTITUDES
Unconventional thought processes, persuasiveness

FAMOUS BIRTHS
Ludwig van Beethoven (1770)
Jane Austen (1775)
Margaret Mead (1901)
Billy Gibbons (1949)

COMPATIBLE WITH
April 11–20

Blessed with original imaginations and the desire to explore concepts that less visionary types would condemn as unfeasible, December 16 people are profound thinkers with the potential to make significant contributions. They are also articulate and persuasive and tend to make strong first impressions on others. Their logical and objective approach to new issues precludes any tendency to succumb to flights of fancy. While open-minded enough to consider a wide variety of opinions and possibilities, they subject the ideas that attract their interest to rigorous examination.

Once convinced of the validity of their theses, December 16 people tend to pursue their goals with vigor, concentration and tenacity, rarely deflected by the opposition they might encounter. In many respects they therefore present somewhat solitary figures, for although they possess the courage of their convictions, they may find themselves isolated from others by their need to pursue their own agenda.

Those born on this day will flourish when unconstrained by society's norms and conventions, and will almost certainly feel stifled within corporate structures. They are better suited for careers as academic or scientific researchers and innovators in such problem-solving fields as software development or production management. They thrive in jobs where they can express their own ideas, whether designing software, building plumbing systems, or writing copy. Their ultimate purpose is usually unselfish and they often have a social concern that may not be immediately apparent. Their deep affection for those closest to them sometimes appears compromised by their drive to achieve, but they are capable of forming loyal partnerships.

DECEMBER 17

✳ ✳ ✳ ✳ ✳ ✳ ✳ ✳ ✳ ✳ ✳ ✳ ✳ ✳

♃ ☉   UNWAVERING PROTECTORS

Their desire to effect results marks out December 17 people, who are go-getters and have little patience with those who prefer to ponder interminably rather than make a decision. This is not to say that they are unthinking or impulsive—on the contrary—rather that those born on this day are blessed with the ability quickly to sum up and assess the components of a situation and then to devise straightforward strategies with which to move forward. Vigorous, practical and progressive types, they undertake nothing half-heartedly. This uncompromisingly direct attitude characterizes their approach to all their endeavors, and also defines their preferred stance within their interpersonal relationships, often with mixed success. Although these natural leaders have a gift for firing the enthusiasm of, directing and organizing, their colleagues, their attempts to marshal their nearest and dearest along the lines that they are convinced are the best (especially if they are men) may not always be appreciated. They may also find it difficult to embark on new relationships, as they can often appear unapproachable and are rarely demonstrative, although they are sociable, cheerful and ebullient.

Despite their somewhat abrupt manner, however, December 17 individuals feel a strong and benevolent sense of connection with, and responsibility for their families, friends, coworkers and others. They will readily spring to the defense of their loved ones and are dependable allies. Their capacity to pinpoint faults within situations and remedy them suits them well for management careers; they may also be attracted to the business sphere or other fields in which they can make their mark on the wider world.

PLANETARY INFLUENCES
Ruling planet: Jupiter
Third decan: Personal planet is Sun

VIRTUES
Decisive, practical, charismatic

VICES
Impatient, dominating, intolerant

CAREERS
Business analyst, human-resources manager, sports coach

SKILLS & APTITUDES
Straightforward approach, leadership skills, analytical abilities

FAMOUS BIRTHS
John Greenleaf Whittier (1807)
Pope Francis (1936)
Kerry Packer (1937)
Sarah Paulson (1974)

COMPATIBLE WITH
April 12–20

DECEMBER 18

✳ ✳ ✳ ✳ ✳ ✳ ✳ ✳ ✳ ✳ ✳ ✳ ✳

LEVEL-HEADED PLANNERS ♃ ☉

PLANETARY INFLUENCES
Ruling planet: Jupiter
Third decan: Personal planet is Sun

VIRTUES
Ambitious, charismatic, visionary

VICES
Emotionally detached, workaholic, obsessive

CAREERS
Conceptual artist, sports person, musician

SKILLS & APTITUDES
Single-minded focus, appetite for hard work, leadership skills

FAMOUS BIRTHS
Christopher Fry (1907)
Keith Richards (1943)
Steven Spielberg (1947)
Brad Pitt (1964)

COMPATIBLE WITH
April 14–20, June 4–6

Blessed with soaring imaginations, December 18 people are fascinated by concepts that those of a less original turn of mind might dismiss, but are also determined to translate their dreams into reality. Even from childhood those born on this day may often have formulated a game plan for life that revolves around the specific interests that absorb their attention. They remain resolutely focused, regardless of the vicissitudes they may experience, the tempting diversions that may present themselves, or even the doubts of those to whom they have confided their aspirations. Always keeping their ultimate objectives firmly in mind, they work meticulously toward their achievement, displaying resourcefulness, ingenuity, and practical and organizational talents in the process. These qualities inspire the admiration of those around them, and their effectiveness in terms of results cannot but win over even the most hardened of skeptics.

Those born on this day will flourish in any profession where they can retain their autonomy and are therefore better suited to careers that allow for such independence, perhaps those encompassed by science and technology, the arts or the sporting arena. Innately resistant to toeing the corporate line, December 18 people are nevertheless charismatic leaders, a gift that, when combined with their ability to maintain a broader view, equips them admirably as politicians. Despite the respect they inspire, and their goodwill to those around them, those who seek more intimate relationships with December 18 people (men especially) may find it hard to access the emotional side of their characters.

DECEMBER 19

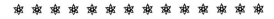

♃ ♄ ☉   Straightforward Debaters

Uncompromisingly individualistic personalities, December 19 people are natural nonconformists who refuse to be bound by what they may regard as the petty conventions of society. They have a strong attraction for what is profound and original and an equally deep dislike—even contempt—for passivity, lack of curiosity, or stodginess. Dismissive of societal norms that do not accord with their own visionary beliefs, they are not afraid to express themselves freely, even relishing the controversy they may provoke with their outspokenness—a propensity that is heightened in those who were born in the Chinese year of the dragon. However, their purpose is not negative, but stems from their desire for stimulating debate. They promote their views with passion and commitment. Among their intellectual strengths are clarity of vision and a strong sense of justice. And because they are rational and clear-sighted individuals, the elevated aims that inspire them are usually realistic, although concentration and sheer hard work will be required for their eventual success.

December 19 people are clearly unsuited to becoming cogs in corporate wheels. Their need for autonomy and exploration bodes well for their success as pioneering artists, scientists or entrepreneurs. Because many will prefer to work alone, the unconditional love and support of those closest to them is especially important. Strong bonds of affection characterize their relationships with friends, partners and family members, who in turn cherish them for their generosity and loyalty.

PLANETARY INFLUENCES
Ruling planets: Jupiter and Saturn
Third decan: Personal planet is Sun
Second cusp: Sagittarius with Capricorn tendencies

VIRTUES
Visionary, passionate, independent

VICES
Rebellious, outspoken, uncompromising

CAREERS
Entrepreneur, contemporary artist, performing artist

SKILLS & APTITUDES
Independence of thought, unconventional methods, articulacy

FAMOUS BIRTHS
Edith Piaf (1915)
Criss Angel (1967)
Alyssa Milano (1973)
Jake Gyllenhaal (1980)

COMPATIBLE WITH
April 18–20, June 4–6

....
....
....

❋ ❋ ❋ ❋ ❋ ❋ ❋ ❋ ❋ ❋ ❋ ❋ ❋

WELL–GROUNDED GUIDES   ♃ ♄ ☉

PLANETARY INFLUENCES
Ruling planets: Jupiter and Saturn
Third decan: Personal planet is Sun
Second cusp: Sagittarius with
    Capricorn tendencies

VIRTUES
Positive, progressive, practical

VICES
Controlling, dismissive, intolerant

CAREERS
Teacher, politician, charity worker

SKILLS & APTITUDES
Social orientation, leadership talent,
motivational skills

FAMOUS BIRTHS
Bob Hayes (1942)
Dick Wolf (1946)
Billy Bragg (1957)
Jonah Hill (1983)

COMPATIBLE WITH
April 19–20, June 4–6

Those born on this day are vigorous individuals who are often concerned with helping society to progress by implementing changes that will materially assist or inform a broad public. These socially responsible people feel a profound sense of connection with those around them and are therefore determined to do their utmost to remedy any perceived failings or abuses or to implement alternative systems of political or intellectual belief, technical innovations, or in some way positively to inspire others to follow the path that they believe to be the optimum one. December 20 individuals are astute and realistic assessors of any situation, and because they are predisposed to initiating responsive action as speedily and efficaciously as possible, are gifted problem-solvers and decision-makers. They supplement their capacity for incisive and direct thought with prodigiously practical skills, and also have a marked talent for motivating and organizing others. Clearly natural leaders, their ability and strength of conviction always shine through.

Their propensity for leading by example, mastery of technical and conceptual issues, and their social orientation suits those born on this day for careers where they can play a coaching role, and they may thus be found excelling in professional fields as varied as teaching, politics, the arts or sciences. Yet it is precisely because they believe so strongly in the importance and veracity of the messages that they communicate to their pupils, compatriots, or even humanity as a global entity, that those who hold alternative viewpoints may come to regard them as overly controlling, a danger that may present especial problems for their children if they are parents, or for their spouses.

DECEMBER 21

✳ ✳ ✳ ✳ ✳ ✳ ✳ ✳ ✳ ✳ ✳ ✳ ✳ ✳

♃ ♄ ☉　　　PASSIONATE IDEALISTS

Those determined individuals born on December 21 are susceptible to extremes in that they are intent on having their way, no matter how high the cost in emotional repercussions—for themselves, or those who stand in their way. They can therefore project an intimidating aura, and are sometimes seen as dogmatic, authoritarian and selfish. Yet their motivation is often based upon ideological convictions with the potential for wide-ranging benefits to others. Their rational intellects and perspicacity enable them to identify systems in need of improvement, which they strive to remedy. They may use confrontation to combat opposition, but usually prefer to rely on their force of will and magnetic charm to win others over. Once people get to know these strong-willed individuals, they will admire their generosity, honor and integrity.

December 21 people may be found working in—and potentially dominating—fields as disparate as commerce, science, sports, construction and the arts, but they are well suited for political or social reform. Their personalities often inspire respect and admiration in those around them, but their single-minded focus may alienate others. The friends and relations on whom they rely deeply (whether or not they are aware of it) for love and support, may come to resent their autocratic tendencies. By giving no quarter in the pursuit of their ambitions, they risk losing the support of loved ones and becoming emotionally and socially isolated, so it is imperative that they remember that a more conciliatory approach than comes naturally to them is often the best way forward.

PLANETARY INFLUENCES
Ruling planets: Jupiter and Saturn
Third decan: Personal planet is Sun
Second cusp: Sagittarius with Capricorn tendencies

VIRTUES
Dedicated, honorable, resourceful

VICES
Intimidating, forceful, autocratic

CAREERS
Social activist, athlete, business innovator

SKILLS & APTITUDES
Leadership skills, unswerving drive, uncompromising vision

FAMOUS BIRTHS
Jane Fonda (1937)
Frank Zappa (1940)
Samuel L. Jackson (1948)
Kiefer Sutherland (1967)

COMPATIBLE WITH
April 20, June 7

♑ CAPRICORN

December 22 to January 19

RULING PLANET: *Saturn* **ELEMENT:** *Cardinal earth* **SYMBOL:** *Goat-fish*
POLARITY: *Negative (feminine)* **COLORS:** *Indigo, gray, dark green*
PHYSICAL CORRESPONDENCE: *Bones, joints, teeth, knees*
STONES: *Onyx, beryl, white sapphire, black diamond, jet, amethyst*
FLOWERS: *Coltsfoot, black poppy, pansy*

The name of the zodiacal sign of Capricorn is derived from the Roman *capricornus* (*caper* "goat," and *cornu*, "horn"). While the image of a horned goat is encapsulated within this constellation, its nether parts represent a fish's tail. This hybrid corpus derives from a Mesopotamian deity, whom the Sumerians equated with the god Enki, and the Babylonians with Ea or Oannes, the ruler of the waters. Other astrological traditions also adopted the goat-fish imagery, including the Persians, the ancient Greeks, and the Hindus. Some scholars believe that the duality inherent in the goat-fish represents the juxtaposition of water—a symbolic metaphor for the unconscious mind—with the mountainous habitat of the ibex, symbolizing intellectual aspiration. Capricorn encompasses the Northern winter solstice (indeed, its sigil is sometimes used to represent the solstice itself). For this reason, the sign was also know in classical times as the "gateway to the gods," *Janua coeli*, or the "gate of death." Its association with death stems from winter's cold, and Capricorn's planetary ruler, Saturn, equates to the Greek god Kronos (also the Greek word for time), whose sickle popularity identifies him with "father time" or the "grim reaper."

The characteristics endowed by Capricorn include a desire for material security, manifested by focused ambition, tenacity and steady reliability, as well as strong loyalty and practical skills—gifts of the element of earth. More negative qualities include pessimism (reflecting the influence of Capricorn's saturnine ruler), and valuing on career achievements over personal relationships.

DECEMBER 22

✳ ✳ ✳ ✳ ✳ ✳ ✳ ✳ ✳ ✳ ✳ ✳ ✳ ✳

♄ ♃　　　　　LONG–TERM PLANNERS

Those born on this day are tenacious and ambitious people; they may act according to a long-term plan formulated as early as childhood. Financial security is important to them, but they are more intent on attaining the high standards they set for themselves, or on implementing ideological concepts that they see as beneficial to society. December 22 people will flourish in professional activities that allow them total autonomy and promise tangible results—for example, as freelancers or self-starting entrepreneurs. Pragmatic realists, they recognize that enduring progress cannot be achieved overnight or without cooperation. Thus they understand the need for meticulous preparation (especially if they were born in the Chinese year of the ox) and have the patience to bide their time, working steadily behind the scenes until they see the opportunity to put their plans into action.

Their ability to focus on visionary goals while paying attention to detail makes them effective directors of their coworkers, who generally respect their strength of purpose and capability. Yet those born on this day are generally more preoccupied with realizing their aims than with fostering congenial working relationships and may appear to stand apart from others. A similar attitude defines their family relationships, especially with their children, of whom they have the highest expectations. Their controlling tendency may stem from the desire to safeguard the welfare of their loved ones, but it often creates resentment. They should bear in mind the negative effects that may result from their focus on achievement, especially its potential to alienate those closest to them, who may not share their ideals.

PLANETARY INFLUENCES
Ruling planets: Saturn and Jupiter
First decan: Personal planet is Saturn
First cusp: Capricorn with Sagittarius tendencies

VIRTUES
Meticulous, patient, determined

VICES
Aloof, controlling, narrow-minded

CAREERS
Entrepreneur, business executive, construction worker

SKILLS & APTITUDES
Single-minded focus, attention to detail, long-term planning

FAMOUS BIRTHS
Giacomo Puccini (1858)
Claudia Alta "Lady Bird" Johnson (1912)
Diane Sawyer (1945)
Ralph Fiennes (1962)

COMPATIBLE WITH
June 7–8, October 23–26

DECEMBER 23

✳ ✳ ✳ ✳ ✳ ✳ ✳ ✳ ✳ ✳ ✳ ✳ ✳ ✳

COMMUNITY ORGANIZERS ♄ ♃

PLANETARY INFLUENCES
Ruling planets: Saturn and Jupiter
First decan: Personal planet is Saturn
First cusp: Capricorn with Sagittarius
    tendencies

VIRTUES
Public-spirited, committed,
resourceful

VICES
Abrupt, controlling, insensitive

CAREERS
Community worker, civil servant,
business executive

SKILLS & APTITUDES
Leadership qualities, focus on
results, organizational skills

FAMOUS BIRTHS
Chet Baker (1929)
Susan Lucci (1949)
Eddie Vedder (1964)
Corey Haim (1971)
Finn Wolfhard (2002)

COMPATIBLE WITH
June 7–8, October 23–26

The fulfillment of many December 23 individuals is bound up with the welfare of the social group with which they identify most strongly—whether family and friends, members of their local community, compatriots or the larger fellowship of humankind. Some feel a real emotional connection; others may be prompted by the recognition that group endeavors can often effect more than individual ventures. However, all are fueled by their drive to lead others along what they believe to be the optimum path to communal success. Their clarity of perception enables them to identify areas in need of improvement, and they can formulate original, yet practical, solutions. Gifted organizers, December 23 people are in many respects suited to positions of leadership in the realms of politics, law enforcement, or commerce, although the more individualistic may be attracted by the opportunities to exert their influence in scientific, artistic or spiritual pursuits.

Others respect their strength of conviction and determination, but do not always view them with affection, sensing the tendency to disregard their emotions and aspirations, and focus on their usefulness. Such negative perceptions are usually inaccurate, resulting from the urgency with which those born on this day (especially men) bring to their tasks. In fact, they can be extremely impatient with those who do conform to their beliefs, especially family members and friends, but they form deep and loyal relationships. Listening to, and, where possible, adopting the viewpoints of others, as well as respecting their right to think and act autonomously, will help them to thrive.

DECEMBER 24

✳ ✳ ✳ ✳ ✳ ✳ ✳ ✳ ✳ ✳ ✳ ✳ ✳

♄ ♃　　　　DEDICATED INNOVATORS

The single-minded focus with which those born on this day pursue the visions that inspire them is awesome in its intensity. Their fulfillment is bound up with the achievement of their goals. Some are determined to better themselves personally; others may be more concerned with benefiting society at large—but all show remarkable vigor and determination in working toward the realization of their aims. Many have identified their goals and principles early in life (perhaps as early as childhood). However, they are not coldly rational individuals—on the contrary, their aspirations usually reflect intuitive responses to the plight of those who are suffering from emotional or physical deprivation.

The careers to which December 24 individuals are drawn offer opportunities for initiating progress. Many will choose to work as commercial, technical, political or educational innovators, or as pioneers in the artistic realm. Coworkers may feel unable to match their dedication, and they often appear isolated within the professional sphere. However, they are positive, reliable people who make devoted friends, partners and especially parents, whose affection is reciprocated by their loved ones. Those born on this day draw upon their astute and rational intellectual talents in all that they do. Sometimes, however, they are so convinced of the veracity of their beliefs and so determined to effect their aims that they have a tendency to focus on their causes and ambitions to the exclusion of all else, including their own needs for physical relaxation and intellectual diversification. Variety is the spice of life!

PLANETARY INFLUENCES
Ruling planets: Saturn and Jupiter
First decan: Personal planet is Saturn
First cusp: Capricorn with Sagittarius tendencies

VIRTUES
Dedicated, progressive, resourceful

VICES
Workaholic, obsessive, intolerant

CAREERS
Business executive, teacher, software developer

SKILLS & APTITUDES
Unwavering focus, goal orientation, practical approach

FAMOUS BIRTHS
King John of England (1167)
Howard Hughes (1905)
Ava Gardner (1922)
Ricky Martin (1971)

COMPATIBLE WITH
September 14–17, October 23–26

DECEMBER 25

✳ ✳ ✳ ✳ ✳ ✳ ✳ ✳ ✳ ✳ ✳ ✳ ✳ ✳

GIFTED COMPROMISERS ♄ ♃

PLANETARY INFLUENCES
Ruling planets: Saturn and Jupiter
First decan: Personal planet is Saturn
First cusp: Capricorn with Sagittarius tendencies

VIRTUES
Resourceful, idealistic, objective

VICES
Impatient, demanding, unsympathetic

CAREERS
Community leader, scientific researcher, architect

SKILLS & APTITUDES
Practical approach, organizational skills, commitment

FAMOUS BIRTHS
Jesus Christ (c.4 bc)
Sir Isaac Newton (1642)
Humphrey Bogart (1899)
Jimmy Buffett (1946)

COMPATIBLE WITH
September 14–17, October 23–26

Those born into Christian families on this day will inevitably have felt themselves marked out as special from an early age, yet they will also have learned to compromise: today's celebrations are not focused exclusively on them. In fact, they receive less attention on their birthdays than their siblings and friends, and may feel that they are missing out. These dual feelings often persist throughout the lives of December 25 people, who are notable for their determination to achieve ambitious aspirations and, usually, their success in life.

Although they are pragmatic and objective, the concepts that fire them reflect an imaginative and progressive outlook. Whether they are drawn to the potential inherent in science, business, politics or the arts, they show a real ability to combine practical skills with intellectual insight. They often make especially effective researchers because of this combination of skills and their aptitude for organization and dedication to their personal goals.

Individualistic as they are, December 25 people also have a sense of social responsibility (especially when they were born in the Chinese year of the snake). This leads them to enlist the support of others for causes they believe will illuminate or otherwise benefit the lives of those around them, or humanity as a whole. Originality, resourcefulness and charisma contribute to their leadership qualities and their easy popularity. However, their ambition, strength of conviction and high standards may place a heavy burden of expectation upon those whose interest they have most deeply at heart. They should remember to show their loved ones how much they care for them.

DECEMBER 26

✳ ✳ ✳ ✳ ✳ ✳ ✳ ✳ ✳ ✳ ✳ ✳ ✳ ✳

♄   NEW–REALITY–BUILDERS

Such is the vigorous nature of the people born on this day that they are not content simply to dream of their visionary aspirations but seek to transform them into reality. December 26 people are blessed with incisive perspicacity, supplemented by profound empathy with those whom they perceive as victims of society's failings or abuses. When they identify such faults, they invariably take remedial action. This combination of characteristics attracts them to fields that are concerned with effecting human progress, perhaps by instituting more enlightened political systems, technical innovations, social service work or creative use of the media. They relish the opportunity to rise to a demanding challenge, but their ultimate goal is to further the common good through their work. While they project themselves as intense, serious people, those born on December 26 are dependable, loyal friends who are admired and loved for their supportive, committed presence. They may, however, be very slow to form their deep relationships, because their ideals sometimes generate unrealistic expectations of others.

Their sense of social concern does not preclude their insistence on freedom of thought and action, which may lead them to adopt a combative stance when they believe their right to personal autonomy is threatened, or when others behave in a manner contrary to their convictions. And although their determination and ability to lead by example marks them out as dynamic team leaders, their unwillingness to brook ideological dissent in coworkers, or even family members and friends, may disrupt the harmony they seek in promoting the common purpose.

PLANETARY INFLUENCES
Ruling planet: Saturn
First decan: Personal planet is Saturn

VIRTUES
Empathetic, community-spirited, committed

VICES
Unreceptive, intolerant, unapproachable

CAREERS
Social worker, local politician, marketing executive

SKILLS & APTITUDES
Progressive instincts, single-minded focus, resourcefulness

FAMOUS BIRTHS
Harry S. Turman (1884)
Jack Benny (1894)
Phil Spector (1940)
Jared Leto (1971)

COMPATIBLE WITH
September 14–17, October 27–31

DECEMBER 27

✺ ✺ ✺ ✺ ✺ ✺ ✺ ✺ ✺ ✺ ✺ ✺ ✺ ✺

DUAL–SIDED PERSONALITIES ♄

PLANETARY INFLUENCES
Ruling planet: Saturn
First decan: Personal planet is Saturn

VIRTUES
Altruistic, dependable, thoughtful

VICES
Unapproachable, isolated, resentful

CAREERS
Community worker, civil servant, lab technician

SKILLS & APTITUDES
Perceptiveness, reliability, problem-solving focus

FAMOUS BIRTHS
Johannes Kepler (1571)
Louis Pasteur (1822)
Marlene Dietrich (1901)
Gerard Depardieu (1948)
Timothée Chalamet (1995)

COMPATIBLE WITH
January 20, October 27–31

The majority of December 27 people have two distinct sides to their personalities: not only do they have a strong feeling of social responsibility and present a positive and dependable persona to the wider world, they are also deep thinkers who need time and space to pursue their own interests. Inherent in this duality is the danger that those born on this day may feel torn between what they perceive as their duty to others and their own personal prerequisites for fulfillment. Any sense of imbalance between these may lead them to become frazzled and frustrated. Because their goodwill makes it difficult for them to refuse requests for help, they may become overburdened with problems not of their own making—especially the women born on this day.

When they can reconcile their desire to help others with their own interests, their potential is truly remarkable. Provided they center themselves emotionally and spiritually, they will attract friends readily for their steady, reliable, supportive qualities, but they can appear unapproachable when immersed in their careers or favorite forms of recreation.

Intellectual and intuitive perception, logical minds and tenacity draw those born on this day to professions wherein they can make contributions to as science, engineering, commerce, sporting or artistic ventures. Despite their concern with the well-being of others, their intellectual focus may isolate them professionally. Typically, they seek an outlet for their emotional needs in their personal relationships and value the comfort and support offered by their nearest and dearest, reciprocating with affection and loyalty.

DECEMBER 28

✵ ✵ ✵ ✵ ✵ ✵ ✵ ✵ ✵ ✵ ✵ ✵ ✵

♄ PILLARS OF SUPPORT

The image that December 28 people present to the world is one of confidence, dependability and capability. They are socially responsible, but their competent exterior overlies a constant and profound search for inner understanding and knowledge in realms that do not necessarily coincide with the more immediate demands that others may make of them. Thus their personal magnetism may be both a gift and a drawback, in that although December 28 individuals may derive transitory satisfaction from lending their energies and talents to the resolution of the problems of others, they may thereby neglect the exploration of interests that are essential to their personal fulfillment. Yet when a serendipitous conjunction of their external and internal orientations occurs—perhaps within their careers—the dynamic synergy produced can have excellent results.

Their natural inclinations, combined with their practical and technical expertise, admirably equip those born on this day for professions in which by furthering their own interests and insights, they may simultaneously help, guide, inform, enlighten or delight a wider audience. Such pursuits include politics, spiritual studies, communications and art. Typically admired for their abilities and self-reliance, there is a risk that these individuals may be regarded primarily as competent providers of support—an image that they themselves may unwittingly foster—and their own emotional needs will be disregarded. It is vital that they and those around them (especially their nearest and dearest) realize that they, too, are emotionally vulnerable and require the mutual support and affection that is inherent in strong emotional bonds.

PLANETARY INFLUENCES
Ruling planet: Saturn
First decan: Personal planet is Saturn

VIRTUES
Dependable, supportive, thoughtful

VICES
Unfocused, unassertive, frustrated

CAREERS
Academic, teacher, nonprofit organizer

SKILLS & APTITUDES
Practical approach, team orientation, research skills

FAMOUS BIRTHS
Woodrow Wilson (1856)
Maggie Smith (1934)
Denzel Washington (1954)
John Legend (1978)

COMPATIBLE WITH
January 20–21, October 27–31

DECEMBER 29

✴ ✴ ✴ ✴ ✴ ✴ ✴ ✴ ✴ ✴ ✴ ✴ ✴ ✴

STRAIGHTFORWARD LEADERS   ♄

PLANETARY INFLUENCES
Ruling planet: Saturn
First decan: Personal planet is Saturn

VIRTUES
Perceptive, responsible, socially concerned

VICES
Stressed, frustrated, exploitable

CAREERS
Self-help author, newspaper columnist, financial adviser

SKILLS & APTITUDES
Resourcefulness, leadership potential, diligence

FAMOUS BIRTHS
Charles Goodyear (1800)
Mary Tyler Moore (1937)
Jon Voight (1938)
Jude Law (1972)

COMPATIBLE WITH
January 20–22, October 27–31

The positive, capable approach of December 29 people inspires admiration and respect: thus they are often seen in leadership positions. Although their strong sense of responsibility leads them to discharge their duties with diligence, those born on this day would often prefer to pursue their own interests unburdened by the demands of others. Harmonizing their external and internal orientations is essential to realizing their own potential for fulfillment, and many—consciously or unconsciously—pursue careers that absorb their personal interests while providing real benefits for the greater good. Along with a penchant for logical and straightforward thought, December 29 people are blessed with keenly perceptive and progressive minds, a combination of qualities that makes them alert to flawed social systems. Because they are vigorous and resourceful, they seek new ways of moving forward, drawing upon their highly developed organizational skills.

Those born on this day will thrive in any career that offers challenging opportunities to assist or enlighten. They are especially suited to those realms where they can provide ideological guidance to others (as parents, politicians or writers, for example), or make innovations that advance knowledge and prosperity (perhaps as scientists or engineers). Others respond to the benevolent aura that December 29 people emanate, but in many respects this personal magnetism can cause unwanted complications in their lives. In essence, they are private individuals who are happiest when working toward their personal goals, bolstered by the love and support of those closest to them, who contribute profoundly to their emotional well-being.

DECEMBER 30

♄ PROPONENTS OF PROGRESS

The thoughts and actions of those born on this day are profoundly influenced by their need to bring order to confused situations and concepts—to effect dynamic progress in place of stasis. These individuals are not only skilled at identifying areas in need of improvement, but also have the vision and imagination to make effective changes. Strong organizational talents and resourcefulness help them to promote the common welfare, whether of family and friends, co-workers, fellow citizens or even the world community. Their ability to channel the energy and talents of those around them makes them natural leaders, successful not only in material terms, but in making significant contributions to the wider world. Their occasionally taciturn demeanor can sometimes mislead others; though prone to pessimism, these are people who prefer a straightforward approach and appreciate humor and the lighter side of life.

The professions to which December 30 people are drawn offer opportunities for innovation and advancement within set—although flexible—parameters (for they prefer to build upon existing foundations rather than branch off in radically new directions). Their talents and inclinations suit them well to business and commercial ventures (especially if they were born in the Chinese year of the snake). Politics, diplomacy and positions that require forceful negotiating skills are other possibilities. Their decisive tendency to take charge of people whom they wish to help can have impressive results, but their associates may resent perceived attempts to limit their personal freedom.

PLANETARY INFLUENCES
Ruling planet: Saturn
First decan: Personal planet is Saturn

VIRTUES
Public-spirited, practical, determined

VICES
Pessimistic, uncommunicative, arrogant

CAREERS
Business executive, nonprofit worker, local politician

SKILLS & APTITUDES
Organizational instincts, leadership skills, progressive focus

FAMOUS BIRTHS
Rudyard Kipling (1865)
Bo Didley (1928)
Davy Jones (1945)

COMPATIBLE WITH
January 20–23, October 27–31

DECEMBER 31

✼ ✼ ✼ ✼ ✼ ✼ ✼ ✼ ✼ ✼ ✼ ✼ ✼ ✼

ENCOURAGING MANAGERS ♄

PLANETARY INFLUENCES
Ruling planet: Saturn
First decan: Personal planet is Saturn

VIRTUES
Dedicated, resourceful, pragmatic

VICES
Impatient, narrow-minded,
self-righteous

CAREERS
Political strategist, business
executive, community leader

SKILLS & APTITUDES
Team orientation, organizational
skills, problem-solving instincts

FAMOUS BIRTHS
Henri Matisse (1869)
Anthony Hopkins (1937)
Ben Kingsley (1943)
Patti Smith (1946)

COMPATIBLE WITH
January 21–24, October 27–31

Those born on December 31 are both idealists and pragmatists. With their progressive objectives, they aim toward perfection, but they possess the insight to recognize personal and practical limitations. As a rule, they are reformers rather than revolutionaries, with good leadership abilities and independent minds. Their talent for devising original strategies to solve problems is joined with tenacity of purpose. Leaders by example, they set high standards for others to follow, but never demand more than they themselves are prepared to give. Reasonable and fair, they are respected and admired by friends and colleagues.

December 31 individuals are well suited to careers in which they can not only satisfy their need to create harmony and excel, but direct coworkers in efforts that will benefit all concerned. Politics, the military or commercial ventures may attract them, and they make skilled and effective team-builders, bringing out the best in others. They are most effective when they temper their own somewhat controlling behavior and encourage others' efforts.

Others admire the dedication of December 31 people, but do not always concur with their convictions and methods. Although their personal relationships are characterized by love and concern for their nearest and dearest, they must beware of imposing their elevated standards and expectations on them. If they are not to become somewhat narrow-minded and intolerant of the individuality of others, those born on this day should temper their occasionally self-righteous tendency to stick rigidly to principles, encouraging those around them to express their opinions, however much they may differ.

JANUARY 1

✸ ✸ ✸ ✸ ✸ ✸ ✸ ✸ ✸ ✸ ✸ ✸ ✸ ✸

♄ ♀   PAST AND FUTURE THINKERS

Those born on January 1 are blessed with the characteristics that caused Janus, the Roman god of doorways, to be named patron of the first month of the year: balance, a willingness to look forward and embrace change, and the ability to recall the lessons learned from past experiences. This duality is an integral part of these people's natures. While they are prized for their affable characters and ability to think rationally and clearly, for example—and nowhere more so than in the workplace, where such qualities usually make them respected and appreciated coworkers—under certain circumstances they may lose their equilibrium. These people are renowned for their determination, capacity for hard work, organizational abilities and strong willpower. They are suited for any career in which their intellectual powers can be stretched, but are especially effective as teachers, lawyers and financial analysts.

Their ability to think coolly and incisively makes January 1 people sought after for advice, all the more because their natural kindness and empathy with others make them loyal friends. Trusted and valued by their peers, they do, however, have a tendency to think the best of people, a quality which makes them popular, but which can lead them to be deceived by those who harbor an ulterior agenda. While their trusting natures may thus set them up to be profoundly let down, January 1 people are wise enough to learn from such experiences and to be more cautious in the future. They also have a pronounced intuitive streak and, if this inner voice is heeded, will achieve a balance of "head" and "heart" which will stand them in good stead in their personal and professional relationships.

PLANETARY INFLUENCES
Ruling planet: Saturn
Second decan: Personal planet is Venus

VIRTUES
Objective, congenial, thoughtful

VICES
Unbalanced, gullible, temperamental

CAREERS
Financial analyst, educator, paralegal

SKILLS & APTITUDES
Drive, goal orientation, analytical mindset

FAMOUS BIRTHS
Paul Revere (1735)
Betsy Ross (1752)
J. Edgar Hoover (1895)
J.D. Salinger (1919)

COMPATIBLE WITH
January 30–31, November 1–5

JANUARY 2

✴ ✴ ✴ ✴ ✴ ✴ ✴ ✴ ✴ ✴ ✴ ✴ ✴ ✴

SENSITIVE OBSERVERS   ♄ ♀

January 2 people are closely attuned to their senses, drinking in the finer details of their surroundings that are invisible to less observant people. This sensitivity to their environment makes them outstanding artists. This quality of perception also applies to their interpersonal relationships, with the result that January 2 people are blessed with an almost uncanny ability to tune in to the nature or moods of others. Strongly committed to their personal ambitions and goals, they also have a critical streak which, when imposed on their work, often produces wonderful results. Less positively, there is a danger that they will demand the impossible of themselves, or that they will set such stringent parameters on their personal relationships that they will be left isolated.

These people are extremely motivated and diligent, requiring the most of themselves and others, qualities which make them valuable employees and exacting bosses. Having intuitively absorbed information, they will then determine their goal and work single-mindedly toward its achievement. Curiously, although they are driven by their desire for perfection, January 2 people often manifest a marked reluctance to have their high ideals disappointed. They are sometimes averse to making irrevocable decisions, preferring to hedge their bets rather than make a commitment about whose outcome they are uncertain. This indecision can be particularly pronounced in January 2 men with regard to their personal relationships. If they throw their natural caution to the wind, however, and apply their undoubted qualities of intuition and self-discipline to the relationship or task as it develops, they will often be successful.

JANUARY 3

CAPRICORNUS

✳ ✳ ✳ ✳ ✳ ✳ ✳ ✳ ✳ ✳ ✳ ✳ ✳ ✳

♄ ♀   UNWAVERING IDEALISTS

The magnetic aura and charm exuded by January 3 people mask the fact that at their core lies a single-minded commitment to the pursuit of their ideals. Once a venture captures their imagination, they will go to almost any lengths to see it through, refusing to compromise or be deflected from their chosen path. Affable, humorous and quirky, their highly individualistic characters draw others to them, and January 3 people can be quick to take advantage of the effect that they have on other people in order to gain their participation in a pet project; this tendency is reinforced if they were born in the Chinese year of the dragon. Such a combination of idealism and manipulative skills makes them imaginative and gifted team leaders, and they will not hesitate to use a whole armory of tactics to ensure that their coworkers achieve a common goal. The quality of wholehearted commitment may be a double-edged sword, however, for it can simultaneously inspire and exasperate others. January 3 people can become obsessive, so convinced of the rightness of their chosen course that they will ignore alternative viewpoints.

Loyalty is a key component in the make-up of January 3 people, and this applies just as much to their domestic as to their professional lives—provided, that is, that their friends and loved ones fall into line with them. Other related features displayed by these people are trustworthiness and reliability, qualities which mean that they will not only deliver anything that is required of them, but will furthermore provide a stable environment for their families. Although others can depend upon their support, January 3 people will suffer disappointment and disillusionment if this loyalty is not reciprocated.

PLANETARY INFLUENCES
Ruling planet: Saturn
Second decan: Personal planet is Venus

VIRTUES
Committed, charming, idealistic

VICES
Obsessive, manipulative, unscrupulous

CAREERS
Community leader, business executive, movie director

SKILLS & APTITUDES
Team orientation, single-minded focus, reliability

FAMOUS BIRTHS
Marcus Tullius Cicero (106 bc)
J.R.R. Tolkien (1892)
Mel Gibson (1956)
Eli Manning (1981)

COMPATIBLE WITH
August 20–22, November 1–5

JANUARY 4

✻ ✻ ✻ ✻ ✻ ✻ ✻ ✻ ✻ ✻ ✻ ✻ ✻

INVENTIVE PROBLEM–SOLVERS   ♄ ♀

PLANETARY INFLUENCES
Ruling planet: Saturn
Second decan: Personal planet is
Venus

VIRTUES
Original, organized, empathetic

VICES
Intolerant, uncompromising,
narrow-minded

CAREERS
Entrepreneur, nonprofit organizer,
educator

SKILLS & APTITUDES
Analytical skills, goal orientation,
practical approach

FAMOUS BIRTHS
Jakob Grimm (1785)
Louis Braille (1809)
George Washington Carver (1861)
Floyd Patterson (1935)

COMPATIBLE WITH
August 20–22, November 1–5

People born on this day combine an impressive capacity for organization in their working and domestic habits with independence of thought, with the result that they often come up with ideas of startling originality, and then implement them with meticulous thoroughness. Their perceptive and incisive minds cut straight to the heart of a problem and, once they have identified their preferred solution, they will be unswerving in its pursuit. They will sometimes manifest a deep and genuine concern for the well-being of humanity and may act on their convictions by becoming involved in political activism. On an individual level, this means that they are sensitive, empathetic and supportive friends and partners, while on a more global scale their desire to improve the lot of those who are less fortunate, as well as their capacity for inventiveness, frequently makes them gifted teachers, charity workers or social pioneers. These people may also prove successful in business ventures, because of their ability to back up their innovative ideas effectively with solid and efficient organizational practices.

Although they enjoy the good things of life and tend to indulge in hedonistic pleasures, especially when young, January 4 people will not be diverted by the trivial for very long, preferring to exert their considerable energies on tasks and projects that will give them a deeper sense of fulfillment. If taken too far, however, such behavior could cut them off from many new experiences and potential friendships. They should also recognize that, while others may not share their goals or methodology, this does not invalidate the worth of alternative opinions, and that there is much to be gained from embracing diversity, whatever form this takes.

JANUARY 5

✻ ✻ ✻ ✻ ✻ ✻ ✻ ✻ ✻ ✻ ✻ ✻ ✻ ✻

♄ ♀   PRAGMATIC PIONEERS

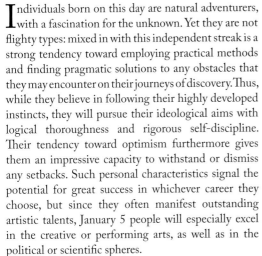

Individuals born on this day are natural adventurers, with a fascination for the unknown. Yet they are not flighty types: mixed in with this independent streak is a strong tendency toward employing practical methods and finding pragmatic solutions to any obstacles that they may encounter on their journeys of discovery. Thus, while they believe in following their highly developed instincts, they will pursue their ideological aims with logical thoroughness and rigorous self-discipline. Their tendency toward optimism furthermore gives them an impressive capacity to withstand or dismiss any setbacks. Such personal characteristics signal the potential for great success in whichever career they choose, but since they often manifest outstanding artistic talents, January 5 people will especially excel in the creative or performing arts, as well as in the political or scientific spheres.

In common with many who rely strongly upon their intuition when it comes to decision-making and questions of judgement, January 5 people are unusually sensitive in tuning in to those around them. Empathetic and understanding, they are valued as friends, but are nevertheless not prepared to give of themselves limitlessly, and may grow impatient if those who seek their support and advice are reluctant to accept the benefit of their wisdom. Having arrived at a carefully considered set of convictions, and having developed a corresponding modus operandi, there is an inevitable tendency for those born on this day to stick rigidly to these preferences and close their minds to alternative approaches. Their self-belief is more often than not justified, but they should remember that there is much to be gained from personal interaction and constant re-evaluation.

PLANETARY INFLUENCES
Ruling planet: Saturn
Second decan: Personal planet is Venus

VIRTUES
Innovative, empathetic, self-disciplined

VICES
Impatient, insular, intolerant

CAREERS
Sculptor, actor, politician

SKILLS & APTITUDES
Practical skills, realistic outlook, leadership instincts

FAMOUS BIRTHS
Robert Duvall (1931)
Charlie Rose (1942)
Diane Keaton (1946)
Bradley Cooper (1975)

COMPATIBLE WITH
August 20–22, November 1–5

JANUARY 6

✳ ✳ ✳ ✳ ✳ ✳ ✳ ✳ ✳ ✳ ✳ ✳ ✳

MORAL COMMUNICATORS ♄ ♀

Underpinning many of the beliefs and actions of people born on January 6 is a profoundly mystical sense of union with the unseen forces that govern the earth. This empathy may take the form of ecological crusades, or else may find its spiritual expression in religion. Either way, these people form firm moral judgements and are determined enough to overcome their natural tendency to gentleness both to defend their convictions and spread their message to others. Such propagation is greatly aided by their ability to connect with others, and thus effectively to impart their vision to the world. This potent combination of intellectual conviction and communication skills makes people born on this day talented teachers, politicians and artists, but they will flourish in any area in which they can provide focused leadership. Depending as they do so deeply on their instincts, there is a danger that these people will rely on these exclusively, politely rejecting alternative viewpoints. Parents of January 6 children should therefore encourage them to appreciate the value of both personal experience and the wisdom of others.

Because they are inherently self-disciplined, service oriented, and driven by their ideals, these people manifest an unusual degree of both tenacity and determination to see a task through, in order that humanity can enjoy the fruits of their visions. Such drive is commendable, but these people should remember that not only is perfection rarely achievable, but that it also exacts a considerable personal toll. They should therefore take care not to neglect their private lives, and should accept the fact that their friends and families appreciate them for what they already are.

JANUARY 7

CAPRICORNVS

♄ ♀   EMPATHETIC ENABLERS

January 7 people have little difficulty in attracting others to them: cheerful, affectionate, loyal and generous in their personal lives, these qualities, which are reinforced if they were born in the Chinese year of the dog, are cherished by friends, family members and coworkers alike. These people have the instinctive gift of being able to sense the moods of other people, a talent which, when combined with their genuine empathy and desire to smooth the way for their fellows, makes their company much sought after. Such qualities make them ideally suited to social work and medicine, or similar activities where their considerable interpersonal and communicative skills can best be employed. It would amaze many to realize, however, that despite their reputation as being pillars of strength, these sensitive people frequently harbor a deep lack of self-confidence and therefore seek to gain a sense of validation and worth from the affection and respect of others.

Personal connection is therefore of great importance to people born on this day, but they also possess a real sense of integration with the natural world, as well as a pronounced otherworldly, mystical side, which fuels an extraordinarily imaginative capacity. It is thus not hard for these people not only to accept, but also to manifest, a marked fascination with unexplained phenomena. Although they would be well advised to pursue their instincts, many do not, apprehensive of being branded cranks. When backed up with the methodical and disciplined approach characteristic of January 7 people, however, this tendency toward original thought can find satisfying fruition.

PLANETARY INFLUENCES
Ruling planet: Saturn
Second decan: Personal planet is Venus

VIRTUES
Empathetic, imaginative, congenial

VICES
Insecure, needy, unassertive

CAREERS
Social worker, scientific researcher, healthcare worker

SKILLS & APTITUDES
Team orientation, unconventional mindset, reliability

FAMOUS BIRTHS
Zora Neale Hurston (1901)
Katie Couric (1957)
Nicolas Cage (1964)
Jeremy Renner (1971)

COMPATIBLE WITH
June 14–16, November 6–11

JANUARY 8

❋ ❋ ❋ ❋ ❋ ❋ ❋ ❋ ❋ ❋ ❋ ❋ ❋ ❋

MOTIVATED STRIVERS   ♄ ♀

Exceptionally single-minded and highly motivated, those born on this day possess the potential to achieve outstanding success in whatever field they choose, be it in the creative arts, where their artistic imaginations can be given full rein; in scientific pursuits, where they can best employ their considerable aptitude for analysis; or in philanthropic work, where their empathetic instincts can be satisfied. These qualities are seen in the achievements of Stephen Hawking for his exceptional, visionary contribution to science and were manifested in the outstanding artistry of Elvis Presley and David Bowie. January 8 people often harbor burning personal ambition but, being pragmatic and somewhat saturnine personalities, realize that the recognition they desire will have to be assiduously worked for. Yet although they possess the necessary radical vision, determination and drive to realize their dreams, they may find that their achievements are somewhat empty if they have sacrificed their personal relationships in pursuit of their cherished goals.

The irony is that while these people may appear almost intimidatingly poised and self-possessed, underneath lies a very real sense of anxiety and inse-curity which is masked by an outward façade of cool reserve. Perhaps January 8 people believe that it is only by spectacular success that they will gain the affection of others, but this is far from the case, and they run the risk of loneliness and disillusionment if they persist in this conviction. They should therefore ensure that they actively seek out and nurture honest and relaxed relationships with others, for it is ultimately from such loving and supportive bonds that they will find the key to personal happiness and fulfillment.

JANUARY 9

♄ ♀　FAMILY-FOCUSED PERFECTIONISTS

Blessed with sharp, analytical intellects, keen powers of perception, and great reserves of energy, January 9 people demand high standards from themselves as well as others, and will not easily accept defeat. They are sometimes intensely ambitious, but their desire is fueled more by perfectionism—by the need to see a task done as well as possible—than by a craving for plaudits or adulation. People born on this day are therefore valued employees, for when given charge of any project they will quickly identify the best course of action, and then set about accomplishing it with characteristic focus and drive. Yet January 9 people are not really corporate animals, cherishing freedom of thought, expression and movement over the restrictions that are usually imposed by large organizations, and they generally thrive better when they are self-employed.

Family is extremely important to people born on this day. Deeply committed to providing the best possible opportunities for their children, they will often work long hours to gain the necessary financial means to achieve them, but in doing so they inevitably sacrifice time spent together. They may also make enormous demands of their children in terms of academic attainments, albeit with the highest motives. It is therefore important that these people do not push their children too hard, but accept their true selves and limitations, love them for who they are, and support them uncritically. They will also gain personally from a more relaxed approach to family life, which will provide a valuable safety valve to release the pressures built up by their professional commitments.

PLANETARY INFLUENCES
Ruling planet: Saturn
Second decan: Personal planet is Venus

VIRTUES
Perceptive, committed, determined

VICES
Demanding, workaholic, unbalanced

CAREERS
Project manager, financial adviser, journalist

SKILLS & APTITUDES
Analytical mindset, problem-solving skills, drive

FAMOUS BIRTHS
Richard Nixon (1913)
Bob Denver (1935)
Jimmy Page (1944)
Kate Middleton (1982)

COMPATIBLE WITH
June 19–21, November 6–11

JANUARY 10

✳ ✳ ✳ ✳ ✳ ✳ ✳ ✳ ✳ ✳ ✳ ✳ ✳ ✳

THRIVING SOCIAL BUTTERFLIES   ♄ ♀

PLANETARY INFLUENCES
Ruling planet: Saturn
Second decan: Personal planet is
Venus

VIRTUES
Self-confident, optimistic, original

VICES
Outspoken, intimidating,
manipulative

CAREERS
Stockbroker, hedge-fund manager,
entrepreneur

SKILLS & APTITUDES
Risk-taking inclinations, positive
focus, motivational powers

FAMOUS BIRTHS
Jim Croce (1943)
Rod Stewart (1945)
George Foreman (1949)
Pat Benatar (1953)

COMPATIBLE WITH
June 19–21, November 6–11

Energetic, realistic and forthright to the point of bluntness, the qualities manifested by people born on January 10 inspire respect and not a little awe in others. The force that drives them is usually their unceasing quest for knowledge, their deep-rooted need to understand, judge the situation and then bring about improvement, never fearing to manipulate others to further their cause. Indeed, such is the boldness of their approach that they will often confidently propose an outrageously radical solution to a problem, and then watch it either fail or succeed spectacularly. Such self-confidence, originality and uncompromising certainty makes these people ideally suited to the speculative end of the financial sector, where their appetite for risk-taking can be amply satisfied, and they can gain the recognition that they feel their talents merit. They will rarely find fulfillment as a small cog in a large wheel, and will only thrive in those situations where their individuality and need to take control can be given full expression.

Blessed with considerable personal charm and an infectious aura of optimism, January 10 people often find themselves the center of attention, but run the risk of hurting others' feelings by their honest observations. They should therefore be aware of the fact that judicious use of tact will often help them achieve their objectives more effectively, and will help to win them the lasting loyalty of their friends. Despite the robust face that they present to the world, these people are also highly sensitive, and perform best when they are bolstered by the affection and esteem of those around them. By actively working on maintaining their friendships, they stand to gain as much as they invest.

JANUARY 11

✱ ✱ ✱ ✱ ✱ ✱ ✱ ✱ ✱ ✱ ✱ ✱ ✱ ✱ ✱

♄ ☿   REPUTABLE DEVOTEES

Those born on January 11 are blessed with unusually sharp powers of perception, which, when combined with their keen intellects, result in a formidable talent for evaluation and decision-making. Little escapes these people, and when there is a problem to be solved they typically display an impressive ability to marshal the facts available to them, impartially weigh up the merits or disadvantages inherent in alternative approaches, and then come to an intelligent, closely argued strategy. This talent for objectivity, logical thought and intellectual clarity makes January 11 people especially well suited to careers in academic research, or else in business, areas in which these qualities—as well as their characteristic refusal to allow their judgement to become clouded by emotional concerns—are greatly prized. Because these people possess such highly developed critical faculties, and are furthermore articulate and quick-witted, they should beware of pronouncing their opinions too forcefully and thereby offending those who may not share their point of view or sense of certainty.

January 11 people are intensely loyal to those people and things that they consider merit their devotion. Though they may seem unapproachable at first, they have the potential to make excellent friends and parents. They should, however, beware of a tendency toward stubbornness and becoming impatient with those who do not quickly fall into line with their own way of thinking, especially as parents. By ensuring that they keep a check on their propensity to judge others against their own exacting standards, and relaxing their inclination to maintain a certain structured formality in their relationships, they will benefit from a richer personal life.

PLANETARY INFLUENCES
Ruling planet: Saturn
Third decan: Personal planet is Mercury

VIRTUES
Objective, efficient, astute

VICES
Arrogant, obstinate, judgmental

CAREERS
Academic, lawyer, business analyst

SKILLS & APTITUDES
Analytical skills, decisiveness, dependability

FAMOUS BIRTHS
Alexander Hamilton (1757)
William James (1842)
Haruki Murakami (1949)
Mary J. Blige (1971)

COMPATIBLE WITH
November 12–16

JANUARY 12

✻ ✻ ✻ ✻ ✻ ✻ ✻ ✻ ✻ ✻ ✻ ✻ ✻ ✻

POPULAR CROWD-PLEASERS   ♄ ☿

PLANETARY INFLUENCES
Ruling planet: Saturn
Third decan: Personal planet is
  Mercury

VIRTUES
Self-confident, original,
emotionally robust

VICES
Critical, arrogant, attention-seeking

CAREERS
Advertising executive, actor,
journalist

SKILLS & APTITUDES
Independent instincts, bold
approach, communicativeness

FAMOUS BIRTHS
Jack London (1876)
Kirstie Alley (1955)
Christiane Amanpour (1958)
Rob Zombie (1965)

COMPATIBLE WITH
November 12–16

Challenging, entertaining, sharp and self-assured, these people tread a fine line between introversion and extroversion. While their incisive intelligence and tendency toward nit-picking criticism may signal an unusual level of self-reliance, they also enjoy the attention that their outspokenness brings them, and frequently relish playing to the crowd. January 12 people do not do things by half-measures, and once they find a topic that intrigues them, they pursue their interests with near-obsessive intensity. They are unafraid of promoting their opinions, and, indeed, welcome a challenging argument in which they will attempt to their utmost to convince others of the veracity of their point of view. Somewhat maverick in their approach, these people flourish best either in those organizations that allow them complete freedom of thought and action, or when working on their own account. They will find the greatest satisfaction engaged in any business activity—such as sales and marketing—within which they can perhaps bend the rules to promote their own beliefs and aims.

In their personal lives, January 12 people often manifest the need to be at the center of attention, and absolutely hate being ignored. They will frequently manufacture confrontational scenarios for the sheer enjoyment of provoking a reaction, and enjoy nothing more than playing devil's advocate. This occasionally pugnacious approach carries its risks, however, and these people should ensure that they do not get carried away with themselves and thus hurt the feelings of those who are less emotionally robust—particularly their family members, whom they may inadvertently discourage by their cynicism.

JANUARY 13

✳ ✳ ✳ ✳ ✳ ✳ ✳ ✳ ✳ ✳ ✳ ✳ ✳ ✳

♄ ☿   MODEST GOOD SAMARITANS

January 13 people are highly motivated—even driven—by the desire to effect improvement, be it in the personal, material sense by "bettering" themselves, or by instituting a global, philanthropic scheme to help the lot of humanity. Nor are such ambitions doomed to remain pipe dreams, for these people have sufficient intellectual capability, directness of approach, and energy to see them realized. When faced with an unsatisfactory position, be it in these people's careers or in society, they will identify a solution and doggedly work toward its implementation, cutting through obstructions and pushing on toward their objective. Whatever it is that inspires them, they will give it their all, but in doing so will inevitably encounter confrontation and resistance, which they will typically handle with perfunctory disdain. Social reform is therefore a natural area of interest for January 13 people, but their imagination and single-mindedness give them the potential to succeed in many arenas.

Although such all-consuming clarity of focus and clear-cut goals are admirable, they may leave little room for human relationships, and those born on this day would do well to remember that, while saving the world is laudable, they may simultaneously neglect those who are close to them, with often far-reaching, destructive consequences. This caveat applies particularly to men, whose partners or children may suffer from a devastating loss of self-esteem if they perceive that their personal needs and concerns are being dismissed or are considered of secondary importance. They should take heed of their own need for relaxation and the simpler pleasures of life, and ensure that they do not sacrifice their physical or emotional health to their aspirations.

PLANETARY INFLUENCES
Ruling planet: Saturn
Third decan: Personal planet is Mercury

VIRTUES
Focused, progressive, determined

VICES
Obsessive, uncaring, unbalanced

CAREERS
Social campaigner, politician, nonprofit project manager

SKILLS & APTITUDES
Problem-solving skills, goal orientation, drive

FAMOUS BIRTHS
Julia-Louis Dreyfus (1961)
Patrick Dempsey (1966)
Orlando Bloom (1977)
Liam Hemsworth (1990)

COMPATIBLE WITH
November 12–16

JANUARY 14

✳ ✳ ✳ ✳ ✳ ✳ ✳ ✳ ✳ ✳ ✳ ✳ ✳ ✳

RIGHTEOUS MORALISTS ♄ ☿

PLANETARY INFLUENCES
Ruling planet: Saturn
Third decan: Personal planet is
Mercury

VIRTUES
Determined, charismatic,
principled

VICES
Self-indulgent, commitment-
phobic, judgmental

CAREERS
Interior designer, social campaigner,
musician

SKILLS & APTITUDES
Esthetic instincts, progressive
mindset, social focus

FAMOUS BIRTHS
Albert Schweitzer (1875)
Andy Rooney (1919)
L.L. Cool J. (1968)
Dave Grohl (1969)

COMPATIBLE WITH
November 12–16

Those born on this day incorporate an intriguing mixture of iron wills and self-indulgence—frequently manifested by their tendency to abandon themselves totally to the pleasures of the senses, to the exquisite. Indeed, their instinctive appreciation of art and music, which is reinforced if they were born in the Chinese year of the snake, as well as their charming and magnetic personalities, mask their very real concern with social injustice and their pronounced determination to change the world for the better. Another apparently paradoxical quirk of their personalities is the juxtaposition of their strongly held ethical beliefs and concomitant desire to impose collective improvements on human society, while at the same time operating on a fiercely individualistic basis. Yet these people, who are governed by a very real sense of right and wrong and are skilled at evaluating the cause of any perceived injustice, will take a fierce personal stance on those issues they hold dear, from which they will refuse to be deflected.

Curiously, for people who are driven by their humanitarian convictions, January 14 people often harbor a deep aversion to making commitments in their personal lives. This may stem from a reluctance to divert their energies from their intellectual ambitions, but may also result from their fear of making the wrong decision. In order to avoid future isolation and loneliness, they should therefore ensure that they do not apply their own ideal moral standards to potential friends and partners, and should learn to appreciate and respect people as they are, compromising accordingly.

JANUARY 15

✵ ✵ ✵ ✵ ✵ ✵ ✵ ✵ ✵ ✵ ✵ ✵ ✵ ✵

♄ ☿   Nurturing Caretakers

January 15 people aspire to perfection, but this desire is generally not fueled by the need to be top dog and reach the pinnacle of their profession (although they frequently do so). Rather than being driven primarily by personal ambition, they are motivated by idealistic and ethical concerns, and demonstrate a strong urge to lead a moral and useful life, thereby often secretly or openly hoping to inspire others by their example. From a very early age these people may manifest a sure, almost intuitive, sense of right and wrong. This tendency may, however, result in a propensity to see things in black and white, and to dismiss the various shades of gray in between without according them the necessary sympathetic and thorough consideration.

These people are especially sensitive to the suffering of others, and because they are blessed with strong analytical and rational intellectual powers, they are also able to channel their emotional responses into the formulation of a carefully considered plan of action in an attempt to alleviate injustice or distress. They perform best within a team framework that offers the mutual support and encouragement of others, and where their strong convictions will provide inspiration and leadership. For this reason January 15 people are particularly suited to careers in the caring professions, or in the emergency services, but some are also talented artists. They are devoted to their family and friends, desiring to bring about their happiness rather than see them succeed at all costs. They should take care to draw a clear demarcation line between their professional and personal concerns so that they do not impose the crushing burden of living up to their own lofty idealistic expectations on those closest to them.

PLANETARY INFLUENCES
Ruling planet: Saturn
Third decan: Personal planet is Mercury

VIRTUES
Idealistic, public-spirited, empathetic

VICES
Judgmental, stubborn, inflexible

CAREERS
Social worker, paramedic, artist

SKILLS & APTITUDES
Analytical skills, team orientation, leadership instincts

FAMOUS BIRTHS
Molière (1622)
Martin Luther King, Jr. (1929)
Charo (1951)
Chad Lowe (1968)

COMPATIBLE WITH
November 17–21

JANUARY 16

✶ ✶ ✶ ✶ ✶ ✶ ✶ ✶ ✶ ✶ ✶ ✶ ✶ ✶

CONSIDERATE SOULS   ♄ ♅ ☿

Those born on January 16 somehow combine an unusual level of sensitivity with razor-sharp, analytical minds. These are often the people who instinctively absorb the indefinable, sublimely elevating qualities of an artistic masterpiece at the same time as consciously deconstructing and evaluating the technicalities of its composition. These multifaceted qualities (an affinity with the finer things in life as well as rigorous intellectual analysis) make them perfectly suited for careers in arts administration or teaching, and doubly so when their gift for communication is taken into consideration. With such a talent for perceiving and integrating both the mystical and rational, little passes them by, and their abilities are such that they are often much sought after for their opinions and advice. In the business sphere, they make successful management consultants or troubleshooters, where their diplomatic skills are also greatly appreciated.

Valued as these people are by others, their sensitive dispositions, when coupled with their tendency toward intellectual criticism, can result in a feeling of internal crisis or angst. Together, their farsightedness and emotional receptiveness may cause January 16 people to become unnecessarily anxious about their future direction, or to believe that they can never live up to their own expectations. The respect and support of their family and friends is therefore of the greatest importance in providing a loving and stable framework in which those born on this day will thrive, particularly when they are young. In turn, January 16 people should remember that little is more important than nurturing personal bonds.

JANUARY 17

✿ ✿ ✿ ✿ ✿ ✿ ✿ ✿ ✿ ✿ ✿ ✿ ✿ ✿

♄ ♅ ☿   DISCERNING FACILITATORS

January 17 people rarely fail to impress others with their forceful sense of purpose and drive. Possessing the enviable ability to evaluate a situation and swiftly discard the chaff from the wheat, these people quickly reach a firm opinion which they then promote with unwavering certainty. Tenacious and strong-willed, people born on this day have the confidence to brush aside their detractors and proceed on their chosen course undeterred. This direct approach is the mark of the leader, a role which January 17 people are happy to assume—not out of a sense of ambition, but because, having applied their considerable judgemental skills to the formation of their convictions, they are genuinely convinced of the correctness of their actions. They also work well as part of a team, being naturally gregarious and appreciative of other people's input, provided, of course, that they share the same motivations. They will find the greatest fulfillment in any career, such as within the military or police force, in which they can combine their strategic talents with their flair for organizational implementation.

The danger of having such a strong sense of self-belief is that if ever these people are thwarted they can lose their tempers in spectacular fashion. They must therefore try to apply their undoubted capacity for intellectual discipline to their emotions, ensuring that they maintain a sense of equilibrium in their dealings with others, and trying not to become temperamentally unsettled when they encounter inevitable obstacles. Furthermore, they should allow their family members freedom of expression and should not try to be all-controlling or to impose unnecessary demands upon them.

PLANETARY INFLUENCES
Ruling planets: Saturn and Uranus
Third decan: Personal planet is Mercury
Second cusp: Capricorn with Aquarian tendencies

VIRTUES
Decisive, confident, tenacious

VICES
Short-tempered, unbalanced, domineering

CAREERS
Law-enforcement officer, sports person, business leader

SKILLS & APTITUDES
Leadership, team orientation, drive

FAMOUS BIRTHS
Benjamin Franklin (1706)
Al Capone (1899)
Betty White (1922)
Muhammad Ali (1942)
Michelle Obama (1964)

COMPATIBLE WITH
August 2–4, November 17–21

JANUARY 18

✴ ✴ ✴ ✴ ✴ ✴ ✴ ✴ ✴ ✴ ✴ ✴ ✴ ✴

BOUNDLESS QUESTERS   ħ ♅ ☿

PLANETARY INFLUENCES
Ruling planets: Saturn and Uranus
Third decan: Personal planet is Mercury
Second cusp: Capricorn with Aquarian tendencies

VIRTUES
Imaginative, fun-loving, enthusiastic

VICES
Impatient, frustrated, subversive

CAREERS
Actor, novelist, artist

SKILLS & APTITUDES
Communication skills, resourcefulness, original mindset

FAMOUS BIRTHS
Daniel Webster (1782)
Cary Grant (1904)
Kevin Costner (1955)
Jason Segel (1980)

COMPATIBLE WITH
August 2–4, November 17–21

....
....
....

Their innate sense of fun and imaginative powers make these people fascinating to others and their company a pleasure. With lively minds, perceptive powers and a desire to explore the world, these people embrace the unusual with enthusiasm, and since they generally find it easy to communicate their ideas to others, will often have a rapt audience. Once they have found a subject that absorbs them, they will pursue it with determination, in doing so demonstrating an impressive level of tenacity and unflagging interest. Although highly self-disciplined, January 18 people chafe under the rules and regulations of others, particularly if they do not appreciate their underlying purpose, and unless they are truly convinced of the merits of a task will not thrive as part of a strictly regulated organization or team. Indeed, given the value that they place on independent thought and their highly developed sense of fantasy, people born on this day have a natural inclination toward such creative activities as writing, acting or painting.

It may take these people some time to find the métier that ideally suits their talents and inclinations, however, and the impatience that may be engendered by adverse circumstances may cause them either to give in to childish displays of willfulness, or to take refuge in their own private world. In children, these strong-willed tendencies may give their parents cause for concern, but such is the resourcefulness of these people that they will eventually find a fulfilling outlet for their intellectual and emotional requirements. They will be happiest if those around them respect their need for freedom, while at the same time providing them with stability and support.

JANUARY 19

❋ ❋ ❋ ❋ ❋ ❋ ❋ ❋ ❋ ❋ ❋ ❋ ❋ ❋

♄ ♅ ☿   FOCUSED INVESTIGATORS

Latent in January 19 people is a tendency toward intensity that can all too easily develop into extremism. Although possessed of inquisitive minds, they will pursue whatever most excites their interest—sometimes mystical and somewhat nebulous concepts—with a single-minded determination that can be obsessive in its attention to detail. Yet if the vision proves short-lived or easily exhausted, such is their desire for intellectual stimulation and knowledge that another subject will soon be found and investigated with equal dedication. This is the day of true originality, of those whose idiosyncrasies may be misunderstood and dismissed by the more conventional, but whose obstinacy will not brook dissuasion from their chosen course. Consequently, people born on this day usually perform their best work in solitary conditions. They frequently receive acclaim in the scientific or artistic fields, and it may well take some time before others appreciate and acknowledge their undoubted talents.

In their personal lives, the restless dynamism of these people will attract baffled admiration, but their natural unconventionality may frighten and alienate those who are not brave or farsighted enough to stand prolonged exposure to them. Indeed, without the grounding support of sympathetic, easy-going friends and relatives, January 19 people may find themselves isolated and, without meaningful personal contact, tend to become prone to depression. They must therefore strive to balance their lives, to ensure that they not only spread their energies equally between work and relaxation, but that they pay genuine attention to the opinions and emotional requirements of those around them; mutually supportive relationships are crucial.

PLANETARY INFLUENCES
Ruling planets: Saturn and Uranus
Third decan: Personal planet is Mercury
Second cusp: Capricorn with Aquarian tendencies

VIRTUES
Determined, curious, visionary

VICES
Obsessive, obstinate, unbalanced

CAREERS
Scientific researcher, artist, musician

SKILLS & APTITUDES
Dynamism, unconventional approach, single-minded focus

FAMOUS BIRTHS
Robert E. Lee (1807)
Edgar Allan Poe (1809)
Janis Joplin (1943)
Dolly Parton (1946)

COMPATIBLE WITH
August 2–4, November 17–21

♒ AQUARIUS

January 20 to February 18

RULING PLANET: *Uranus (traditionally Saturn)* ELEMENT: *Fixed air*
SYMBOL: *Water-carrier* POLARITY: *Positive (masculine)* COLORS: *Violet and blue*
PHYSICAL CORRESPONDENCE: *Blood vessels, calves, ankles, heels*
STONES: *Sapphire, onyx, amethyst, black pearl, hematite*
FLOWERS: *Myrtle, rosemary, dandelion, orchid, goldenrod*

Aquarius is known as the water carrier, personified as a human figure with a pot of water. This corresponds to the ancient Egyptian tales of the god Hapi, who filled the sacred River Nile with water, and to the Greek myth of Ganymede, the youth whom the enamored Zeus (Jupiter), in the form of an eagle, transported into the heavens to act as his cup-bearer. Other astrological traditions depersonalized Aquarius and identified it as a vessel containing water: in Hindu astrology it is called Khumba; and in Mesopotamian belief it was Dul, both names that signify a water-pot. Yet the Babylonians equated this sign with the goddess Gula, the deity who regulated childbirth and possessed the gift of healing. Until the planet Uranus was discovered in 1781, Aquarius was believed to be governed by Saturn (the Greek Kronos, an agricultural deity), but since the Greek god Ouranos was a sky god, whose domain was the element of air that influences this sign—and who was additionally the consort of the mother goddess Gaia (associated with the fecund powers of water)—in many respects the more recent pairing is appropriate.

The defining characteristics of Aquarians are independence, manifested in their intellectual originality and progressiveness (with which Uranus is also credited), and the water that Aquarius represents is symbolically equated with knowledge. Yet since this is a sign that is governed by the element of air—which not only signifies a desire for freedom of thought and action, but may also imply a lack of staying power—those born under this sign may tend toward aloofness and impulsiveness, while their personal relationships are often relegated to second place, behind exploring abstract ideas.

JANUARY 20

✳ ✳ ✳ ✳ ✳ ✳ ✳ ✳ ✳ ✳ ✳ ✳ ✳

♒ ♄　　　POPULAR PERFORMERS

These exuberant individuals relish the attention that their manifold interests, outgoing personalities and love of life attract. Their kindness and sense of fun make them popular companions, but unless these people keep their feet on the ground and develop a more pragmatic attitude their heads may be turned by the admiration that they inspire. In their efforts to entertain others (and humor is strongly indicated by this day) they have a tendency to become somewhat out of control.

This is not to say that people born on this day lack discipline (far from it), but if bored or frustrated they may either withdraw completely, succumb to temper tantrums or play the fool in an attempt to enliven things. Indeed, this need for stimulation is paramount for January 20 people, and when they find a subject that truly interests them they display unusually intense powers of concentration and tenacity, rarely giving up on a task until it is completed.

Running parallel with these people's capacity for solid, intellectual pursuits is a marked sensitivity for the feelings of others, as well as a desire to please their audience. These qualities mark them out as natural performers and also indicate a latent talent for diplomacy and politics—particularly if they were born in the Chinese year of snake—areas in which their resilience, self-belief and aptitude for problem-solving may find their full expression.

In their personal relationships, people born on this day should cultivate patience and try to develop a more relaxed and accepting attitude toward both themselves and others.

PLANETARY INFLUENCES
Ruling planets: Uranus and Saturn
First decan: Personal planet is Uranus
First cusp: Aquarius with Capricorn tendencies

VIRTUES
Energetic, self-confident, charming

VICES
Arrogant, egotistical, condescending

CAREERS
Actor, politician, entertainer

SKILLS & APTITUDES
Impressive capacity for hard work, analytical minds, ability to tune into the moods of others

FAMOUS BIRTHS
George Burns (1896)
Joy Adamson (1910)
Frederico Fellini (1920)
Edwin "Buzz" Aldrin (1930)
Evan Peters (1987)

COMPATIBLE WITH
September 23–25, December 27–30

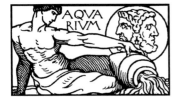

JANUARY 21

✳ ✳ ✳ ✳ ✳ ✳ ✳ ✳ ✳ ✳ ✳ ✳ ✳ ✳

FREEDOM-FINDERS
♒ ♄

PLANETARY INFLUENCES
Ruling planets: Uranus and Saturn
First decan: Personal planet is
  Uranus
First cusp: Aquarius with Capricorn
  tendencies

VIRTUES
Free-spirited, sensitive, idealistic

VICES
Unpredictable, indecisive, escapist

CAREERS
Public relations, social worker,
activist

SKILLS & APTITUDES
Sensitivity to emotions and
instincts, originality

FAMOUS BIRTHS
Thomas "Stonewall" Jackson (1824)
Christian Dior (1905)
Wolfman Jack (1938)
Geena Davis (1957)
Emma Bunton (1976)

COMPATIBLE WITH
September 23–26, December 28–31

....
....
....

Crucial to January 21 people is their profound thirst both for unfettered freedom of expression and for an emotional haven to which they can retreat for the privacy that is so essential to them. These people will never find fulfillment if they are forced to submit unquestioningly to the rules of others, for their urge to explore and follow their natural inclinations is as vital to them as the air that is their element. Indeed, in order to understand what exactly it is that makes these libertarian people tick, one must appreciate their need to be allowed to act upon their instincts. The important thing is that even if they end up following the wrong course, the decision to do so was their own and, indeed, they will be quick to learn from their experiences. These twin qualities of sensitivity and waywardness, as well as a marked sensuality, bestow upon people born on this day the especial potential to succeed in the world of the arts.

Inevitably somewhat unpredictable, their idiosyncratic behavior may ultimately exasperate those around them who prefer a more logical approach. Any attempt to place impositions upon January 21 people is, however, doomed to disaster; they must be accepted as they are. Related to their individuality is their occasional craving for solitude, the time for reflection and to be themselves, and this too should be respected. Yet while people born on this day are stubbornly resistant to coercion, their inherent respect for personal liberty means that they will never consciously attempt to dominate others, despite their talent for persuasion. Since they are consumed by a strong desire for the happiness of other people, their ideals will often lead them into humanitarian activities and pursuits.

JANUARY 22

✳ ✳ ✳ ✳ ✳ ✳ ✳ ✳ ✳ ✳ ✳ ✳ ✳ ✳ ✳

♅ ♄ ASTUTE ENVIRONMENTALISTS

People born on this day have a craving for stimulation, a need that endows them with the potential to be polymaths, provided that they are disciplined enough to develop their interests beyond the superficial level. Because they are quick-witted and instinctual, they are gifted at speedily summing up a situation, but may then persist with their initial response and fail to explore it deeper.

Tedium is among the greatest enemies of January 22 people, and if forced to carry on with a task that bores them, their impatience may lead them into performing hastily or carelessly, or, indeed, to abandon the project altogether in favor of the lure of pastures new.

Whichever profession they choose, whether it be in the arts or not, people born on this day tend to blossom when allowed to express their creativity unhindered, and when not stultified by petty procedures or bureaucratic rules and restrictions.

In common with most Aquarians, January 22 people are not generally motivated primarily by personal ambition or monetary aims, but rather by the desire for personal and collective human improvement. They often also feel strong empathy and appreciation for the natural world and environmental issues, and their ideals and inclinations may lead them to become environmentalists.

In order to enjoy fulfilling personal lives, people born on this day must control their inherent tendency to behave impetuously and inconsiderately, and should seek to ground themselves in stable, mutually respectful relationships.

PLANETARY INFLUENCES
Ruling planets: Uranus and Saturn
First decan: Personal planet is Uranus
First cusp: Aquarius with Capricorn tendencies

VIRTUES
Versatile, enthusiastic, multifaceted

VICES
Fickle, impatient, temperamental

CAREERS
Artist, writer, environmentalist

SKILLS & APTITUDES
Wide-ranging interests, restless vigor, connection to nature and humanity

FAMOUS BIRTHS
Francis Bacon (1561)
Beatrice Potter Webb (1858)
Sam Cooke (1931)
John Hurt (1940)

COMPATIBLE WITH
September 23–27, December 29–31

JANUARY 23

✻ ✻ ✻ ✻ ✻ ✻ ✻ ✻ ✻ ✻ ✻ ✻ ✻ ✻

UNINTENTIONAL ROLE MODELS   ♒ ♄

PLANETARY INFLUENCES
Ruling planets: Uranus and Saturn
First decan: Personal planet is Uranus
First cusp: Aquarius with Capricorn tendencies

VIRTUES
Unconventional, magnetic, grounded

VICES
Single-minded, withdrawn, aloof

CAREERS
Researcher, scientist, artist

SKILLS & APTITUDES
Highly original, natural sense of style, disregard for convention

FAMOUS BIRTHS
John Hancock (1737)
Humphrey Bogart (1899)
Chita Rivera (1933)
Princess Caroline of Monaco (1957)

COMPATIBLE WITH
September 24–27, December 30–31

To their enthusiasts, their deep convictions, original thinking, manifest integrity and natural sense of style make those born on this day inspirational figures. Yet January 23 people are unintentional and reluctant role models, and often feel uneasy at being regarded as such. While they might well occasionally seek to influence others, they are motivated by the wish to achieve impersonal ideals, and not by the desire to become the subjects of admiration. Yet it is precisely this refreshing disregard for human vanity that, along with their individualistic approach, other people find so magnetic. The intellectual qualities of people born on this day (curiosity, objectivity, inventiveness and a dash of adventurousness) signal a distinct aptitude for science, as well as for those artistic spheres in which they can combine their natural sensitivity with their independent approach. Naturally open to outside influences, and enthusiastic travelers, these people will drink in new experiences and then reinterpret them in their inimitably unique fashion.

Because January 23 people are easily absorbed by intellectual pursuits and are highly self-reliant (especially if they were also born in the Chinese year of the tiger), their friends and relatives may feel somewhat excluded. Although they are usually considerate and generous partners who tend to think the best of others (and thus also make extremely good parents), there are times when their fascination with ideas will cause them to withdraw into their own world and to neglect those close to them. They benefit by remembering that, in their desire to advance the greater good of humanity, they must not sacrifice the individual.

JANUARY 24

✤ ✤ ✤ ✤ ✤ ✤ ✤ ✤ ✤ ✤ ✤ ✤ ✤ ✤

♒ RELUCTANT ECCENTRICS

Those born on this day are imaginative to the point of feyness, and are fascinated by topics that less free-thinking people might dismiss as being oddball. Indeed, so accustomed are they to being branded eccentric when they moot their wildly original ideas and theories, that to avoid experiencing the hurt of a negative reaction, they frequently keep quiet about what it is that really excites them. This defensive mechanism may be effective in the short term, but such suppression of the true self will ultimately cause emotional damage.

The paradox governing their personalities and behavior is that although January 24 people are generally greatly admired for their original qualities, they are reluctant to believe that the people around them appreciate them just as they are. They may completely reject such esteem, either suspecting underlying motives or feeling that their essence has been misunderstood.

Their sensitivity, love of nature, and genuine desire to work for good propels many January 24 people into working with animals, with whom they feel a deep empathy and trust that they sometimes feel are lacking in their relationships with their human peers. They thrive best in those small-scale, more personal, working environments in which they do not feel inhibited or under pressure to perform artificially. Similarly, they need to be constantly reassured by the love and support of their friends and family if they are to achieve their true potential.

PLANETARY INFLUENCES
Ruling planet: Uranus
First decan: Personal planet is Uranus

VIRTUES
Empathetic, unique, imaginative

VICES
Oversensitive, hesitant, aloof

CAREERS
Veterinarian, zookeeper, non-profit organizer

SKILLS & APTITUDES
Effortlessly draw others to them, attraction to all that is different, outstanding intellectual abilities

FAMOUS BIRTHS
Edith Wharton (1862)
Neil Diamond (1941)
John Belushi (1949)
Mary Lou Retton (1968)

COMPATIBLE WITH
September 24–28, December 31

JANUARY 25

✺ ✺ ✺ ✺ ✺ ✺ ✺ ✺ ✺ ✺ ✺ ✺ ✺ ✺

EXTREME ENIGMAS

To the less sensitive, those born on January 25 present something of an enigma. Such is the complexity of their characters that they may at one moment entertain others with their humor, wit and charisma, and at the next retreat into a shell of introversion and solitude. Indeed, these people are drawn to extremes, a reflection of their inherent curiosity, craving for stimulation and thirst to explore and satisfy the many facets of their personalities.

Their behavior, pursuits and moods may sometimes appear erratic, but underlying them is an overwhelming interest in all aspects of life, which may often be manifested in an enthusiasm for travel and a willingness to experience new things.

Those born on January 25 are extremely sensitive and are highly receptive to the feelings of others. This gift, combined with their powers of perception and genuine interest in the welfare of others, suits them especially to the caring professions, in which they often make outstanding contributions.

There will be times, however, when people born on this day will feel almost overwhelmed by the strength of their empathy, which may be intensified by the strong sense of fatalism to which they are prone. On such occasions they must actively strive to be positive and not to succumb to feelings of helplessness and despair. The unqualified love and support of those close to them is crucial to these people's emotional well-being, and will in turn be amply and loyally rewarded.

JANUARY 26

✳ ✳ ✳ ✳ ✳ ✳ ✳ ✳ ✳ ✳ ✳ ✳ ✳ ✳

♒ BOLD RISK-TAKERS

Their energy, drive and boldly expressed convictions make many January 26 people larger-than-life figures who follow their hunches and deeply held convictions in characteristically individual style. There is a dual side to these personalities: on the one hand they are physically vibrant, combative and confident in their sensitivity and intellects, while on the other they are prone to follow their instincts and beliefs with steely determination, thereby also demonstrating their capacity for organization and tenacity. The combination of their highly developed talents of intuition, ambitious vision and intellectual perceptiveness, as well as their willingness to take risks if they feel these justify the potential rewards, mark these people out as potentially successful players of the financial markets, where they often have a gift for investment. Yet despite this commercial bent, people born on this day also have a propensity to spend their money as though it were water.

In their personal lives, these people must beware of using the same tactic of determined confrontation that frequently serves them so well in their careers. Although they may have a deep and genuine affection for their loved ones, they may inadvertently cause upset if they give their well-meant words of advice too bluntly, or try to make others follow a course of action to which they are not suited. These people therefore benefit by becoming less controlling and more accepting of the limitations and viewpoints of others; when they apply this strategy to their own lives, they will also discover that there is much to be gained from a more relaxed attitude and willingness to compromise.

PLANETARY INFLUENCES
Ruling planet: Uranus
First decan: Personal planet is Uranus

VIRTUES
Strong-willed, quick-witted, confident

VICES
Blunt, intimidating, short-sighted

CAREERS
Accountant, banker, marketer

SKILLS & APTITUDES
Resounding impact on others, outstanding intellectual gifts, bold and vibrant personalities

FAMOUS BIRTHS
Paul Newman (1925)
Eddie Van Halen (1955)
Ellen DeGeneres (1958)
Wayne Gretzky (1961)

COMPATIBLE WITH
January 28–31, September 25–28

Planetary Influences

Ruling planet: Uranus
First decan: Personal planet is Uranus

Virtues

Determined, benevolent, relaxed

Vices

Frustrated, self-indulgent, restless

Careers

Business owner, designer, consultant

Skills & Aptitudes

Pioneering spirits, respond instinctively to challenge, accept others as they are

Famous Births

Wolfgang Amadeus Mozart (1756)
Lewis Carroll (or Charles Lutwidge Dodgson) (1832)
William Randolph Hearst (1863)
Bridget Fonda (1964)

Compatible With

January 28–31, September 25–29

JANUARY 27

Courageous Challengers ♅

Perhaps the strongest characteristic of January 27 people is their inherent need to be challenged and stimulated, and this is often manifested by a ceaseless questing to experience and master all that life has to offer. Running parallel to their strong sense of purpose and deep desire to succeed is a pronounced streak of courage, which enables them doggedly, and sometimes apparently recklessly, to tread new paths without being deflected from their purpose. Yet although they are daring, those born on this day will generally not take chances without first having weighed up the risks and having carefully examined potential pitfalls. Although they are personally ambitious, these people are rarely motivated by a desire for financial reward, instead being driven by a desire to test and prove themselves. Their intellectual talents, including those of perceptiveness and objectivity, suit them for most professions, that is, as long as their attention is held and they are allowed to be creative.

Away from work, these people greatly enjoy the good things of life and as appreciative gourmets are ever willing to sample new sensual experiences. Unusually, for such active people, their propensity for self-indulgence and love of luxury can seduce them into idleness, especially if they were born in the Chinese year of the snake. Generous to a fault, they are deeply attached to their family and friends, desiring their happiness above all. In turn—perhaps as a result of their intellectual restlessness—they need a stable and secure personal life, and to receive the constant reassurance and encouragement of those closest to them, as well as the occasional firm hand.

JANUARY 28

✳ ✳ ✳ ✳ ✳ ✳ ✳ ✳ ✳ ✳ ✳ ✳ ✳ ✳

♒︎ TOLERANT JUDGES

Although these people have extremely strong views regarding what is right and what is wrong, and relish the stimulating cut and thrust of intellectual debate, these qualities are motivated more by a sense of justice than by a need to impose their convictions by dominating others. Indeed, while they may not always agree with them, January 28 people are remarkably tolerant in their appreciation of inevitable differences of opinion, respecting what other people have to say but not allowing their integrity to be swayed in the process. These qualities are often best employed in the judicial, diplomatic or political sphere, in which they can objectively seek to advance the humanitarian causes that are dear to them without dismissively rejecting alternative convictions. Their natural charm, capacity for penetrative thought and compelling articulateness will also stand them in good stead in such pursuits. January 28 people are also intuitive, and if they nurture their creative impulses, they can achieve memorable artistic success.

Just as they are frequently motivated by humanitarian aims in their professional lives, in their personal relationships people born on this day place the happiness and well-being of their families above all else. They greatly value the sense of security that they gain from strong, supportive relationships. Highly sensitive, they have an instinctive distaste for emotional conflict and will do their utmost to avoid unpleasant confrontation with members of their family, whom they may often infuriate by appearing to duck issues and retreating into their own world.

PLANETARY INFLUENCES
Ruling planet: Uranus
First decan: Personal planet is Uranus

VIRTUES
Compassionate, objective, persuasive

VICES
Hypersensitive, avoiding, vulnerable

CAREERS
Judge, lawyer, humanitarian

SKILLS & APTITUDES
Tolerance toward others, powers of persuasion, sense of justice

FAMOUS BIRTHS
Jackson Pollock (1912)
Alan Alda (1936)
Mikhail Baryshnikov (1948)
Elijah Wood (1981)

COMPATIBLE WITH
January 25–27, September 25–30

JANUARY 29

✺ ✺ ✺ ✺ ✺ ✺ ✺ ✺ ✺ ✺ ✺ ✺ ✺ ✺

ASSERTIVE CAMPAIGNERS ♒

PLANETARY INFLUENCES
Ruling planet: Uranus
First decan: Personal planet is
Uranus

VIRTUES
Bright, ardent, inspiring

VICES
Oversensitive, petulant, prone to
fatigue

CAREERS
Political campaigner, social activist,
lobbyist, charity worker

SKILLS & APTITUDES
Possessed of a burning desire to
right perceived wrongs, ardent
espousal of ideals, potential to
inspire others

FAMOUS BIRTHS
Thomas Paine (1737)
Tom Selleck (1945)
Oprah Winfrey (1954)
Greg Louganis (1960)

COMPATIBLE WITH
January 25–27, September 26–30

The forceful personalities and profound convictions of January 29 people frequently evoke extremes of emotion in others, to whom they may be either the subject of deep esteem or dismissive derision. Either way, they consistently refuse to be ignored, a quality for which they are sneakingly admired even by their loudest detractors.

Inherently empathetic to the plight of others, and blessed with quick-witted minds, those born on this day are, invariably drawn to social causes, impelled by their natural sense of justice to fight for those whom they feel have been wronged.

When inspired by their principles, January 29 people make formidably determined campaigners, despite—or perhaps because of—the fact that they usually prefer to achieve their ends through reasoned argument rather than direct confrontation. Such qualities indicate that these people are predisposed to be politicians or social campaigners. They may often be found volunteering for charities and causes even if they have jobs in a completely different field.

The downside of their innate sensitivity is that when they provoke negative responses January 29 people may feel deeply hurt by this rejection. This makes it all the more important that they are supported by stable personal relationships so that they are buoyed up by the love and understanding of those who appreciate their qualities. A happy personal life will also put a brake on these people's martyr and obsessive tendencies, and will help to provide them with a sense of perspective.

JANUARY 30

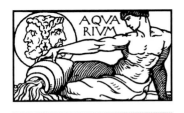

✷ ✷ ✷ ✷ ✷ ✷ ✷ ✷ ✷ ✷ ✷ ✷ ✷

♒ INSTINCTUAL INDIVIDUALS

These dynamic people have a burning desire to impose their own stamp on all that they undertake, confident as they are in the truth of their convictions. Although they will have arrived at their judgments by means of reasoned thought, January 30 people rely on their instincts to guide them, and often retrospectively justify their initial responses with rational arguments. This remarkable ability to channel their sensitivity through their intellects and then transmit their opinions lucidly and convincingly is a rare one, and will gain them acclaim, especially when employed in artistic pursuits, but also in politics or the military forces. Whichever professional path they follow, however, it is important that these people be allowed to follow their natural urge to lead others and to act independently. They do not function well in subordinate roles, either in the professional or personal realm, and can be somewhat passive-aggressive toward anyone who tries to dominate them.

There is a distinct danger that such a high level of self-belief, particularly when it is apparently confirmed by others, can result in excessive egotism or complacency. These people furthermore crave the approval of their peers and may play to their audience, instinctively picking up on the prevailing mood and mirroring it. On such occasions they should step back and calm their propensity to respond impulsively and instead remain true to themselves and their own convictions. They may demand (and receive) the unquestioning support of their family and friends, but should remember that any dissension is not a personal betrayal, but rather a healthy manifestation of the rich benefits that are gained from diverse opinions and approaches.

PLANETARY INFLUENCES
Ruling planet: Uranus
First decan: Personal planet is Uranus

VIRTUES
Empathetic, intuitive, persuasive

VICES
Vain, impatient, dismissive

CAREERS
Soldier, artist, politician

SKILLS & APTITUDES
Strength of character, ability to transform empathy into action, talent for persuasion

FAMOUS BIRTHS
Franklin Delano Roosevelt (1882)
Roy Eldridge (1911)
Gene Hackman (1930)
Phil Collins (1951)

COMPATIBLE WITH
January 1, January 25–27, September 26–30

JANUARY 31

✵ ✵ ✵ ✵ ✵ ✵ ✵ ✵ ✵ ✵ ✵ ✵ ✵ ✵

RECOGNITION–SEEKERS ♒

PLANETARY INFLUENCES
Ruling planet: Uranus
First decan: Personal planet is
Uranus

VIRTUES
Idealistic, magnetic, visionary

VICES
Oversensitive, wayward, prone to
melancholia

CAREERS
Writer, actor, philosopher

SKILLS & APTITUDES
Attractive personality, sensitivity to
others, ability to inspire

FAMOUS BIRTHS
Jackie Robinson (1919)
Carol Channing and
Norman Mailer (1923)
Johnny Rotten (1956)
Portia de Rossi (1973)

COMPATIBLE WITH
January 1–2, January 25–27,
September 27–30

January 31 people have an all-consuming need to be taken seriously, to gain the regard of their peers for those qualities that they value most in themselves: their originality, compassion, sensitivity and vision. And indeed these people are admired by others yet, despite their best efforts, it may be for entirely different, and perhaps more superficial, reasons—such as for their personal charm, physical appearance or the entertainment that they give others.

Perhaps these people have a tendency to send mixed messages in their attempts to gain the undivided attention of others, but it is frequently the case that they undervalue the particular talents that attract others to them. They have a tendency often to place greater worth on their more profound characteristics. Their extreme sensitivity, fascination with mystical concepts and innate appreciation of beauty will often find fulfilling expression in the artistic world, but their considerable intellectual powers will also bring them success if they're willing to work for ir.

To console and reinforce them in the throes of their personal struggles to be accepted on their own terms, it is vital that January 31 people receive frequent demonstrations of the unconditional support of those closest to them, whose encouragement they will reward many times over. Yet, as in all other areas of their lives, people born on this day must beware of making unreasonable demands on the good will of others. Developing a more relaxed, pragmatic and less intense approach will benefit them in all areas of their lives.

FEBRUARY 1

❅ ❅ ❅ ❅ ❅ ❅ ❅ ❅ ❅ ❅ ❅ ❅ ❅ ❅

♅ ☿   JACKS OF ALL TRADES

February 1 people are blessed with so many talents that they often have difficulty in deciding which to concentrate on, a tendency that is complicated by the conflict between their heads and hearts. Indeed, these people have powerful perceptive qualities, as well as the enviable ability to evaluate a situation quickly and formulate an appropriate course of action—often a humanitarian course motivated by their natural sense of justice and desire to effect improvement. Their gifts and disposition suit them for careers in politics or education, as well as the medical and other caring professions, but since they are sensitive and communicative, they may also find success in the arts. Whichever area they decide to favor, however, these strong-willed people must be allowed to follow their own course, for if frustrated or forced to espouse a cause in which they do not believe, they will become obdurate and uncooperative.

Their grounded and sensible intellectual approach does not mean that these people are dull and plodding. On the contrary, their empathetic and intuitive qualities can result in startlingly impulsive behavior. February 1 people are often extremely sensual and sociable, giving themselves over to the enjoyment of the good things of life with enthusiasm. These characteristics make them popular and attractive to others, who are drawn to their company for the fun and excitement that they generate. Children and less disciplined individuals may become carried away by their wayward impulses and propensity for self-indulgence, a predilection toward the extreme that should be curbed.

PLANETARY INFLUENCES
Ruling planet: Uranus
Second decan: Personal planet is Mercury

VIRTUES
Multitalented, tenacious, charismatic

VICES
Stubborn, self-indulgent, blunt

CAREERS
Educator, doctor, diplomat

SKILLS & APTITUDES
Outstanding powers of communication, boldness, compassionate nature

FAMOUS BIRTHS
Clark Gable (1901)
Langston Hughes (1902)
Sherman Hemsley (1938)
Lisa Marie Presley (1968)
Harry Styles (1994)

COMPATIBLE WITH
September 28–30, October 1

FEBRUARY 2

✳ ✳ ✳ ✳ ✳ ✳ ✳ ✳ ✳ ✳ ✳ ✳ ✳ ✳

ANALYTICAL COMMANDERS ♅ ☿

PLANETARY INFLUENCES
Ruling planet: Uranus
Second decan: Personal planet is Mercury

VIRTUES
Driven, strategic, disciplined

VICES
Cold, impersonal, restrained

CAREERS
Corporate sales, athlete, CEO

SKILLS & APTITUDES
Intellectual capacity to cut straight to the heart of the issue, masters of detail, enviable faculty of seeing the larger picture

FAMOUS BIRTHS
James Joyce (1882)
Stan Getz (1927)
Farrah Fawcett (1947)
Christie Brinkley (1953)

COMPATIBLE WITH
September 29–30, October 1–2

....

....

....

Control is vitally important to February 2 people, who need to feel in command of a given situation, of their emotions, as well as of their image and how others perceive them. There are many possible reasons for this fundamental necessity, including a wish to hide perceived weakness, a yearning to attain perfection, or, perhaps, a genuine desire for domination.

The uncompromising people born on February 2 will frequently cultivate a suave exterior or a coldly logical approach—whatever the personal implications of such a stance—and may terrify others by the apparently unattainable level of their demands. Yet it must be remembered that, despite their tough image, these people aspire to the approval and admiration of their peers for their outstanding qualities, which are, indeed, considerable.

People born on this day possess the talent to analyze a problem with crystal clarity, weigh alternative courses of action dispassionately, and strive to achieve their objectives with single-minded determination. They revel in competition: when not climbing their way to the top of the corporate tree—and they usually excel in the business sphere, especially in sales—they will often be winners in the sporting field, or in politics.

Unfortunately, particularly if they are male, their preferred tactics may be less welcome in more intimate relationships, where, in spite of their willingness to offer instant and practical advice, their reluctance to appear vulnerable may be seen as a hurtful lack of interest.

FEBRUARY 3

✶ ✶ ✶ ✶ ✶ ✶ ✶ ✶ ✶ ✶ ✶ ✶ ✶ ✶

♅ ☿   FREE—SPIRITED PARTNERS

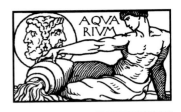

Easy-going, affable and kind to those whom they perceive as vulnerable, February 3 people are popular individuals, whose apparently relaxed approach to relationships draws others to them. While they generally enjoy their powers of attraction, their personal magnetism can also create the unwelcome feeling of being trapped by the attention of others.

The greatest fear of many of those born on this day is of having their wings clipped and their freedom curtailed by the stifling demands of partners or friends for wholehearted commitment. This is not to say that these people do not experience deep and genuine emotions, but that they need to feel they have not sacrificed the personal liberty that is so dear to them. This tendency is particularly pronounced in February 3 men, and in those also born in the Chinese year of the horse: partners who desire an enduring relationship with them should accept the fact that February 3 people simply cannot tolerate being "suffocated."

However, these people are not usually intellectual butterflies who flit from subject to subject without stopping long enough to delve deeper. When a concept truly stimulates them, they will probe every minute aspect of it, driven by their insatiable curiosity and determination to master attendant challenges. Their inherent sensitivity, originality and technical aptitude is an ideal combination for success in the arts—a career in music may be particularly auspicious—or in the scientific field, where their willingness to strike out boldly may lead them along previously untrodden paths.

PLANETARY INFLUENCES
Ruling planet: Uranus
Second decan: Personal planet is Mercury

VIRTUES
Charming, adventurous, original

VICES
Fickle, unreliable, stifled

CAREERS
IT specialist, musician, geneticist

SKILLS & APTITUDES
Open-mindedness, bold individualism, quick intellect

FAMOUS BIRTHS
Gertrude Stein (1874)
Norman Rockwell (1894)
Glen Tetley (1926)
Morgan Fairchild (1950)

COMPATIBLE WITH
September 30, October 1–3

FEBRUARY 4

✵ ✵ ✵ ✵ ✵ ✵ ✵ ✵ ✵ ✵ ✵ ✵ ✵ ✵

ENERGETIC DISCOVERERS ♅ ☿

PLANETARY INFLUENCES

Ruling planet: Uranus
Second decan: Personal planet is
Mercury

VIRTUES
Inquisitive, positive, innovative

VICES
Impulsive, distracted, flighty

CAREERS
Political activist, journalist, artist

SKILLS & APTITUDES
Quick-thinking personalities,
remarkable originality,
unconstrained and exuberant
imaginative powers

FAMOUS BIRTHS
Charles Lindbergh (1902)
Betty Friedan (1921)
Alice Cooper (1948)
Lawrence Taylor (1959)

COMPATIBLE WITH
October 1–4

Such is their originality, their speed of thought and their prodigious energy that people born on this day sometimes exhaust their less mercurial companions. The whirlwind of activity that they create around them is driven by their darting curiosity and compulsion to act—characteristics that, if focused, may lead them into uncharted realms. Lacking such focus, their relish for discovery and variety may cause them to bounce from one enthusiasm to the next, often spending vast quantities of money in the process. Indeed, if bored, they tend to lack staying power, dismissing an unstimulating project or relationship as unworthy of their attention. They should make an effort to curb this impatience, especially in their personal lives in which, because of their flighty behavior, they may be seen as superficial and unable to reciprocate profound emotions.

Yet despite their sometimes inconsistent image, February 4 people do harbor great emotional depths: the level of their empathy with others, or the strength of their humanitarian vision, will often manifest itself in a stubbornly brave refusal to be deflected from their position.

When February 4 people are truly fired up by a cause they will pursue it with fierce intensity and such a tenacious sense of purpose that others may label them eccentric. They will fare especially well in the artistic field, where their idiosyncratic blend of sensitivity and originality will be accepted and appreciated, but their potential may generate success in any professional area they choose, as long as they remember the importance of self-discipline.

FEBRUARY 5

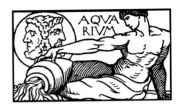

✴ ✴ ✴ ✴ ✴ ✴ ✴ ✴ ✴ ✴ ✴ ✴ ✴

♅ ☿   PERFECTION-SEEKERS

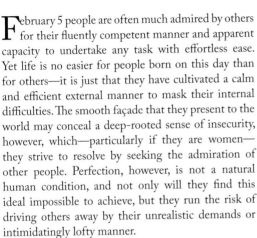

February 5 people are often much admired by others for their fluently competent manner and apparent capacity to undertake any task with effortless ease. Yet life is no easier for people born on this day than for others—it is just that they have cultivated a calm and efficient external manner to mask their internal difficulties. The smooth façade that they present to the world may conceal a deep-rooted sense of insecurity, however, which—particularly if they are women—they strive to resolve by seeking the admiration of other people. Perfection, however, is not a natural human condition, and not only will they find this ideal impossible to achieve, but they run the risk of driving others away by their unrealistic demands or intimidatingly lofty manner.

Their hypersensitivity is perhaps the key to February 5 people, who respond instinctively to the moods of others. Their twin qualities of intuition and mental farsightedness may, however, cause them great emotional anxiety, which they will suppress with a polished veneer that falsely indicates control. Indeed, the combination of their desire to be seen in the best possible light and their perceptive intellectual powers may sometimes lead them to offer practical help over the emotional support that is perhaps more valuable to others and which, moreover, they also crave for themselves. Their unusually diverse personal talents make them naturally well-rounded, with the potential to excel in either the arts or in academic or scientific pursuits. They generally work better as part of a team or cause, where they can simultaneously satisfy their need for human contact and utilize their flair for administration and management.

PLANETARY INFLUENCES
Ruling planet: Uranus
Second decan: Personal planet is Mercury

VIRTUES
Self-disciplined, sensitive, organized

VICES
Tendencies to overidealize and mislead, arrogant

CAREERS
Manager, administrator, professor

SKILLS & APTITUDES
Clarity of vision, highly controlled competence, extraordinary potential for achievement

FAMOUS BIRTHS
William Seward Burroughs (1914)
Red Buttons (1919)
Hank Aaron (1934)
Bob Marley (1945)

COMPATIBLE WITH
October 2–5

FEBRUARY 6

✳ ✳ ✳ ✳ ✳ ✳ ✳ ✳ ✳ ✳ ✳ ✳ ✳ ✳

UNRESTRICTED RESEARCHERS

PLANETARY INFLUENCES
Ruling planet: Uranus
Second decan: Personal planet is
  Mercury

VIRTUES
Stimulating, knowledgeable,
ever-curious

VICES
Bored, skittish, inconstant

CAREERS
Researcher, publisher, band
director

SKILLS & APTITUDES
Exceptionally responsive to sensory
and intellectual stimuli, powers of
intuition and curiosity, intelligent
and original reactions to challenges

FAMOUS BIRTHS
Babe Ruth (1895)
Ronald Reagan (1911)
Zsa Zsa Gabor (1915)
Tom Brokaw (1940)
Bob Marley (1945)

COMPATIBLE WITH
October 3–6

In common with most Aquarians, February 6 people have a profound need for liberty, not necessarily in the physical sense—although these people may be restless and have a love of travel and sporting pursuits—but more crucially in their intellectual pursuits and dealings with others. They hate feeling constrained by the demands of others and will rarely thrive in tightly run organizations or in relationships in which they feel that too great a level of commitment is being required of them. That having been said, they will often display remarkable focus when they find a topic or person that intrigues them, and will be driven by the almost irresistible urge to investigate further. For this reason they show a special aptitude for scientific research, into which their willingness to anticipate the unexpected and explore new avenues will be profitably channeled. More artistically inclined February 6 people may find similar satisfaction in the realms of music and literature.

Ironically, given their fiercely independent outlook, people born on this day prize the approval of others. This desire for popularity is generally not motivated by the desire to have their talents recognized, but rather by a more emotional craving to be cocooned by the love and admiration of those around them. Since they are intuitive beings, they will absorb the prevailing mood of the company within which they find themselves, and are prone to reflect it—a policy which may endear them to others in the short term, but which may ultimately gain them a reputation for inconstancy. Even so, others frequently feel affinity and enthusiasm for these people, and may elevate them to positions of leadership.

FEBRUARY 7

✳ ✳ ✳ ✳ ✳ ✳ ✳ ✳ ✳ ✳ ✳ ✳ ✳ ✳ ✳

♒ ☿   PROGRESSIVE PROBLEM-SOLVERS

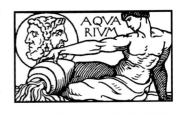

Those born on February 7 often tend to view the world around them in a somewhat naive way, in that they have an inherent sense of justice and respond on a deeply emotional level to any perceived social abuse. They are quick to identify solutions to problems, which they will then pursue with idealistic enthusiasm, but in their zeal they are unlikely to have thought their plans through sufficiently, and thus they're often seen as somewhat gullible.

The majority of February 7 people, who are quick-witted and original thinkers, are furthermore possessed with great communicative and persuasive skills, which they will characteristically employ to enlist the support of others. Such interpersonal talents indicate potentially successful salespeople, but they will often also thrive in social work. For those who can rein in their more idealistic propensities and offset them with practical and rational considerations, they can make gifted journalists and technicians, too.

A vital characteristic of these people is their instinctive aversion to authority. It is not that they lack discipline—far from it—just that they chafe under regulations with which they do not agree and, if constricted, they will typically resort to subversion as a manifestation of their independence. Self-starters, they will always perform best when given autonomy and freedom of action; this applies as much to their personal as to their professional lives. If this crucial criterion is satisfied, they make empathetic and even indulgent partners, and—since they always maintain a youthful outlook and tend to persuade rather than dictate—are often particularly good parents.

PLANETARY INFLUENCES
Ruling planet: Uranus
Second decan: Personal planet is Mercury

VIRTUES
Forward-thinking, energetic, analytical

VICES
Tendencies toward disappointment and disillusionment, cynical

CAREERS
Reporter, salesperson, social worker

SKILLS & APTITUDES
Endearing sense of optimism, problem-solving abilities, capacity for original thought

FAMOUS BIRTHS
Charles Dickens (1812)
Frederick Douglass (1817)
Laura Ingalls Wilder (1867)
Garth Brooks (1962)

COMPATIBLE WITH
October 3–6, January 8

FEBRUARY 8

✹ ✹ ✹ ✹ ✹ ✹ ✹ ✹ ✹ ✹ ✹ ✹ ✹

INTERPRETIVE ARTISANS ♅ ☿

PLANETARY INFLUENCES
Ruling planet: Uranus
Second decan: Personal planet is Mercury

VIRTUES
Personable, creative, accomplished

VICES
Anxious, concealing, vulnerable

CAREERS
Theater worker, poet, musician

SKILLS & APTITUDES
Vision, respect for colleagues, skilled at establishing consensus

FAMOUS BIRTHS
Jules Verne (1828)
Dimitri Ivanovich Mendeleyev (1834)
James Dean (1931)
John Williams (1932)

COMPATIBLE WITH
October 4–7, January 8–9

Inherent in February 8 people is a curious mixture of extreme intuition and technical flair which, if balanced, can make them extraordinarily successful in the world of the arts—especially if they were also born in the Chinese year of the tiger. Of further benefit to them in their musical, artistic, dramatic or literary pursuits are their strong imaginative powers, which, in combination with their instinctive ability to assess a situation and their gift of interpretation, will delight their audiences with their originality. Although intellectual freedom is as vital to these people as the air that is their element, they do not limit this requirement to themselves alone and are always ready to respect and consider other people's opinions. Furthermore, they shrink from confrontation, and therefore generally seek to smooth over conflict by finding a compromise.

It is their profound—occasionally almost psychic—sensitivity that drives these people to try to create peace and harmony around them. They delight others with their unique sense of humor and refreshing company, although they remain reserved and avoid personal topics of conversation. Their ability to effortlessly attune themselves to the moods of other people, as well as their limitless imaginations, leads them not only to identify themselves with others' situations, but also to envisage possibly negative future scenarios. Thus the easy-going façade that they generally adopt may mask a deep sense of distress and emotional turmoil. Their friends and partners should therefore give them unquestioning support and understanding in order to create the stable, loving background which is so important to them.

FEBRUARY 9

❊ ❊ ❊ ❊ ❊ ❊ ❊ ❊ ❊ ❊ ❊ ❊ ❊

♅ ☿   ENCOURAGING COUNSELORS

For many who are close to them, February 9 people appear to possess two diametrically opposed characteristics: whereas they are unfailingly optimistic while addressing other people's problems, when it comes to their own situation, they often appear unduly negative. This apparent inability to apply their considerable gift for encouraging others to themselves has many possible causes—perhaps it results from a feeling of fatalism founded on the accumulation of previously unhappy experiences, or it may be the manifestation of an unjustified sense of unworthiness.

Such is their natural vigor and appetite for tasting all that life has to offer that people born on February 9 will indeed be exposed to a wide variety of situations—with both positive and negative ramifications—in their lives, and will draw upon their wealth of experience to assist those who seek their advice.

The complex personal qualities displayed by those born on this day are the products of their great sensitivity and highly developed powers of perception and imagination. Practical as well as empathetic, they make gifted counselors, as well as excellent parents (especially in the case of February 9 women). Yet when they apply their talent for penetrating insight to their own personalities, they have a tendency to measure themselves against an impossible ideal and will inevitably consider themselves lacking. By reciprocating the love and support of these people, their friends and family members will give them the stability and sense of self-affirmation that they need if they are to thrive.

PLANETARY INFLUENCES
Ruling planet: Uranus
Second decan: Personal planet is Mercury

VIRTUES
Benevolent, devoted, insightful

VICES
Exploitable, overburdened, self-doubting

CAREERS
Counselor, pyschiatrist, child-development worker

SKILLS & APTITUDES
Strongly motivated by humanitarian concerns, devotion to worthy causes, sympathetic natures

FAMOUS BIRTHS
Carole King (1942)
Joe Pesci (1943)
Alice Walker (1944)
Mia Farrow (1945)

COMPATIBLE WITH
January 9–10, October 5–8

FEBRUARY 10

✶ ✶ ✶ ✶ ✶ ✶ ✶ ✶ ✶ ✶ ✶ ✶ ✶ ✶

ACHIEVEMENT–HUNTERS ♅ ♀

PLANETARY INFLUENCES
Ruling planet: Uranus
Third decan: Personal planet is Venus

VIRTUES
Original, ambitious, determined

VICES
Obsessive, insecure, isolated

CAREERS
Professional athlete, delegator, human-resources personnel

SKILLS & APTITUDES
Clear-sighted with regard to aspirations, multiple talents, single-minded focus

FAMOUS BIRTHS
Boris Pasternak (1890)
Jimmy "Schnozzle" Durante (1893)
Peter Allen (1944)
Mark Spitz (1950)

COMPATIBLE WITH
January 11, October 6–10

Those people born on February 10 are centered on achievement. It is vitally important to them to win the respect and recognition of others—possibly as a result of a sneaking sense of insecurity—and it is generally to this end that they concentrate their considerable talents. Blessed with great determination, imagination and a confident belief in their own potential, they will strive to make their mark on the world, secretly hoping to have their sense of self validated by the approval of others. Yet however great their ambition, these are not people who trample roughshod over others on their upward path; intuitive and kind, their aspiration is to achieve their goals and not to harm others in the process. Indeed, when channeled toward problem-solving, their gift of empathy and genuine desire for progress makes them notable peacemakers. Inevitably, however, these people will experience competition, particularly since many are drawn to active sports.

Because they are so oriented toward realizing their goals, these people may not pay adequate heed to their undoubted gift of empathy, and may inadvertently neglect those close to them, becoming emotionally isolated. They have a tendency to externalize their sensitivity, picking up the mood of others and in turn projecting it back again to gain approval—a propensity that suits many February 10 people to careers in the performing arts. Ironically, given that much of their energies are ultimately directed toward gaining the esteem and affirmation of others—whether or not they are consciously aware of it—they may find themselves admired from afar but lacking intimate friends to rejoice and share in their success.

FEBRUARY 11

✳ ✳ ✳ ✳ ✳ ✳ ✳ ✳ ✳ ✳ ✳ ✳ ✳ ✳ ✳

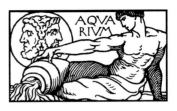

♅ ♀   HOUSEHOLD INVENTORS

The urge to implement progress is a vital component of February 11 people's personal makeup. With their complementary need for mental stimulation and natural capacity for problem-solving, they are constantly casting around for a challenge against which they can apply their talents and, because they are usually rather domesticated beings, will often find it close to home. Indeed, these cheerfully original and multitalented people have something of a knack for invention and, when also technically minded, enjoy nothing more than designing and constructing their own, improved version of a household appliance, or devising a scheme to make everyday life easier. Yet their wish to bring about improvement is not merely limited to their immediate sphere of influence, and people born on this day may, for example, become charity workers or dedicated volunteers, actively pioneering practical ways in which to help others.

Their originality and optimism frequently exert a magnetic influence on other people, who are drawn irresistibly to their affability and sense of fun. In turn, February 11 people, who are in any case naturally gregarious, relish the cut-and-thrust excitement of intellectual sparring. Extremely hospitable, they are welcoming and solicitous in their care of their guests. The combination of their great sociability and intellectual enthusiasms, however, can mean that they may not devote enough attention to the emotional needs of their family and friends, and they should therefore ensure that they do not neglect the less tangible needs of their nearest and dearest, especially as parents.

PLANETARY INFLUENCES
Ruling planet: Uranus
Third decan: Personal planet is Venus

VIRTUES
Creative, enthusiastic, helpful

VICES
Self-absorbed, forgetful, eccentric

CAREERS
Inventor, scholar, non-profit organizer

SKILLS & APTITUDES
Originality of thought, desire to see dreams realized, ability to invent and/or innovate

FAMOUS BIRTHS
Thomas Alva Edison (1847)
Leslie Nielson (1926)
Sheryl Crow (1963)
Jennifer Aniston (1969)

COMPATIBLE WITH
October 7–12

FEBRUARY 12

✳ ✳ ✳ ✳ ✳ ✳ ✳ ✳ ✳ ✳ ✳ ✳ ✳ ✳ ✳

ENLIGHTENED LEADERS ♅ ♀

PLANETARY INFLUENCES
Ruling planet: Uranus
Third decan: Personal planet is Venus

VIRTUES
Assured, objective, progressive

VICES
Polarizing, opinionated, uncompromising

CAREERS
Military command, legal aid, state representative

SKILLS & APTITUDES
Great powers of perception and original thought, progressive instincts, strong beliefs

FAMOUS BIRTHS
Charles Darwin and Abraham Lincoln (1809)
Franco Zeffirelli (1923)
Judy Blume (1938)

COMPATIBLE WITH
October 8–13

Admired by others for their inspirational qualities and concern for social justice, these people often find themselves in leadership positions. And while they are indeed sympathetic to the plight of others, February 12 people are motivated less by feelings of empathy than by a burning desire to right perceived wrongs and to set the world moving along a more enlightened course. When faced with a situation that requires resolution, they have an enviable facility to marshal the facts available to them, evaluate them impartially, and then determine an effective plan of action.

Such is their faith in the veracity of their moral judgments that people born on February 12 will rarely be deflected from their chosen path, and will work toward their goal with confidence and single-minded tenacity. Such qualities may make them ideally equipped for senior positions in military or political careers, especially if they were also born in the Chinese year of the dragon.

Yet although they are driven, these people are not all earnestness and ambitious zeal—far from it. They are also highly sensual beings, who have a real and instinctive appreciation for the good things in life, including the arts, fine cuisine and stimulating company. Indeed, most recognize that indulging their hedonistic side is a necessary release from the pressures of their intellectual or professional pursuits. They also typically make loving and concerned partners and parents, although they should beware of being overly paternalistic and should allow their children in particular to follow their own course.

FEBRUARY 13

✳ ✳ ✳ ✳ ✳ ✳ ✳ ✳ ✳ ✳ ✳ ✳ ✳ ✳

⛢ ♀ ☿   SPOTLIT TRENDSETTERS

February 13 people are often natural extroverts. Brimming with energy, sensation-seeking, and open and unaffected in just about everything they undertake, they are always difficult to ignore and relish being the center of attention. Their strong imaginative powers and irresistible urge to seek out new paths, combined with their boldness and a tendency toward exhibitionism, mean that these people are often regarded as trend-setters, especially within the realm of the arts. Indeed, these people are oriented toward interpersonal contact, and shine brightest when playing to an audience.

Whichever career they choose, it is likely that February 13 individuals will not flourish if they feel themselves constricted by petty rules and regulations, and they rarely find satisfaction in solitary pursuits that deprive them of acclaim.

Despite their need for intellectual stimulation and love of novelty, these good-hearted people are genuinely and deeply attached to their family and friends, desiring nothing more than their happiness and comfort. In turn, they require profound love and a large amount of emotional support, and may thereby unwittingly demand that those dear to them sacrifice a certain amount of independence of action and thought.

While they appreciate the material things that money can buy, and aspire to surround themselves with luxurious objects, this yearning is motivated less by a wish to flaunt wealth than by the sheer sensory pleasure derived from beauty and opulence.

PLANETARY INFLUENCES
Ruling planets Uranus
Third decan: Personal planet is Venus

VIRTUES
Exuberant, outgoing, quick-witted

VICES
Unruly, erratic, boisterous

CAREERS
Fashion designer, actor, performer

SKILLS & APTITUDES
Original and daring nature, propensity to make waves, inexhaustible vigor

FAMOUS BIRTHS
Rosa Parks (1913)
Kim Novak (1933)
George Segal (1934)
Peter Gabriel (1950)

COMPATIBLE WITH
October 8–14

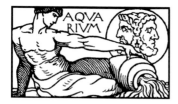

FEBRUARY 14

✿ ✿ ✿ ✿ ✿ ✿ ✿ ✿ ✿ ✿ ✿ ✿ ✿ ✿ ✿ ✿

LOFTY APPRECIATORS ♅ ♀

PLANETARY INFLUENCES
Ruling planet: Uranus
Third decan: Personal planet is Venus

VIRTUES
Incisive, articulate, sensual

VICES
Impatient, demanding, frustrated

CAREERS
Chef, business owner, consultant

SKILLS & APTITUDES
Strong intellect, highly developed communication skills, impeccable taste

FAMOUS BIRTHS
Jack Benny (1894)
Florence Henderson (1934)
Carl Bernstein (1944)
Gregory Hines (1946)

COMPATIBLE WITH
October 9–15

February 14 people think quickly and analytically, express themselves succinctly and often wittily, and are progressive—both in their ceaseless personal need to move onward and upward, and in their desire to set the world to rights. While the purposeful and clear-thinking manner in which they direct their considerable energies frequently garners them admiration, their impatience with those who think and act less quickly may well intimidate others, usually with the effect of driving them away. Furthermore, their biting sense of humor, when combined with their great articulateness can, if not checked, be a deeply wounding weapon.

February 14 people must remember to respect the sensibilities of other people—especially those closest to them—and anticipate the consequence of impulsive words, however satisfying their impact may be in the short term. Should they fail to keep this in mind, they may end up isolated.

Yet these people are not solely governed by their intellectual qualities. They are extremely receptive to their instincts, and respond on a profound level to such sensual stimuli as a wonderful painting, a haunting piece of music, a gourmet dish or a fine vintage wine. Such is the varied nature of their talents that they have the potential to be equally successful in the artistic or scientific fields, but their compulsion for action gives them an especial aptitude for such business spheres as manufacturing. They enjoy making money, but mainly so that they have the financial means to be able to surround themselves with beautiful objects.

FEBRUARY 15

✲ ✲ ✲ ✲ ✲ ✲ ✲ ✲ ✲ ✲ ✲ ✲ ✲ ✲

♅ ♆ ♀ HAPPY EXPLORERS

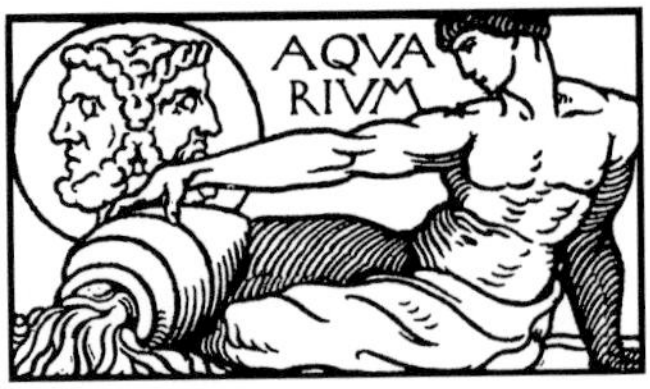

Perhaps the overriding characteristics inherent in February 15 people are their need for stimulation and their related enthusiasm for exploring new areas of interest, both in their intellectual pursuits, and—since these energetic people often feel a strong connection with the natural world—also in the more physical sense. They furthermore rely to a large extent upon their highly developed instincts in their dealings with other people, attuning themselves to others' moods and most of the time responding with kindness and courtesy.

Motivated by their desire to bring happiness to those closest to them, as well as to the wider world, they will employ their skills of communication and diplomacy to smooth over potentially explosive situations. They are thus greatly valued by their friends and family, who may, however, become irritated by what is sometimes perceived as a certain waywardness and aversion to being hemmed in by parameters that have been dictated by others.

Because they are multitalented, people born on this day will find professional success in a variety of fields—science, the creative arts, outdoor and sporting pursuits, as well as business—just as long as they are allowed to follow their own, idiosyncratic course.

If they feel themselves to be stifled by external constrictions, February 15 people have a marked propensity to escape into the more congenial world of the senses, compensating for their frustration by indulging their love for entertainment, company and the good life, especially if they were also born in the Chinese year of the rabbit.

PLANETARY INFLUENCES
Ruling planets: Uranus and Neptune
Third decan: Personal planet is Venus
Second cusp: Aquarius with Piscean tendencies

VIRTUES
Charming, enthusiastic, kind

VICES
Overexcited, undisciplined, frustrated

CAREERS
Communications worker, park ranger, management

SKILLS & APTITUDES
Genuine desire to help others, originality, connection to nature

FAMOUS BIRTHS
Galileo Galilei (1564)
Susan B. Anthony (1820)
Cesar Romero (1907)
Chris Farley (1964)

COMPATIBLE WITH
March 11, October 11–17

FEBRUARY 16

✻ ✻ ✻ ✻ ✻ ✻ ✻ ✻ ✻ ✻ ✻ ✻ ✻

THE WORLD'S CAREGIVERS ♅ ♆ ♀

February 16 people respect life in all its forms, and are troubled by manifestations of social injustice, since they feel an instinctive empathy and a burning desire to effect improvement. Yet although these people may be guided by their intuition and compassion, they rarely act impulsively, preferring instead to apply their highly developed powers of intellectual analysis and foresight to a problem before deciding upon their preferred course of action. Furthermore—perhaps because they are so perceptive—they have an impressive capacity to be realistic, both in their assessment of others and in their personal goals. Such qualities, along with their originality and energy, give them the potential to perform particularly well in business, especially if they are able to take charge. Since these people are profoundly receptive to the intuitive, life-enhancing quality inherent in the arts, they may also find success as entertainers and performers.

Many February 16 people consciously control their propensity toward extreme sensitivity, applying a rational system of checks and balances to their emotional responses in what may be a self-defensive mechanism. Indeed, such is their concern for others that they may believe they will be overwhelmed with sadness and anxiety unless they maintain a level of emotional detachment. They have a tendency, however, to internalize their deepest feelings, and may therefore become beset with feelings of inadequacy, while their quality of vivid foresight may cause them to resist, or even avoid, emotional commitment. Their partners should therefore be patient, considerate and encouraging in their treatment of these sensitive people.

FEBRUARY 17

♅ ♆ ♀ **Crusading Motivators**

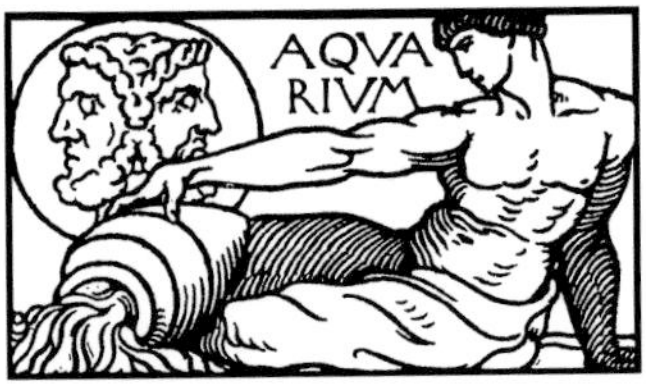

These people are often extraordinarily sensitive individuals, who never miss a detail, nuance or undertone of a situation. Their inherent powers of perception, combined with their soft hearts and their profoundly empathetic identification with the weak and defenseless, are rare qualities, but may often cause emotional complications for February 17 people. Indeed, as children they will often be deeply hurt by the careless words or actions of others, and their parents should recognize this propensity and support them with consistently kind and considerate behavior and reinforcement. As they mature, they will be forced to develop self-protective strategies and will mask their vulnerability with a veneer of toughness, but although they may often thus present a hardened image, their sensitivity will always remain an integral part of their natures.

Building a better world is of vital importance to those born on this day, and this desire to effect improvement may take a variety of forms, depending on the particular talents of the individual. Although they are not especially organized types, they will typically devote their passions toward implementing national, social, physical or technical ideals in a characteristically determined manner. Because they are such firm believers in individual freedom, and, being free spirits, chafe at being subjected to the unimaginative regimes of others' making, they will be unhappy (and possibly insecure) unless they are allowed to operate either independently or within an unstructured and enlightened framework.

Planetary Influences
Ruling planets: Uranus and Neptune
Third decan: Personal planet is Venus
Second cusp: Aquarius with Piscean tendencies

Virtues
Sensitive, trusting, determined

Vices
Susceptible, emotional, inflexible

Careers
Motivational speaker, IT specialist, human-rights activist

Skills & Aptitudes
Empathy for the downtrodden, instinctual responses, crusading energy

Famous Births
Yasser Arafat (1929)
Rene Russo (1954)
Lou Diamond Phillips (1962)
Michael Jordan (1963)

Compatible With
March 12–13, October 13–20

FEBRUARY 18

✸ ✸ ✸ ✸ ✸ ✸ ✸ ✸ ✸ ✸ ✸ ✸ ✸ ✸

SINCERE HERALDS   ♅ ♆ ♀

PLANETARY INFLUENCES
Ruling planets: Uranus and Neptune
Third decan: Personal planet is Venus
Second cusp: Aquarius with Piscean tendencies

VIRTUES
Fasighted, tenacious, incisive

VICES
Exclusive, unrealistic, alienating

CAREERS
Leadership trainer, investment analyst, negotiator

SKILLS & APTITUDES
Guided by the heart, single-minded in approach, positive personality

FAMOUS BIRTHS
Toni Morrison (1931)
Yoko Ono (1933)
John Travolta (1954)
Molly Ringwald (1968)

COMPATIBLE WITH
March 13–14, October 14–22

Their strong convictions—which are often shaped by their hearts rather than their heads—may give February 18 people an idiosyncratic and optimistic view of the world which, although altruistic, may not be entirely realistic. These sensitive, spiritual people are quick to perceive those areas in which humanity's lot could be improved and, being idealistic and determined types, will energetically marshal their talents to the cause. Since they are inspired by the desire to realize their sometimes grandiose utopian visions, and impatiently refuse to allow themselves to be distracted by petty details in the urgent promotion of their aims, those born on this day have the potential to achieve remarkable success. Although they care deeply for those closest to them, and, indeed, have a profound need to receive their support and encouragement, they may inadvertently neglect their loved ones in favor of their cherished cause, particularly if they are men.

Despite their propensity to pursue their ambitions with apparently boundless vigor and tenacity, these people are not solely given over to their instinctual responses. They have a tendency to rationalize their predilections, and will evolve a sense of certainty from knowing that they have verified their instincts by means of their talents for analysis and perception. Moreover, they will listen to other people's points of view and, if convinced of their veracity, will adopt certain tenets. Because they are charismatic and inspiring figures, others are drawn to them for leadership, and these multitalented individuals will therefore flourish in any professional discipline, provided they can follow their own path.

⚹ PISCES

February 19 to March 20

RULING PLANET: *Neptune (traditionally Jupiter)*   ELEMENT: *Mutable water*
SYMBOL: *Two fishes*   POLARITY: *Negative (feminine)*   COLORS: *White, mauve, red*
PHYSICAL CORRESPONDENCE: *Feet*
STONES: *Coral, jasper, bloodstone, white opal, pearl, amethyst, moonstone*
FLOWERS: *Poppy, water lily, pink, thyme*

Many astrological traditions have identified this constellation with a marine creature. The ancient Greeks and Persians envisaged Pisces as a single fish, as did Hindu astrologers, who linked it to Vishnu's *avatar* as a fish, Matsya. It was the Babylonians who first conceived of the constellation as a pair of fishes. An ancient Greco-Roman myth tells of how the ogre Typhon pursued the goddess Aphrodite/Venus and her son Eros/Cupid until they escaped him by transforming themselves into fishes. Because Aphrodite/Venus was born from the sea, and since the sign is ruled by the sea god Neptune (who supplanted Jupiter following the planet's discovery in 1846), it is appropriate that the element of water governs this sign. It's also associated with the Moon, whose ability to regulate the oceanic tides links it unequivocally with water. The twin curves of Pisces' sigil mimic the crescents that represent the waxing and waning of the Moon. This duality is mirrored within the annual cycle, for since Pisces' realm of influence is the last month of winter, it simultaneously looks back over the past agricultural year and forward to the next.

Pisces represents duality, often taken to denote the spiritual and worldly realms. The Piscean personality may be symbolically linked to a fish swimming through the water seeking enlightenment, but the potential for undirected restlessness and emotional instability is also indicated. Many iconic representations of Pisces show the two fishes bound together by the Nodus, or silver cord, which represents the link to the spirit world, suggesting Pisceans' dreamy natures.

FEBRUARY 19

✻ ✻ ✻ ✻ ✻ ✻ ✻ ✻ ✻ ✻ ✻ ✻ ✻ ✻ ✻

INDIVIDUALISTIC HUMANITARIANS ♆ ♅ ♃

PLANETARY INFLUENCES
Ruling planets: Neptune and Uranus
First decan: Personal planets are
Neptune and Jupiter
First cusp: Pisces with Aquarian
tendencies

VIRTUES
Problem-solving, energetic,
global-thinking

VICES
Addictive, suppressing, impersonal

CAREERS
Carer, social worker, entertainer

SKILLS & APTITUDES
Perceptiveness, practical problem-
solving, thirst for challenges

FAMOUS BIRTHS
Nicolaus Copernicus (1473)
Smokey Robinson (1940)
Cass Elliot (1943)
Jeff Daniels (1955)

COMPATIBLE WITH
February 19–22, March 12–14

February 19 people value independence of thought and action and many exhibit a near-compulsive need to impose the stamp of their individuality on everything that they undertake. Although they are undoubtedly sensitive to the needs of other people, they usually direct their concern more toward humanity as a collective entity rather than toward individuals. Like the rather global quality of their empathy, their powers of perception are conditioned by their predilection to rational thought, and they therefore cultivate a rather lofty air of impartiality. Yet despite the impersonal projection of their empathetic insights, February 19 people nurture deep aspirations to affect progress and contribute to the greater good. For this reason they often make outstanding social and care workers who do not allow themselves to become ineffective through overidentification with their clients, as well as gifted environmental campaigners. The more artistically inclined among them—and many have a mystical side—possess the enviable potential to delight and inspire others with the power and focus of their performances.

Because they are able to balance empathy and rational idealism, these people typically exude a sense of stability. They make responsible and supportive parents—particularly if they are women—whose natural sense of authority, combined with their respect for individual opinions, draws others to them. On the other hand, their quest for knowledge and need to be challenged can lead them to take increasingly hair-raising risks, bolstered as they are by their self-confidence and faith in their own abilities.

FEBRUARY 20

✳ ✳ ✳ ✳ ✳ ✳ ✳ ✳ ✳ ✳ ✳ ✳ ✳ ✳

Ψ ♓ ♃   SECRET ATTENTION-SEEKERS

It is ironic that although those born on this day are thoughtful and highly oriented toward pleasing other people, they may sometimes cause hurt to those who are drawn to them. For while they usually feel a global concern for the welfare of others, it is the acclaim and validation of their contemporaries that brings them security, and in seeking this recognition they may disregard the sensibilities of individuals. These people are intuitively perceptive, and find it easy to attune themselves to the moods of those around them, adjusting their responses accordingly.

February 20 people are possessed with considerable personal charm, which they may sometimes consciously exploit in order to manipulate others in the furtherance of their ambitions—although those ambitions are often related to helping others. Given such driving personal qualities, these people have the potential to achieve great success in the caring professions, but especially in the artistic sphere, where they can employ their sensitivity and energy and in turn receive the attention and applause that they so deeply desire.

Coupled with this yearning to be appreciated for their achievements is a need to be stimulated, to experience novel sensations and excitement. February 20 people have an urge to travel, and will often choose to work in tourism, where they can satisfy their sense of adventure while also retaining the interpersonal contact that is so important to them. This restlessness may cause them difficulties in their personal lives, however, especially since they have a fear of emotional commitment in the first place.

PLANETARY INFLUENCES
Ruling planets: Neptune and Uranus
First decan: Personal planets are Neptune and Jupiter
First cusp: Pisces with Aquarian tendencies

VIRTUES
Charismatic, sympathetic, perceptive

VICES
Restless, needy, hypersensitive

CAREERS
Nurse, daycare worker, art teacher

SKILLS & APTITUDES
Emotional intelligence, originality, energy

FAMOUS BIRTHS
Sidney Poitier (1924)
Kelsey Grammer (1955)
Cindy Crawford (1966)
Kurt Cobain (1967)
Olivia Rodrigo (2003)

COMPATIBLE WITH
February 19–23, March 12–14

FEBRUARY 21

❊ ❊ ❊ ❊ ❊ ❊ ❊ ❊ ❊ ❊ ❊ ❊ ❊ ❊

SOFT-CENTERED SOULS   ♆ ♅ ♃

PLANETARY INFLUENCES
Ruling planets: Neptune and Uranus
First decan: Personal planets are
   Neptune and Jupiter
First cusp: Pisces with Aquarian
   tendencies

VIRTUES
Caring, self-perceptive, trusting

VICES
Steely, suppressed, guarded

CAREERS
Research scientist, builder, artist

SKILLS & APTITUDES
Intuition, high standards, faith in
colleagues and team members

FAMOUS BIRTHS
Cardinal John Newman (1801)
W.H. Auden (1907)
Rue McClanahan (1936)
Jennifer Love Hewitt (1979)

COMPATIBLE WITH
February 19–24, March 13–14

Their profound sensitivity is the defining characteristic of February 21 people, although this may not be immediately apparent to those who do not know them well, for they may have developed a tough outer shell in order to protect themselves from experiencing pain. These inherently guileless and trusting people instinctively think the best of others, an endearing characteristic which, unfortunately, means that unscrupulous individuals are liable to abuse their confidence and take advantage of them. Having suffered as a result of such disappointments, those born on this day will therefore consciously harden themselves, building a protective wall around their soft centers. They must, however, ensure that they do not take this strategy too far and become overly cynical—especially if they are men—for their emotions are at the core of their being.

When they have achieved the perfect balance between their intuitive and emotional urges and their rational consciousness, these highly original people have the potential to make outstanding artists and craftsmen in particular, although their intellectual inquisitiveness, predilection toward careful consideration and natural spirit of adventurousness also indicate possible success in the fields of science, business and research. They should, however, ensure that their inherent restlessness, as well as their fear of being hurt if they commit themselves to one individual totally, does not prevent them from finding the fulfillment in their closest personal relationships that is so vital to them.

FEBRUARY 22

♆ ♅ ♃

RATIONAL ALTRUISTS

Strong-willed and determined, February 22 people are inspired by high humanitarian ideals, toward the achievement of which they direct their considerable powers of mental clarity and great energy. These are sensitive individuals, whose empathy with the less fortunate and concurrent desire to improve their lot drives them to formulate a well-thought-out plan of action and then implement it with characteristic tenacity.

Although those born on this day respond to their instincts, they rarely allow themselves to be deflected from pursuing the realization of their aims by strictly rational means. This combination of qualities is a particularly powerful one, and suits them to a variety of careers, including those within the realm of scientific research—especially if they were also born in the Chinese year of the rooster—the military and politics, but also within the performing arts.

These are steady and responsible people, who are relied upon by their families and friends for the advice and support that they rarely fail to provide. Because they are also generally self-reliant types and desire to protect their loved ones from anxiety, they may, however, fail to share their personal worries with those closest to them, thereby denying themselves emotional comfort and release. A further danger that results from their lofty ideals and high personal standards is that they will inevitably experience disappointment when others fail to live up to them, a feeling that they find hard to conceal. In some cases, this could lead to depression, so it's important they learn to relax.

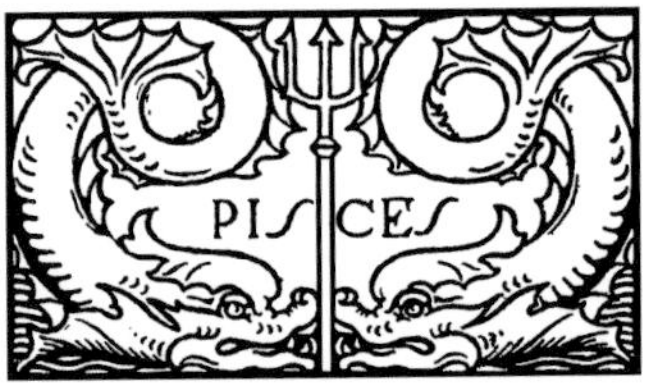

PLANETARY INFLUENCES
Ruling planets: Neptune and Uranus
First decan: Personal planets are Neptune and Jupiter
First cusp: Pisces with Aquarian tendencies

VIRTUES
Focused, compassionate, principled

VICES
Overburdened, autonomous, disappointed

CAREERS
Military recruiter, research scientist, politician

SKILLS & APTITUDES
Rationality, integrity, drive

FAMOUS BIRTHS
George Washington (1732)
Eric Gill (1872)
Julie Walters (1950)
Drew Barrymore (1975)
Rajon Rondo (1986)

COMPATIBLE WITH
February 19–25, March 14

FEBRUARY 23

✱ ✱ ✱ ✱ ✱ ✱ ✱ ✱ ✱ ✱ ✱ ✱ ✱

THOUGHTFUL GO–GETTERS   ♆ ♃

PLANETARY INFLUENCES
Ruling planet: Neptune
First decan: Personal planets are Neptune and Jupiter

VIRTUES
Perceptive, determined, practical

VICES
Sulky, resentful, overthinking

CAREERS
Poet, performer, business leader or manager

SKILLS & APTITUDES
Pragmatism, empathy, imagination

FAMOUS BIRTHS
George Frederic Handel (1685)
Victor Fleming (1883)
Peter Fonda (1939)
Emily Blunt (1983)

COMPATIBLE WITH
February 20–25, August 29–31

Although other people are drawn to them for their cheerful, "can-do" approach to life, underneath their confident exterior February 23 people are in reality less optimistic and certain than their projected image suggests. Those born on this day are blessed with both great analytical skills and tenacity, and gain much satisfaction from worrying away at an issue, examining every angle and thinking through all the possible permutations and consequences of a proposed solution. Their self-confidence is born of a recognition of their talents, and also of an awareness of the respect and affection that they engender in others. These characteristics make them particularly well equipped to attain success in business, where their positive approach and natural gregariousness will further endear them to their coworkers. Since their intellectual talents are complemented by profound sensitivity, they also have the potential to make their marks as artists, writers or actors.

Geared as they are toward smoothing the path for other people, unless they feel as though they are supported by the uncritical love and encouragement of their loved ones, however, the sensitivity of those born on this day may be manifested in negative feelings. If they feel that their efforts are not being appreciated by others, they will feel exploited and may therefore become resentful. Another disadvantage of being simultaneously mentally perceptive, imaginative and responsive to their intuitive side is that not only do they have the propensity to envisage a variety of scenarios, but they also have a natural predilection to focusing on the less positive ones.

FEBRUARY 24

✳ ✳ ✳ ✳ ✳ ✳ ✳ ✳ ✳ ✳ ✳ ✳ ✳ ✳

Ψ ♃   HUMANITY'S HELPERS

Others turn to February 24 people when they are in need of a helping hand—be it practical aid or emotional support—knowing that not only will they not be turned away, but that they will receive committed and sympathetic assistance. Those born on this day generally have a real desire to engage their energies on behalf of their fellow human beings. Their motivations may vary. It may be that they have experienced unhappiness at the hands of others—especially during their childhoods—and are determined to save others from a similar plight; many believe in the power of karma and the notion that they will benefit spiritually from their unselfishness; some have a real humanitarian vision; while others experience the superiority of martyrdom from self-sacrifice.

Whatever it is that fuels them, these people will find satisfaction in such public services as the military or police force, or else in the caring and medical professions, where they can feel that they are actively doing good. The empathy that informs many of their actions is a manifestation of the extreme sensitivity of these people, but these are not vague and dreamy types—on the contrary, they are resolutely practical and will harness their intuitive tendencies to their impressive capacity for self-discipline and intellectual clarity. There are twin dangers inherent in this devotion to others, however: that the no less pressing needs of those closest to February 24 people are neglected in favor of the greater good, or that they suppress their own, less "worthy"—but no less important—urges.

PLANETARY INFLUENCES
Ruling planet: Neptune
First decan: Personal planets are Neptune and Jupiter

VIRTUES
Vigorous, empathic, practical

VICES
Forgetful, polarizing, neglectful

CAREERS
Police officer, doctor, nurse

SKILLS & APTITUDES
Single-minded focus, philanthropic attitude, interest in others

FAMOUS BIRTHS
Wilhelm Grimm (1786)
Barry Bostwick (1945)
Edward James Olmos (1947)
Alain Prost (1955)

COMPATIBLE WITH
February 21–26, August 29–31

FEBRUARY 25

✳ ✳ ✳ ✳ ✳ ✳ ✳ ✳ ✳ ✳ ✳ ✳ ✳ ✳ ✳

SOCIAL–JUSTICE ADVOCATES ♆ ♃

February 25 people nurture passionately held convictions and ideals, world views that are dictated by their emotional response to perceived social injustices and abuses of power. They are profoundly empathetic to the vulnerable—and their pity is often directed toward animals—who arouse in them a fiercely protective instinct and a single-minded desire to reverse their situation. Although they are tenacious, perceptive and visionary, they are guided more by their emotions than by dispassionate, intellectual considerations, and will therefore often act impulsively and thereby sabotage their efforts through their overhasty and rash enthusiasm. Moreover, since they are convinced that theirs is the right course of action, they may contemptuously dismiss those who express their reservations, not believing it worth the effort to recruit a potential convert by patient and reasoned argument; this dismissive attitude is particularly pronounced during adolescence.

Other people admire them for their energy and ardent commitment, but may regard them as being radical to the point of eccentricity and erratic when disappointment causes them to move on to a new crusade. Friends and family members should be tolerant of, and patient with, these people, always keeping in mind the truly noble motivations that fuel them. When these people accept that there are limitations to everything, and become more realistic and self-disciplined, they will often fulfill their enormous potential in such intellectual fields as scientific research, but also within the artistic world.

FEBRUARY 26

✳ ✳ ✳ ✳ ✳ ✳ ✳ ✳ ✳ ✳ ✳ ✳ ✳ ✳

Ψ ♃　　　　MASKED STRATEGISTS

The authoritative, somewhat detached, persona that these people often adopt masks a profoundly sensitive and caring nature. Thus while others stand in awe of the rather impersonal and abrupt image that those born on this day project, underneath the façade lies an intuitive and compassionate being. Indeed, their natural powers of perception and moral certainty arouse in February 26 people a determined desire to improve the world around them.

Rather than impulsively launching themselves into their mission, February 26 people prefer to stand back, rationally consider the merits of a strategy, and then work quietly but tenaciously toward its implementation. Personal independence is vital to those born on this day, and they demand to be allowed to follow their consciences. They are not willing to compromise their beliefs, but as a result, they often have a tendency to take themselves a little too seriously—which can be annoying for those around them.

The natural empathy that informs these people's conscious actions remains a guiding principle, and the combination of humanitarianism, shrewd pragmatism and originality that is inherent in these people suits them for careers in the judiciary, as well as in the arts, where they will typically put forward their critical message in a misleadingly palatable—but in fact subversive—form. In their personal lives, they are steady and caring, but they do have a tendency to be authoritarian or caustic when those close to them appear to deviate from the straight and narrow path of which they approve.

PLANETARY INFLUENCES
Ruling planet: Neptune
First decan: Personal planets are Neptune and Jupiter

VIRTUES
Compassionate, thoughtful, independent

VICES
Rigid, isolated, opinionated

CAREERS
Court clerk, attorney, judge

SKILLS & APTITUDES
Sensitivity, serious-mindedness, natural empathy

FAMOUS BIRTHS
Victor Hugo (1802)
"Buffalo Bill" Cody (1846)
"Fats" Domino (1928)
Johnny Cash (1932)
Corinne Bailey Rae (1979)

COMPATIBLE WITH
February 24–28

FEBRUARY 27

✳ ✳ ✳ ✳ ✳ ✳ ✳ ✳ ✳ ✳ ✳ ✳ ✳

PASSIONATE BUSINESSPEOPLE   ♆ ♃

PLANETARY INFLUENCES
Ruling planet: Neptune
First decan: Personal planets are
Neptune and Jupiter

VIRTUES
Independent, observant,
inspirational

VICES
Distracted, impulsive, irrational

CAREERS
Entrepreneur, entertainer,
marketing executive

SKILLS & APTITUDES
Confidence, passion, charisma

FAMOUS BIRTHS
John Steinbeck (1902)
Elizabeth Taylor (1932)
Ralph Nader (1934)
Chelsea Clinton (1980)

COMPATIBLE WITH
February 25–29, March 1

....
....
....

As these pragmatic and charismatic people stride confidently through their professional lives, others admire them for their apparent sense of certainty and purpose, but may secretly wonder why it is that they often have such tumultuous personal lives. The answer to this apparent contradiction is that those born on this day are highly responsive to their often explosive emotions, and while they may successful conquer their impulse to listen exclusively to their hearts in impersonal situations, they find this strategy virtually impossible in their dealings with those closest to them—in those relationships that are, after all, founded on passionate emotions. Another exacerbating factor is that while these people demand the right of freedom of action and thought for themselves, they expect total commitment and support from others. Those who wish to build a stable relationship with February 27 people should therefore recognize this inconsistency and avoid head-on confrontations in favor of more subtle approaches.

While they may be prone to extremely impulsive behavior when "off duty," these people tend to show greater focus when it comes to their careers. Hand-in-hand with their sensitivity go highly developed powers of perception, and those born on this day find it easy to absorb all the various elements of a situation and then decide on the appropriate course of action. They perform particularly well in business ventures, where their empathy for others will also stand them in good stead when working as part of a team, but they will probably find greatest fulfillment in the artistic sphere, where they can project their intuition outward to inform or entertain other people.

FEBRUARY 28

✳ ✳ ✳ ✳ ✳ ✳ ✳ ✳ ✳ ✳ ✳ ✳ ✳

Ψ ♃ HYPERACTIVE ADVENTURERS

February 28 people are adventurers on the sea of life, following wherever their impulses lead them in their search for the gratification of sensual excitement. These highly intuitive people will always their instincts, and, since they tend to be hyperactive as well as hypersensitive, will bounce from one enthusiasm to the next with breathtaking speed, particularly if they were also born in the Chinese year of the horse. This sensation-seeking behavior is compounded by a horror of standing still and of the risk of boredom. Although more steady people are drawn to those born on this day for the hedonistic excitement that they generate, they will rarely be able to stand the erratic pace. February 28 people are regarded with deep affection by others, especially since they wish to please and entertain those around them, and harbor no ulterior motives. They may find it difficult to stay committed in their personal relationships, however.

It is vitally important that these endearing people learn to develop greater self-control, otherwise they will find themselves spiraling on a path to self-destruction at breakneck speed, and parents of February 28 people should do their utmost to instill a sense of realism—as well as an understanding of cause and effect—in their children when young. Those born on this day will thrive in professions in which they can channel their vigor and natural inquisitiveness along a more focused course; tourism is a particularly propitious field for them, while the arts and sport will allow them to fulfill their twin needs for sensuality and action. Financial careers should be avoided, since these people have a tendency to be as extravagant with their money as they are with their emotions.

PLANETARY INFLUENCES
Ruling planet: Neptune
First decan: Personal planets are Neptune and Jupiter

VIRTUES
Charismatic, energetic, pioneering

VICES
Erratic, undisciplined, lacking in self-control

CAREERS
Tour guide, sports trainer, photographer

SKILLS & APTITUDES
Charm, enthusiasm, creativity

FAMOUS BIRTHS
Zero Mostel (1915)
Tommy Tune (1939)
Mario Andretti (1940)
Bernadette Peters (1948)

COMPATIBLE WITH
February 26–29, March 1–2

FEBRUARY 29

❊ ❊ ❊ ❊ ❊ ❊ ❊ ❊ ❊ ❊ ❊ ❊

ETERNAL YOUTHS   ♆ ♃

PLANETARY INFLUENCES
Ruling planet: Neptune
First decan: Personal planets are
  Neptune and Jupiter

VIRTUES
Original, pragmatic, optimistic

VICES
Immature, aggressive, excessive

CAREERS
Investment banker, arts
entrepreneur, actor

SKILLS & APTITUDES
Self-reliance, confidence,
willingness to embrace risk

FAMOUS BIRTHS
Gioacchino Rossini (1792)
Jimmy Dorsey (1904)
Dennis Farina (1944)
Tony Robbins (1960)
Ja Rule (1976)

COMPATIBLE WITH
February 27–29, March 1–2

....
....
....

From their earliest years, these people will have felt different from those around them, and, indeed, so they are, since they can only celebrate their true birthdate every four years. As a further result of this quirk of the calendar, they will have had to learn the value of pragmatism and of entering into the spirit of compromise by choosing an alternative date upon which to mark the passing of the years. A positive side effect of their unusual birthday, however, is that in chronological terms these people are technically still children when they reach middle age, and adolescents in old age. Their characteristic youthful vibrancy, sense of optimism and risk-taking, and determination to experience all that life has to offer moreover seems to confirm their youthfulness in years.

Their natural tendency to indulge their senses in hedonistic pursuits is therefore tempered by a more grounded intellectual attitude to life, although February 29 people still retain their restlessness and inquisitive qualities, which are augmented by a streak of daring.

Those born on this particular date have a strong sense that they are special individuals, a belief that manifests in their self-confidence, as well as in a compulsion to make others appreciate their unique qualities. They will therefore flourish in any competitive profession—especially if they are men—where they can harness their instincts, realism and need to prove their worth. In their personal lives, they should, however, try to temper any aggressive tendencies and recognize that others already accept them as they are. Failure to work on these tendencies will result in alienating those around them.

MARCH 1

Ψ ☽   LAID-BACK ARTISTS

Beneath the charming and easy-going manner of March 1 people lies a real concern for other people's well-being, and with social issues and humanitarian causes. These people are sensitive in the extreme, but instinctively recognize that acting impulsively, or revealing their often tumultuous emotions, may result in disastrous consequences. By controlling the more erratic urges that may lead them into irreversible situations, and by cultivating a calm and nonconfrontational approach, they therefore not only provide themselves with a safety net, but inspire confidence in others, although they may not feel this confidence themselves. Indeed, when their problems appear insurmountable, the rising panic felt by those born on this day may cause them to abandon the situation altogether and resort to a comforting strategy of cutting themselves off from the cause of their emotional distress by ignoring it or moving on.

Despite the propensity toward self-doubt and depression that is engendered by their sensitivity, these people are blessed with remarkably positive qualities. As well as possessing great personal magnetism, they have a highly original intellectual approach and an optimism that is inspired by their fascination with new and stimulating ideas. In their professional lives they will generally find personal satisfaction as artists, or when they run their own enterprises, in which they can operate independently of alienating regulations and exploit their imaginative concepts profitably. And when they achieve the financial rewards that they unashamedly relish, they will generously share the fruits of their success with those whose unstinting emotional support and affection has played such a crucial part in its achievement.

PLANETARY INFLUENCES
Ruling planet: Neptune
Second decan: Personal planet is Moon

VIRTUES
Imaginative, sensitive, thoughtful

VICES
Overwhelmed, anxious, detached

CAREERS
Artist, small-business owner, freelancer

SKILLS & APTITUDES
Independence, sound instincts, creativity

FAMOUS BIRTHS
Frédéric Chopin (1810)
David Niven (1910)
Harry Belafonte (1927)
Ron Howard (1954)

COMPATIBLE WITH
February 27–29, March 1–3

PISCE/

MARCH 2

✳ ✳ ✳ ✳ ✳ ✳ ✳ ✳ ✳ ✳ ✳ ✳ ✳ ✳

DEEP DREAMERS   ♆ ☽

Still rivers run deep, as the saying goes, and this maxim certainly applies to those born on March 2. These people are deeply intuitive beings, who generally would rather explore their own inner world of thoughts and dreams than launch themselves at the challenges of the real world. Indeed, although they are often passionate about social issues, these gentle people detest the emotional upset that direct confrontation causes them, and will do their utmost to promote a peaceful resolution to problems—if they have not previously managed to avoid them altogether. It therefore goes without saying that March 2 people will be unhappy in competitive business situations, and are better suited to the artistic world. However, they are also suited to those careers, such as politics or the caring professions, in which they feel that their services can make a real contribution to the welfare of others.

Despite—or perhaps because of—their rather introverted personalities, these people crave the security that results from happy and stable personal relationships. They have a deep need to receive the unconditional love of those closest to them, which they will reciprocate loyally. The unstinting devotion—and even uncritical adoration—that they have a propensity to direct toward their partners, children or individuals that inspire them, creates the risk of stifling the objects of their affection, however. These people should therefore try to develop a more detached approach within their personal liaisons. Indeed, a less dependent attitude to others will benefit them in all areas of their lives.

MARCH 3

Ψ ☽   BALANCED PARTNERS

It may surprise those who do not know them intimately that beneath the confident and direct manner of people born on March 3 lie deeply sensitive and reflective beings. Indeed, some of these people may consciously have cultivated a brisk, no-nonsense approach to shield their emotional vulnerability and their unfounded sense of insecurity. In general, however, they are naturally inclined toward combining their considerable powers of intellectual clarity with their instincts.

The inherent ability of March 3 people to unite such qualities of compassion and rational perspicuity is a rare gift, and augurs well for success in such careers as charity or social work, in which they can promote their desire for human progress by means of a carefully considered and logical plan of action. This conjunction of sensitivity, rationality and discipline also bestows great potential for artistic pursuits or innovation upon those born on this day.

These empathetic and caring people make loyal and affectionate partners and parents, supplying the right balance of emotional support and domestic organization. It is essential, however, that they do not allow their propensity for intellectual criticism to become overdeveloped. Because—whether they realize it or not—these people are motivated by their emotional responses, they have a tendency to promote the beliefs that are supported by their intuition with convincing justifications, and then to discredit counterarguments by picking holes in them. They should beware of allowing themselves to become dismissive of others.

PLANETARY INFLUENCES
Ruling planet: Neptune
Second decan: Personal planet is
Moon

VIRTUES
Gentle, incisive, tenacious

VICES
Dismissive, resistant, insecure

CAREERS
Caseworker, charity advocate,
fundraiser

SKILLS & APTITUDES
Self-discipline, competence,
caring attitude

FAMOUS BIRTHS
Alexander Graham Bell (1847)
Jean Harlow (1911)
John Irving (1942)
Jackie Joyner-Kersee (1962)
Jessica Biel (1982)

COMPATIBLE WITH
February 9, March 1–5

MARCH 4

✳ ✳ ✳ ✳ ✳ ✳ ✳ ✳ ✳ ✳ ✳ ✳ ✳ ✳

EXPLORERS OF INTERNAL WORLDS   ♆ ☽

March 4 people are typically self-contained individuals, whose rich imagination and profound sensitivity do not require the trigger of external stimuli. Those born on this day are fascinated by abstract concepts, and their compulsion to explore these further will be expressed with remarkable tenacity—indeed, sometimes to the exclusion of all else. Yet despite their twin intellectual talents of great concentration and inquisitiveness, these intuitive and humanitarian people are governed by their hearts rather than their heads and not only respond to their emotional impulses, but experience deeply empathetic feelings with regard to the problems of others. Therefore, although they may isolate themselves from the world when exploring an idea that absorbs their full attention, they are never completely unaware of the parallel world of reality.

These are gentle people, who abhor confrontation and will withdraw smartly within themselves at the first sign of discord. This tendency, combined with their other personal characteristics, means that they will be unhappy in competitive professional situations, but will flourish when they can move within parameters set by themselves. Careers as artists, musicians and writers are especially well starred, but they may also make gifted teachers, whose infectious enthusiasm for their subject will inspire their pupils. Receiving the emotional support of friends and family members is vital to these people's holistic well-being, but they may involuntarily neglect the needs of those closest to them when their minds are in thrall to an impersonal interest.

MARCH 5

✳ ✳ ✳ ✳ ✳ ✳ ✳ ✳ ✳ ✳ ✳ ✳ ✳

♆ ☽ EMOTIONAL WAVE–SURFERS

L ike the water that is the ruling element of March 5, people born on this day can at one moment appear calm and tranquil, and at the next be making spectacular waves. The emotional undercurrent that flows beneath these people's attractive exterior is a strong one and, since they are sensitive types who respond to their instincts, they may feel powerless to resist the shifting directions to which they are being drawn. When they feel happy and secure, those born on this day are capable of being charming and sympathetic companions who will do their utmost to put others at their ease; when their equilibrium is unbalanced, however, the passionate expression of their frustration can be manifested in a veritable squall of temper. Given the emotional extremes to which they are prone, these people need to receive the unconditional understanding and support of those closest to them, who in many ways may be equated to ports in a storm.

The empathy which gives them such a strong rapport with others frequently manifests itself in a fervent desire to work toward the good of humanity, and these people will find satisfaction in careers which allow them to pursue this aim—in such areas as social or volunteer work, for example. But underneath the often assured and gregarious façade presented by these people lies a more pensive soul, which needs occasionally to retreat from the demands of the world to indulge in quiet and solitary reflection—a mark of the artist. Their intellectual powers of perception and analysis are great and, when harnessed to their empathy, can achieve remarkable results.

PLANETARY INFLUENCES
Ruling planet: Neptune
Second decan: Personal planet is Moon

VIRTUES
Charming, sympathetic, caring

VICES
Irrational, temperamental, fragile

CAREERS
Nonprofit or charitable work, social advocacy, artist

SKILLS & APTITUDES
Sympathy for others, imagination, humanitarian beliefs

FAMOUS BIRTHS
James Madison (1751)
Rex Harrison (1908)
Dean Stockwell (1936)
Andy Gibb (1958)
Aarthi Agarwal (1984)

COMPATIBLE WITH
March 3–7, November 1–5

MARCH 6

✳ ✳ ✳ ✳ ✳ ✳ ✳ ✳ ✳ ✳ ✳ ✳ ✳ ✳

AESTHETIC IDEALISTS   ♆ ☽

PLANETARY INFLUENCES
Ruling planet: Neptune
Second decan: Personal planet is
Moon

VIRTUES
Motivated, sensitive, tenacious

VICES
Easily disillusioned, demanding,
unrealistic

CAREERS
Fine artist, graphic designer,
nurse

SKILLS & APTITUDES
Drive for perfection, willingness to
work hard, creativity

FAMOUS BIRTHS
Michelangelo Buonarroti (1475)
Lou Costello (1908)
Valentina Nikolayeva-Tereshkova
(1937)
Shaquille O'Neal (1972)
Nicole Fox (1991)

COMPATIBLE WITH
March 4–9, November 1–5

Those born on this day are idealists, but their quest for perfection is not motivated by austerely intellectual objectives, but rather by a desire to experience the pleasure and satisfaction that are engendered by true excellence. The orientation of this overriding ambition may vary according to the personal interests of March 6 individuals, but since all are profoundly sensitive and thus inherently appreciative of the arts, this sphere of life is particularly important to them.

Whether or not they actively direct their highly imaginative talents toward the creation of sublime pieces of music, paintings, sculptures or poems, those born on this day are stimulated and uplifted by aesthetic beauty above all else. Some of these people passionately wish to create an ideal political or social regime. Whatever their career choice, be it in business, the arts or in the caring professions, these people will typically invest their considerable gifts of energy and perception in the attainment of their high ideals.

The disadvantage of this high regard for excellence, however—and this is especially true for March 6 men—is that others will inevitably fail to match their lofty standards. In their personal lives especially, the disappointment that these people feel when the object of their affection turns out to have feet of clay can be shattering, and they may therefore have difficulty in making and maintaining emotional commitments. They must therefore try to develop a more realistic and less demanding attitude to those closest to them.

MARCH 7

✽ ✽ ✽ ✽ ✽ ✽ ✽ ✽ ✽ ✽ ✽ ✽ ✽ ✽

Ψ ☽   RECEPTIVE VISIONARIES

Although they can be immensely practical and, as a result of their sensitivity, empathetic toward other people, those born on March 7 have a propensity to direct their interest and attention to what really fascinates them—the ideas and ideals that are products of their vivid imaginations. People with March 7 birthdays often possess the gift of extraordinary vision. They will perceptively survey their surroundings, analyze the situation's faults and merits and formulate an ideal scenario, which they will then strive to achieve, to the best of their abilities.

Although they may be gripped by one specific aim, since March 7 people are extremely receptive to all kinds of emotional and intellectual stimuli, this perspicuity and urge to act may be manifested in a wide range of enthusiasms. Within whichever area they ultimately choose to make their profession—be it in the arts, for which they have such a natural affinity, or in politics or sport—they will generally mount a determined and organized campaign to attain their ambitions.

There is a danger, however, given their focus on impersonal concepts, that those born on this day may allow their focus to be diverted from the very real needs of their family and friends, who will not necessarily understand these people's frequent desire for periods of solitary reflection or their enthusiastic devotion to a cause that may seem remote. Cultivating a spirit of compromise and give and take is therefore vital in giving March 7 people the balance that will result in self-fulfillment.

PLANETARY INFLUENCES
Ruling planet: Neptune
Second decan: Personal planet is Moon

VIRTUES
Visionary, idealistic, intellectual

VICES
Blinkered, neglectful, unwilling to compromise

CAREERS
Politician, lawyer, artist

SKILLS & APTITUDES
Intuition, determination, enthusiasm

FAMOUS BIRTHS
John Herschel (1792)
Luther Burbank (1849)
Piet Mondrian (1872)
Willard Scott (1934)
John Heard (1947)
Rachel Weisz (1970)

COMPATIBLE WITH
March 5–10, November 1–5

MARCH 8

✳ ✳ ✳ ✳ ✳ ✳ ✳ ✳ ✳ ✳ ✳ ✳ ✳

Unconventional Trailblazers ♆ ☽

March 8 people harbor a fiercely independent spirit beneath their outward veneer of endearing affability, so while they may give the impression of conforming to the norm, to some extent they are often actually working to undermine accepted conventions. This somewhat subversive approach is not prompted by a need to be perverse for defiance's sake—although the free-spirited individuals born on this day are naturally resistant to submitting to hidebound rules and regulations—but rather because they find it easy to identify the flaws and contradictions of a previously unchallenged approach and to formulate a better solution.

Indeed, people born on March 8 are often blessed with highly developed intellectual qualities of inquiry and lateral thinking, as well as being inherently sensitive and empathetic toward others. Such characteristics mark them out as potentially great reformers or inspirational trailblazers, especially in the academic, scientific, artistic, literary and social spheres.

As children, March 8 people will have to accept the hard lesson that society demands adherence to its mores, but if their parents respect their individuality and give them understanding and a sufficient degree of sympathetic guidance, they will benefit from the opportunity to learn to channel their talents positively. Otherwise there is a danger that the compulsion experienced by these people will find negative outlets, or that they will cut themselves off from others altogether. This is not to say that they should suppress their independence of thought, but simply to remember the value of compromise.

MARCH 9

♆ ☽ TRUTH–SEEKERS

Those born on this day are uncompromisingly individualistic in every aspect of their lives. Their energy is fueled by a burning compulsion to gather knowledge and seek out the truth of a situation for themselves rather than accepting the interpretation of others. And, because they are extraordinarily imaginative, their curiosity will lead them to explore a variety of avenues, then to evaluate their findings objectively before expressing them in their unique fashion.

March 9 people have high nonmaterialistic ideals—a result both of their visionary qualities and of their sensitivity. Because they desire harmony in life, and because their empathy with others bestows on them a profound sense of natural justice, these people will often make gifted social campaigners and reformers. Indeed, into whatever career their interests lead them—be it in the artistic realm, politics or sport—these people will never allow the excitement of discovery to obliterate their humanitarian concerns.

Because they retain their inherent feeling of connection with other people, especially if they were also born in the Chinese year of the horse, March 9 people will rarely forsake the real world for the isolation of an ivory tower. Yet this does not mean that these profound thinkers will not withdraw temporarily from the society of others in order to ponder an irresistibly absorbing concept. Those closest to them should therefore respect that occasional periods of solitude are crucial to these normally gregarious people.

PLANETARY INFLUENCES
Ruling planet: Neptune
Second decan: Personal planet is Moon

VIRTUES
Original, supportive, enthusiastic

VICES
Easily confused or distracted, impulsive, self-obsessed

CAREERS
Humanitarian, social campaigner, reformer

SKILLS & APTITUDES
Charisma, innovativeness, imagination

FAMOUS BIRTHS
Samuel Barber (1910)
Yuri Alekseyevich Gagarin (1934)
Bobby Fischer (1943)
Micky Dolenz (1945)
Bobby Sands (1954)

COMPATIBLE WITH
March 6–12, November 6–11

MARCH 10

✻ ✻ ✻ ✻ ✻ ✻ ✻ ✻ ✻ ✻ ✻ ✻ ✻ ✻

SERVERS OF THE COMMON GOOD   ♆ ☽

Although they are blessed with the intellectual gifts of objectivity and discernment, as well as with practical, organizational skills, it is their inner world of visions and ideals that primarily defines and occupies March 10 people. These are profoundly sensitive and thoughtful people, whose deeply felt compassion with those who are less fortunate arouses in them the ardent ambition to bring about improvement.

Because they are inclined to think both innovatively and seriously, people born on March 10 will often come up with a visionary, but also pragmatic, plan of action. Most will find greatest fulfillment when serving the common good, and they are therefore especially well suited to such caring professions as social work or medicine, or in fields in which they can devote their considerable talents to bringing happiness to others in less tangible ways, such as in entertainment, the arts or digital technology.

Despite their humanitarian concerns, and the value that they place on the intimacy of family life, these people are relatively solitary beings who need to retreat within themselves every so often for periods of reflection. Their sensitivity furthermore instills in them an inherent dislike of conflict, and when they feel upset or under pressure they will go within rather than confront an unpleasant situation; this tendency is particularly pronounced in March 10 males. They therefore need to receive frequent manifestations of the unconditional love and support of their friends and family if they are to thrive.

MARCH 11

✳ ✳ ✳ ✳ ✳ ✳ ✳ ✳ ✳ ✳ ✳ ✳ ✳ ✳ ✳

Ψ ♂ ♇   CLEAR–SIGHTED CEOs

People born on this day share the intuition that characterizes their Piscean fellows, but in their case it is less static and contemplative in quality, since they tend to use it more as a tool for gathering information and, if necessary, manipulating others. Indeed, March 11 people are shrewd judges of character, a talent partly informed by their instincts and partly by their gifts of observation. Similarly, although they nurture high ambitions, these are generally personal rather than global, and are realistically pitched. These people are geared toward making progress, especially in their professional lives, within which they will work tirelessly, not only to reach the top of the corporate ladder, but also to make their organization the best of its type. Because they are also imaginative and positive people who are willing to put aside personal differences in favor of building team spirit, they usually fare well when directing commercial enterprises and managing complex projects, particularly when they were also born in the Chinese years of the monkey or snake.

Domestic harmony is also important to March 11 people, who regard their personal sphere as a retreat from the hurly-burly of work in which they can relax and be themselves. They make indulgent parents, partners and friends, although—especially if they are men—they may occasionally adopt their professional persona in their relationships with those closest to them and behave in a somewhat high-handed manner. They furthermore expect the unquestioning loyalty and support of their loved ones, and have a tendency to lose their tempers spectacularly if they detect dissent.

PLANETARY INFLUENCES
Ruling planet: Neptune
Third decan: Personal planets are Mars and Pluto

VIRTUES
Personable, imaginative, ambitious

VICES
Manipulative, easily frustrated, temperamental

CAREERS
Business management, marketing, human resources

SKILLS & APTITUDES
Leadership skills, team-building, clear-sightedness

FAMOUS BIRTHS
Lawrence Welk (1903)
Ralph Abernathy (1926)
Rupert Murdoch (1931)
Douglas Adams (1952)
Jesse Jackson, Jr. (1965)

COMPATIBLE WITH
February 15–16, March 8–14

MARCH 12

✳ ✳ ✳ ✳ ✳ ✳ ✳ ✳ ✳ ✳ ✳ ✳ ✳ ✳

LIFE–EXPERIENCERS   Ψ ♂ ♇

A crucial component of the characters of those born on this day is the need to explore as many aspects of life as they can, in order to gain knowledge, to expose themselves to new experiences, and often also to test themselves against demanding challenges. In view of their adventurous spirits, it is hardly surprising that March 12 people are also energetic and daring individuals, who carry the less imaginative along on the tide of their enthusiasm, although few would dare to travel as impulsively or, indeed, as far. Some regard these individuals as reckless—and they unquestionably sometimes are—but since they have the gift of clarity of vision they will generally have considered any risks and will have evaluated the odds. These people have the potential to succeed as stockbrokers, or in any field in which they can take gambles. Yet it is not only external stimuli that invigorate those born on this day: they possess an originality and vision—as well as a fascination with the metaphysical—that borders on the radical, and augurs well for personal success in such diverse realms as politics or the arts.

Although they relish competition—against themselves rather more than against others—March 12 individuals are not motivated by the need to score victories over other people. They are empathetic and compassionate beings who have no real desire to succeed at another's expense, and who moreover also need to be rooted in the secure bonds of an emotionally stable and happy personal life. They sometimes find it hard to reciprocate the quiet and unconditional support that they crave from their friends and family, however, a difficulty that is caused by their inherent mental restlessness.

MARCH 13

Ψ ♂ ♇   OTHERWORLDLY INVESTIGATORS

With their marked interest in metaphysical and even paranormal concepts, March 13 people are instinctively fascinated by ideas and ideals that less imaginative types would brand as being fanciful or naive at best, and outrageously implausible at worst. Such is their acceptance of otherworldly possibilities, as well as their consequent tendency to challenge conventional "truths," that as children these people will have taxed their parents to the limit with their endless questioning as to the hows and whys of life. And they may well have immersed themselves for hours on end browsing the Internet.

If properly channeled, the curiosity and free-ranging intellects of March 13 people, coupled with their refusal to be dissuaded from pursuing the interests that excite them, can have remarkable consequences. Those born on this day will not find fulfillment by following a structured career path, and will be stifled within large organizations. If their many talents are to flourish, they must be allowed to follow their own route, and they are therefore best suited to working in the academic, artistic, digital or sporting sphere, in which they will be relatively unconstrained.

There is a danger that other people's denigration of their world views and opinions may wound these deeply sensitive individuals, causing them to conceal their true natures in an attempt to conform to a less original norm. Alternatively, they may feel tempted to opt out of conventional society altogether. It is therefore important that those closest to them not only bolster their self-belief, but that they gently steer them on to a straighter course when their equilibrium threatens to become unbalanced.

PLANETARY INFLUENCES
Ruling planet: Neptune
Third decan: Personal planets are Mars and Pluto

VIRTUES
Imaginative, enthusiastic, courageous

VICES
Hypersensitive, vulnerable, insecure

CAREERS
Academic, digital innovator, actor

SKILLS & APTITUDES
Originality, independence, self-motivation

FAMOUS BIRTHS
Percival Lowell (1855)
L. Ron Hubbard (1911)
William Casey (1913)
Neil Sedaka (1939)
Noel Fisher (1984)

COMPATIBLE WITH
February 18–21, March 10–19

MARCH 14

✳ ✳ ✳ ✳ ✳ ✳ ✳ ✳ ✳ ✳ ✳ ✳ ✳ ✳

VIEWPOINT VISUALIZERS ♆ ♂ ♇

Those born on March 14 frequently exasperate others by their apparent inability to make a decision and stick by it. Yet this indecisive tendency is not the result of a lack of perception or conviction—on the contrary, these sensitive individuals are extremely astute, and furthermore possess strong principles. It is just that because they have the ability to evaluate a situation and then visualize many possible future scenarios, they find it hard to decide on a single course of action when the alternatives seem equally viable or fraught with problems.

Since March 14 people are furthermore intellectually open to a variety of viewpoints, as well as being profoundly intuitive when it comes to the emotions of those around them, they shrink from bigotry and intolerance and from accepting other people's certainties. It is precisely their combination of open-mindedness, empathy and abhorrence of injustice that informs their deeply humanitarian concern, and their refusal to rush to judgement.

Human company is important to these sociable people, and others are drawn to them on account of their cheerful kindness, sympathy and infectious originality. Wonderful friends, they also have potential to make exceptionally good, nonjudgemental parents, but—as in all things—may initially find it hard to commit themselves to a single partner. Professionally, they will thrive when working within small teams, although they instinctively rebel against the rigidity of large corporations. The artistic sphere is especially auspicious for March 14 people, in which their powers of imagination and sensuality can be given the opportunity to flower.

MARCH 15

ΨσΡ VIVACIOUS VENTURERS

The adventurousness of March 15 people may take many forms: they may be intrepid travelers, fearless athletes, dynamic business people, visionary scientists or inspirational artists. In whatever area these people choose to make their careers, their progress will be rapid, driven by their compulsion for exploration of the world—real and virtual—and their inherent courage when it comes to taking risks.

Yet despite their ceaseless quest to be stimulated by new experiences, those born on this day will not generally set off blindly on a voyage of discovery, for they are furthermore blessed with keen and perceptive intellectual powers, as well as the capacity for great concentration in the pursuit of their aims. These individuals will inform themselves of the facts of a particular situation and impartially evaluate alternative approaches before throwing themselves at a challenge with their typical enthusiasm and energy.

Their need for independence of thought and action defines those born on this day, and their strength of purpose—as well as their natural magnetism—make them charismatic figures who have great leadership potential. Despite their undoubted empathy, they have a tendency to become impatient with those who do not share their visions and willingness to take chances, dismissing such individuals as being dull or obstinate. It is therefore important that they do not isolate themselves from other people—particularly their family and friends—by failing to acknowledge the merits of less intrepid viewpoints and approaches.

PLANETARY INFLUENCES
Ruling planet: Neptune
Third decan: Personal planets are Mars and Pluto

VIRTUES
Independent, bold, decisive

VICES
Restless, dismissive, impatient

CAREERS
Feature journalist, business leader, actor/director

SKILLS & APTITUDES
Out-of-the-box thinking, good research skills, self-confidence

FAMOUS BIRTHS
Andrew Jackson (1767)
Judd Hirsch (1935)
Sylvester Stone (1944)
Sananda Maitreya (formerly Terence Trent D'Arby) (1962)
Eva Longoria (1975)

COMPATIBLE WITH
March 11–20

MARCH 16

✵ ✵ ✵ ✵ ✵ ✵ ✵ ✵ ✵ ✵ ✵ ✵ ✵ ✵

BALANCED LEADERS   ♆ ♂ ♇

PLANETARY INFLUENCES
Ruling planet: Neptune
Third decan: Personal planets are
  Mars and Pluto

VIRTUES
Multitalented, visionary, realistic

VICES
Sulky, dismissive, self-indulgent

CAREERS
Lecturer, CEO, manager

SKILLS & APTITUDES
Intellectual focus, logical analysis,
leadership

FAMOUS BIRTHS
James Madison (1751)
Jerry Lewis (1926)
Bernardo Bertolucci (1940)
Erik Estrada (1949)
Alice Hoffman (1952)
Isabelle Huppert (1953)

COMPATIBLE WITH
March 12–20

Those born on March 16 generally appear to others to be exceptionally well-balanced characters, who somehow manage to reconcile their imaginative and fun-loving qualities with a steady and practical approach. These people are blessed with incisive powers of perception, logic and penetrating vision, all of which they utilize in formulating effective plans with which to attain their goals.

March 16 people may often be personally ambitious, and enjoy the trappings that material success can bring as an affirmation of their status, but because of their sensitive nature, they are more anxious to gain respect and friendship. They will flourish in those professional situations in which they can lead and inspire a team, and are therefore especially suited to careers in teaching or business. They may also devote a great deal of personal time blogging, engaging with current controversies or expressing their opinions on social media.

Such is their originality of thought that these people will remain unsatisfied if they cannot impress their personal stamp on everything that they do, especially if they were also born in the Chinese year of the dragon. In their personal lives, they are active types who will competently organize a vibrant social event or recreational expedition, but have a tendency to sulk if others fail to fall into line with their current enthusiasm. Similarly, although they make generous and gregarious friends and family members, they may have a propensity to become overly authoritarian, particularly with regard to their children.

MARCH 17

✳ ✳ ✳ ✳ ✳ ✳ ✳ ✳ ✳ ✳ ✳ ✳ ✳

♆ ♂ ♇   FLUID CREATORS

The natures of March 17 people can be compared to that of their watery element, for they have a propensity to drift fluidly from interest to interest, and, rather than be impeded by a difficult obstacle, simply to sidetrack and flow around it. This characteristic behavioral pattern has many possible causes, including these people's inquisitiveness and desire for progress, their dislike of confrontation, or, indeed, often a fundamental sense of insecurity and lack of self-esteem which discourages them from standing their ground.

Whatever the reason for their restless and elusive nature, those born on this day are unsuited to strictly structured careers in which they are subject to external controls and the rule of others, and must be indulged in their need for independence of action and thought. Their talents will often find their best expression in crafts, design and the arts, in which they can delight others with their sensitive interpretations of the beauty that inspires them.

Although they are fired by humanitarian concern and hate witnessing others' unhappiness, these people may inadvertently hurt those closest to them by their inherent aversion to commitment in close relationships (especially if they are men) and to the mundane constraints imposed by domestic life. They may therefore initially find it difficult to settle down, and, when they do, have a propensity to shirk responsibility. Their partners will thus need to be tolerant types, who can respect March 17 people's need for freedom and imaginatively work around their fear of entrapment.

PLANETARY INFLUENCES
Ruling planet: Neptune
Third decan: Personal planets are Mars and Pluto
Second cusp: Pisces with Arian tendencies

VIRTUES
Creative, instinctive, optimistic

VICES
Evasive, insecure, unreliable

CAREERS
Interior designer, artist, artisanal or craft businessperson

SKILLS & APTITUDES
Imagination, creativity, practical skills

FAMOUS BIRTHS
Patrick Brontë (1777)
Nat "King" Cole (1919)
Kurt Russell (1951)
Rob Lowe (1964)
Alexander McQueen (1969)

COMPATIBLE WITH
March 12–20, November 22

MARCH 18

✳ ✳ ✳ ✳ ✳ ✳ ✳ ✳ ✳ ✳ ✳ ✳ ✳ ✳

PROGRESSIVE PEACEKEEPERS   ♆ ♂ ♇

PLANETARY INFLUENCES

Ruling planet: Neptune
Third decan: Personal planets are Mars and Pluto
Second cusp: Pisces with Arian tendencies

VIRTUES

Sensitive, empathetic, positive

VICES

Weak, deceptive, unable to withstand pressure

CAREERS

Caregiver, artist, nanny

SKILLS & APTITUDES

Broad vision, sense of justice, diplomacy skills

FAMOUS BIRTHS

Stephen Grover Cleveland (1837)
John Updike (1932)
Vanessa Williams (1963)
Queen Latifah (1970)

COMPATIBLE WITH

March 12–21, November 22–23

Individuals born on March 18 are fueled by a constant quest to make progress, to move a step further on in life, and while this compulsion may be manifested in personal ambition, these compassionate people are typically motivated by a more global concern to improve the lot of humanity. Indeed, these visionary people have the gift of seeing the wider picture—of how things are and how they ought to be—a talent that results primarily from their perceptiveness and also from their profound sense of natural justice. While this ability, combined with their trademark enthusiasm, gives them the potential to achieve real success, it also can influence them to ignore the seemingly minor, yet often crucial, details of a situation.

This tendency to run away from situations of potential conflict is particularly true if the details involve unpleasant or controversial issues, which those born on this day would prefer not to confront. Their aversion to conflict can result in these people employing their considerable skills of diplomacy in the pursuit of a solution, but may equally cause them to make inadvisable concessions or to prevaricate.

March 18 people are particularly suited to careers as sympathetic caregivers, or in the arts, in which they will not be forced to compromise their principles, and in which they can use their talents to inspire a larger audience. Similarly, in their personal liaisons, they will thrive best if they are not pushed into following a lifestyle or complying with emotional demands that are alien to their natures.

MARCH 19

Ψ ♂ ♇   ORIGINAL THINKERS

Inherent in the characters of March 19 people is a curious mixture of imaginative qualities that tend toward the fanciful and a blunt directness and tenacity that will seldom be swayed. If properly channeled, this combination of visionary idealism and single-minded determination can give these people the potential to be startlingly successful in the pursuit of their aims, that is, as long as they have focused on a realistically achievable target.

While people born on March 19 are fueled by a righteous desire to effect social improvements, because they are highly original thinkers, their seemingly radical solutions may cause others to balk. However, once those born on this day have identified a worthy task to which to devote their prodigious energies, they will work unswervingly toward its completion, employing their considerable powers of organization and persistence in the process.

As a result of these qualities, March 19 people are happiest working in fields in which they feel that they are actively doing good, a requirement that encompasses a diversity of professional interests, including politics, science, the military, the caring professions and, of course, the arts, particularly drama.

Because they frequently encounter opposition to their ideas, it is important to these people's emotional well-being that they receive the consistent and unjudgemental support of their nearest and dearest, so that their homes become havens of security in which they can retire from the battle and simply be themselves.

PLANETARY INFLUENCES
Ruling planet: Neptune
Third decan: Personal planets are Mars and Pluto
Second cusp: Pisces with Arian tendencies

VIRTUES
Sensitive, fair, forward-thinking

VICES
Radical, obsessive, single-minded

CAREERS
Armed-forces personnel, scientist, artist

SKILLS & APTITUDES
Self-motivation, focus, organizational skills

FAMOUS BIRTHS
David Livingstone (1813)
Ornette Coleman (1930)
Glenn Close (1947)
Bruce Willis (1955)
Rachel Blanchard (1976)

COMPATIBLE WITH
March 13–22, November 23–24

MARCH 20

PLANETARY INFLUENCES
Ruling planet: Neptune
Third decan: Personal planets are Mars and Pluto
Second cusp: Pisces with Arian tendencies

VIRTUES
Multitalented, positive, compassionate

VICES
Hypersensitive, vulnerable, indecisive

CAREERS
Artist, humanitarian, caregiver

SKILLS & APTITUDES
Idealism, vision, imagination

FAMOUS BIRTHS
Ovid (43 BC)
Fred Rogers (1928)
Pat Riley (1945)
Spike Lee (1957)
Touré Neblett (1971)

COMPATIBLE WITH
March 14–23, November 23–24

....
....
....

Those born on this day possess such a wealth of attributes that it is difficult to identify a specific quality as a defining characteristic. But underlying their perceptiveness, tenacity, imagination and idealism is their great sensitivity, a gift that can have both negative and positive consequences for March 20 people. Although their inherent ability to relate to others with kindness and empathy makes them valued colleagues and friends, these people may sometimes feel overwhelmed by the intensity of their feelings of compassion, and therefore have a propensity to become depressed in the face of human suffering, particularly if they are women.

Yet March 20 individuals are natural optimists and, when buoyed up by their enthusiastic determination to make the world a better place, and in the absence of excessive criticism, they will intuitively follow a clear-sighted and logically considered plan of action.

A further characteristic that results from March 20 people's humanitarianism is their endearing propensity to think the best of others; sadly, this may make them vulnerable to being taken advantage of by less scrupulous types, and such abuses of trust will wound them deeply. A stable and supportive domestic background is vital in maintaining these people's emotional equilibrium, since they need to be assured of the love of those closest to them and will reciprocate it unflaggingly. Professionally, the best—and potentially least damaging—outlet for the sensitivity of those born on this day lies in the realm of the arts, especially if they were also born in the Chinese year of the rat, or in the service industries.